# European Union

An historical and political survey
Second edition

**Richard McAllister**

Routledge
Taylor & Francis Group

LONDON AND NEW YORK

First edition published 1997 by Routledge
Second Edition published 2010 by Routledge
2 Park Square, Milton Park, Abingdon, Oxon OX14 4RN

Simultaneously published in the USA and Canada
by Routledge
270 Madison Avenue, New York, NY 10016

Reprinted 2009

*Routledge is an imprint of the Taylor & Francis Group, an informa business*

© 1997, 2010 Richard McAllister
The author asserts the moral right to be identified as the author of this work.

Typeset in Times New Roman by Swales and Willis Ltd, Exeter, Devon
Printed and bound in Great Britain by CPI Antony Rowe, Chippenham, Wiltshire

*British Library Cataloguing in Publication Data*
A catalogue record for this book is available from the British Library

*Library of Congress Cataloging in Publication Data*
McAllister, Richard, MA
    European Union: an historical and political survey/
    Richard McAllister. — 2nd ed.
    p. cm.
    Rev. ed. of: From EC to EU. 1997.
    Includes bibliographical references and index.
    1. European communities—History. 2. European federation—History.
    3. European Union—History. I. McAllister, Richard, M.A. From EC to
    EU. II. Title.
    JN30.M36 2009
    341.242'2—dc22
    2008054238


ISBN10: 0–415–40762–1 (hbk)
ISBN10: 0–415–40761–3 (pbk)
ISBN10: 0–203–87569–9 (ebk)


ISBN13: 978–0–415–40762–5 (hbk)
ISBN13: 978–0–415–40761–8 (pbk)
ISBN13: 978–0–203–87569–8 (ebk)

To the memory of my parents

# Contents

# Preface

It may be better to begin by saying what this book does *not* purport to do, before indicating what it *does* try to do. It does not purport to be a comprehensive account of the European Community and its evolution into the European Union. It does not aim to chronicle all developments; it does not set out to describe the institutions in detail, one by one or even in interaction; it does not give a systematic account of the policies and policy areas in which the institutions of the European Union are involved. The reason for this is quite simple: such things have been admirably done in several other books; and this book assumes some familiarity with, or access to, the kind of information they provide.

Neither does this book try to set out some new 'grand theory' or 'explanation' of the whole process. Many years ago, writers such as Charles Pentland and Reg Harrison discussed the relevance of functionalism and neofunctionalism; of federalism and pluralism or intergovernmentalism, to the development of the (then) EC. More recently, Michael Shackleton has made use of 'cultural theory' from anthropology to provide insights into the future possibilities. In the United States especially, scholars such as Robert Putnam, Robert Keohane, Joseph Nye, Andrew Moravcsik and others have contributed understandings in terms of two- or multi-level games: 'liberal intergovernmentalism' and so forth. I am not here trying to challenge – let alone 'improve on' – their efforts.

Rather, this book aims to offer a fairly straightforward framework in terms of which to consider what the EC/EU has (always) had to be about; and it then goes on to focus mainly on a selective range of episodes, moments and developments in the history of the enterprise, ones that seem to me to have been significant for its subsequent path.

Further, I have concentrated a good deal on what was said and thought about these developments *at the time*: how issues were perceived, reported on and presented; how far major difficulties and issues were foreseen and anticipated; how far EC/EU institutions were merely reacting to events. This means that I have often reported official and semi-official reactions close to the events in question.

This account is offered for the reader (whether student, researcher, person having business or other concerns involving the EU, or the famous 'interested lay reader') to ponder how far this evidence squares with any single account of where the enterprise is going, its 'destination', purposes or limits. Or does it rather support the view that this was indeed from the beginning a voyage of both escape and exploration, undertaken, to be sure, out of a sense of necessity, but without very clear notions of maps and certainties and the perils that might be found out there?

# Preface to the second edition

The first edition of this book appeared in 1997. Since then much has changed. Academic writing on every aspect of the European Union (EU) has cascaded forth. 'Theories' and 'approaches' have multiplied. EU membership and diversity have grown along with the reach of its policy competences. Several attempts have been made to alter its institutional arrangements and to set out anew its purposes and limits.

As this edition goes to press, the EU – and the wider world – is in the midst of a major financial, and indeed wider economic, crisis, one that will, once more, test severely the efficacy and legitimacy, the fragility or robustness, of the EU setup.

This hardly seems a propitious time for prognostications: fortunately, these are not the purpose of the book, which looks, rather, at the course of and change in the EC/EU since its foundation. It tries to do so in a spirit that is, for the most part, closest to that of (to use a phrase current among 'devotees' of such matters) 'historical institutionalism'.

Chapters 10, 11 and 12 of this edition, dealing with the period 1994–2008, are almost entirely new. I have made a number of alterations and additions to earlier chapters, but retained their essential layout. Brief suggestions for 'further reading' have been appended to each chapter.

## Note on terminology

Throughout, the term 'EC' is used where appropriate in the period prior to ratification of the Treaty on European Union (TEU); 'EU' is used thereafter if referring generally to the whole operation, not just the 'EC pillar'; and 'EC/EU' or 'EC/U' are used to refer generally to the whole period before and after the TEU.

# Acknowledgements

For reasons too tedious to relate, work on this book has had to proceed in a rhythm that sometimes imitated its subject: by fits and starts. Because of this, I am grateful for the support, encouragement and cajoling that I received from several friends.

I would like in particular to acknowledge certain debts. Several people, colleagues and friends at Edinburgh and elsewhere, were kind enough to read parts or all of the work at various stages and to offer comments and criticisms. I would like in particular to thank Werner Bonefeld, Alice Brown, Jill Hanna and Kenneth Robbie. Richard Brodie and Paul Norris were kind enough to read and comment on what is now Chapter 10. None of them is in any way responsible for my views or my inaccuracies, although they saved me from some of the latter: I am most grateful to them. In a slightly different vein, I would like to thank Chris Brewin of the University of Keele, with whom I collaborated in sporadic annual bursts some time ago on the annual review of the activities of the EC, first for the University Association for Contemporary European Studies, then for the *Journal of Common Market Studies*. My thanks also go to the staff of various libraries, especially those of the Europa Library and the Main University Library at Edinburgh University. Permission to reproduce short extracts from the *Europe Daily Bulletin* is also gratefully acknowledged.

Finally, I should like to thank the editorial staff at Routledge for encouragement and assistance and their anonymous readers for their comments: they likewise are not responsible for errors that remain or for what may seem to them my ignoring the advice they offered. I am most grateful to all of them.

# Abbreviations

| | |
|---|---|
| ACP | African, Caribbean and Pacific states (Lomé Conventions) |
| *ACQ* | *Atlantic Community Quarterly* |
| ASEAN | Association of South-East Asian Nations |
| Benelux | Belgium, Netherlands and Luxembourg Customs Union |
| *BJPIR* | *British Journal of Politics and International Relations* |
| *BQE* | *Bulletin Quotidien Europe* (also *EDB*) |
| BTO | Brussels Treaty Organisation |
| *Bull. der PIB* | *Bulletin der Presse- und Informationsamt der Bundesregierung* |
| *Bull. EC* | *Bulletin of the European Communities* |
| *Bull. Supp.* | *Supplement to the Bulletin of the EC* |
| CAP | common agricultural policy |
| CCP | common commercial policy |
| CCT | common customs tariff |
| CDU/CSU | German Christian Democratic Union/Christian Social Union |
| CEN | European Committee for Standardisation |
| CENELEC | European Committee for Electrotechnical Standardisation |
| CET | common external tariff |
| CFP | common fisheries policy |
| CFR | Charter of Fundamental Rights |
| CFSP | common foreign and security policy |
| CJEC | Court of Justice of the EC (also ECJ) |
| CMEA | Council for Mutual Economic Assistance (also Comecon) |
| *CMLR* | *Common Market Law Reports* |
| *CMLRev.* | *Common Market Law Review* |
| COM | Commission document |
| Comecon | Council for Mutual Economic Assistance (also CMEA) |
| COPA | Committee of Professional Agricultural Organisations |
| COREPER | Committee of Permanent Representatives |
| CSCE | Conference on Security and Cooperation in Europe (also OSCE) |
| DC | Italian Christian Democratic Party |
| DDR | German Democratic Republic |

| | |
|---|---|
| *DEP* | *Debates of the European Parliament* |
| DG | Directorate-General (in the Commission) |
| DTEU | Draft Treaty on European Union |
| EAEC | European Atomic Energy Community ('Euratom') |
| EAGGF | European Agricultural Guidance and Guarantee Fund |
| EC | European Community |
| ECA | European Co-operation Administration |
| ECB | European Central Bank |
| ECJ | see CJEC |
| *ECR* | *European Court Reports* |
| ECSC | European Coal and Steel Community |
| ECU | European currency unit |
| *EDB* | *Europe Daily Bulletin* (also *BQE*) |
| EDC | European Defence Community |
| EEA/EEZ | European economic area/zone |
| EEC | European Economic Community |
| EES | European economic space |
| EFTA | European Free Trade Association |
| *EI* | *Europe Information* |
| EIB | European Investment Bank |
| EMCF | European Monetary Cooperation Fund |
| EMI | European Monetary Institute |
| EMS | European Monetary System |
| EMU | economic and monetary union |
| ENP | European neighbourhood policy |
| EPC | (a) 1959–62: European Political Community; |
| | (b) from December 1969: European political cooperation |
| EP | European Parliament |
| EP docs | documents of the European Parliament |
| EPU | (a) 1950–58: European Payments Union; |
| | (b) European political union |
| *ER* | *European Report* |
| ERDF | European Regional Development Fund |
| ERM | exchange rate mechanism |
| ESC | Economic and Social Committee |
| ESF | European social fund |
| EU | European Union |
| *FAZ* | *Frankfurter Allgemeine Zeitung* |
| FCO | Foreign and Commonwealth Office (UK) |
| FDP | German Free Democratic Party |
| FRG | Federal Republic of Germany (also BRD; 'West Germany' until 1990) |
| *FT* | *Financial Times* |
| G7 | Group of Seven |
| GATT | General Agreement on Tariffs and Trade |

| | |
|---|---|
| GDP | gross domestic product |
| GDR | German Democratic Republic (also DDR; 'East Germany' until 1990) |
| *GRA* | *General Report on the Activities of the Community* (annual: Commission) |
| HOSG | heads of state or government |
| IEA | International Energy Agency |
| IGC | intergovernmental conference |
| *IHT* | *International Herald Tribune* |
| IMP | integrated Mediterranean programme |
| *JCMS* | *Journal of Common Market Studies* |
| JHA | justice and home affairs |
| *JO* | *Official Journal* (of EC) |
| MBFR | mutual and balanced force reductions |
| MCA | monetary compensation amount |
| MEP | member of the European Parliament |
| MFA | multi-fibre arrangement |
| NAFTA | North American Free Trade Area |
| NATO | North Atlantic Treaty Organisation |
| NCE | non-compulsory expenditure |
| NPT | non-proliferation treaty |
| NTB | non-tariff barrier |
| *NZZ* | *Neue Zürcher Zeitung* |
| OCA | optimum currency area |
| OECD | Organisation for Economic Cooperation and Development |
| OEEC | Organisation for European Economic Cooperation |
| *OJ* | *Official Journal* (of EC; also *JO*) |
| *OJC* | *Official Journal* communications series (information and notices) |
| *OJL* | *Official Journal* legislation series |
| OMC | open method of coordination |
| OPEC | Organisation of Petroleum Exporting Countries |
| PAC | Political Affairs Committee |
| PCI | Partito Comunista Italiano |
| PHARE | Poland–Hungary Aid for Reconstruction (of Economy) |
| PoCo | political cooperation |
| QMV | qualified majority vote |
| *RCP* | *Report on Competition Policy* (annual) |
| *RCW* | *Review of the Council's Work* (annual) |
| RDG | regional development grant |
| SAA | stabilisation and association agreement |
| SAD | single administrative document |
| SALT | strategic arms limitation talks |
| SEA | Single European Act |
| SEM | single European market |

| | |
|---|---|
| SGP | stability and growth pact |
| SPD | Social Democratic Party |
| STC | state trading countries |
| TAC | total allowable catch (fish) |
| TCE | treaty establishing a constitution for Europe (also CT) |
| TEU | Treaty on European Union |
| The Six | the six founding member states of the EC: Belgium, France, FRG, Italy, Luxembourg, the Netherlands |
| The Nine | the Six plus Denmark, Ireland, the UK (1973) |
| The Ten | the Nine plus Greece (1981) |
| The Twelve | the Ten plus Spain, Portugal (1986) |
| The Fifteen | the Twelve plus Austria, Finland, Sweden (1995) |
| The Twenty-five | the Fifteen plus Cyprus, Czech Republic, Estonia, Hungary, Latvia, Lithuania, Malta, Poland, Slovakia, Slovenia (2004) |
| The Twenty-seven | the Twenty-five plus Bulgaria, Romania (2007) |
| TREVI | terrorism, radicalism, extremism and violence |
| ua | unit of account |
| UN | United Nations |
| UNCTAD | United Nations Conference on Trade and Development |
| UNEP | UN environmental programme |
| VAT | value added tax |
| VER/VERA/VRA | voluntary export restraint agreement |
| WEU | Western European Union |
| WTO | World Trade Organisation |

# Chronology

**1946**

| | |
|---|---|
| 16 March | Churchill's 'Iron Curtain' speech, Fulton, MI |
| 19 September | Churchill's Zurich speech: 'a kind of United States of Europe' |

**1947**

| | |
|---|---|
| 12 March | Truman urges Congress to give direct financial aid to Greece and Turkey; Truman Doctrine' – 'to support free peoples' |
| 5 June | announcement of 'Marshall Plan': US aid for economic rehabilitation in Europe |
| 2 July | Soviet Union announces it will not take part. Czechoslovakia and Poland do not either |
| 5 October | Cominform announced |
| 29 October | Benelux set up |

**1948**

| | |
|---|---|
| 22 February | Communist Party of Czechoslovakia gains control of the Prague government: 'the Prague coup' |
| 17 March | Brussels Treaty (BTO): Benelux, France, UK. 'Collective self-defence' |
| 16 April | Convention for European Cooperation signed. OEEC set up (later to become OECD) |
| May | Resolution of Congress of Europe (Hague Congress): urges European nations to 'transfer and merge some portion of their sovereign rights' |
| 24 June | Berlin blockade begins |
| 6 July | US/BTO/Canada begin discussions on North Atlantic defence |

**1949**

| | |
|---|---|
| January | communiqué on CMEA (Comecon) |
| 4 April | NATO Treaty signed. On 31 March Soviet Union had claimed Treaty contrary to UN Charter |

| | |
|---|---|
| 5 May | statute of the Council of Europe signed (London Agreement). Specifically excludes defence matters |
| 9 May | Berlin blockade lifted |
| 20 September | German Federal Republic constituted |
| 22 September | western announcement of atomic explosion by USSR |

**1950**

| | |
|---|---|
| 9 May | Schuman Plan proposed by France. Origin of European Coal and Steel Community (ECSC) |
| October | Pleven Plan for a unified West European army with German contingents; NATO discussions on West German participation |

**1951**

| | |
|---|---|
| 18 April | ECSC set up (Treaty of Paris) |

**1954**

| | |
|---|---|
| January/ February | abortive Berlin Conference on German reunification |
| 29 August | French National Assembly refuses to ratify EDC project |

**1955**

| | |
|---|---|
| 5 May | West Germany officially becomes a NATO member |
| 14 May | Warsaw Pact set up |
| 15 May | Austrian state treaty signed: ends four-power occupation |
| 1–3 June | Messina Conference: foreign ministers of 'Six' propose further steps of 'integration' |

**1956**

| | |
|---|---|
| 26 June | negotiations on Rome treaties start |

**1957**

| | |
|---|---|
| 24 March | Rome treaties signed setting up EEC and Euratom, by 'Six' |

**1958**

| | |
|---|---|
| 1 June | government of de Gaulle accepted by French assembly |

**1959**

| | |
|---|---|
| 20 November | European Free Trade Association (EFTA) set up |

**1961**

| | |
|---|---|
| August | Ireland, UK, Denmark request negotiations for EEC membership |

**1962**

| | |
|---|---|
| December | Kennedy–Macmillan meeting at Nassau. Polaris to be supplied to UK: offer to France, rejected January 1963 |

**1963**
| | |
|---|---|
| 7 January | de Gaulle rejects Polaris offer |
| 14 January | 1st de Gaulle veto of UK EEC entry |
| 22 January | Franco-German Treaty of Cooperation signed in Paris |

**1965**
| | |
|---|---|
| 8 April | 'Merger Treaty' establishes single Council and Commission of the three European Communities – EEC, Euratom, ECSC |
| 1 July | France leaves EEC Council over opposition to majority voting and serious crisis in Community begins: lasts 7 months |

**1966**
| | |
|---|---|
| 29 January | EEC crisis 'ends' with 'Luxembourg agreements' |
| 7 March | France announces intention to withdraw from NATO integrated military commands |

**1967**
| | |
|---|---|
| 24 April | Greek association 'on ice' following colonels' coup |
| 25 May | UK reapplies to join, followed by Denmark, Ireland, Norway |
| 30 June | conclusion of GATT 'Kennedy Round'; signed by member states and Commission |
| 1 July | Merger Treaty (1965) enters into force |

**1968**
| | |
|---|---|
| 1 July | customs union completed, 18 months ahead of schedule |
| 18 December | launching of the Mansholt Plan for agriculture |

**1969**
| | |
|---|---|
| 4 February | Soames–de Gaulle meeting in Paris – 'l'affaire Soames' |
| 12 February | Barre Plan on EMU launched as Commission memorandum |
| 14 February | 'meeting of WEU' in London, which France contests and from which absents itself |
| 21–2 February | press stories about Franco-British crisis break |
| 27–8 April | referendum in France on regional/senate reform: de Gaulle loses and steps down |
| 15 June | Pompidou elected President of France |
| 10 July | Pompidou commits himself to a (Hague) summit |
| August | French devaluation |
| September | FRG elections: Brandt heads SPD–FDP coalition |
| September | FRG revaluation |
| 2 December | Hague Summit: completion, deepening, enlargement formula |

**1970**

| | |
|---|---|
| January | Council resolution on EMU |
| 6 March | 1st moves on 'Davignon' political cooperation proposals |
| 21–2 April | (First) Budget Treaty: agreement on 'own resources' |
| May | Werner (EMU) Interim Report |
| 30 June | new negotiations for enlargement begin |
| 2 July | Malfatti Commission takes over |
| 20 July | 1st Davignon Report on PoCo |
| 12 August | FRG–Soviet Union *Grundvertrag* signed |
| 7 October | presentation of Werner Report on EMU |
| 8 December | agreement with UK on 5-year transition |

**1971**

| | |
|---|---|
| | Community introduces GSP |
| 25 January | Franco-German Summit: EMU agreement |
| 18 March | Swedish cabinet announces membership not compatible with neutrality |
| 3–5 May | Huge $ inflows into FRG |
| 7 May | FRG opts for floating currency |
| 10 May | joined by Dutch |
| 11–12 May | emergency agriculture ministers' meeting as result: implications for 'common prices' |
| 20–1 May | Heath–Pompidou meeting breaks logjam on UK entry |
| 15 August | 'Nixon package' – surcharge, devaluation |
| 20 August | Community finance ministers' meeting |
| 2–3 September | G10 deputies' meeting: UK lines up with EC against USA |
| 3–4 December | Brandt–Pompidou Summit |
| 13–14 December | Pompidou–Nixon meeting in the Azores |
| 17–18 December | 'Smithsonian' Agreement on monetary matters |

**1972**

| | |
|---|---|
| 22 January | treaties of accession signed |
| 21 March | 'Snake' set up |
| 25 March | Vedel Report on the powers of the EP |
| 23 April | French referendum on enlargement |
| May | Denmark, Ireland, Norway, UK join Snake |
| June | big speculation against sterling; leaves Snake, with punt |
| 22 July | agreements with non-applicant EFTA countries |
| 9 October | Norwegian government informs EC withdrawing application to join |
| 19–21 October | Paris Summit |
| 21 December | FRG–GDR Treaty signed |

**1973**

| | |
|---|---|
| I January | 1st enlargement Denmark, Ireland, UK |

| | |
|---|---|
| 6 January | Ortoli Commission comes in |
| February | France withdraws from Snake |
| February | dollar devalued 10%: Italy leaves Snake |
| II March | Snake leaves tunnel (joint float) |
| 23 April | Kissinger's Year of Europe speech |
| 10–11 September | EC-9 reply to Kissinger: 'two documents' |
| 21 October | 2nd PoCo Report |
| 6 October-November | Yom Kippur war (25 October US 'strategic alert') |
| 30 November | Jobert proposal for Euro-Arab dialogue |
| 14–15 December | Copenhagen Summit: EC-9 fail to agree common response to oil price crisis |
| 17–18 December | failure to agree regional policy; death of EMU |

**1974**

| | |
|---|---|
| 20 January | France again leaves Snake |
| 12–13 February | Washington 'energy conference'; disarray; IEA emerges later |
| April | 'Gymnich' procedure devised for consultation with USA over 'matters of common concern' |
| May | 'new impetus': Giscard president, Schmidt chancellor |
| July | France rejoins Snake |
| Autumn | French government presses for 'European Council' formula |
| 9–10 December | Paris Summit: paves way for European Councils; strengthens COREPER; decision to begin moves to direct elections; Tindemans mandate on European Union Report |

**1975**

| | |
|---|---|
| 28 February | 1st Lomé Convention |
| March | Dublin Summit: British 'renegotiations' declared completed |
| March | Marjolin Report |
| March | introduction of 'conciliation procedure', EP/Council of Ministers |
| June | UK referendum: 67.2% of those voting favour continued membership |
| 26 June | Commission presents its report on European union: calls for big institutional and constitutional changes; gets no response from Council of Ministers |
| 12 June | Greek membership application received |
| 10 July | Second Budget Treaty |
| 1 August | CSCE Helsinki 'Final Act' |
| December | Rome Summit |
| 29 December | Tindemans Report |

**1976**

| | |
|---|---|
| 16 February | contacts with CMEA (Comecon) about 'outline agreement' – inconclusive |
| March | France again leaves the Snake |
| April | agreements with Maghreb – Algeria, Morocco, Tunisia |
| 20 September | Council finally approves legislation for direct elections to EP |

**1977**

| | |
|---|---|
| January | agreement with Mashreq (Egypt, Jordan, Lebanon, Syria) |
| 28 March | Portugal applies for membership |
| 28 September | Spain applies |
| 4 October | CSCE follow-up meeting in Belgrade begins |

**1978**

| | |
|---|---|
| April | trade agreement with China signed |
| April | Copenhagen Summit |
| July | Bremen Summit |
| December | Brussels Summit: all concentrate on mitigation of economic problems and especially on moves toward EMS |

**1979**

| | |
|---|---|
| 9–10 March | Paris Summit – EMS finally sealed; set up 12th |
| 29 May | Greek accession signed |
| 7–10 June | 1st direct elections to the EP |
| 24 September | Spierenburg II Report |
| October | 'Three Wise Men' Report on European institutions |
| 31 October | Lomé II signed |
| 20 November | Council endorses Tokyo Round GATT negotiations |

**1980**

| | |
|---|---|
| 30 May | 'British budget deal' agreed; proves shortlived |
| 30 October | steel crisis measures |

**1981**

| | |
|---|---|
| 1 January | Greece joins |
| 1 January | ECU replaces European ua in Community's general budget |
| March | result of Isoglucose case: EP adopts new consultative procedure |
| 9 July | EP vote commits it to 'taking initiative' on European union; sets up Committee on Institutional Affairs |
| October | French franc devaluation |
| 15 October | 'Carrington' Report on PoCo adopted |
| 6 November | Genscher–Colombo Report produced |

**1982**

| | |
|---|---|
| 23 February | Greenland leaves the EC |
| March | limited trade sanctions against Soviet Union following martial law in Poland |
| Autumn | FRG–Schmidt–Genscher crisis |
| November | Soviet Union 'sanctions' crisis patched up |

**1983**

| | |
|---|---|
| 25 January | CFP established |
| 6 May | Commission presents proposals on future financing of the Community |
| June | Stuttgart Summit: 'solemn declaration' on European union (waters down Genscher–Colombo proposals drastically) |
| December | EC quietly ends limited sanctions imposed on Soviet Union March 1982 |

**1984**

| | |
|---|---|
| February | EP votes for Draft Treaty on European Union (DTEU – 'Spinelli') |
| March | Brussels Summit sets up Dooge and Adonnino committees |
| June | 2nd direct elections to EP |
| December | internal market council agrees principle of 'single customs document' |

**1985**

| | |
|---|---|
| 1 January | Delors Commission takes office |
| January | Delors speech to EP underlines internal market commitment |
| March | Brussels Summit. Interim Dooge Report: suggests convening of intergovernmental conference (IGC) |
| Spring | 'new approach' to technical harmonisation agreed |
| June | Milan Summit: UK outvoted on IGC proposal |
| June | Cockfield White Paper on internal market agreed |
| Autumn | main work of IGC on SEA takes place |
| December | Luxembourg Summit: SEA virtually agreed |

**1986**

| | |
|---|---|
| 1 January | Spain and Portugal formally join |

**1987**

| | |
|---|---|
| April/May | Turkish application for accession |
| Summer | SEA finally comes into force |
| Autumn | Émil Noël retires as Commission Secretary-General after 29 years; replaced by David Williamson (UK) |

**1988**

| | |
|---|---|
| February | 'Delors package' on CAP/budget/finances finally agreed |

| | |
|---|---|
| April | Cecchini Report on 1992 issued |
| September | Mrs Thatcher's 'Bruges speech' |

**1989**

| | |
|---|---|
| January | 2nd Delors Commission |
| January/February | EFTA meetings about strategy vis-à-vis '1992' and EFTA's future |
| 12 April | Delors Committee presents report on EMU |
| 15–18 June | 3rd direct elections to EP |
| 26–7 June | Madrid European Council |
| 17 July | Austria applies to join |
| 9 November | Berlin Wall breached |
| 8–9 December | Strasbourg European Council: 'requisite majority for convening EMU IGC' |

**1990**

| | |
|---|---|
| 8 February | Bangemann heads Commission group on 'the German future' |
| 18 March | free elections in DDR |
| 28 April | extraordinary European Council in Dublin welcomes 'German unification … without revision of the treaties' |
| 25–6 June | Dublin European Council: two IGCs convened: EMU and Political Union |
| 4 July | Cyprus applies to join |
| 16 July | Malta applies to join |
| 21–3 August | Commission adopts 'emergency procedures' to handle German unification |
| 21 September | Merger Control Regulation comes into force |
| 3 October | Germany unified |
| 6 October | sterling joins ERM of EMS |
| 19–21 November | CSCE (34) meeting in Paris sign charter for a New Europe |
| 30 November | Thatcher leaves office |
| 2 December | all-German elections |
| 14–15 December | Rome European Council: opening of the two IGCs |

**1991**

| | |
|---|---|
| December | Maastricht European Council. European Union Treaty signed: to be ratified by member states |

**1992**

| | |
|---|---|
| 2 June | Danish Maastricht referendum: 'no' majority |
| June | Lisbon European Council |
| September | sterling leaves the ERM |
| 11–12 December | Edinburgh European Council: agrees Danish opt-outs and opening of Austrian, Finnish, Norwegian, Swedish accession negotiations |

**1993**

| | |
|---|---|
| 18 May | 2nd Danish Maastricht referendum: 'yes' majority |
| Early August | major ERM/EMS crisis: 'wide bands' agreed |

**1994**

| | |
|---|---|
| 1 January | 2nd stage of EMU; European economic area comes into being |
| 1 February | 'Europe agreements' with Hungary and Poland come into force |
| July | 'partnership and cooperation agreements' with Russia and Ukraine signed; free trade agreements concluded with Baltic states |
| November | Norwegian referendum on membership – 'no' |

**1995**

| | |
|---|---|
| 1 January | Austria, Finland, Sweden join EU |
| January | Santer Commission takes over |
| 7 March | agreement preparing for an EU–Turkey customs union signed |
| 26 March | seven states implement Schengen Accord |
| 3 June | 'reflection group' to prepare 1996 IGC begins work |
| 22 June | Romania applies to join EU |
| 27 June | Slovakia applies to join EU |
| 26 July | signature of: Europol Convention; Customs Information System Convention; Convention on Protection of Communities' Financial Interests |
| September | (more) major currency instability as finance ministers/central bank governors meet to discuss single currency arrangements |
| 27 October | Latvia applies to join EU |
| 3 December | 'new transatlantic agenda' between EU and USA signed in Madrid |
| 8 December | Lithuania applies to join EU |
| 15–16 Dec | Madrid European Council: 'euro' to be name of single currency |
| 16 December | Bulgaria applies to join EU |

**1996**

| | |
|---|---|
| January | Italian presidency: priorities: preparing IGC; enlargement, EMU |
| 3 March | Spanish elections: PP/Aznar head governing coalition |
| 29 March | IGC opens at Turin |
| 21 April | Italian elections: Prodi eventually forms government 16 May |
| 10 June | Slovenia signs a 'Europe agreement' and applies to join |

| | |
|---|---|
| 25 November | Italy rejoins the ERM |
| 13–14 December | Dublin European Council: progress on EMU including agreement on stability and growth pact (SGP) |

**1997**

| | |
|---|---|
| 1 May | UK elections: large Labour majority |
| 12–13 May | 'Paris Declaration' on cooperation between EU and WEU; and WEU and NATO |
| 25 May | French legislative elections, 1st round: big losses by right; blow to Chirac |
| June | French PM Jospin sets out 'four conditions' for joining EMU |
| October | UK: Chancellor Brown sets out 'five conditions' for possible EMU membership: 'not in this parliament' |
| 2 October | EU foreign ministers sign draft 'Amsterdam' Treaty: then has to be ratified |
| 1–10 December | Kyoto climate change conference |
| 12–13 December | Luxembourg European Council: announces accession process for 10 CEEs plus Cyprus, to begin from end March 1998 |

**1998**

| | |
|---|---|
| 1 January | UK presidency: priorities include enlargement; foreign policy; environment; EMU |
| 1 February | 'Europe agreements' with Latvia, Lithuania, Estonia |
| 2 February | 'accession partnership agreements' (APAs) with 10 pre-accession states |
| 12 March | Standing Conference on Enlargement starts in London |
| 25 March | Commission initially recommends 11 states for eurozone |
| 30 March | enlargement: Six '1st wave' states begin formal process: Cyprus, Czech Republic, Estonia, Hungary, Poland, Slovenia |
| 3 April | 'accession and screening' for five other eastern applicants: Bulgaria, Latvia, Lithuania, Romania, Slovakia |
| 30 June | ECB starts work in Frankfurt; Duisenberg 1st President |
| mid-July | Commission President Santer presents *Agenda 2000* to EP |
| 27 September | German elections: Schröder (SPD) plus Greens replace Kohl. Swedish elections: Social Democrats lose seats but stay in power |
| 30 September | negotiations begin between EU and ACP states on 'successor' to Lomé IV |
| 1 October | Europol convention comes into force |
| 24–25 October | Pörtschach informal HOSG meeting: discussions on defence and WEU: origin of Franco-British St Malo agreement |

**1999**

| | |
|---|---|
| 1 January | German presidency starts. Euro launched: initially 11 members of single currency ('euro–11'). Exchange rates 'irrevocably fixed'. ECU replaced by euro |
| 27–28 January | 'Committee of Five' announced to investigate allegations of mismanagement and fraud in the Commission |
| 15 March | 1st report of Committee of Five: whole Santer Commission resigns; though remaining in 'caretaker capacity' until September |
| 24–25 March | Prodi nominated as next Commission President |
| April | situation in Kosovo worsens: EU foreign ministers hold out possibility of accession for Balkan states to try to calm the situation |
| 1 May | Amsterdam Treaty comes into force |
| 3–5 June | Cologne European Council: Solana chosen as High Representative for CFSP |
| 10–13 June | 5th EP elections: lowest turnout to date. EPP largest single party |
| 1 July | Europol begins work |
| 15 September | EP approves Prodi Commission |
| 23 September | Solana becomes (also) WEU Secretary-General |
| 10–11 December | Helsinki European Council: accession invitation to six more states: Bulgaria, Latvia, Lithuania, Malta, Romania, Slovakia |

**2000**

| | |
|---|---|
| January | Portuguese presidency: priorities include enlargement, economic reform, reduction of unemployment |
| 15 February | accession negotiations begin with '2nd wave six': see 10 December 1999 |
| 23–24 March | Lisbon 'extraordinary' Council on employment etc.: the 'dotcom' summit |
| 19–20 June | Greece approved for EMU/euro membership |
| 28 July | draft charter of fundamental rights published |
| 12 September | 'sanctions' against Austria, imposed in February because of inclusion of Haider's party in government, are 'lifted' (abandoned) |
| 28 September | Danish 'no' to joining euro |
| 2 October | a convention drafts the Charter of Fundamental Rights |
| 7–9 December | Nice European Council: tries to deal with the 'leftovers from Amsterdam' |

**2001**

| | |
|---|---|
| 1 January | Greece becomes 12th member of eurozone |
| 26 February | Treaty of Nice signed by foreign ministers |

| | |
|---|---|
| 7 June | Ireland votes 'no' to Nice Treaty |
| 11 September | 9/11 attacks on targets in the USA |
| 14 November | 'Doha Round' trade negotiations launched |
| 14–15 December | Laeken European Council adopts Declaration on Future of EU; arranges convention preparatory to 2004 IGC; takes decisions on common ESDP |

**2002**

| | |
|---|---|
| 1 January | introduction of euro notes and coins |
| 28 February | 1st meeting of the 'Convention on the Future of Europe' |
| 28 February | 'Eurojust' established: to promote cooperation in the investigation and prosecution of 'serious cross-border and organised crime' |
| 4 May | Commission paper on management of external borders published |
| 13 June | European arrest warrant: framework agreed by Council |
| 23 July | Treaty of Paris expires |
| 25 August | Johannesburg world summit on sustainable development meets |
| 19 October | Ireland holds 2nd referendum on Nice Treaty: votes 'yes' |
| 28 October | Convention: praesidium presents draft 'Constitutional Treaty' to plenary session |
| 12–13 December | Copenhagen Council: accession negotiations concluded with 10 candidates; 'roadmaps' agreed concerning Bulgaria and Romania |

**2003**

| | |
|---|---|
| 1 February | Treaty of Nice comes into force |
| 17 February | 'extraordinary' Council in Brussels on Iraq |
| 28 February | Croatia applies to join EU |
| 10 March | Malta accession referendum: 'yes' |
| 23 March | Slovenia accession referendum: 'yes' |
| March | EU deeply divided over Iraq invasion |
| 12 April | Hungary accession referendum: 'yes' |
| 16 April | accession treaty signed with 10 new members joining in 2004 |
| May | Lithuania, Slovakia accession referenda: large 'yes' majorities |
| June | Czech Republic, Poland accession referenda: 'yes' |
| 19–20 June | Thessaloniki European Council: draft 'constitution' presented |
| 14 July | Cyprus parliament votes for accession: no referendum |
| September | Estonia, Latvia accession referendum: 'yes' |
| 14 September | Swedish referendum on euro membership: 56% 'no' |
| 4 October | IGC opens in Rome, to negotiate the 'Constitutional Treaty' |

| | |
|---|---|
| 12–13 December | Brussels European Council fails to agree on 'Constitutional Treaty': IGC suspended |

**2004**

| | |
|---|---|
| 13 January | Commission proposal on services sector: the 'Bolkestein Directive' |
| 11 March | Madrid bombings |
| 14 March | Spanish elections: Rodriguez Zapatero (PSOE) forms government |
| 1 May | Ten states join EU: which then has 25 members |
| 12 May | Commission 'European neighbourhood policy' paper published |
| 10–13 June | 6th EP direct elections |
| 17–18 June | Brussels European Council: general agreement on Constitutional Treaty |
| 29 October | Constitutional Treaty signed in Rome |
| 22 November | Barroso Commission takes office |

**2005**

| | |
|---|---|
| 18 January | Council drops 'excess deficit procedure' against Germany and France |
| 22–23 March | European Council: 'reform' of SGP; 'mid-term review' of 'Lisbon process' |
| 29 May | France votes 'no' on Constitutional Treaty |
| 1 June | Netherlands votes 'no' on Constitutional Treaty |
| 17 June | European Council: ratification of Constitutional Treaty 'suspended'; 'period of reflection' |
| 18 September | German elections: 'grand coalition' eventually formed, headed by Merkel |
| 3–4 October | accession negotiations officially 'opened' with Croatia and Turkey |
| 15–16 December | European Council agrees 'financial framework' for 2007–13; Macedonia accorded 'candidate status' |

**2006**

| | |
|---|---|
| April | parliamentary elections in Italy and Hungary |
| 29 May | Council reaches 'political agreement' on Services Directive |
| 15–16 June | Council agrees 'twin-track' approach over institutions: to make 'maximum use' of the existing treaties, but also prepare for reforms |
| 11 December | Council 'partially suspends' Turkey's accession negotiations |

**2007**

| | |
|---|---|
| 1 January | Slovenia joins eurozone; Bulgaria and Romania join EU |

| | |
|---|---|
| Spring | French presidential elections: Sarkozy victorious. Blair hands over to Brown as UK PM |
| July | new IGC opens on what is to be referred to as the 'Lisbon Treaty' |
| October | agreement reached on Lisbon Treaty |
| 13 December | European Council: signature of Lisbon Treaty; ratification required |

**2008**

| | |
|---|---|
| June | Ireland votes 'no' to Lisbon Treaty |
| 1 July | French presidency |
| Autumn | deepening financial and economic crisis worldwide |

# Introduction

## A disputed community

This book offers an account of the European Union (EU) from its beginnings in the European Coal and Steel Community (ECSC) of the early 1950s up to 2008. In doing so, it does not attempt comprehensive coverage, which would be literally impossible. Rather, it discusses certain episodes and developments that seem to have had a great influence on the evolution and subsequent history of the EC/U – whether for good or ill.

### Politics of design and the gremlins of history

The purpose of this book is thus rather different from that of a standard textbook. The story that it tells is, in essence, about the interplay between, on the one hand, the 'politics of design' and, on the other, the part played by contingency or by accident. It invites the reader to reflect on the history – the course, development and changes – through which the EC/U has passed so far. It aims to give some evidence and some commentary that may provide a perspective, or modify perspectives. It has a schema, but it does not seek to peddle a single, simple message – whether (to use terms current in the UK) 'eurofederalist', 'eurosceptical' or something other. This is because, for this observer, the reality is, as usual, more complex than that.

### Four continuing issues

The book portrays what the EC/U has been about in terms of four clusters of issues, or 'battles', as some might prefer to call them. It is further concerned to stress, and to illustrate, that these clusters of issues do not exist in neat, separated boxes: on the contrary, they overlap, interact, get in one another's way, but in ways and with results that are not always predictable. The first of the four 'battles' concerns *interinstitutional* matters: essentially, what is to be the distribution of power and influence between the various institutions of the EC/U? The second is the issue of the *internal policies* of the EC/U: what should they be and how far should they extend? The third leads on quite inevitably from the second, even though for a long while this was less clear: it concerns the *external persona* of the EC/U – what kind of entity it can agree to be or may be forced to be on the wider stage. The fourth, simply, is the issue of the EC/U's *geographical extent*: the question of who comes on board and under what conditions or constraints.

It is claimed, first, that this distinction, although 'merely analytical', will also prove helpful and enlightening as a way of describing what has been going on; and second, that it in fact adequately encompasses many other questions raised about the EC/U. For example, it seems clear that the question 'What of the balance of power between member states and the EC/U?' is not a separate issue, but covered by those mentioned.

### A process replete with ambiguities

The starting point and basic point of view may be stated as follows. Only a few years after World War II, it was apparent to many that even the truncated western Federal Republic of Germany would rapidly re-emerge as an economic power of vital importance for all its neighbours. *How* they were to reckon with it was less clear: but at a minimum, most of them came to believe that reliable market access – both to what the FRG produced, and to its markets for their exports – was vital for future prosperity; and that that prosperity in turn was vital both to underpin postwar welfare states and to fend off political extremisms of left and right (see Milward 1992: Chs 1–4; Dinan (ed.) 2006: Chs 2 and 3). Such views were also strongly supported by their external backer, the USA (Lundestad 1998: *passim*).

There was less agreement about precisely how to ensure this: about what kind of arrangements and institutions would, at key moments, prove acceptable to enough key office holders. If the general *imperative* were clear, the precise modalities were far from clear. The precise form of the bodies that came to make up the EC/U emerged, with no inevitability, out of the confusion and 'fog of war' between contending notions of 'what needed to be done', how and who should be involved. Very little about the process was tidy or planned, although it came to be widely agreed that, to guarantee that element of *reliability*, something more than simple 'cooperative' arrangements was required. Although there were from the beginning *elements* of 'design' about the bodies that made up the European Community, now Union, no notion of its 'ultimate destination' was stated at the outset. Nevertheless it was clear that what was involved was intended to be a process and a movement in a certain direction.

This process and direction were described in the very first lines of the preamble to the 1957 (Rome) EEC Treaty as 'to lay the foundations of an ever closer union among the peoples of Europe'. That formula already indicated not only the nature of the process and the general direction, but also some of the ambiguities, the potential for differences of opinion and scope for misunderstanding and disagreement that were to appear, which form a central theme of this book.

'Ever closer union' (the inclusion of the phrase is thought to emanate from J.-F. Deniau, one of Jean Monnet's acolytes) clearly meant a progressive growing together. It did not, however, specify the nature of an 'end product': it did not, for instance, speak of a single state, a state-like entity or a federation. On the other hand, the union was described as being 'among the peoples of Europe': this appeared to indicate something other than simply a 'union of states' and it clearly (and crucially) left the membership open to other states, as long as they were European, but without defining where that stopped.

'Ever closer' might also be held to imply that the process might never stop – might never be held to be 'complete'. In turn, this might be held to commit the signatories to further, and certainly not to obstruct, *any* proposal to develop the union. Moreover, those forming the union were committing themselves to a degree of 'special relationship' with one another. Henceforth, there were things that they would share with other members that would not be shared with non-members: but again, it was not stated precisely what these things would be and what might be excluded. Just how 'exclusive' the relationship was to be, how far it might preclude or constrain *other* relationships of member states was also unclear.

So we see that what was being set in train was a general process and a general direction. But we also see that the project was, from the start, open ended and imprecise, having about it qualities of aspiration and ambition and not only narrow obligation; and that the destination remained unclear.

But just as there were elements of design, and of programme, so there were also the gremlins of history: a whole series of developments or events, which may perhaps be described as exogenous shocks, that have impacted on the EC/U and to which it has had to try to respond. 'History' has always had the ability to throw difficulties in the way of the EC/U. Equally, the 'design' itself could only aim and claim to anticipate just so much: unanticipated events occurred, just as the growth, change and development of the EC/U itself brought about consequences also frequently unanticipated. How far the exogenous shocks would throw out the original design or intentions ('blow it off course', in a famous phrase), and how far they would merely delay, irritate or cause tactical changes of speed or of tack, are also worth investigating, for this throws light on how powerful or robust have been the 'politics of implication', the logic of the design.

## Criteria for the material discussed

Quite clearly a book on this scale cannot be comprehensive. What follows concentrates more on some periods, episodes and incidents than on others; some are hardly mentioned. The basis for the selection may be fairly simply stated, although it is open to challenge. On the one hand, the book has a more or less chronological tale to tell: it is important to be reminded which things happened before, at about the same time as or after others: thus I hope to have included at least sufficient reminder of most developments which, by common consent, have been thought important. Further, I try to remind the reader what was thought or said about some of these events *at the time* and not just with the benefit of hindsight.

On the other hand, however, there have occurred certain 'moments' in the history of the EC/U: sometimes, a new 'grand design' has been announced; at other times, events have occurred that seem clearly to have impacted on the EC/U system and what it announced it was trying to do or to be. These are the aspects on which I concentrate most: on battles about becoming – about change and resistance to change

– which have so clearly marked the history so far of this rather strange, *sui generis* polity – the EC and, now, EU.

Broadly, then, four criteria are borne in mind in selecting matter for discussion from among the almost infinite possibilities. The first is major turning points, whether 'positive' or 'negative': something needs to be said about these milestones. The second is the early airing of issues or matters that were to cast long shadows before them. The third is that there are some events that appear to have been insufficiently commented on generally in the literature. The fourth is that certain episodes or moments illustrate quite sharply the kinds of interconnection that often exist between different parts of the agenda. The first criterion speaks for itself: but developments and episodes of this kind will often have been commented on by others and may tend to receive somewhat brief treatment here. I have tended to be more interested in matters that also meet one or more of the other criteria: certain such episodes are explored at some length. It is my hope that what the book risks losing in balance thereby may be compensated for by some insights and explorations that are a little fuller than in most other accounts. The choice may appear somewhat idiosyncratic, but I hope it will illustrate some of the tugging and pulling that is central to the EC/U.

The EC/U is, to amend Trollope, about the 'way we fight now'. Those who do the 'fighting', whether working for the institutions or for the member states, come in all shapes and sizes and with varying beliefs. They include, first, those we may call the zealots, the 'maximalists', the keepers of the ark of the covenant, according to taste. Such, whether they approve of the original 'Monnet design' or not, are committed to pursuing the politics of implication, progress by crisis, 'dynamic disequilibrium' in which the 'resolution' of one issue creates problems in surrounding areas which only Community/Union machinery should solve. Some others may be described as 'trimmers', prepared to bend and tack with wind and tide, but equally determined to stay in the game and not to be seen as forever questioning the purpose of the voyage. Some are of a quite different hue. They may have thought the destination was one place, only to discover to their discomfiture that, in fact, it appears different. Some never really relished boarding at all, but felt that time and tide offered them no alternative. In charting their views and reactions, I have made quite extensive use of official and semi-official outpourings, in the hope of illustrating *how the agenda and the issues appeared at the time*, as well as later.

In particular, some of the economic issues receive more, some of the institutional issues perhaps less attention than might be expected. This reflects a double judgment: first, that a good deal of what the EC/U does and does not accomplish is very much influenced by the prevailing economic climate; second, that, while visions of 'political union' continue to be present and play their part, they remain to date to a considerable extent just that – visions.

The first is perhaps not surprising. It will be pointed out that the period up to about 1968 provided generally favourable economic weather for the Community to sail in. The 1970s were a period of economic turbulence and of stagflation: also of 'euro-sclerosis'. From the early 1980s, there was a period when the economic outlook appeared somewhat more favourable, culminating in a heady boom. It was also a period when the Community was said to have regained its *élan*. But in the early 1990s, the economic gods smiled less kindly and the Community again seemed destined to haul in sail and at best ride out the storm. In the new millennium, forces of globalisation helped create contrasting problems across the enlarged Union and thus more differentiated views about its utility and the desired extent of its competences. The suggestion is, then, that a good deal depends on the state of the economic barometer.

Early developments are briefly sketched in Chapter 1, to set the scene. However, the book concentrates on the period since about 1968. There are several reasons for this. First, a good deal has been written about the earlier period, of the 'founding fathers', the treaties themselves and the so-called transitional period (see, particularly, Gillingham 1991; Milward 1992: esp. Chs 2–5; Milward et al. 1993: esp. Chs 1, 3, 5, 6; Gillingham 2003 esp. Part I; Dinan (ed.) 2006: esp. Chs 1–5). That last phrase, indeed, provides a second reason. The EEC Treaty set out a 12-year 'transition', composed of three 4-year slices, each of which could be speeded up or slowed down a little: it sought to 'programme' fairly closely the main things that were supposed to happen in that time. The 'completion' of the industrial customs union was indeed announced a little ahead of schedule. My main concern in this book is rather with what was to happen next: in the period *beyond* that in which things were intended to be thus programmed. Third, as we shall see in more detail below, a number of developments occurred in several states in or around 1968 which together constitute something of a watershed. However, to set the scene, and to remind the reader less *au fait* with the history of the EC, it is necessary to sketch the background; to remind ourselves what the EC had become by about 1968, before taking the story forward. This is the purpose of Chapter 1. It is important to do this for another reason. Already, before 1968, certain events had occurred that were to cast long shadows before them in terms of the development of the EC.

One event, familiar from most sketches of the EC, was of course the 'crisis' of 1965–6, in which France, angered at the boldness of certain Commission proposals, absented itself from meetings of the Council of Ministers for a period of some 7 months (the so-called 'policy of the empty chair'). Another event, less well known but in its own way just as revealing, had happened even earlier: the early discussions on the development of a so-called European political union; the 'Fouchet–Cattani' negotiations which began in 1959, dragged on in some disagreement and acrimony in 1960–1 and ran into the sand during 1962.

So it may be seen that a list of disarmingly simple but also alarmingly wide questions has concerned the EC/U for a long time. They include, in telegraphic form, the questions of what, why, how, who, how fast and whither. Of what was the EC/U to consist, in policy terms? Why should just *these* items be included, rather than others? How, by what means, were certain things to be accomplished or attempted? Who was to form part of the crew; and should that change before, as a condition that, or only after certain things were accomplished? 'How fast' is obvious enough; and 'whither' implied the ongoing debates about destination or *finalité politique*.

Many volumes on the EC/U deal with policy areas discretely – a chapter on competition policy, a chapter on agriculture and so forth: or with the institutions discretely – a section on the Commission, on the EP, on the Court. This has the great advantage, from the writers' point of view, of rendering the material much more manageable, easier to handle, less speculative. It may also give the reader the false impression that it constitutes an adequate account. The approach adopted in the current volume begins with the twin notions that the EC/U is both a constantly *changing* set of relationships and an *ambiguous* set of relationships – where possibilities open up or close down in particular areas sometimes because of 'felt needs', sometimes because of developments quite elsewhere – the famous exogenous factors. It (even the 'it' invites questions) has not always been about the same things. The agenda has changed, several times and sometimes markedly. Notions of destination have changed. Nautical or navigational metaphors come readily to mind, but just as obvious is the fact that the 'crew' is frequently, perhaps routinely, divided – both about destination and about tactics and even about who does or should make up the crew.

Thus this whole *newish* level of governance, the EC/U, throws up a number of questions, including that of *what kind of political system it is*. Taxonomy and classification will prove difficult and may even prove futile: but the attempt is important, in order to highlight certain things that the EC/U is and is not (analogies, etc.); certain 'logics' that are thought to lead from X to Y; and certain (perennial?) controversies in which the enterprise has found itself enmeshed. (Is there a 'democratic deficit'? Is it important? If so, can anything be done about it? What? To what would that lead?) Then there is the question of just how dependent on/autonomous of the rest of the political processes in Europe and the wider world the EC/U actually is and, thus, what may be expected of it. There is, further, the issue of the link between its reputation and its future prospects. The EC/U is not completely chained by its history, yet it is fair to say that it carries its history around with it somewhat like a ball and chain.

## Politics, economics and law

The topic lies within a triangle formed by politics, economics and law and the main practitioners include, prominently, all three: politicians, economists and lawyers. We are concerned with 'forms of economic logic' – i.e. the assumption that certain economic benefits will flow from specific forms of economic rearrangement of a specifically integrative (not just cooperative) kind. Political means/mechanisms are needed to bring these changes about. Do they/will they do so (i.e. instrumentally, will they 'succeed', on their own terms?)? These economic changes are not just self-standing, but *intended* to lead to (profound) further changes in political outlook, configuration, interrelationships (*inter se*) and status (vis-à-vis the external world) of the states and peoples concerned. Have they so far? Will they? In this process, legal means also assume a most prominent part. How far can they/do they substitute for 'political will'? Do they have autonomous influence over what happens?

Thus the book is about the 'politics' of the EC/U in two senses. First, the EC/U is an animal in motion, whose destination, as often remarked, is not fixed. Part of its 'politics', therefore, is its modern history, tracing its main lines of development, its main changes and failures to change. Second, in this process, the operation of certain mechanisms and tendencies, not necessarily prescribed in the formal documentation, has become apparent. These appear to influence its policymaking, its outputs and its capacity for implementation and monitoring. This in turn influences its reputation which, in a 'feedback loop', may affect the willingness of states to make over to it other competences or to allow its organs to interfere in certain ways.

The EC/U is not something quite separate from and independent of the states that set it up or later joined. It is a compound of several bodies: some possess a degree of constitutional independence (more or less honoured in practice) – Commission and Court of Justice being the prime examples; others obviously derive from and work to the states and their governments (Councils of Ministers and European Councils particularly).

Thus the EC/U is a strange creature, a kind of hybrid, which has been variously described as 'a union of States without unity of government' (Brewin 1987: 1); as 'less than a federation, more than a regime' (Wallace, Wallace and Webb 1983: 403) and so on. Thus it seems that, to borrow from another context, 'your theology depends upon where you stand': different people occupying various positions would not give similar accounts of the nature or the prospects of the EC/U.

We have seen that its evolution has been a paradoxical business. The verdicts given on its performance vary greatly with the position and, interestingly, often with the profession of the observer. In general, the lawyers are the least dissatisfied with the way things have gone. They can point to the degree of independence achieved by the Court; to its early and firm assertion of the concepts of primacy and direct effect; to the fact that its judgments are usually enforced, its rulings usually effective – although arguably not always consistent. Of course they have also worried about tendencies to flout the Court's rulings or to bypass it and about the law's delays. But the EC/U is a highly legal world, an aspect that cannot be emphasised too strongly. It is also one in which, as lawyers are not slow to remind us, the Court has often acted as the political glue or cement of the whole system when political will in other quarters appeared to be lacking.

Economists tend, sometimes, to appear the most critical. They are so sometimes on grounds of *theoretical* revisionism – suggesting, for instance, that gains from a customs union may be far more limited and problematical than earlier formulations suggested; and sometimes on grounds of straightforward observation of developments – in several of which they cast the Community as one of the villains of the piece.

And this time it is the political scientists who sometimes occupy the middle ground and are heard to utter 'on the one hand, … on the other hand', as they try to balance the achievements of the EC/U and the problems to which its existence has given rise or contributed.

At times its dynamism has seemed to flag, at others to pick up; and often, unexpected or unanticipated consequences have flowed from particular events. The world of the EC/U is full of paradox and irony, as we shall see. Its founding documents have certain constitution-like characteristics; they continue to be amended;

yet their exact status and effect continue to be disputed, as they seek to extend their reach.

Those documents – originally the Treaties of Paris and Rome – meant for the member states a highly *legal* world; an arrangement intended to produce, not least, *political* change; and to do so by – initially at least – mainly *economic* means. It is important to be aware of this strategy, as it is precisely its validity and its unanticipated consequences that have been and remain contested.

Since the end of the 1960s, Community institutions have announced a number of intentions and goals. They have sought to extend the range of activity internally; to develop the EC/U's external role; and to enlarge its membership. (In a related but slightly different formula, then French President Pompidou had spoken in 1969 of 'completion, deepening and enlargement' – *achèvement, approfondissement, élargissement.*) But like every other political system, the EC/U has had to face two kinds of challenge: one concerned with the consistency or coherence of the objectives being pursued; the other concerned with changes in the environment that might either render its efforts nugatory or more difficult or, of course, might prove favourable to it.

So although the EC/U has been in movement, it should be clear that there was never an agreed 'end product' or destination. Andrew Shonfield's 1973 title, *Europe: Journey to an Unknown Destination*, points this up sharply. It was clear that the very concept of a 'common market', never precisely defined, was a piece of elastic: everyone was sure of the minimum lengths to which they were supposed to go – a customs union, with agriculture somehow included; moving from free movement of goods to free movement of persons, services and capital as well. But just how far things could or should stretch; just what else should be included; what else would come to be seen or would be presented as implied or required, especially in pursuit of the second of the 'strategies' of Article 2 EEC – 'progressively approximating the economic policies of Member States' – was to be a matter of continuing debate.

In another context, I wrote: 'Beyond that, between that minimal state which the Treaty sought to programme fairly closely, and some distant peak which came later to be known as "full economic and monetary union", there was a good deal of mist and dead ground' (McAllister 1975: 180). Here I intend to explore a good deal of what went on in that mist and dead ground and to find out why it is that, to some, EMU seems a promised land; to others, distinctly unalluring.

If war is, as the nineteenth-century German strategist Clausewitz would have it, the continuation of diplomacy by other means, it is also the case in recent times, when 'war' might mean annihilation, that 'war' itself is largely pursued by 'other means' and these are often economic. It is against this background that the rocky ride of the EC/U should be seen.

Several 'wars' have been waged at once, closely allied to the four main themes I introduced earlier. There has been the 'external war': to define, establish and sustain a place for the EC/U in the world at large. There have been 'internal wars': to promote 'national interests' through the Community; to try to shape it in conformity with states' perceived interests; to avoid or mitigate undesirable consequences of the creature's actions. And the weaknesses and strengths of the EC/U are the mirror image of that. They arise from the same fundamental sources: from the exogenous shocks and impulses to which it is subject; from the attitudes of states and interests in fighting the internal wars; and from the institutional and structural features of the craft itself, designed perhaps for other cargoes and other waters and conditions.

There have been, then, several 'wars' and several sources of difficulty since the heady days of the founding fathers. Yet, as I hope to show in Chapter 2, 1968–9 marked a particular kind of change. With one of those ironies that seem to mock human endeavour, it was to be simultaneously a change upwards in ambition and rhetoric, and downwards in fortune and performance. But first, in Chapter 1, I trace the origins and early development of the original three communities (Coal and Steel Community; the Economic Community; the Atomic Energy Community) through the 1950s and up to the late 1960s.

# 1 Birth, childhood and adolescence

On the afternoon of 9 May 1950 Robert Schuman, born in Luxembourg and an auxiliary with the German army during World War I, stepped as Foreign Minister of France into the Salon de l'Horloge at the Quai d'Orsay and asserted: 'It is no longer the moment for vain words, but for a bold act – a constructive act.' With these words he launched, with the offer to the Federal Republic of Germany (FRG) specifically and to any other European state that so wished, the idea of pooling its resources of coal and steel in a European Coal and Steel Community (ECSC) (McAllister 1975: 177; Monnet 1978: 304). Unbeknown to anyone at the time, this was to become the first of three 'European communities' – together with the European Economic Community (EEC) and the European Atomic Energy Community (Euratom).

Schuman's natural style was anything but dramatic. One who knew him well said that he had the manner of a provincial priest, slightly hunched, with a hesitant voice. But he was certainly right about the 'vain words': this was, if anything, an understatement for some of the misunderstanding and mistrust that had marked relations between France and the government of the fledgling Federal Germany – then only a few months old (Willis 1965: Chs 3, 4).

The initiative that bore his name was largely the work of a man from the opposite end of France, Jean Monnet, head of the French national Planning Commission, native of Cognac, who had spent a good deal of *his* wars coordinating Allied efforts against Germany. The 'Schuman Declaration' followed at least three serious perceived failures, arguably more. There had been the perceived failures of the Organisation for European Economic Cooperation (OEEC), particularly associated with the UK's devaluation of September 1949. There had been the disappointments and minimalism associated with the first months of the Council of Europe which, its proponents had originally hoped, could be the political germ of a European federation, with limited but real powers. And there had been the rejection by France of Konrad Adenauer's suggestion on 9 March 1950 of a complete Franco-German union, beginning with a customs union.

However, there had also been some key 'successes' and these were also to have considerable influence over what did and did not happen. They were mainly in two areas: first, defence and security; second, economic reconstruction and trade.

On 17 March 1948 the Brussels Treaty had been signed by the 'Benelux' three, France and the UK. Its most important aspect was probably the last item of its title:

'collective self-defence'. The signatories resolved, among other things, to 'afford assistance to each other ... in resisting any policy of aggression' (preamble). It was no accident that it was concluded some 3 weeks after the Communist Party of Czechoslovakia gained control of that country in what was referred to as the 'Prague coup': some 3 months later the Soviet blockade of Berlin began.

The importance of this for our story is that the 'defence' angle was thus already covered; it included the UK from the start; it was greatly extended the following year with the signing of the North Atlantic Treaty Organisation (NATO) Treaty in April 1949; and in the early years, to no one's initial surprise, the FRG was excluded. With the defence flank covered, minds could turn to other things; and, by the same token, when 'other things' were set up, they would not cover defence, although the possibility was occasionally raised. Defence matters were also specifically excluded when the Statute of the Council of Europe was signed in May 1949.

The second, crucial, area – economic reconstruction and the revival of trade – had been the subject of an array of initiatives and proposals beginning right at the start of the 'cold war'. Pride of place here should go to the June 1947 proposal by US Secretary of State George Marshall to revitalise the European economy: the 'Marshall Plan' or European Recovery Programme (speech at Harvard, 5 June: text: *FRUS* (1947), III: 237–9; *DAFR* (1947), IX: 9–11). Marshall thought it essential that Europeans should work together in this, not in national boxes; and that thus what would become Germany's economic preponderance would be diffused. He also expected the UK to give an initial lead: and in this was disappointed. But in July, European officials, meeting in Paris, agreed to form the Committee on (later Organisation for) European Economic Cooperation – OEEC. Its early work however was, in American eyes, marked by timidity and lack of ambition: it did not propose a customs union or powerful institutions to give it direction (*FRUS* (1948), III: esp. 352–501; Lundestad 1998: 30–1; Messenger in Dinan (ed.) 2006: 37–9).

Slowly, however, a learning process set in: several states came to see that it was essential to tie Germany in; and the USA, increasingly disillusioned with British attitudes, found more receptive and proactive minds in France. Among these, Monnet was prominent. A great 'networker', he had long cultivated powerful friends in the United States and was more feted there than in his home country.

Another body, set up in June 1950, the month after the Schuman Declaration, was to provide crucial underpinning for west European cooperation and the achievement of prosperity. This was the 'child' of OEEC, the European Payments Union (EPU), promoted by the Economic Cooperation Administration and the State Department in Washington, to facilitate multilateral payments (thus enabling trade to grow) and ultimately (1958) full currency convertibility among OEEC members. In this it was successful and this growth of trade was the other key background factor of the 1950s. (West) German growth was heavily export biased, but this growth also made access to the German market of crucial importance for that country's neighbours (Milward 1992: esp. 134–8; Gillingham 2003: 40–3; Brusse in Dinan (ed.) 2006: 92–9; Gillingham in Dinan (ed.) 2006: 56–9). These developments were more immediately important for western Europe than the ECSC, to which we must now return.

Elsewhere I have argued that 'to some extent the strategy pursued by the "founding fathers" had a positive logic of its own; to some extent it was also a reactive one, a response to the perceived failures or shortcomings of any alternative approach' (McAllister 1975: 174). This is clear in a number of respects regarding Monnet's intellectual debts, and the 'lessons' that he believed a rich life experience had taught him. Having been part of a quasi-global body, the League of Nations, in the interwar period, he believed that the functions of such bodies as the United Nations (UN) would be largely restricted to those of a switchboard; there was insufficient common interest to go much further. He had, however, worked on inter-Allied coordination and equally knew the shortcomings of that kind of setup. But his wartime experience in Washington marked him deeply: 'In the United States Monnet learned how to organize Europe' (Gillingham 1991: 52). He believed passionately, as his autobiography makes clear, in the virtues of institutions, appropriately structured ('Nothing is possible without men [*sic*]: nothing is lasting without institutions' – Monnet 1978: 304–5). This aspect will be of great importance later in our discussion. He believed that much could be gained by pooling perspectives, if necessary banging heads together, by 'upgrading the common interest', by iconoclastic negotiating styles: that there was much to be said, in other words, for the sort of exercise in which the French Planning Commission, which he headed, was engaged. The US example told him that large markets were desirable. He borrowed from David Mitrany's functionalist thinking, but changed the scale in a way that Mitrany would not have approved: downwards from the global level, but upwards from the level of the single state, to the 'in-between' level of a (regional) group of states.

His natural bent, and lifelong orientation, was toward the Atlantic, Anglo-Saxon worlds including the UK, although he doubted its readiness to participate in his schemes. 'The British will not find their future role by themselves. Only outside pressure will induce them to accept change', he reports himself as saying to Schuman and Massigli in London in June 1950 (Monnet 1978: 307). And so it proved. The British, to whom Schuman fatally offered some form of 'association' falling short of total commitment, left it at that. Schuman made it clear that, if necessary, he would proceed with only two countries involved: in the event, France and Germany were joined by Italy and Benelux and 'Europe of the Six' was born.

The negotiations were fraught with difficulty; so were the operations of the Coal and Steel Community. At one point the Germans threatened to pull out entirely: the US civil commissioner for Germany, John McCloy, had to 'read the riot act' to Adenauer. Neither, in the event, did Monnet's schemes emerge unscathed; and there was a protracted battle over economic ideology between his (muddled) liberal–plus–*dirigiste* notions and a resurgent – and mostly triumphant – German corporatism (Gillingham 1991: esp. 137–77, 228–347; Milward 1992: esp. 333–7; Gillingham in Dinan (ed.) 2006: 66–76).

But for now, a few key points should be noted. First, the starting point was to be a common market: this starting point was to prove – and was intended – to have important political consequences. Second, it was limited to two key sectors (psychologically as well as materially – although the history and actual characteristics of these sectors made them highly *un*likely candidates for anything resembling 'market integration'). Third, there were significant institutional innovation and clear departure from 'intergovernmental' approaches. Fourth, although Monnet was no 'technocrat', the keystone of his institutional arch and most original feature was the small college of independent experts, the High Authority, of which Monnet himself became the first head. Institutions, indeed, claimed a prominent place in the Coal and Steel (Paris) Treaty. There were to be four, designated by Article 7: the High Authority; a 'Common Assembly'; a Council of Ministers; and a Court of Justice. To a marked degree these, both in their respective roles and powers, and in the doctrines that were to guide them, reflected notions and practices then current in France (see McAllister 1975: 179; McAllister 1988: 212–15). But although Monnet got his High Authority, the concept was not widely welcomed. The Germans to a degree eviscerated it, and were successfully to re-cartelise (Gillingham 1991: 319–30).

The general direction also found favour in Washington, but expectations were not over-sanguine. A CIA assessment dated 24 September 1951 stated: 'Supranational institutions of European unity – specifically the European Defense Force and the Schuman plan administration – should develop during the next 2 years, but *there is no indication that any European state is yet prepared to form a true federation with its neighbors*' (*FRUS* (1951), I: 202 [then classified top secret]). In November Riddleberger, Acting Deputy Special Representative for Europe to the ECA, cabled: 'We start from the conviction that ... we must continue to promote European economic unification (and political federation)' (*FRUS* (1951), I: 1500).

So, from early on, ECSC was not intended to be the only organisation. Already later in 1950, soon after war broke out in Korea, the Pleven Plan for a united West European army with German contingents was unveiled. It was seen as a French alternative to the inclusion of German units within NATO, for which the USA continued to press vigorously. The Pleven Plan became the basis of the proposal for a European Defence Community (EDC), mentioned earlier.

Again, the UK, whose support was particularly important to reassure France, refused to become involved. Nonetheless, the proposal, although weakened, was not yet abandoned. Indeed the opportunity was taken to try to add a 'third leg' to the organisational setup: a European Political Community (EPC) to be established under Article 38 of the EDC draft. Had these plans gone ahead, there would have been three bodies: ECSC, EDC and EPC. It was not to be: after increasingly bitter debates, the French National Assembly at the end of August 1954 voted not to proceed with consideration of the EDC proposal, and with it fell the EPC.

Other proposals for 'sectoral' organisations paralleling the ECSC, for transport, agriculture and health, proposals usually made under a Council of Europe umbrella, also had little success. In consequence, by the end of 1954 the organisational and institutional landscape was beginning to resemble a breaker's yard: there were far more wrecks than going concerns. In particular, it was far from clear at the time whether the 'sectoral approach' could really be proclaimed a great success, as cartels and price fixing rapidly entrenched themselves and as Monnet's stratagems seemed marginalised (Gillingham 1991: esp. Chs 5, 6; Gillingham 2003: Chs 2, 3; Gillingham in Dinan (ed.) 2006: 72–6): and he himself resigned from the presidency of the High Authority.

At this point, some advocated moving to a much wider approach to economic integration. In the year and a half following the EDC failure, 'over a dozen new proposals appeared' for some measure of trade liberalisation (Moravcsik 1999: 139). What eventually proved the most persuasive – despite Monnet's initial attempts to sabotage it – lay conveniently to hand in the form of the progress being made with the Benelux Economic Union. (For a detailed account, see Meade, Liesner and Wells 1962: 61–194.) Willem Beyen of the Netherlands took the lead in promoting the notion of a customs union of the Six, with some elements of a common market. Again timing was to be of the essence. The replacement of Mendès by Edgar Faure as French prime minister helped greatly.

But Monnet did not give up on his sectoralist preferences: the one then thought most promising appeared to be the great technological hope – it was much favoured by France in particular and there were few established interests to offend (except military ones): the nuclear energy industry.

Thus it was that the foreign ministers of the six members of ECSC came together at the Messina Conference in Sicily, at the beginning of June 1955, with both the Benelux and atomic energy proposals before them. The UK, invited at the insistence of the Benelux states, did not participate. Again the air had been cleared on some other questions: after the EDC failure had come the agreement to bring the FRG and Italy into NATO on 5 May 1955. Military difficulties were off the agenda, resolved elsewhere. The conference was chaired by Luxembourg's Joseph Bech, and, on this occasion, it was the 'Benelux three' who played the leading part. The conference concentrated on the two proposals – for a general common market, championed especially by Benelux; and for an atomic energy community, proposed by France. The resolution at the end of the conference incorporated both (Weigall and Stirk 1992: 94–7). It was thought best to keep the two separate, however, as they evoked differing reservations: France was doubtful of the benefits for itself of the common market idea; the FRG was doubtful about the atomic energy scheme (Urwin 1991: 74–5).

It was further agreed to set up an intergovernmental committee to work out the detail of the proposals and to report back. It was known to posterity as the Spaak Committee, after Belgium's Foreign Minister Paul-Henri Spaak, who chaired it. Its report was finally issued in Brussels on 21 April 1956 and accepted as the basis for negotiations by the six foreign ministers on 30 May. Since its influence on the subsequent Rome Treaties is so clear – sometimes the very same concepts and terms are used – a brief glance at its approach is warranted.

The Spaak Report asserted that a large market would facilitate mass production without monopoly. But the advantages of a common market could only come about if the requisite time were given to enable enterprises to adapt. This 'phasing', the transitional period, was of course spelled out in the EEC Treaty. It spoke also of the need for geographical limitation and added (this was crucial) that a common market was inconceivable without 'common rules, joint action, and finally an institutional system to watch over it': this last was music to the ears of a Monnet. It discussed such matters as the difficulty of distinguishing between (state) aids that were 'useful in the general interest' from those that had 'as their object or effect the distortion of competition' – the exact wording of the subsequent Article 85 EEC. It insisted that 'agriculture would have to be included' (Spaak Report: 44) – but did not say *how*, although the notion of 'agriculture as special' – subscribed to by all involved – was promptly and probably inevitably to appear in Article 39.2 of the EEC Treaty. It spoke about the 'need to override the unanimity rule, in defined cases, or after a certain period' (Spaak Report: 23–4): this was one of four 'principles', giving effect to which would require setting up four institutions – exactly those that are found in the Rome Treaties. It talked about the inclusion of services (Spaak Report: 40). It is, in brief, the 'open sesame' to the thinking behind the Rome Treaties, because the committee was then given the drafting task.

That certainly did not mark the end of the difficulties. Indeed, in France especially, initial responses to the Spaak Report were far from universal enthusiasm. The members of the committee had been operating *à titre personnel*, even though they had kept in fairly close touch with governments. There followed the difficult business of thrashing out national responses to it. And over this, there were serious disagreements at the time about several key questions: the separation of the two areas, atomic energy and general common market, and to which of them priority should be given; the institutional scheme; the underlying economic 'philosophies' – the balance of *dirigisme* and protectionism versus 'liberal' principles; and the whole question of how feasible a 'federal'-style ambition might be. All of these received an early, and vigorous, airing at the time: all were to come back time and again onto the agenda of the EC/EU.

Because France's role was so central – France was the *sine qua non* of the whole enterprise – differences between leading French figures assumed great significance. They were not lacking in the Fourth Republic. The most highly dramatised differences – to become more important once de Gaulle re-emerged from the political wilderness to lead the Fifth Republic in 1958 – were between de Gaulle and Monnet. But many even of Monnet's closest collaborators, notably Robert Marjolin who first met him in 1940 and worked closely with him from 1943, were far from sharing Monnet's apparently 'simplistic' federal vision. Marjolin, indeed, believed that it was not *necessary* to be so lofty: a common market could function perfectly well and achieve a critical enough transformation of the political relations of the states concerned, without 'going all the way' to political union. However, as he later wrote, '[I]t did not take me long to understand that Monnet was right in that to succeed one absolutely had to simplify' (Marjolin 1989: 173).

By the time of the Messina meetings and the setting up of the Spaak Committee, there was general acceptance that there would be no war between the states of *western* Europe again: nuclear weapons had rendered former great powers powerless. The greater security in other respects felt by most people meant that this could be a moment for bold experiment. It was clear that the US warmly supported the notion of a large market: for the wider political gain of creating a bulwark against communism, the USA was willing to make some sacrifices in the area of its apparent immediate economic interests. But there was still great hesitation and considerable resistance to the proposals, albeit from contrasting sources and for different reasons, in both France and Federal Germany (see, for example, Milward 1992: 198ff.).

France at the time of the Spaak Report remained for the most part strongly protectionist. The Germans, especially Economics Minister Erhard, preferred a liberal *global* order and worried about closed blocs. In working out the details and the mechanics, Spaak was much aided by another close Monnet aide, Pierre Uri, and by Hans von der Groeben of Germany, later a Commissioner.

Once the report was produced, in April 1956, it fell to national administrations to take positions. Because French reactions were of most importance, I deal mainly with them here. In France, initial reactions were far from favourable. (For rival accounts, see Willis 1965: 227–72; Monnet 1978: 418–26; Marjolin 1989: 284–307.) However, in the elections of 2 January 1956 the Gaullist group in the French National Assembly had shrunk from 121 to 21 (Grosser 1980: 127). But most representatives of French officialdom, of agriculture and of the *patronat* were also hostile. Marjolin reported that at the first French heads of department meeting to consider the matter, on 24 April 1956, apart from his own 'positive, though guarded' response, at the *tour de table*: 'All were against, except Bernard Clappier' – who had been Schuman's *chef de cabinet* when Monnet produced the coal and steel draft in 1950 (Marjolin 1989: 285).

So the French government response in May contained many caveats and called into question much of the Spaak approach. Main worries included the competitive position of French industry, in the light of France's supposedly higher social protection; the whole issue of how 'irreversible' the process was to be and whether states could back out if a trial period proved unsatisfactory; worries about capital movements; worries about labour migration, both from Italy to France, and from France to Germany; worries about German industrial hegemony; worries about 'overambitious' institutional schemes. These last were resolved by leaving out all mention of a 'High Authority' – to be replaced by the Commission, but with non-identical powers – and all mention of 'supranationality'.

The objections found full expression in Pierre Mendès-France's speech in the National Assembly on 18 January 1957. He claimed that the common market project as presented was 'based on the classical liberalism of the 19th century': and that it represented the abdication of democracy to an outside authority which 'in the name of technical efficiency, will in fact wield the political power' (Marjolin 1989: 293). Communists claimed that it was all an American plot, a German plot and a papal plot (see Willis 1965: 262–3). But by that stage, they and those of the Mendès persuasion were losing the battle. At the close of the debate of 17–18 January 1957, the motion expressing satisfaction with the progress on a Common Market Treaty was passed by 332 to 207. One factor which appears to have contributed to a change of gear, from the snail's pace of summer 1956 to a much speedier progress, was the humiliation of the Suez episode, which convinced Prime Minister Guy Mollet in particular that it was vital to show some positive achievement. He was powerfully aided by his own *chef de cabinet*, a certain Émile Noël, who in due course was rewarded for his pains with the key post of Secretary-General to the Commission, where he remained for an amazing tenure of some 29 years.

It is, however, to the Germans that most credit goes for keeping the *two* projects on the road in parallel and in contrast to Monnet's apparent preference for Euratom. Several areas of the common market agreement in particular represent delicate compromises, sometimes downright fudges, of contrasting French and German positions. Such include the issue of capital movements, where the text spoke of '*progressively* eliminating' them 'to the extent required for the efficient functioning of the common market' – without defining how far that went. There was also the question of systems of ownership of enterprises, again a delicate compromise between German preference for a system 'ensuring that competition in the common market is not distorted' (Art. 3f EEC) and French wishes not to have wider nationalisation called into question: 'This Treaty shall in no way prejudice the rules in Member States governing the system of property ownership' (Art. 222 EEC). (See McAllister 1988: *passim.*) Overall, there is little doubt that the French obtained most, although not all, of what they sought. They themselves acknowledged this: for instance, Lucien de Sainte Lorette, Secretary-General of the French section of the *Ligue Européenne de Coopération Économique*, spoke of the 'spirit of European understanding' shown by France's partners, who 'allowed her [France] to determine the course of the debate, not only because her representatives were of excellent quality, but also because her favors were worth having' (Sainte Lorette 1961: 71ff., quoted in Willis 1965: 247). In the final, lengthy debates on ratification in July 1957, government representatives were able to claim, 'It is the French coloring that has most marked and inspired [the Treaties]' (Willis 1965: 264).

The Treaty discussed in only the vaguest terms an area of crucial importance for France – agriculture. But even in that vagueness there was cause for satisfaction: Article 39.2 spoke of taking account of 'the particular nature of agricultural activity' – implying that the policies to be developed would maintain the supportive and interventionist relationships already built up in all the member states, 'in contrast to the more liberal tone that rang through most of the treaty' (Knudsen in Dinan (ed.) 2006: 193).

Two matters that might have proved more controversial in France appeared to have been compromised on or passed over. First was the notion of 'reversibility', desired by many in France but opposed by almost all its partners and contrary to the GATT requirement that customs union projects must proceed to complete tariff disarmament between the members. The second was what Marjolin described as 'the sole element of supranationality' – the Council of Ministers' power to take certain decisions by qualified (weighted) majority as of 1966. He reported:

> Curiously enough, few at the time, at any rate as far as I remember, were sufficiently worried about this eventuality to make a stand against clauses that would one day enable the majority to impose its law, with the risk that France might be in the minority.
>
> (Marjolin 1989: 305)

This issue forcefully resurfaced, on cue, 8 years later, as we shall see.

The treaties were ratified in the French National Assembly by 342 to 239. It was in the very middle of the French debate that ratification by the German Bundestag took place, on 5 July, followed by unanimous ratification by the Bundesrat on 19 July. Thus the two treaties of Rome – EEC and Euratom – originally signed in Rome on 25 March 1957, came into effect from 1 January 1958.

Any thoughts that, for France in particular, this meant some access of stability were rapidly shown to be an illusion. The Fourth Republic was in its death throes, battered by a sea of closely related internal and external crises. The most serious of the internal ones concerned the budget and the balance of payments; the most critical 'external' one was the war in Algeria and the resultant crisis of May 1958. On 13 May came the right-wing putsch in Algiers and the establishment of a 'Committee of Public Safety'; on the 15th, General Salan in Algiers ended his speech with the cry 'Vive de Gaulle!' and that gentleman obligingly declared himself 'ready to take over the powers of the Republic'. On the 19th de Gaulle spoke about the need to break with 'customary procedure' if he took over, but abjured dictatorship. On the 24th, paratroops from Algeria landed in Corsica: it was thought certain that Paris was their next objective. On the 28th, Pflimlin resigned as premier and President Coty announced to the National Assembly that he had called on de Gaulle to save the Republic.

Exactly 5 months after the entry into force of the Rome treaties, on 1 June, de Gaulle was invested as premier: and many both inside and outside France thought that he, as 'a vitriolic critic of European supranationalism, would smother the new Community at birth' (Willis 1965: 273–5). They were wrong: instead, the general proclaimed that he would defend the Rome treaties against their detractors.

However, during the 1960s, the Community faced a number of problems concerning its nature, scope and membership in which de Gaulle's central concept of a Europe of states came into conflict with the integrationists' aim of a United States of Europe. In this battle Adenauer, with, it is clear, major misgivings, felt constrained to support de Gaulle's line. This caused splits inside both France and the FRG and between them. These developments also caused many to see the Franco–German 'axis' not as the cornerstone of 'European' construction but as its rival. Three episodes were particularly prominent: the issue of UK membership; the issue of 'political union'; and the issue of the balance of power between the several institutions. I shall look at each in turn.

The period between 1958 and 1962 has been described as a 'honeymoon' period for the new Communities. This is not totally true, but insofar as it was, it owed a good deal to the facts that de Gaulle's most urgent priorities lay elsewhere and that the Germans, even when they had reservations about what was done, seldom got too far out of line with France.

Yet de Gaulle's role remains both crucial and controversial. It is perhaps not surprising that interpretations of his actions, intentions and ambitions tend to vary rather strikingly with the nationality of the observer. Probably he aimed, quite simply, at maximising France's room for manoeuvre and thus, he hoped, its prestige: at ensuring that it could not be taken for granted. Beyond that, he aimed to test and probe, confident in the double gamble that to do so would raise France's profile and that if France so dared, others would not dare to imitate, for fear of 'rocking the boat'. Also he made, and probably intended to make, embarrassing and tantalising offers to his interlocutors: knowing that *any* response they gave, *or none*, could be used by him and could damage them. His proposal, for instance, for a 'defence directoire' in the 17 September 1958 memorandum to Eisenhower and Macmillan (discussed later) was of such a kind.

As the 1960s proceeded, there were crises aplenty. Marjolin was right to argue that, to understand what went on in this first decade (up to about 1968), it is important to distinguish between 'what was actually spelled out in the treaty and the much more ambitious and often confused aspirations that reigned in the minds of some of the treaty's authors' (Marjolin 1989: 310). The confusions came to centre on de Gaulle's wishes and the UK and its motives. Most political 'federalists' wanted a federal Europe but with UK participation; but they asked themselves whether the UK was ready. 'Gaullists' wanted neither 'federalism' nor UK membership, but wondered if they might have to accept the second to prevent the first. And the UK certainly did not want political federalism either, but found its US friend and backer clearly asserting that this should be the destination, part of the 'grand design'. At several points in the 1960s (especially 1963 and 1965, perhaps also 1967) it looked as if the Community might reach a breaking point, as we shall see later in this chapter.

The early period produced two major attempts to 'haul' the Community structure in certain directions. The first was led by the UK and was in the direction, essentially, of a wide free trade area. These were the proposals of the 'Maudling Committee'. The second was to be led by France and sought to limit Community competence in another way: by setting up separate and different structures to deal with 'non-economic' matters. This concerned the so-called political union, or 'Fouchet', negotiations.

## Sixes and sevens

The first test was not slow in coming. This concerned the reactions to the establishment of the EEC by its excluded neighbours. The UK, having rejected membership for itself at the time of the ratification of the Rome treaties, had for some time sought to create a wide free trade area within the framework of OEEC. The ('Maudling') intergovernmental committee to consider this met from late 1957 to late 1958. Its proposals highlighted and rekindled divisions in the FRG in particular. Economics Minister Erhard and most business leaders were well disposed to the idea, both on general principle and on grounds of concrete commercial interest. It was clear, however, that the Fifth Republic's new government 'took a firm decision against commitment to the free trade area proposal ... *before* the opening of what the British government saw as the first true negotiations with the Six in October [1958]' (Milward 2002: 266, emphasis added). Would Adenauer again support French views in opposition to those of his minister, as he had already done during the EEC negotiations? On 14 September 1958 the Chancellor paid his first visit to General de Gaulle's country retreat at Colombey-les-deux-Églises. Willis reports that that Sunday afternoon, de Gaulle succeeded in persuading Adenauer 'of his devotion to the reconciliation of their two peoples, to the economic unification of the Six, and to the *association* of Britain and others in the work of integration' (Willis 1965: 279, emphasis added). It was a significant order – and a significant nuance.

Having first achieved this striking success with Adenauer, de Gaulle fired off his 17 September memorandum on the Atlantic Alliance, declaring that within it, the USA, France and the UK should form a special grouping. This *directoire* of three should 'function on a worldwide political and strategic level', averred the then secret memo (text reprinted in Grosser 1980: 187). The point was, of course, that within such an arrangement, France uniquely would 'speak for Europe', the one state to be both a member of the 'group of three' and of the European Community.

Then came the tense negotiations of the Maudling Committee on a 'wide free trade area' in October. Of these, Monnet wrote that it was one thing to preserve the interests of third parties; it was quite another to preserve the unity of the Six. 'And if Germany and the Benelux countries were infinitely more concerned about the former than France was, everyone was agreed on the latter' (Monnet 1978: 448). Again, this is a refrain worth bearing in mind: a pattern that has been repeated time and again in negotiations between the Community and its interlocutors. The UK argued, by contrast, that 'integration of this sort would divide the members of the OEEC between themselves and create two rival trading blocs ... Such a division of Europe would be bad economically and dangerous *politically*' (de la Mahotière 1970: 23, emphasis added).

There was no way through. The UK saw 'the Six' dividing Europe: France especially saw the UK dividing, perhaps deliberately trying to subvert, the Six, and saw the free trade area and EEC proposals as incompatible (see Milward 2002: Ch. 10). Indeed Marjolin, who had after all been OEEC Secretary-General until 1955, described the British proposal as 'too ingenious for its own good' (Marjolin 1989: 319). Although talks were due to reconvene on 19 November, French Information Minister Jacques Soustelle announced on the 14th that 'it was clear to France that it was not possible to create the free trade area in the way the British wanted' (Willis 1965: 280; see also Camps 1964: 174). The UK announced that Maudling would not be going to Paris for the scheduled meeting and that negotiations were suspended.

In the first of a series of uncannily similar episodes, de Gaulle immediately played the German card and requested an urgent meeting with Adenauer. At this, France made rather small concessions to the wishes of Erhard, on whom the British had relied to salvage something from the wreck. In December negotiations were formally broken off; the two groups went their separate ways and seven of the remaining eleven members of OEEC –Austria, Denmark, Norway, Portugal, Sweden, Switzerland and the UK – began the negotiations for a free trade association that were to lead to the Stockholm (EFTA) Convention, finalised on 20 November 1959 and signed in January 1960. Thus western Europe arrived at the stage of 'sixes and sevens'. The whole episode had confirmed the UK's isolation from the other major players, the political dimension inherent in the 'common market' starting point of the Communities, and the singular importance of the Paris–Bonn axis.

## The Fouchet negotiations on 'political union'

It was not long, however, before the third of these – the Paris–Bonn axis – was to come under strain as a result of an attempt to pursue the second – the 'political dimension'. Work on the customs union went forward, but there were different views about 'acceleration'. In the debate that took place on this between February and May 1960, France supported the acceleration proposals as a step toward 'political union': again, Erhard in the FRG led those urging caution and not widening the schism with EFTA and the UK in particular. Again Erhard lost most of the battle. Progress over the main mechanisms and speed of the common agricultural policy (CAP) was closely linked to this: at one point the agricultural dossier came close to derailing the talks. Agriculture having been included in the Treaty (Articles 38–47), discussion on how to put these into effect had begun early, at the Stresa Conference of July 1958. More detailed proposals were produced by the Commission during 1959, under Vice-President Sicco Mansholt: they were finalised and presented to national ministers on 30 June 1960, then passed to a special committee on agriculture which reported back to the Council of Ministers in November 1960 (Willis 1965: 289).

It was in the middle of this phase, on 5 September 1960, that de Gaulle held one of his seismic press conferences. Here he proposed regular cooperation in western Europe on political, economic, cultural and defence matters. The system he advocated was essentially intergovernmental – 'regular organised consultation by the governments responsible'. For this was also the occasion when he set forth the famous view: 'What are the realities in Europe? What are the pillars on which it can be built? In truth, they are the States … the only entities that have the right to command and the authority to act.' Once again, de Gaulle had forewarned his most important interlocutor, Chancellor Adenauer, at their meeting at Rambouillet on 29–30 July, of his views on 'political cooperation' and 'political union'. Although Adenauer's personal response had been generally positive, more general German reactions were negative (Silj 1967: 3, 5).

It seems fairly clear that de Gaulle was seeking to link several items of his preferred agenda. Acceleration of the customs union could go ahead if there were parallel progress on agriculture: both would entail a greater economic 'identity' for the Six. But the specifically Community machinery should be circumscribed: the best way to do this was to set out alternative and clearly intergovernmental mechanisms for handling all proximate policy areas. A key part of the French proposals was to hold the consultations at the highest political level – of heads of state or government – and to institutionalise them.

To consider how to take things forward, the first conference of heads of state or government in February 1961 set up an intergovernmental committee with the French ambassador to Denmark, Christian Fouchet, as chairman: the negotiations bear his name and that of his successor, Cattani of Italy. Marked differences of view rapidly emerged: the Dutch took the strongest stand against French views on NATO, the relationship with the existing Community bodies and with the UK. The other four countries were roughly in between, 'with Germany and Italy either willing or resigned to accept the French formula (only marginally modified)' (Silj 1967: 9). It is worth noting that only much later, towards the end of the negotiations, did the position come to resemble 'France versus the Five'. For this is one of several respects in which the Fouchet negotiations of the early 1960s resembled the later 'constitutional' crisis in the Community in 1965–6 (discussed later), which culminated in the so-called Luxembourg Agreements.

The discussions became linked to the UK attitude concerning accession. Although the 'political union' negotiations were kept separate from negotiations on UK membership, '[T]he two sets of negotiations interacted in a number of ways' (Camps 1964: 414) – beginning with the very decision to apply and its timing (31 July 1961). The British government decided not to wait, either for a more favourable climate of opinion on the continent or a more convincing mood of European enthusiasm by public opinion and domestic political forces.

The UK's decision to apply came quickly after the second, July, summit meeting in the Fouchet framework. The Bonn Declaration (18 July) of that meeting was a masterpiece of doors left ajar and options not foreclosed. The preamble spoke of strengthening ties 'especially in the framework of the European Communities' and of a united Europe 'allied to the United States of America and to other free peoples': it declared that they wished for 'the adhesion to the European Communities of other European States ready to assume in all spheres the same responsibilities and the same obligations' – a weighty qualification. They spoke *both* of 'further[ing] the application of the Rome and Paris Treaties' and of 'facilitat[ing] those *reforms* which might seem opportune in the interests of the Communities' greater efficiency'. Clearly France had gone some way to placate the fears of the Five over the Atlantic Alliance and the ECs. Finally, the Fouchet Committee was instructed to make proposals on ways to enable 'a statutory character to be given to the union of their peoples' (Camps 1964: 415; text: Camps 1964: 523–4).

This was where it came unstuck: 'exogenous shocks' played their part, in the shape of the August Berlin crisis; the building of the Wall; the non-response of the west; a most awkward hiatus in the FRG's foreign policy; and the relatively poor showing of Adenauer's coalition in the elections of 17 September (Grosser 1980: 197). At all events, little progress was made in the 'political union' discussions and the draft submitted by the French to the others in November 1961, entitled a 'union of states', was widely seen as retreating from the formulae of the Bonn Declaration in a distinctly Gaullist direction.

The grounds of disagreement cast remarkably long shadows before them. First there was the whole 'states' versus 'peoples' formula, redolent of completely different philosophies and approaches – constantly fudged ever since, usually by the careful inclusion of both terms and still very much with us. The other issues read almost like an agenda of Community business for the rest of the 1960s and beyond. Second was the institutional issue, specifically whether an intergovernmental body at the level of heads should be institutionalised, as it finally was with the emergence of regular European Councils in 1974; and the issue of whether the existing Community institutions should be sacrosanct, the basis of France's challenge in the 1965–6 crisis. Third was the issue of defence, where again the Gaullist programme was fully revealed in the decision to quit the NATO integrated military commands in 1966, hot on the heels of the 'Luxembourg Agreements'. Fourth was the issue of relations with the UK and other possible applicants, which again was to result in the two French vetoes of the UK in 1963 and 1967.

By this stage things had much more firmly assumed the shape of 'France versus the rest': but this was reinforced yet further by a second French draft in January 1962, which seemed to the other Five to be even worse than the first. Again France sought to make some concessions to save the plan: its attempts were directed almost entirely to the Germans and Italians and the small states felt marginalised. The Dutch and Belgians, although having differing views about what was proposed, both refused to sign any such treaty until the UK had joined the EEC. Rounds of frantic diplomatic activity got nowhere. In April, the (now Cattani) Committee adjourned – its report simply rejected by the Netherlands – and was not reconvened. The whole episode had been most revealing: it had involved all four of the battles, or issue clusters, discussed earlier; and it had shown some of the 'contrary logics' at work, in terms of the approaches adopted by the contending philosophies.

January 1962 had seen not only the Fouchet revised French draft. It saw also two other important episodes. The first was the protracted crisis over an agricultural deal, finally ending with agreement on 14 January. Without that agreement, it seems quite likely that France would have forced a major crisis on the Community, perhaps even have left (5 *GRA*: 10; Marjolin 1989: 325). As it was, the agricultural agreement was heralded by Rolf Lahr of the German Ministry of Foreign Affairs as 'a new Treaty of Rome'. The hyperbole was understandable. The Six had proved their seriousness to one another and this enabled them to move to the second stage: for better or worse it set major parameters to the kind of CAP that could possibly emerge thereafter and, again for better or worse, it imposed a degree of solidarity – over agriculture – among the Six in their subsequent dealings with the UK (see Camps 1964: 391–2; Willis 1965: 287–92).

It also set up cumbersome, bureaucratic, autarkic arrangements, committing the Community to internal preference, 'financial solidarity' and a Byzantine policy that few would lightly challenge lest the whole thing fall apart. The compromise was one in which, by common consent, France gained most and gave way least. In all those senses of 'importance for the future' then, the agreements of 14 January 1962 were indeed to prove 'historic'.

The second development was the proclamation of President Kennedy's 'grand design', followed by several authoritative statements in the same sense by US administration heavyweights such as George Ball and McGeorge Bundy and on 4 July by the president again, this time calling, on Independence Day, for European–US 'interdependence'. It is fairly clear that neither of these speeches had the intended effect on de Gaulle.

The year 1962, like 1973 in this respect although not in others, was thus both a year of grand American declarations and also a year in which the Atlantic seemed for some, especially in France, to grow much wider. Two episodes above all seemed to de Gaulle and those around him to confirm their worst fears about both the USA and Britain: the Cuban Missile crisis of October and the issue of the US–UK military nuclear relationship, culminating in the Kennedy–Macmillan talks at Nassau in December and the American offer of Polaris to Britain.

But there was a further revealing lesson. The 'successes' of 14 January did not 'spill over' to influence the Fouchet discussions. And de Gaulle's response to the failure of 'Fouchet' and to the other events of 1962 just described, became clear in the following months. It was 'to conclude with Germany alone the political union he had offered the Six' (Willis 1965: 299). This time his timing was fine. For while France and the FRG shared certain political interests, their economic interests – concerning the admission of the UK – were in conflict. 'When de Gaulle vetoed British membership … in January 1963, he did so knowing he would precipitate a major crisis in Franco-German relations' (Willis 1965: 299).

## The first UK accession bid and the road to January 1963

My concern here is not with what motivated the UK's decision to apply for membership (see Camps 1964: *passim*; Milward 2002: esp. Ch. 11); rather it is with the effects that had on the relations between the existing members and on the work programme of the Community. Nonetheless, several points that Prime Minister Harold Macmillan made, in the initial announcement of the decision to open negotiations on 31 July 1961, and in debates in the Commons on 2 and 3 August, were to be influential. (See Camps 1964: 356–66; Willis 1965: 299–305; Kitzinger 1973: *passim;* Marjolin 1989: 332–40.)

First, Macmillan stressed that if a closer relationship between the UK and EEC were to disrupt Commonwealth ties, 'the loss would be greater than the gain'. That gave de Gaulle one hostage. Second, he rejected the strategy of going for early entry and then, from within, trying to deal with the issues of EFTA, the Commonwealth and UK agriculture. Third, he emphasised that exploratory talks had gone as far as they could and that to discover the terms of entry now required submission of a formal application for accession (Camps 1964: 357; *Hansard*, HoC, 31 July 1961, cols 928–31).

Macmillan made clear that he agreed with the General on *Europe des patries*. By a fine irony, his most feared opponent from his own side, former minister Sir Derek Walker-Smith, used formulae that were to be taken up and thrown back at the British by de Gaulle in his famous 14 January 1963 press conference. Clearly, the French Embassy in London and the Quai d'Orsay had done a fine job of collecting and conserving quotable quotes. Walker-Smith said that the Six's evolution had been 'continental and collective. Ours has been insular and imperial'. Seventeen months later, de Gaulle said, 'England [*sic*] … is insular, maritime, linked through her trade, markets and supply lines to … very distant countries' (Camps 1964: 362; Urwin 1991: 124).

Negotiations began in September 1961. We do not need to relate their course in detail here. (For full accounts see Camps 1964: Chs XI, XIV; Milward 2002: Chs 10–14; also Grosser 1980: 199–208; Marjolin 1989: 332–40.) At one time, they appeared to be going well, with conclusion at least envisageable. Yet, as is well known, they failed in January 1963. Why?

First, the UK had a hard hand to play. If the British appeared too enthusiastic to join at any price, the price was likely to be raised. If they appeared too cool, their sincerity and intentions would be questioned.

Yet by August 1962 considerable progress had been made. But it appears that, in regard to arrangements for the Commonwealth, the British tried too hard to get open-ended concessions from the Six and waited too long before making concessions. As a result, the 'outline agreement' that Heath had set as a goal for the summer was not complete. 'Six weeks saved in the summer of 1962 might have made the difference between failure and success' (Camps 1964: 411).

Second, it is clear too that the differences of view over political union, between 'Gaullists' and 'Europeans' and between each of these and the UK, 'helped create the political climate in which the breakdown ... occurred' (Camps 1964: 414). Thus even by the time of the 17 April 1962 breakdown of the Fouchet negotiations, a great deal of mutual suspicion and bad blood had been created. If the Fouchet failure hardened de Gaulle's stance, military matters made things worse. In May, US Defence Secretary McNamara presented his strategic conception for NATO 'without any prior consultation' (Grosser 1980: 204). Then there was Cuba: this was ambiguous, since it is noted both that France saw it as the USA 'going it alone', but also that de Gaulle offered the Americans much appreciated support. Then the Anglo-American missile tangle came to a head in December just after de Gaulle had met Macmillan at Rambouillet.

The Kennedy–Macmillan meeting at Nassau in December was crucial. At Nassau, the unexpected, perhaps unintended, happened. The USA offered initially the British and then the French the Polaris missile. It happened in part to sooth battered British egos and accusations of treachery following the US decision to cancel the Skybolt missile, promised to the UK and without which she was indeed, in the nuclear sense, bare. It was not the outcome intended at the start of a badly prepared rendezvous. It seemed to turn on the odd personal chemistry between a young president and an avuncular but difficult prime minister. It carried a heavy price.

Nassau ended with a long communiqué and a yet longer statement on nuclear defence, a sure sign that explanations were felt to be required (Grosser 1980: 205–7). Polaris was also offered to de Gaulle. Kennedy appears to have thought that de Gaulle would accept; Macmillan, rightly, that he would not. He was not likely to accede to something agreed by others for him: and in any case he did not then have the submarines in which to put the missiles. For him, the whole thing smelt of dependence; and the British were the midwives of it.

Nassau was at any rate a pretext for General de Gaulle to say no. There was probably no longstanding French plot to refuse British accession, partly because it seems that de Gaulle did not believe until summer 1962 that their 'necessary conversion' would be other than a lengthy process. Until that point, France was able to present as pure 'defence of the hard-won treaties' what undoubtedly conformed to its concept of its own interests. Camps is surely right – once it seemed that the UK adaptation might be swift, de Gaulle had only two options: to change his own policy and take the British on board or to 'take action to give his assumptions continuing validity. It is in character that he chose the latter' (Camps 1964: 501). For the UK presented a double threat to French power as he conceived of it: 'an immediate threat to French dominance of the Continent' and 'a continuing threat to the emergence of his preferred kind of "third force" Europe' (Camps 1964: 504). Nonetheless, there is evidence that contingency plans had been laid. In June 1962 *Agence Europe* published a document written, it said, 2 years earlier by the 'young Turk' Alain Peyrefitte, a close collaborator of Debré and other senior French political figures. It discussed ways of 'exploiting the hopes and making use of the forms and language of the "Europeans" to attain Gaullist ends' and set out a strategy for dealing with the UK issue very close to that adopted by the French government (see Camps 1964: 500n). Needless to say, he became minister of information!

Nassau fell into General de Gaulle's hands, but as such it significantly helped to shape the Community. De Gaulle had other, less instant, and more clearly economic, reasons for resisting – at least postponing – UK accession. He had never liked the British 'free trade area' approach and had rejected it in late 1958. That had been followed by long wrangles over the economic terms. Meanwhile, between then and 1963, he had seen the French economy do extremely well within the (proto-)customs union. To try to accommodate UK commonwealth concerns would be costly and, for him, undesirable. There were thus durable economic objections – until, as he made clear in the January press conference, the UK's attitudes and policies had further evolved. Even if 'the *language* of de Gaulle's veto was shaped by the United Kingdom's close military alliance with the USA ... [T]he course of the negotiations for accession suggests that the veto was pronounced for economic reasons' (Milward 2002: 472, emphasis added).

But the veto meant that things happened between 1963 and the early 1970s which were most unlikely to have occurred in the same way, if at all, had the UK and others completed accession around 1963. These things were both positive and negative. Some, while de Gaulle was still around, reflected his own determination to prevent or restrain certain Community developments: this is particularly the case with the 'crisis' of 1965–6 and the Luxembourg Agreements. Later, as we shall see, other and more ambitious *démarches* were begun. These too, little though de Gaulle would have approved them, would have been most unlikely had the UK been on board; we may note especially the proposals for 'deepening' that were to emerge at The Hague in 1969.

January 1963 was another crucial month: crucial for the whole shape of the Community and not just for narrower relations. At the beginning of the month came de Gaulle's rejection of the Nassau offer. On the 14th came the famous press conference at which he indicated that the UK was not ready to join the Community without restriction, reservation or preferences. A week later Couve asked for negotiations to be suspended *sine die*; on the 30th they were. But that week later also marked the signature of the Franco-German Treaty of Cooperation, on the 22nd. In the circumstances, the Treaty, which should have crowned Adenauer's career, was regarded in the FRG with deep suspicion. *Die Zeit* put a direct antithesis: 'De Gaulle or Europe?', it asked (Willis 1965: 310). It was regarded with equal suspicion among France's other partners, who hastened to try to apply balm to the British.

The dust took time to settle. But it slowly became clear that, as a result of what had happened, the construction phase of the Community would continue to be largely Franco-German led and dominated by French concerns. If the UK thought that it could move on from the original free trade area proposals of 1956–8 and instead ride on the back of the Kennedy 'grand design' as a way of squaring the circle – 'Atlantic plus European free trade' with a Commonwealth add-on; entry to the Community followed by modification from within – it was sadly disillusioned. It was, in fact, left awkwardly hanging in the middle, though helped by the 'Kennedy Round' of tariff reductions. In Acheson's famous expression, it had lost an empire but not yet found a role.

Although most were shocked at the 'brutal' way that de Gaulle had forced a breach, many shared some of his views. The British had shown that they were not ready. The negotiations had been a major distraction. Once out of the way, 1963 and 1964 were described as 'among the most productive' years in the building of the Community (Marjolin 1989: 346).

These dramatic events clearly shaped the Community for the rest of the 1960s. But they were followed by others, some connected. For my purposes, four further episodes should be noted for their importance in shaping what the Community was to become by 1968–9.

They are: first, the 'constitutional crisis' of 1965–6 and the Luxembourg Agreements concluding it; second, the 'Merger Treaty' of 1965, not effective until 1967; third, France's decision to leave the integrated military command of NATO in March 1966; fourth, the second British membership application and second French veto of 1967, following which the application was left 'on the table'.

The furore in the Five that greeted the 1963 French veto was quickly followed by action in the Bundestag over the Franco-German Treaty. At ratification, that body added a preamble quite at variance with Gaullist notions of European identity and foreign policy. The signing of the treaty was virtually Adenauer's last major act of office. In October 1963 he demitted to Erhard: in what time remained, there continued to be little love lost between them.

The years 1963 and 1964 saw the consolidation of the CAP in two ways: first, it was extended to new sectors (dairy products, rice, beef and veal); second, actual common prices were agreed for the 'foundation stone' sector of cereals. Further steps were taken on tariffs both internal and external. A start was made on attempts at 'economic coordination', even though the 'first medium-term economic policy programme' remained largely a dead letter (Denton 1967; McAllister 1979: 63–6).

## The crisis of 1965–6 and the 'Luxembourg Agreements'

But in March 1965 broke the violent storm that was to shake the Community to its foundations. This episode was about both policy scope and the balance between the institutions – and thus about the powers of member states to halt the process. Its causes and course have been well described (Lambert 1966; Newhouse 1967; de la Serre 1971) and will be only sketched here. It should be noted that, while the start of the crisis did not prevent the signing of the Treaty of Merger, or Fusion, of the executives of the three Communities (Treaty Establishing a Single Council and a Single Commission; Brussels, 8 April 1965), it did delay bringing that Treaty into effect – until 1967.

It was Marjolin's judgment that, when that period of crisis (March 1965–January 1966) was over, the Community assumed 'if not its definitive form, at least the form it would retain for the next twenty years' – in other words, until ratification of the Single European Act (Marjolin 1989: 347). It meant the victory of essentially Gaullist conceptions about the institutions, but it left the Community in an awkward limbo, for there was no formal revision of the treaties, and the 'Luxembourg compromise' was a so-called 'gentleman's agreement', having no legal status. The few 'supranational' elements in the Rome Treaty were removed *in practice*: but if 'federal' Europe were in full retreat, France's partners were not willing to see Europe of the states formally erected instead.

The crisis broke over France and agriculture. The most contested issue is whether it could *only* have broken over a matter so important to that country or whether in principle at least it could have centred on another country, another issue – and in that sense could be said to be a crisis about the very nature of institutions that forced states into a corner. What was no coincidence was that it occurred *when* it did: at the approach of the move from second to third stage of the transitional period, to be accompanied, according to the Treaty, by moves to qualified majority vote on a range of issues.

There was one important reason, frequently overlooked, why the swing towards a 'power of the states' notion could not go further, or all the way. It was *not* that the other states were able completely to resist. The point to note is that the battle took place between the states (at first in the Council of Ministers until France withdrew – the 'policy of the empty chair'), and concerned *two* of the other institutions, the Commission and the Assembly. It could not reverse what had *already happened* in the other institution – the Court of Justice.

Already, in two key judgments in particular between 1962 and 1964, the Court had established the doctrines of the primacy/supremacy of Community law and that of direct effects. The latter was enunciated in Case 26/62 *Van Gend en Loos*; the former in Case 6/64, *Costa* v. *ENEL* (see [1963] *ECR* 1; [1964] *ECR* 585; Usher 1981: 19–38; Wyatt and Dashwood 1987: 28–30).

Although the Court played no role in the dénouement of the 1965–6 crisis (and this itself is significant), it yet retained the capacity to act as a crucial 'political cement' in the system when the other institutions, more overtly endowed with such a mission, were disabled. The Court could not 'do it all', but it was not powerless either, as was painstakingly to be proved by the end of the 1970s.

What, then, of the causes and course of the 1965–6 crisis? Once again, as in January 1962, there was the coincidence of the need to take key decisions concerning agriculture and the timetable of a move from one to another stage of the transitional period. Once again, France was the key actor. The January 1962 marathon session had adopted financial regulations valid until 1 July 1965. The question thus arose of what arrangements to make for the period between 1 July 1965 and the adoption of a 'definitive' financing regime later, when both agricultural levies and import duties would become the Community's 'own resources'. The Council, in agreeing a major *CAP* package in December 1964, asked the Commission to present proposals on the CAP aspects, by 1 April 1965.

Commission President Walter Hallstein presented outline proposals in a speech to the Assembly in Strasbourg on 24 March. Outline proposals did not require formal agreement of the whole Commission. But both this manner of proceeding and the radical content caused raised eyebrows: normal practice was for the Council of Ministers to be informed first. The proposals went well beyond just agriculture. Hallstein proposed that both the agricultural and industrial common market should be completed in mid-July 1967. From that date the proceeds of the agricultural levies should be payable direct to the Community, while the payment of industrial import duties also direct to the Community should be phased in over some few years. The member states realised that this meant the Community would be in receipt of funds well beyond its immediate needs.

Further compounding its audacity, the Commission proposed changes to the *institutional competences* in budgetary matters. The Commission should be given power to accept or reject amendments to the draft budget put forward by simple majority of the Assembly. If it accepted, then the Council could only reject that by a five-sixths majority (non-weighted: one country, one vote). If the Commission rejected the Assembly proposal, the Council, on the basis of four-sixths, could support the Commission. In all other cases, the Assembly's amendments would be adopted. What lay behind this was very simple. In budgetary matters, the Commission would become in effect 'a kind of government of the Community' (Marjolin 1989: 350): as long as it received the support of a majority of the Assembly and of two states, perhaps small ones, its proposals would carry the day. A majority, even of large states, would not prevail.

Commissioner Marjolin was himself opposed to it and convinced that, far from triumphing, the plan was bound to provoke hostility and would probably set back Community construction severely. His comment that '[W]ith this strange legal construct the idea of a federal Europe made its last appearance' (Marjolin 1989: 350) is probably correct as far as the ensuing near 20-year period is concerned. It is clear that it was the brainchild mainly of Hallstein and of agriculture commissioner Mansholt; the plan was kept secret from many in the Commission.

What lent a false note to the proceedings was that states began to strike poses, to take up positions not because they believed in them but in order to embarrass other states. It is important to underline this point. Although this was a key example, it was by no means the only one. The technique of 'shaming the other' and of striking a *communautaire* pose to see who would crack first has become a central part of the games people play in the EC/U. We shall encounter it often.

This time, other states and some Commissioners were trying to force France's hand, mainly in retribution for the veto on Britain. Few were ready to agree to the

Commission's institutional proposals, but many found it convenient to hide behind France, which could be relied on to refuse even to discuss these. From late 1964 the French government had insisted on the centrality of the agricultural deal and threatened dire but somewhat unspecified consequences if it did not happen. But it was also determined to stop the move to majority voting and the Commission's quasi-governmental ambitions.

Thus in the early hours of 1 July 1965, when the deadline for agreeing agricultural finance had passed and no deal had been concluded, Couve de Murville said that only an interim agriculture deal was required and the issue of the Assembly's powers must not and need not be discussed. France recalled its Permanent Representative and began the policy of the 'empty chair' in the Council of Ministers which was to continue until January 1966. But the Community did not, despite dire predictions, break up; neither did it even stand completely still. Although France was now represented only at meetings concerned with the operation of the CAP (and association of Greece and Turkey), a 'written procedure' was devised, whereby routine business not objected to could go ahead.

The Commission, realising that it had over-reached, tried to rescue the situation by a compromise, in a July memorandum, that would have given France most of what it had publicly argued for. This had the effect only of evoking from the General the full broadside of his real objections. In another press conference (9 September) he argued that what had happened was not just about agriculture, but highlighted 'certain errors or ambiguities in the Treaties … That is why the crisis was, sooner or later, inevitable' (Newhouse 1967: 120–1). He went on to cite majority voting in particular. Marjolin was clear: France was asking that provisions of the Treaty, to which it had subscribed, not be applied. Would the others go ahead nevertheless, take majority decisions and haul France before the Court as they were entitled to do? 'It was conceivable, but absurd. The Community would have fallen to pieces' (Marjolin 1989: 354).

But de Gaulle's position was not unassailable: presidential elections loomed, his popularity sagged. And he had other fish to fry in the dispute developing over NATO. France set forth its demands in a document known as the 'decalogue'. A first round of negotiations by foreign ministers failed. It was held in Luxembourg to emphasise its 'separateness' from Brussels. The Commission was not present: it was no more part of the immediate solution than the Court. At a second meeting on 28–30 January, the 'compromise' was hammered out. Its deft wording seems to have owed much to Joseph Luns (Newhouse 1967: 156–7). It stated, first, that states would do everything possible to agree; next, that France considered that, where very important interests were at stake, the discussion must be continued until unanimity was reached; third, that there was thus a divergence of views on what should be done in the event of a failure to reach complete agreement. Finally came the masterstroke: 'The six delegations nevertheless consider that this divergence does not prevent the Community's work being resumed in accordance with the normal procedure' – *selon la procédure normale.* Seldom has the definite article been so indefinite! But one thing was definite: from thenceforth, the Council did not proceed to majority voting where the Treaty allowed, and the search for unanimity became the norm.

The main consequences of the whole affair may be briefly summarised. First, there is little doubt that the balance of power between Commission and Council of Ministers, rather delicately crafted by the framers of the treaties, tilted away from the former. It had been given a sharp rap over the knuckles, lost much *élan*, and failed to gain the ground that 'stage 3' promised, let alone that which it had tried to claim for itself. The Commission certainly had to drop some of its 'executive' pretension and content itself more with the role of mediator. But second, that did not quite equate to saying that the Council(s) 'gained' power: rather that its (negative) power to stall was confirmed, with the potential that held for slowing down a decision process that might otherwise have been expected to *accelerate* as the Community moved beyond its 'set' agenda. Third, in that situation, for anything to move at all, there would be greater propensity to adopt the methods of package deals, log rolling, tradeoffs and pork barrel, as indeed proved the case. Fourth, that tendency was magnified by a decline in morale and in the initiative and innovating features of the Commission. Fifth – a consequence that emerged in the fairly short term – the 'Merger' Treaty having formally recognised the role of the Committee of Permanent Representatives (COREPER), that body found its real influence in practice very much enhanced. That was where deals were increasingly brokered (see Newhouse 1967: 161–2). Sixth – a longer range 'consequence' – the situation resulting from the crisis contributed to two later and more distant developments of considerable importance: one, the re-emergence of 'summits' and their formalisation as the European Councils of Heads of State or Government; two, the Parliament's strengthened attempts, especially once directly elected, to control the budget.

Opinions differ about the importance and extent of each of these points and how far they may be regarded as 'resulting' from the 1965–6 crisis, but overall there is little doubting its significance in setting parameters for what was to happen for a long time to come. In the meantime, the Commission itself, due for renovation under the Merger Treaty, had no mandate and the French insisted that Hallstein not be in charge: Jean Rey of Belgium was to become president.

It has been said often that the Luxembourg 'Agreement' was an agreement to disagree. It should be added that few, if any, of the member states really wanted majority voting in 'important matters' and that was to remain true for most. To a great extent they agreed about precisely what the 'compromise' said they disagreed about.

## The second accession bid

Business was resumed. In 1966 a financial regulation largely met French demands. The date of 1 July 1968 was set for the simultaneous completion of the 'common market' in both industrial and agricultural aspects. May 1967 saw agreement on the Kennedy Round. It also saw the submission of the second UK accession application.

Again France stated her opposition: this was to be the so-called 'velvet veto'. This time there was no Nassau. But there was another event in which France had played no small part: in November sterling was devalued. This was not a trivial event. Not merely did it enable de Gaulle to say with some plausibility 'I told you so!' in regard to the UK's 'fitness' to join, but it was also part of the war waged with increasing fierceness by those Johnson called the 'continental conservatives' in monetary matters, against the 'Anglo-Saxon profligates' (Johnson 1970: Ch. 9). Yet more important were two much greater paradoxes, as we shall see in the next chapter. First, the 'costs' of this war proved damaging to de Gaulle, and to the franc. Second, this set in train a turbulence in the world monetary system which in turn contributed to derailing the best laid schemes of the Community in the monetary field.

De Gaulle used the sterling devaluation to rub in the message of the UK's economic weakness and general unsuitability. By yet another fine irony, it was just prior to the completion of the customs union stage, 18 months ahead of schedule on 1 July 1968, that the famous May–June 'events' of 1968 revealed that the French economy had feet of clay too. At the point of maximum risk to de Gaulle's Republic, it was Prime Minister Pompidou who took charge in Paris while de Gaulle went to Baden-Baden to assure himself of the reliability, in case of need, of General Massu's crack divisions. Pompidou's reward, after the crushing victory of the right in the elections that followed, was to be stood down from his office, but asked to hold himself in readiness for whatever duty the Republic might require.

The call was not long in coming. The year 1969 brought, first, the curious 'Soames affair' to poison Franco-British relations yet further; then the April referendum on regional and senate reform, lost by de Gaulle and immediately followed by his resignation. His replacement by Pompidou, who devalued the franc, revealed a more positive approach to the accession requests, and provided the 'open sesame' to the further development of the Community. For, clearly, somewhere between the attainment of the customs union and the formal end of the transitional phase at the end of 1969, it would have been possible for the Community and member states to declare its essential aims complete: to declare that the 'process' was at an end and that all that remained was continuing management. This is not what happened.

Instead the Commission, in a declaration on 1 July 1968, announced: 'All – or nearly all – still remains to be done.' It spoke of harmonisation in commercial, fiscal, transport, social and other fields; of gradually replacing 'the old national policies with Community policies'; of monetary union and its coping stone, 'a common currency superseding the old national currencies'; of a political union, enlarged, with federal institutions. 'This is work on a grand scale which will keep a whole generation busy.' The last phrase certainly came true. There was to be no respite if the Commission had its way (Hodges 1972: 69–73). What happened to those mighty plans will be looked at in the next two chapters.

Meantime, the untidier real world obtruded. In February 1969, misunderstandings were further increased by the so-called 'Soames affair' – clashing interpretations given to conversations between the British ambassador and the French president concerning the future shape of 'Europe' (see Kitzinger 1973: 45–58; rival texts, de la Serre 1972: 75–7). It remains unclear how far the whole episode should be read as conspiracy, how far as confusion. It is unnecessary to recount the entire controverted saga here, for, in the end, it was to matter less than appeared at the time. De Gaulle departed the political scene less than 3 months later; Labour and Harold Wilson lost office the following year, at which point the opportunity was taken for a fresh start in British–French relations.

But a number of points appear relevant. First, from July 1968 there was a considerable battle within the French government for influence over policy. Second, this may well have been just one more attempt by General de Gaulle to shake the Community tree to see if loose fruit fell. As reported, French 'ideas' included, again, a *directoire* – of four: France, Germany, Italy and the UK. Again, this would infuriate the UK's then staunchest Benelux allies. Last, it is probably more than coincidence that the episodes of late 1961 to January 1962, 1965–6 and early 1969 were so closely linked to the completion of each phase of the transitional period.

How, then, should we characterise the period up to 1968? The 1950s were par excellence the age of projects, full of stops and starts of course. The impulses at work were both positive and negative (McAllister 1975: *passim*). They included, in Europe, the fear of the old hegemony – of Germany (DePorte 1979: *passim*) and the new threat perceived to arise from Soviet ambitions. 'Outside–inside' Europe, as it were, were the hardly compatible but variously voiced fears about US intentions – that the original acts of US assistance and support would be chopped off if the west Europeans could not demonstrate some 'self-help': fears of isolationism and withdrawal, and, by contrast, fears of being overwhelmed, economically and culturally, as the American shark crunched the European minnows.

The 1960s, by contrast, may be characterised as the age of implementation – of carrying forward, although not quite carrying through, the original projects, in a basically favourable environment. But it was also a period of 'defence' rather than expansion: of a refusal to change either the original membership or the original aims, but rather to push ahead with the original crew toward the original destinations. France especially refused to contemplate anything more; and indeed, at several points, showed that it wanted, if anything, less in terms of the strictly Community agenda. There is little doubt that, during the 1960s, France above all set the agenda and dictated the pace.

By about 1969, things were different. They were different in a number of crucial ways, all fraught with consequences for the EC. First let us look at the factors then thought to be positive.

Many people could be forgiven for being optimistic in 1969. For a start, they had survived. The year 1968 had not been too easy: the 'events' of May–June in France and their repercussions in the rest of the world, or at least in the west, had been followed by the supine western response to the Soviet 'fraternal assistance' to Czechoslovakia in August.

One of the many ironies that we shall encounter was that important turning points were indeed reached around 1968–9, but they were almost certainly not of the kind imagined at the time. General de Gaulle had survived the test of May–June 1968 and even insisted on reinforcing his stance of *hauteur* on the monetary front – refusing to devalue the franc, gloating not a little over the November 1967 'success' of sterling devaluation, the most tangible sign of the war of calculated pinpricks against the Anglo-Saxons. He succumbed (needlessly, some thought) in the referendum of April 1969 on regional and senate reform and resigned.

For many, General de Gaulle's political passing was a blessing: with it, they thought, had vanished a great stumbling block to 'progress' in western Europe and not least in the affairs of Community Europe. Neither was this all. Optimists also detected a sea change in French defence policy: when, on 9 March 1969, the then French Chief of Staff, General Fourquet, set forth his strategic views, not a few thought that France 'the prodigal' was about to return to the NATO fold; that the baffling (to some) and unhelpful neo-neutralist *tous azimuts* doctrine of Ailleret, Fourquet's predecessor, was now to be set aside, in belated recognition of the seriousness of the Czech 'road accident', in favour of 'realistic' western cooperation (Mendl 1970; Irwin 1971; McAllister 1972).

Certainly Fourquet's lecture seemed to provide the sweet scent of defence cooperation; of France cooperating with its allies against an enemy 'in the east'; of a western Europe where France, although not formally returning to the NATO fold, was at least providing depth, divisions and believable doctrine. Although all this was not 'Community business', yet it seemed to provide a helpful atmosphere, and the not inconsiderable hopes that were entertained of the Pompidou regime appeared justified by the lifting of the veto on British membership. This, in turn, encouraged the hopes for a *relance communautaire* and the grand schemes of the Hague Summit of December 1969.

In the FRG too, political change seemed propitious. The demise of the Kiesinger government was not widely lamented. If the direct implications for the EC were not clear, the new start in the *Ostpolitik* appeared to be firmly underlined, and was supported, in a public show of unity at least, by France as well as the USA and UK (Grosser 1980: 251). Less noticed outside was the rapid resurgence of trade with the GDR (often referred to as the 'extra member' of the EEC because of the 'intra-German' second Protocol of the EEC Treaty) (Aubert de la Rüe 1970: *passim*; Levi and Schütze 1970: 460ff.).

Other reasons for optimism were advanced. The Community seemed to have survived its major constitutional crisis, that terminating in the Luxembourg 'Agreements' of January 1966 and seemed to have survived even the commotion over the second veto on enlargement in 1967. Obstruction had given way to a more positive line, even from France: the acceleration of the customs union had been followed by the Barre proposals, intended not merely to guarantee actual common agricultural prices but also to discourage parity changes and hence act as a stepping stone to monetary union by stealth. And the economies were for the most part still growing satisfactorily (Shonfield 1976; Strange 1976; Hodges and Wallace 1981: esp. Ch. 2; Hu 1981).

Yet on the horizon, storm clouds were gathering. These duly turned into the storms that were to buffet the Community, restrict its speed and blow it about in the 1970s and early 1980s. Some of the problems were internally generated. That is to say, they were the result of unacknowledged ambiguities or contradictions, of assumptions allowed to pass without very great challenge in the early years. Others were more the result of exogenous factors, factors coming from the world outside.

For at the outset, the Community had enjoyed something of a 'free ride', in the sense that its main competitor, the USA, was also its greatest friend, with a declared stake in its success. It could take advantage of something of a 'vacuum' in the international economy and indeed, to some extent due to America's diversions on 'imperial missions', could fill it. It was not confronted, as later it was to be, by a world of 'super-competitors'. These two sources of difficulty, internal and external, are examined later.

What then were the first storm clouds? First, the very mechanics of the 'success' of the CAP gave rise to one source of difficulty. As just noted, common agricultural prices were just being achieved when the CAP was washed over by the first waves of the international currency crisis.

Second was the way in which the monetary crisis itself developed. It was no accident that the relatively most successful period for the EC to date, coincided so closely with the 'Bretton Woods convertibility phase', as Brian Tew called it (Tew 1977). It was *European* actions in resentment at the *effects* of this, pursued to prick the 'Anglo-Saxon bubble' in the name of 'Europe' and its 'disciplines', that brought about the demise of the system: but with that demise came also a body blow to that first attempt at a closer monetary Europe in whose name all this had been done. As we shall see, if the dollar seemed dented by 1971, so did the plans of the 'Europeans' led by Werner, although this only became clear a little later.

Third, France did not satisfactorily fulfil the role of the prodigal in defence matters – so much so that Michel Debré excelled himself in 1971 in declaring that 'European solutions' were a chimera and a delusion (Debré 1971: 1411–31).

Fourth, on the energy front, western Europe had put itself far out on a limb already half sawn through. The sirens were already warning of the end of cheap oil with the founding of the Organisation of Petroleum Exporting Countries (OPEC) and the first Libyan moves.

Such were the impending developments. It is time to retrace our steps and examine in a little more detail how the agenda looked to participants in 1968–9 and how they wished to present their plans and actions.

## Further reading

D. Dinan (ed.), *Origins and Evolution of the European Union*. Oxford: Oxford University Press, 2006. (Part II: The Postwar Context and Part III: Shaping the European Community.)

J. Gillingham, *Coal, Steel and the Rebirth of Europe, 1945–1955: The Germans and French from Ruhr Conflict to Economic Community*. Cambridge: Cambridge University Press, 1991.

J. Gillingham, *European Integration, 1950–2003*. Cambridge: Cambridge University Press, 2003. (Part I: A German Solution to Europe's Problems?)

M. Hogan, *The Marshall Plan: America, Britain and the Reconstruction of Western Europe, 1947–1952*. Cambridge: Cambridge University Press, 1987.

G. Lundestad, *'Empire' by Integration: The US and European Integration 1945–1997*. Oxford: Oxford University Press, 1998.

A. Milward, *The Reconstruction of Western Europe, 1945–51*. London: Methuen, 1984.

A. Milward, *The European Rescue of the Nation-State*. London: Routledge, 1992.

A. Moravcsik, *The Choice for Europe*. London: UCL Press, 1999. (Chapters 2 and 3.)

J. Newhouse, *Collision in Brussels: The Common Market Crisis of 30 June 1965*. New York: Norton, 1967.

P. Weigall and D. Stirk (eds), *The Origins and Development of the European Community*. Leicester: Leicester University Press, 1992. (Chapters 3–7 especially.)

The *Journal of European Integration History (JEIH)* is a valuable source of specialist articles on many of the historical developments and issues discussed in this and later chapters.

Key US government views and documents may be found in the series *Foreign Relations of the United States (FRUS)*, Washington, DC; and *Documents on American Foreign Policy*, Washington, DC.

# 2    The Community at the end of the 1960s

In this chapter, we examine the situation reached in the Community in 1968 and more especially 1969, up to and including the 'summit' at The Hague in December that year. We have seen that the customs union phase was completed ahead of schedule in mid-1968 – ironically, immediately following the 'events' of May–June in France, which revealed her economic weakness relative to the FRG and, in some eyes, came near to toppling de Gaulle's regime. But, by common consent, the year 1969 too opened badly, with much of March and parts of April taken up with the consequences of and recriminations over the Soames affair.

Among other landmarks to notice are the following. In April 1969 General de Gaulle lost the referendum on regional and senate reform and, as he had said he would do, resigned. Pompidou became president and in his keenly anticipated July press conference spoke both about the famous formula – 'completion, deepening and enlargement' – but also of the need for a summit gathering of the Six to discuss these. At the end of July, the second Yaoundé Convention, on cooperation with certain African countries, was signed. In August an episode occurred on which we will need to pause: the devaluation of the French franc. The elections in the FRG in September led to a change of government, bringing in the SPD–FDP coalition under Brandt. Immediately after the elections, the Deutschmark was floated. On 1 and 2 December the summit took place at The Hague, the Commission being invited to be present although, as was delicately said, the conference was 'not a Treaty institution'. Following the summit, much optimism was expressed about the outlook for the Community. We will see how far it was justified.

## The Soames affair

The year 1969 began badly, as we have seen, with a classic episode of Anglo-French 'ruffled feathers' and damaged pride over Western European Union (WEU) and the so-called Soames affair. Its origins lay in the response of the 'other Five' to France's second veto of UK membership of the Community (19 December 1967), following so conveniently on the UK devaluation of November, which France had done much to help precipitate. The second veto was significantly followed by British determination to 'keep the application on the table', as well as by the proposals, originated by Belgium's Harmel, to use WEU to keep open the discussion on the desirable shape and development of cooperation between the states of western Europe. To an extent, the British were successful in their strategy of keeping a foot in the door, as well as in forcing France to react more positively. WEU, as the one body then containing the 'Six' plus the UK, might help to keep the pressure on France, to prevent it 'getting off the hook' on the UK accession question and to maintain dialogue.

These were some of the issues that lay behind the conversations between de Gaulle and Christopher Soames, then British Ambassador in Paris. Soames had been sent there specifically to mend fences and improve the diplomatic climate. This was badly needed, following a decade of strained relations. What caused the sudden change of heart was de Gaulle's swift reappraisal of France's weakening position relative to the FRG. The volte face – to suddenly privilege relations with the UK above those with Germany – was too sudden for a good outcome (see Vanke in Dinan (ed.) 2006: 160–1). Debré, it seems, had smoothed the path to a meeting between Soames and de Gaulle, originally scheduled for early January, but rearranged for 4 February because Soames had been ill.

The key issue was how far WEU machinery could be used, while UK accession remained blocked, to further political cooperation between the UK and the Six, but this time avoiding the risk of 'France claiming to speak for all'. At their Luxembourg meeting on 5 February 1969 all the other governments except France agreed on the principle of 'compulsory' – later modified to 'prior' – consultation on matters of the political organisation of western Europe. The agreement to have 'prior consultations' was put into immediate operation over the Middle East in February. France had not agreed to take part and blew hot and cold about the whole procedure, in ways that more alarmist accounts regarded as likely to damage not just WEU but also NATO and the Community.

On the eve of President Nixon's February visit to western Europe, France capped this by 'revelations' of the content of the de Gaulle–Soames conversations, which let it be understood that the UK was itself prepared to leave NATO and to help to transform the EC into essentially a free trade area rather than a body pursuing notions of European Union (*EDB* 280, 24 February 1969: 3). The British version of what had transpired was inevitably different. According to Britain, de Gaulle had raised the question of the nature of a 'European' identity; had stressed that, while France had been able to regain its independence (signalled by its 1966 departure from the NATO integrated military commands), other western European countries remained firmly tied to US coattails; that he had no particular love for the form of the Common Market, foresaw that UK membership would in any case transform it and that this might be of benefit. The form of any new association would have to be agreed by the major partners; this implied a *directoire* of four – France, FRG, Italy and UK. The vital aspect was agreement between Britain and France, and it would be best if the UK were to take the initiative (an obvious trap).

Of course, the Soames affair was bound to appear as ultimately of little consequence. It did not, finally, prevent UK entry to the EC neither did it result in any change to the institutions or to the Community. Yet it remains of interest as an indication of the degree of mistrust that characterised both Franco-German and

Anglo-French relations during the de Gaulle–Wilson years and also serves to remind us how the ground was subsequently cleared. This occurred as a result partly of changes of personnel: not just that Pompidou replaced de Gaulle, important though this was, but also that, as Soames apparently may have hinted to de Gaulle, Labour was on its way out of office too. And it occurred partly because of revelations of the *weaknesses* of France's position, shown dramatically by the monetary events later in 1969 and also by the growing fear of the FRG manifested by large segments of French political life, which had finally brought many to view a suitably humbled UK as a 'necessary counterweight' to German power.

What seemed clear was that, at least from the French side, the Soames–de Gaulle conversations were meant to be an exploration of several major unanswered problems of the 'European construction', reflecting both France's (de Gaulle's) concern at the lack of a foreign policy and defence 'personality' and its less than total enthusiasm for the existing Community structure, particularly in its allegedly 'supranational' elements. Of course it might alternatively be construed, or used, to show the Five that the UK was engaging in backstairs treachery and discussing notions that they, its supporters, heartily deprecated. It could thus serve to delay UK membership yet further, until Britain's weakness was more fully apparent to all and she was even less able to dictate terms or help to set a tone of which France would disapprove, although the Dutch, notably, might approve.

## Political change in France and Federal Germany

The twofold political change in France and the FRG provides our next focus. A great deal was expected in many quarters of each of these, not least in what they might portend for an EC that was widely perceived to have 'come through', albeit somewhat battered and bruised, from the crisis of 1965–6. Those who expected much to result for the EC from these political changes were espousing, whether they knew it or not, a particular view of the political processes most relevant to the EC: that the Community was indeed highly dependent on the benevolence of national political forces and that those most important in setting national attitudes were, 'ultimately', the politicians rather than bureaucrats, senior officials and other 'technocrats'.

Take, for example, the (political) demise of General de Gaulle at the end of April. In Brussels, the *Europe Daily Bulletin (EDB)* declared:

> As of today, Europe can again count on France ... Nothing was more depressing than to have to observe that France was renouncing, increasingly from day to day, the role that had been hers since the war – to be the driving force of a European unification which could hardly be imagined without France's total and unreserved participation ... there is no doubt that France will have to change her policy, particularly her European policy.
>
> (*EDB* 28 April 1969: 1)

The problems, it was widely acknowledged, remained considerable. The French political transition would take time and absorb energies, just at a time when the end of the Community's transitional period was approaching and a case could clearly be made for pressing on the accelerator and not the brakes. Neither, of course, was it yet clear that the successor as president would be Pompidou. Yet in anticipation, the *EDB* added the next day that, with other factors (such as the WEU's Anglo-Italian declaration on Europe and the Monnet Committee's deliberations on the problem of UK membership): 'This will make possible a *fresh start*, and will allow France to get back into the "movement" without, however, being constrained to make a sudden change of direction' (*EDB* 29 April 1969).

At all events, as we have seen, change followed fairly swiftly the arrival in power of Pompidou, elected French president in June 1969. That victory was not a foregone conclusion and owed not a little to the support that Pompidou won from the previously opportunist Duhamel and the 'oui-mais' Giscard d'Estaing, who had associated himself (March 1969) with Monnet's Action Committee for the United States of Europe, which clearly favoured British entry. Both of these gentlemen felt sufficiently convinced of Pompidou's bona fides to back him (de la Serre 1970: 24–5).

The direction was amply confirmed in the makeup of the new government with Chaban-Delmas as prime minister and Maurice Schumann as foreign minister. It was crystallised in the famous Pompidolian triptych: 'completion, deepening, enlargement', which he set forth in his press conference on 10 July 1969. To achieve a suitable agreement on enlargement, Pompidou suggested a summit meeting of the Six, which took place at The Hague on 1 and 2 December (de la Serre 1972: 25). The Commission was invited to present to it an update of its document on problems of enlargement.

The French initiative clearly improved the climate of Community business later in 1969. The Commission's proposals for further development were taken up, especially over the harmonisation of economic policy and over monetary and external commercial policy.

Pompidou visited Bonn as soon as decently possible after the summer break (8–9 September). His conversations with Chancellor Kiesinger helped to clear the way for a summit that Kiesinger himself was not to attend, displaced by Willi Brandt's Social Democrats in coalition with the German Free Democratic Party (FDP) but a few weeks later. On 15 September, the Community's Council of Ministers set the seal not just on the summit but on a quite important implicit compromise about the negotiating framework. This entailed that the Five abandon their attempt to convene WEU immediately afterwards, and that France both allow the participation of the Commission at The Hague and also not insist on the summit as any kind of precedent for 'institutionalising' conferences of heads of state and government, which, as de la Serre remarked, 'might have been interpreted [by France's partners] as an attempt to return to the Fouchet plan of 1962' (1972: 26). A nice irony, this: for France's 'graceful withdrawal' of any such insistence was to play no small part in precisely that institutionalisation of summits which, in fact, eventually came about.

The change of government (*Machtwechsel*) in the FRG in September 1969 took place about 7 weeks after the French devaluation of 8 August, which many had expected earlier. This change did not, perhaps, lead to such high blown language when people reflected on its implications for the European Community.

But a further irony is also worth noting here: in bringing the FDP back into government, the 1969 West German election ushered on to centre stage a man whose influence on the future course of events should in no way be underestimated. Herr Josef Ertl became federal agriculture minister, a post that he was to retain through thick and thin for 14 years until 1983. He was to have an enormous influence on the (non-)reform of the CAP. His presence and the 'pact' whereby the Free Democrat ministers of successive coalitions agreed to act on the basis of 'anyone threatened, all out' (i.e. their ability to unmake a government at will) were important not only for their direct impact on the CAP. They also help to explain some of the more important ambiguities (to choose a fairly polite term) of West German policy and the consequent frictions that resulted, at a later stage, in the FRG's relations with the UK in particular. There was to be a recurring tendency for the UK to expect the FRG to take up cudgels in its cause, not least with France, or to propose solutions benefiting the UK even more than the FRG itself and to be disappointed.

## Monetary turbulence impacts on the Community

But 1969 was important for another and very different reason also. It witnessed a series of events of the type that focus attention on another 'explanation' of what does and does not happen in the EC: an explanation that concentrates on the influence of 'exogenous' factors in the evolution of the Community – factors in the international economy, notably, which may 'blow off course' or, alternatively, consolidate the Community. It was no accident that the period of greatest 'success' for the EC coincided so closely with the period of greatest stability in the postwar international monetary regime: the period *between* the establishment of full multilateral convertibility in western Europe in 1958–9 and the first seismic shocks that were to topple the Bretton Woods system. These shocks began, arguably, with the British devaluation of sterling in November 1967 (the French role in engineering that provides, as we have seen, an ironic counterpoint to France's own devaluation of August 1969, one of the first acts of Pompidou on becoming president) but that went on through 1971 and were finally confirmed in early 1973 with the recognition that 'floating rates were here to stay'.

These events, in turn, highlighted dramatically a 'missing step' in the presumed link between the 'internal' Community agenda and the external environment. They showed how *dependent* the Community was, for certain key lines of its own development, on the maintenance of certain key conditions in that external environment. The failure of these 'props' could indeed cause the structure to weaken and totter. For this was exactly the period when the CAP was due to move to its 'second stage' – from agreement about the *system* of price mechanisms and arrangements that had marked the first steps, to agreement about actual *common prices* for the commodities concerned, which was intended to be the second. The common prices, it had been agreed at the CAP's inception in 1962, were to be denominated, for accounting purposes, in a *numeraire*, the unit of account (ua) – which would be 'translated' into the national currencies in which farmers were actually paid.

There was no doubt that France, when devaluing, had not engaged in the prior consultation to which it was committed. Its timing indeed was a master stroke and it would be testing credibility too far to assume that it was an accident. The Community's rate of activity and capacity for response are usually at their lowest in the month of August. The major event of this period of torpor was the French devaluation. A special meeting of the Council of Ministers was called for the late afternoon of Friday 8 August. After it, the devaluation 'in principle' was announced at about 7.15 pm, to 'take effect' from midnight on Monday 11 August. The Community's Monetary Committee met on Sunday 10 August, and, as it tartly stated in its Opinion:

> In accordance with the decision of the EEC Council of Ministers, on 8 May 1964, concerning preliminary consultation in cases of changes in monetary parities, the Monetary Committee met on 10 August 1969 and *recorded* the decision of the French government to adjust the parity of the French franc and the economic and financial reasons which motivated this decision.
> *(Bull. EC* 9/10 1969: 41–3; *EDB* 392, 25/6.8.69: 4–7)

In particular, they indicated, they had faced up to the problem of the implications of the decision for the hard won *acquis* of the CAP. It is at this point that again we see the key importance of these events of 1969 for the future directions of the Community. These events were to lead directly to modifications of the CAP with effects that endured throughout the 1970s and 1980s. They also involved directly the plans then being developed for moves toward greater economic and monetary union (EMU). Thus:

> The Monetary Committee also examined the problems raised by the change in … parity … as regards the definition of the unit of account (ua) and common agricultural prices by the terms of Council Regulation No. 653/68 of 30 May 1968. In present circumstances, the Monetary Committee does not think it opportune to express an opinion aimed at modifying the agricultural ua or agricultural prices. However, it expresses the opinion that it is important to place the agricultural problems within the wide framework of its repercussions on medium and long-term economic policy.
>
> The Monetary Committee draws attention to the grave consequences which could result from the automatic adjustment of agricultural prices expressed in actual currency for the French economy. It considers, in consequence, that it would be opportune for the French Authorities to adopt *temporary graded measures* to counter these consequences, *as long as the measures adopted did not involve distortions in trade.*

The Opinion has been quoted at length because its implications for the future, not just of the CAP or of moves to economic and monetary union, but of the Community as a whole, were most important.

The manner in which the matter had to be handled is also worth notice. Most members of the Commission were, it appears, on holiday when the French government's communiqué reached Brussels. Albert Coppé (of Belgium) was, however, still available and had, it appears, already had a telephone conversation with the President of the Commission, Jean Rey, on Friday evening. A first short meeting took place in Brussels on Sunday 10 August, followed by a plenary meeting of the Commission at 8 am on Monday 11 August, to precede the Council of Ministers' meeting beginning at 11 am.

The Commission set out its own position on the several aspects of the problem, including the outlines of a proposal on the *agricultural* implications, which had been worked on by officials in the monetary and agricultural directorates of the Commission on the basis that no change in the parity of the units of account in agriculture should be allowed.

The Council of Ministers indeed found itself obliged to bow to the fait accompli. Devaluations are like that; either the secret is well kept or it is not, with inevitable consequences. This one was well kept. The key part of the discussion in the Council of Ministers revolved around a statement from Raymond Barre of France. The significance of this was that he was also heavily involved in the 'Barre plans' bearing his name, on economic and monetary union.

Barre stated that these events showed once again the need to organise without delay and implement immediately a *coordinated economic and monetary policy* in the member states; if not, the Common Market risked being subjected to regular upheavals which would undermine and destroy it.

Note that this is new talk. It announces a new vista of risks and troubles which had not greatly preoccupied the Community until then; it was, however, to be a dominant motif from that time forward. As it was, France had, not for the first or last time, presented the Community with a finely executed fait accompli and left its partners to pick up the pieces and make the best of it in Community terms. To re-emphasise: the episode confirmed the predominance of *national* priorities and agenda over Community ones; it was not the case that the Community's hoped for linkages had triumphed – rather France's agenda triumphed, and wide and crucial implications followed for its partners and the whole shape of the Community.

For the Community, the hope had been that the move to actual common prices in agriculture, denominated in units of account, rather than in actual currencies, would serve to 'proof' the agricultural prices against national meddling. But it would also have the effect of making national parity changes more problematic and less likely, by giving the national authorities powerful cause for pause and thus contribute to monetary union by stealth. Barre indeed appeared to approve of these objectives.

The situation that now faced the Community, therefore, was that the French devaluation posed two dangers. The effect of the devaluation would be an increase in French agricultural prices, expressed in national currency. This would both encourage France to produce more (and those surpluses, being unsellable in the Community market, would have to be exported via the export-rebate mechanism) and would also cause a considerable increase in the cost of living in France, thus reducing the effectiveness of the devaluation itself.

In the face of such likely consequences, Agriculture Commissioner Mansholt of the Netherlands explained that another approach would have to be pursued: the *temporary* isolation of the French agricultural market. These notions he had discussed on Sunday 10 August, with Messrs Rey and Duhamel (French Agriculture Minister) but the debate on them lasted right through Monday and until 5 am on Tuesday 12 August.

The Commission put forward a preliminary draft for a Council Regulation to resolve the problem. Its essence, contained in Article 3, was to oblige France to grant subsidies to *imports* from member states and third countries and to oblige it to levy compensatory amounts on *exports* to other countries. This became Regulation 1586/69 (*OJL* 202 12 August 1969) published immediately: the detailed application of taxes and payments was left to be worked out by the management committees for agriculture, which completed their highly complex business on the night of 22 August.

One further reason for regarding 1969 as an interesting benchmark (but not necessarily turning point) for west European interrelationships in this era again refers to France. Here the dimension is the defence and security debate, to which I referred in Chapter 1. When in March 1969 the then French Chief of Staff, General Fourquet, set forth his strategic views, there was an audible sigh of relief in many western countries. The prodigal, they seemed to think, might yet return to the NATO fold. Yet it did not work out that way and instead reflected much more a power vacuum in de Gaulle's last weeks and immediately after.

By contrast, Italy witnessed no change in its governing political groups, but this did not mean no action of importance for the European construction. Italy's involvement in the student/worker unrest of the late 1960s was crucial, culminating in the 'hot autumn' of 1969. The expectation of not a few observers that Italy would 'go left' had been confounded in 1968 despite the fact that the elections coincided almost exactly (19–20 May) with the French 'events' and preceded by some 3 months the invasion of Czechoslovakia which was to be such a seminal event not only for the debate within the Partito Comunista Italiano (PCI), but for the emergence of the notion of 'eurocommunism'.

The year 1969 did, however, as we have seen, bring change to the FRG, ushering in what was to prove a long period of SPD–FDP government. The August 1969 pre-election speeches of Kiesinger and Brandt showed contrasting emphases. With Brandt, the stress was on consolidation and enlargement of the EC, over and above any notion of relaunching a 'political union' in western Europe or of a European Defence Community, albeit within a NATO framework. In his view, that the European calendar must be mainly devoted to the 'consolidation, deepening and widening' of the Common Market, he echoed Pompidou's 'completion, deepening and enlargement'.

Kiesinger, in an interview with *Die Welt* in August, had spoken of the priority of 'the political unification of western Europe' over 'the policy of opening up to the East', and suggested that this could be accomplished by a compact secretariat, as originally proposed in the Fouchet Plan in the early 1960s. He was markedly cool on UK membership, indicating that Britain had first to put its own house in order to qualify for membership; and that at the time it did 'not yet quite know the path [it] was to take'. And so his departure after the elections of late September and replacement by the SPD–FDP coalition led by Brandt were also welcomed as providing new opportunities for the Community.

## The Hague Summit

The Hague Summit of December 1969 provided an important occasion to demonstrate just how far these changes might go. However, it also gave a clear indication of something just as crucial: of the extent to which the Community failed to take account of recent changes in its environment and continued to peddle wares embedded in the agenda of its bureaucracy, regardless of their having been rendered inoperable.

The new powerhouse of the Community, the Brandt–Pompidou axis, was clearly better disposed to UK membership than its predecessors, and the summit communiqué made this clear. However, the determination to prove that 'things had changed', the mood of euphoria, was such that grand designs and loose talk were allowed to slip in, ill considered, at the edges. This was true in two areas above all, each soon to be graced, as is the way of these things, by its own committee, which would feel bound to report that something had to happen, regardless of the longer term efficacy. One area was 'political cooperation', that degree of closer cooperation in external matters, which, on the one hand, did not fall neatly within existing treaty competences, yet which, on the other hand, fell short of a unified foreign policy. The other was the commitment in the communiqué to an 'economic and monetary union', to be established in three stages by 1980. These committees (when set up in March 1970) were to be graced by famous names: the first by Étienne Davignon of Belgium, the second, under Luxembourg's Pierre Werner. The first was to slip quietly and unobtrusively into gear, as we shall see. The second was to roar off in first gear in an impressive cloud, but to break down rather badly not far up the road.

Of more immediate concern, however, was the question of the first enlargement of the Community, intended to take it from six to ten by the addition of Denmark, Ireland, the UK and, it was hoped, Norway. On this matter, the Commission had, at the instigation of the Council of Ministers at its 22–3 July 1969 meeting, updated its opinion. The Commission was equally firm about the importance of moving from the transitional period to a final stage on schedule, i.e. at the end of 1969.

In paragraph 8 of the summit communiqué, the leaders 'reaffirmed their will to press forward with the further developments needed' to promote the Community's 'development into an economic union'. They continued, in a kind of swansong to the unprecedented growth that western Europe had known: 'They are of the opinion that the integration process should result in a Community of stability and growth.' This was, of course, just what it was in several respects about to cease to be, as instability and 'economic divergence' came increasingly to the fore in the 1970s. To this end, said the communiqué:

> [T]hey agreed that within the Council, on the basis of the Memorandum presented by the Commission on 12 February 1969 … a plan in stages should be

worked out during 1970 with a view to the creation of an economic and monetary union ... The development of monetary co-operation should be backed up
by the harmonization of economic policies.

(*Bull EC* 1–1970: 11–16)

The Commission added, in its press statement, that the 'decisions taken at the
Summit Conference prove how utterly wrong were those who thought that the communities were paralysed and losing momentum'. On the basic troika – of completion, deepening and enlargement – it concluded that progress had been most
satisfactory. The close of the 1960s, thus, was marked by considerable optimism in
Community circles. The end of the transitional period had been accomplished –
more or less – on time. 'More or less', because there remained loose ends: agricultural finance was not finally settled between the Six until April 1970. The
Community appeared to be set on a new and ambitious agenda, although the
Commission regretted that the summit had not provided an opportunity for any
progress towards political union.

But, as we have seen, it was clear too that storm clouds were gathering. To be
sure, several of these were not of the Community's own making, but they were to
affect it deeply as the 1970s wore on. The transitional period, 1958–70, although of
course far from troublefree, had been in many ways a period of *communitas felix*.
There had been something of a vacuum in the world economy, in which the Six
were able to float without much effort. The major ground rules of the international
economy had been laid down, and guaranteed, by the American protector. They had
indeed been challenged (especially by France over the role of the dollar and sterling) but had only just begun to crumble. The western world in general floated on a
sea of cheap oil. Its economies adapted to a moderate, if continuing, inflation. A
whole generation knew nearly full employment. Europe's industries were not yet
visibly threatened by super-competitors. The US defensive umbrella, and hegemony in security also, were only just being ruffled: by the French withdrawal from
the NATO integrated military command in 1966 (but then there were many, clutch-
ing at straws, who saw in Fourquet's speech a potential return of the prodigal); and
by the Soviet naval build-up in the Mediterranean at the time of the Six Days' War.
The Commission, and many others, could perhaps be forgiven their relative
optimism.

In summary, what then had been accomplished by 1969 and what problems were
beginning to cast a shadow? For a start, the Community system had survived intact,
at least in formal terms. It had survived the presence of General de Gaulle. It had
survived the arguments of the early 1960s, of the deliberations of the
Fouchet–Cattani period on political union, which had raised for the first but far
from the last time the question of just what was to be the relationship of such proposals to the *existing* Community structure. In particular, would it be necessary to
modify the original treaty structure; to subtract from the powers of the original
institutions; to alter their competences; or to link them in some specific way with
such other, 'outside' bodies as NATO? To all of these questions the answer was

essentially no: no treaty revision, no modification of competences or institution-alised linkage with other bodies. The Community would continue on its own.

In policy terms, it was going to be possible to announce success, even if on closer inspection the success looked distinctly partial. The announced successes – i.e. 'completion' on schedule – concerned essentially the customs union and the agri-cultural policy. It was not just that they were to be accomplished by the due date (i.e. end of 1969). Also of importance, because it had been contested before, was the notion of parallel progress on the two fronts of the industrial customs union and agriculture. This had been one bone of contention at the time of the 1965–6 crisis.

There were further developments, both positive and negative, which indicated likely limits and a likely shape to the enterprise. On the one hand, the outcome of 'Fouchet' appeared to mean that the Community system would go on autonomously, that it would not be conflated or confused with anything else. (The French, indeed, had been highly critical of Dutch tactics in this regard, purporting to sense in the stance of the Netherlands that of a 'Trojan horse' for perfidious Albion.) Equally clearly, notions of a 'political union' and of a 'political secre-tariat' were not easy to get off the ground. This meant that for many, there was a risk that the building blocks of the Community might lack political cement. It was Walter Hallstein, the German first president of the Commission, after all, who had sold the pass – certainly as de Gaulle saw it – in declaring that 'our business is poli-tics', that economic means were to be used to attain an essentially political goal.

Could there be an alternative source of 'cement' to hold together the Community which, contrary to Monnet's original wishes, had ensconced the power of national governments in the Council of Ministers? The answer that the 1960s seemed to pro-vide, and in a perhaps unexpected quarter, was to be yes. That quarter, we have seen, was the Court of Justice of the European Community (CJEC), which grasped the nettle early in certain memorable judgments, in particular the two mentioned in Chapter 1. It sought to clarify the nature and role of Community law in such a way that that law could itself become, it was hoped, a vital cement of the system, strong enough to hold the edifice together even in the face of the kind of direct political challenge to aspects of it presented, for instance, by the 1965–6 crisis.

These two judgments were given in the cases *Van Gend en Loos* ([1963] *CMLR*: 105) and *Costa* v. *ENEL* ([1964] *CMLR*: *425*). Since they have about them more than a little of the grand ring of certain key early judgments of the US Supreme Court (despite the fact that clearly the CJEC is not in the same position as the Supreme Court), it is perhaps worth citing them at some length here.

In its judgment in *Van Gend en Loos*, the Court stated:

> [T]he role of the Court of Justice in the framework of Article 177, the aim of which is to ensure uniformity of interpretation of the Treaty by the national courts, confirms that the States recognised in Community law have an author-ity capable of being invoked by their nationals before those Courts. We must conclude from this that the Community constitutes a *new legal order* in inter-national law, for whose benefit the States have limited their sovereign rights, albeit within limited fields, and the subjects of which comprise not only the

member-States but also their nationals. Community law, therefore, apart from
legislation by the member-States, not only imposes obligations on individuals
but also confers on them legal rights. The latter arise not only when an explicit
grant is made by the Treaty, but also through obligations imposed, in a clearly
defined manner, by the Treaty on individuals as well as on member-States and
the Community institutions.

Of equal importance, the judgment in *Costa* v. *ENEL* stated, in part:

As opposed to other international Treaties, the Treaty instituting the EEC has
created its own order which was integrated with the national order of the member-States the moment the Treaty came into force; as such, it is binding upon
them. In fact, creating a Community of unlimited duration, having its own
institutions, its own personality and its own capacity in law, apart from having
international standing and more particularly, real powers resulting from a limitation of competence or a transfer of powers from the States to the
Community, the member-States, albeit within limited spheres, have restricted
their sovereign rights and created a body of law applicable both to their nationals and to themselves.

We have noted that these two judgments were given before the crisis of 1965–6
broke and that the Court and other Community institutions played no active role in
its resolution. It is clear, too, that the crisis of 1965–6 left a great deal unresolved,
and essentially for the making.

## Optimism amid growing uncertainty

Yet the mood of optimism was fully reflected in the Commission's major survey,
the *General Report on the Activities of the Community (GRA)*. The Third Report,
that for the year 1969, summed up as follows:

The year 1969 ended better than it started. On 1 January 1970 the Community
moved into its final stage. Important political decisions were taken with regard
to the completion and strengthening of the Community and to its enlargement.
Happily, the atmosphere in which the Community is embarking on the new
phase of its existence is far more serene.

(3 *GRA*, 1969: 11)

Although the Report did not say more serene than what, it was clear that the reference was to the earlier problems mentioned above.

The *shape* of the debate was also of great importance. The importance lay not
merely in the *manner* in which 'completion, deepening and enlargement' were to
be linked and related to each other, but also the *context*. And the context of monetary disruption was the most important element. Both of these elements – the linkages between major agenda items and the importance of external factors blowing

the Community 'off course' – will be recurring themes here. Both were clearly apparent at The Hague.

The 'core' elements discussed at The Hague were agricultural finance and enlargement. On the morning of Tuesday 2 December, Pompidou added several surprises, especially as regards the second aspect of the 'triptych' – deepening. On this he called for a complete economic and monetary union and for plans for it to be completed within one year. In doing this, he certainly appeared to have snatched the initiative; but equally, this was an example of something leaping onto the Community agenda as a 'commitment' at very short notice, when it was not clear how much thought had been given to the reasons for it, or the difficulties in the way of its fulfilment.

By the same token, the final communiqué committed the Community leaders to another *démarche*. They instructed the ministers of foreign affairs to 'study the best way of achieving progress in the matter of political unification, within the context of enlargement. The ministers are to make proposals before the end of July 1970.' Thus they gave birth to the Davignon Committee and the activity to be known as 'political cooperation' – something less than agreement on foreign policy and external affairs, but an attempt to reach common positions.

The conclusions of the Hague Summit seemed to satisfy everyone and to offer reason for self-congratulation to each. The difficulty was that this beautifully cobbled compromise was not robust enough to stand up in the real world. Attention was, perhaps, too much focused on obtaining an 'internal' agreement that would satisfy everyone's *amour propre*, without any great attention to whether it effectively advanced any of the objectives that everyone claimed to be pursuing.

But first, we should note the way in which it appeared to satisfy. For France, the 'final' agricultural financing arrangement was recognised as having priority and to be resolved by year end; the Barre plan on economic and monetary union could be regarded as having the nod of approval; enlargement discussions, although to be undertaken 'in a most positive spirit' (3 *GRA*, 1969, Annex: 489) also contained a 'failsafe' clause ('*in so far as* the applicant States accept the Treaties and their political objective', etc.) (Kitzinger 1973: 58). The Five, too, had satisfaction, notably over the notion of 'parallel progress' in the fields of strengthening and of enlargement (de la Serre 1970: 27) as the Commission too had stated in its opinion of 1 October 1969 and reaffirmed in its 19 November memorandum to the heads of state or government (3 *GRA*, 1969: 485). No firm dates were set for the enlargement negotiations to be held or completed.

So much for the euphoria; indeed, the Commission showed, in its commentary on the summit, that it shared this. Yet both Commission and Parliament had, in October and November, also sounded warning notes that were to prove most pertinent to the problems already emerging (3 *GRA*, 1969: 482, 484).

The European Parliament had described itself, in its Resolution of 3 November, as 'deeply concerned by the present situation, which threatens what the Community has achieved' (3 *GRA*, 1969: 482) and qualified its espousal of the objective of a 'genuine common economic and cyclical policy' by adding 'which alone will make it possible to work out the difficult problems that have arisen … particularly with regard to agriculture and monetary matters'. These same 'recent difficulties of an agricultural and monetary nature' were alluded to in the Commission's memorandum to the heads of state or government (3 *GRA*, 1969: 484). The Commission made explicit, too, the linkage it saw between 'common economic and monetary policies, the Community's industrial and technological development, and social and regional measures' (3 *GRA*, 1969: 485), and evoked too the need for reform and strengthening of the institutions. '[The Community] needs stronger institutions to ensure its internal government. It needs them equally to enable it to cope with the danger of unwieldiness inherent in enlargement.'

There was, thus, an increasing if uneasy perception of the ways in which 'everything was linked to everything else' in the agenda that the Community faced. There was not, however, agreement as to what to do about this 'inevitably' linked agenda; neither was there the confidence that those things that appeared likely to lie within the Community's competence to agree or achieve, would actually prove efficacious in protecting even the *acquis communautaire*, let alone its further development, in the face of the much rougher seas that were now running.

What were such linkages and how far had the treaties anticipated and provided for them? First, as we have seen, the achievement of actual common prices for many agricultural products in the CAP was seen to be clearly linked to the relationship between one currency and another. Rather than use a national currency, agricultural prices were to be calculated in units of account (uas). Farmers in a particular country would thus, in principle, receive the same amount of this *numeraire* for the same output as those in another. But if one country devalued, or revalued, its currency and another did not, the effects could be serious. Farmers in the devaluing country would be better off than non-farmers; food prices would rise, and output would be stimulated in that country without a corresponding increase in internal demand; such price rises would contribute directly to inflation, thus reducing the effectiveness of the original devaluation and contributing to surpluses; farmers would become a kind of 'foreign sector' within the home economy. These problems, of course, would be avoided if the parities of the currencies concerned did not change; in other words, if there were a monetary union between them. That in turn, it seemed, was not conceivable without the other aspects of an economic union, as in the USA, for example.

But the effects of economic and monetary union, in any of its conceivable variants, on weaker, poorer and peripheral regions were, history and theory seemed to agree, likely to be severe unless adequate compensatory (including regional) policies were to be developed too, to counteract the tendency of wealth, capital and jobs to flow to the centre, which, in turn, might threaten the political cohesion of the entity. While it was not clear what scale of compensatory policies might be needed, it was certain that national policies themselves had failed to make much impact on the (by later standards) relatively modest problems of the 1960s. Ironically, the exception – relatively effective in the context of the 1960s – had been UK regional policy (Moore and Rhodes 1973). Equally, it was clear that none of this was at all closely programmed, with a framework of actions, obligations and sanctions, in the Treaty. In embarking on this terrain therefore (aspects of what was sometimes referred to as 'positive' integration, as opposed to the 'negative' integration of removal of tariff barriers, etc. – see Pinder 1968), the Community was indeed moving into uncharted waters where what should or could be done was not prescribed in any detail by the treaties. The EEC Treaty, for example, specified the 'four freedoms' necessary to a common market, but did not always detail how they were to be established; neither did it give to any other policy area the status of such specified common policies as CAP (agriculture), competition, commercial policy and transport. Thus references to monetary cooperation were limited to Article 105, while references that might give rise to a 'regional policy' were scattered throughout the Treaty under other headings.

This was not particularly surprising. In some cases, such policy notions had been in their infancy in most member states in the 'founding' period of the 1950s; in others, there was clear disagreement about the role that government ought to play, as between some of the founding members (McAllister 1979). Thus, at the close of the transitional period (end of 1969), the scene was set for the new agenda of 'what do we do next?' And it was precisely this that the Commission, and European Parliament (EP), and indeed the Hague Summit, sought to address. As we have seen, though, they did so in circumstances where several of the key foundations and assumptions of the postwar order in western Europe were showing cracks.

Contemplating 'tomorrow's tasks' at the close of the decade, the Commission declared: 'First on the list comes economic union.' Next, 'though ... the Community has laid the foundations of an industrial policy, it has not yet produced its answer to the major changes already taking place.'

The events of 1969 focused attention on the lack of coherence in the economic policies of the member states and the fragility of the Community's infrastructures 'when set against the common policies now being elaborated' and finally they underlined the need for political union (3 *GRA*, 1969: 19–21).

What of their evaluation (undertaken at the behest of the EP) of the consequences of Community policy for the economies of member states and of the Community? Again, it is useful to see how the Commission saw the position at the end of the decade. With due acknowledgement to problems of methodology and non-availability of data and studies (3 *GRA*, 1969: 23) which meant that 'trying to trace cause and effect runs into enormous difficulties', the Commission concluded that the 'indicators compare favourably with those in the leading industrialised non-member countries'. While this is true, a couple of comparisons might have given pause. Annual GNP volumes, employment *and* GNP per employed person had all grown faster on average, in percentage terms, in the period 1950–8 (i.e. *before* the EEC Treaty came into force) than in the first 10 years of the EEC, 1958–68. What had taken place, however, was a fairly marked trade diversion: trade between member states had, in total, grown twice as fast in the decade 1958–68, as had trade between members and non-members. This applied almost equally to imports and to exports (3 *GRA*, 1969: 30). How much diversion had occurred depended on the basis of calculation, but the Commission averred that 'in proportion to the Community's domestic product, imports from non-member countries are still *of the same order of magnitude*' (3 *GRA*, 1969: 31, emphasis added).

The employment figures, although their significance was not fully grasped at the time, also cast a shadow before them into the 'low growth' period post-1973. 'The Community', noted the Commission, 'has had to cope with a smaller total growth of employment than that of the U.S.' (EEC 0.3% pa, USA 2% pa, 1958–67 average). The Commission added comfortingly: 'As regards the creation of jobs, however, the difference is far less marked, since the Community has had to offset a bigger reduction in the number of jobs in the primary sector.' This was true; but the question, looking forward, became what would happen when the 'minus' side of that net figure – agricultural job loss – dropped out.

The report pointed to an imbalance in policy terms also, again with clear implications for later debates. This was the 'negative/positive' integration distinction: between liberalisation and dismantling barriers, on the one hand, and active common policies, on the other. The first had gone ahead fast; the second had lagged. 'The construction of the Community', concluded the Commission, '*cannot go ahead* unless, in the years to come, there is a change of emphasis between these two aspects' (3 *GRA*, 1969: 41, emphasis added).

The Hague Summit was thus a landmark of importance. Although there had been 'summit' gatherings on occasion before, this one was to become the first of a more or less regular series. It offered at least some promise of breaking the impasse over enlargement. It also offered a broader picture of what the EC might next be about. Whether its promise would be fulfilled, however, would prove to depend on a great deal more than agreement and goodwill between the existing members.

## Further reading

F. de la Serre, 'La Grande-Bretagne s'éloigne-t-elle de l'Europe?', *Revue Française de Science Politique*, 20 (I), 1970: 37–50.

D. Dinan (ed.), *Origins and Evolution of the European Union*. Oxford: Oxford University Press, 2006. (Chapters 6 and 7.)

A. Moravcsik, *The Choice for Europe*. London: UCL Press, 1999. (Chapter 3.)

P. Stirk and D. Weigall (eds), *The Origins and Development of European Integration*. London: Pinter, 1999. (Chapter 8.)

D. Urwin, *The Community of Europe: A History of European Integration since 1945*. London: Longman, 1991.

J. Young, *Britain and European Unity, 1945–1999*. Basingstoke: Macmillan, 2000.

# 3  From The Hague to Paris

## 1969–1972

Several issues dominated the period between the Hague Summit and that at Paris nearly 3 years later. First, from the Community's point of view, was the triptych cluster – completion, deepening and enlargement. Moving outward, as it were, from this 'central core' conceived in Community terms, the second cluster concerned the issues raised by the international monetary upheavals both for the Community's ambition to move toward an economic and monetary union and also directly for the 'common price' ambition of the CAP. The third cluster may be loosely labelled *détente*: although encapsulated in another 'triptych' – mutual and balanced force reductions (MBFR), the Strategic Arms Limitation Talks (SALT) and the beginnings of the process leading to the Conference on Security and Cooperation in Europe (CSCE) – it clearly contained a dimension of more direct relevance to the Community and the mutual suspicions felt within it, in the FRG's Ostpolitik and the resultant eastern treaties. Fourth was the 'defence' cluster: the arguments in and outside France about its position; the arguments about a 'nuclear component' of western European security; and the rumblings over US troop reductions and western European responses.

Looking forward (from the vantage point of 1971) to the problems that the Community would have to face in the rest of the 1970s, Miriam Camps aptly summed up the Community's situation: '[T]he decisions that will soon have to be taken about the tasks needing to be done will confront the member countries with large new choices: there is very little guidance in the existing agreements' (Camps 1971: 674). The injunctions of the founding treaties had been carried out (as in the case of the customs union), outlived (as for much coal and steel business), run into the sand (Euratom) or, she argued, they were so general in character that the decisions yet to be taken on how to implement them would be the key decisions, as was the case with monetary union and the other statements of intent in the Hague communiqué. If the Community were not merely to remain on the plateau that it had attained, very important decisions would thus have to be taken.

Yet, in the taking of these decisions, 'there is very little clear guidance in what might be called the imperatives of the European situation' (Camps 1971: 674). Revived prosperity and reduced perceptions of threat and likely armed conflict combined with reduced plausibility for ideas of 'spillover' from one policy area to another. Thus:

It is easy enough to enumerate tasks that an enlarged Community might now undertake; but ... difficult to list many that either the objective facts of the European situation, or the results of past actions, or the obligations of commitments already entered into require it to undertake ... The rhetoric of European unity, is, today, no guide to specific action.

(Camps 1971: 674–5)

Camps argued that an 'unfortunate by-product' of the 1960s' battle between de Gaulle and such 'Europeans' as Monnet and Hallstein had been that the latter, in their determination to defend their creation, had become 'conservative and overly doctrinaire' (Camps 1971: 671). The need to 'think new thoughts' was underlined by three sets of changes: 'first, changes in the character of the political security setting; second, changes in the nature of relationships among states and in attitudes within states; and third, changes in the nature of the agenda of the enlarged Community' (Camps 1971: 672).

She further argued that, while the third set of changes allowed of a wide latitude in thinking about what tasks the Community might undertake, the first two sets of changes offered some clues as to what action might be appropriate. The first set – a multipolar world configuration – implied that western Europe could have a substantial role to play if it could speak with one voice. The second set suggested that:

[C]ertain functions should now be performed at the 'European level' rather than the national level because that is the level that corresponds to the dimension of the problem and not because of some compulsion to push to the European level anything and everything that the concept of 'Europe as a power' might seem to imply.

(Camps 1971: 675)

At this point the argument advanced by Miriam Camps parallels that put forward at almost the same time by this writer (McAllister 1971). The argument has not gone away: it looks both at the range and nature of functions requiring to be handled at some level or shared between certain levels in the system and attempts to discover where given functions might most appropriately be handled. The more recent debates about 'subsidiarity' are closely linked to it. I pointed out that there were new, emerging, functions as well as 'old' ones; and that particular agenda items might require a shared competence between different levels of governance, identified under the rubric of 'region, nation, Europe'. Camps too suggested that there were 'constraints from below' – from sub-state levels, as well as from above, influencing the 'where' and 'how' of the handling of issues. She asked whether the two roles could be combined: whether 'Europe' could be both a world power 'and a "layer" or "level" in the continuum of organised society ... I see no reason why it cannot ... [This] seems to me to be in accord with the real needs of the times. But it is a lot harder to break new ground' (Camps 1971: 677). So it was to prove. In what follows, we shall see that the European Community of the 1970s was, for the most part, unable to break out of the mould of those earlier quarrels between de Gaulle's views and those of such as Monnet or Hallstein; and I shall seek to identify why this proved so.

As we have seen, the Hague Summit spawned a number of policy initiatives: some were long to preoccupy the Community. The main cluster of concerns ran on from the 'triptych': completion, deepening and enlargement. 'Completion' was both an acknowledgement of the achievement of the customs union and more 'final' arrangements about agricultural financing, even if common prices had bitten the dust ('temporarily', of course). Deepening included the remits both of Davignon ('political cooperation ... especially on foreign policy' having slipped into the vocabulary instead of 'achieving progress in the matter of political unification') and of Werner (EMU). The implications of the latter for the weaker brethren (especially in the context of enlargement) were widely held to provide an opportunity to give a higher profile to regional policy which until then had progressed at snail's pace: this line of development was to encompass the Thomson Report on the Regional Problems in the Enlarged Community (COM (73) 550; 3 May 1973), of which more will be said in the next chapter.

But the crucial point about this period was that it witnessed a serious test of some of the key assumptions that had, until then, been widely held. In particular, key pillars of the postwar economic framework were visibly cracking, and the question was how far the Community could act as a force in its own right to influence the course of events and to identify and defend 'common west European' interests, or how far it would be a rudderless victim of the economic storm. While some aspects of that storm were not revealed until 1973 and even afterwards, others, particularly as regards the international monetary system, were all too immediate. Another legacy of the Hague Summit, however, was quite simply agreement to meet again, with a date and a place. Not least important was the notion: 'We must go on meeting like this.'

The preoccupations of the years 1969–73 can be sketched briefly as follows. 'Completion' had been announced and, even though it was quite clear that it was 'incomplete', most evidently in regard to the 'four freedoms', yet certain activities flowed directly from the end of the transitional period. 'Deepening' could mean all things to all people and to some extent was witness to the incompleteness of the project. 'Enlargement' was more self-evident and although there were elements of 'touch and go', it appeared to be clinched by the Heath–Pompidou meeting of May 1971.

The optimism of 1968 about economic prospects was underlined in successive numbers of the Commission's quarterly survey publication *The Economic Situation in the Community (Ec. Sit.)*. 'The Community's economy is expanding vigorously' (*Ec. Sit.* 2–1968: 3): 'The year 1968 has been one of very vigorous economic expansion for the Community' (*Ec. Sit.* 3/4–1968: 3); yet certain clouds had appeared. These were both local (the working through of the effects of the French 'events' of May–June 1968) and more global – including measures to curb demand in both the USA and the UK.

A good illustration of the linkages perceived to exist between different areas of activity and also of the way in which matters, once on the agenda, tend not to vanish but rather, after a tactical retreat to the 'back burner', to revive, also appears at this time. At the time of the crisis of 1965–6, the Commission had held that moves over agricultural finance entailed 'own resources' and that the issue of control of 'own resources' raised the question of the role of the European Parliament in that. At the time, France appeared to have 'disentangled' these elements, insisting that the situation called only for the completion of agricultural financing and not the institutional reforms.

The Hague Summit of 1969 had spoken not only of completion as involving the laying down of 'a definitive financial arrangement for the CAP by the end of 1969' (3 *GRA*, 1969: 487), but also of the need to replace member states' contributions by Community 'own resources' and said that this in turn was 'with the object … of strengthening the budgetary powers of the European Parliament'. This was followed immediately by a short, significantly separate, paragraph reminding the reader that 'the problem of the method of direct elections is still being studied by the Council of Ministers' – a remark whose truth was to prove durable indeed (3 *GRA*, 1969: 488). All of this, in turn, was linked with the urgently felt need to produce 'a plan in stages … during 1970 with a view to the creation of an economic and monetary union' (3 *GRA*, 1969: 488).

## The Vedel and Werner Reports

These linkages continued to be made and led to the creation of the ad hoc working party examining the problem of the enlargement of the powers of the European Parliament under the chairmanship of Professor Georges Vedel of Paris (decided on 22 July 1971; the Vedel Report was dated 25 March 1972) (*Bull. Supp.* 4/72). The Vedel Report provides a useful vantage point on the problems of the Community at the beginning of the 1970s, as do the arguments over the economic and monetary union proposals.

What became equally clear at this time was the importance of outside forces which, quite independently of what might be happening within the Community, might blow things off course. We have already noted the beginnings of the monetary disruptions: these, and the later (1973) first 'oil price shock' which was in some respects their sequel, were to mark the Community deeply as the decade proceeded.

The Vedel Report reminded its readers that the Community 'has by no means done all it set out to do, even in regard to matters on which specific actions should have been completed before the end of the transitional period': it cited transport, free movement of capital and freedom of establishment for liberal professions among the 'laggard' areas (Vedel 1972: 15). More serious, it was acknowledged, had been the problems with 'coordination of economic policies' as required by Article 105. The report declared that 'distortions in … national economies have often been alarming' and that these had in part caused erratic exchange rate movements since 1969, and added: '[T]he makers of the Treaty never visualised the possibility of the problems assuming such proportions, and provided only for incidental ad hoc action, notably in Article 107 EEC.' Underlining how exchange rate changes had interfered with 'the whole concept of a common market', especially in agriculture, the report added: 'It is becoming apparent that unless the very foundations of the Common Market are to be ruined monetary policy must be a European-level affair. Upon this premise is based the project for economic and monetary union' (Vedel 1972: 16).

Vedel then reminded its readers that it was 'governments themselves' that had made the first moves towards EMU, with the Council decision to set up the Werner Working Party whose final report had gone to Council and Commission on 13 October 1970. There followed the Council resolution of 22 March 1971 on the establishment by stages (by 1980) of an economic and monetary union and which also provided a working definition of what that somewhat contested concept was being taken to mean. Vedel noted that the Council resolution had not referred to a controversial institutional proposal of the Werner Report, that there should be 'a centre of decision for economic policy' to 'exercise *independently*, in accordance with the *Community* interest, a *decisive* influence over the general economic policy of the Community' (Vedel 1972: 18, quoting Werner, emphasis added).

Werner had himself shown that he realised how controversial his proposals might be, in his lecture at Lausanne University on 22 February 1971. In it he said:

> The report points to a centre of decision for Community economic policy, and to a centre of decision for monetary policy. While the functions of the second are clearly envisageable, since this would mean a 'community system' of central banks, there remained a wide margin of interpretation as far as the 'decision-centre' of economic policy was concerned. With regard to this, the problem of democratic parliamentary control must be faced, [an] indispensable [element] insofar as important decisions are transferred to the Community level. In this area, conflicting views will surface, depending upon first what concept people hold of the Europe to be.
>
> (Werner 1971: 23)

In hindsight, it may well appear that EMU was not likely to get off the ground, in the midst of the monetary and other turmoils of the time. Yet at the time it was taken most seriously, and indeed figures at the head of the matters of substance referred to in the communiqué of the Paris Summit of October 1972. It is worth noting, too, that these proposals, which were to have several and very varied impacts on the future course of events, were the product of a particular experience and set of lenses. It has often been remarked that the Werner proposals emerged after a battle between the 'monetarists', led by France (Barre) and Belgium, and the 'economists', led by Schiller for the FRG. The 'economists' emphasised that convergence of economic performance was the essential precondition for a successful monetary union; the monetarists that the move to monetary union would be the catalyst that enforced economic convergence. But also Werner, a Luxembourger, was, as he himself admitted, heavily influenced by his 'local' experience with the Belgian–Luxembourg Union in the view he took of what was (institutionally) necessary; his proposals appeared to espouse the view that to do something 'equivalent' on a larger scale would not involve totally new problems. As he said in the Lausanne lecture:

> For myself, I have had the conviction since 1960, that the fullness of objectives of the Common Market could not be attained except through a far-reaching monetary co-operation, going beyond the prudent thoughts of the Treaty. The experience of my own country with economic unions was such as to make me particularly aware of this aspect of affairs.
>
> (Werner 1971: 15)

On one matter, both Werner and the European Parliament, in its resolution on the report, were agreed: any substantial transfer of powers in these areas must be accompanied by an increase in the Parliament's powers; equally, a Parliament not directly elected would lack the legitimacy to exercise such powers. Werner said that a decision centre for economic policy would have to be politically responsible to a European Parliament, whose status must correspond to these tasks not just by a formal grant of authority, but also 'having regard to the method of election of its members'. The EP resolution stated that any such transfer of powers 'must be accompanied, to ensure democratic control, by an increase in the powers of the European Parliament'.

Of course, things were not to come to pass in this way at this time. The point is that the world was configured, or perceived to be configured, in a particular way. A certain set of 'logics' was espoused by those favouring the proposals. These views included the following:

1    that one could not 'stop' at the level of a customs union, that the way forward was toward EMU and that this would incidentally 'solve' the problem of CAP prices;
2    that EMU would in any case be economically beneficial and especially that it would have benefits in terms of 'efficiency';
3    that it would entail institutional changes;
4    that it would also help to reinforce western Europe's 'economic personality', especially with regard to the international monetary order.

There were also contrary logics and each of the views just given was also strongly attacked, both at the time and since. Among the more trenchant one-liners was from the governor of the Danish Central Bank, who was reported as saying: 'I shall begin to believe in European economic and monetary union when someone explains how you control nine horses that are all running at different speeds within the same harness' (*FT*, 23 January 1973). Fred Hirsch spelled out the interests that he felt underlay the proposals in *The World Today* (Hirsch 1972: 424–33). Its supporters included the Commission (in the name of logic and 'completion'), the monetarists (in the name of discipline – as it was pointedly put at the time, both of labour and of Labour) and the City of London (also in the name of 'discipline', but hoping too for a new Europe-wide arena in which to act). Thus, for example, the proposals were lent influential support by ex-Commissioner Ralf Dahrendorf in another piece in *The World Today*:

> It is imperative for the Community to pursue its own course towards Economic and Monetary Union along the lines which have been suggested in the past. And it is important that the crucial step towards Economic and Monetary Union – a step towards a commitment in the monetary as well as the economic field – is taken at the time which has been set for it. It should be clear that the next two years will be as decisive for the E.C. as for the world system in respect of monetary policy.
>
> (Dahrendorf 1973: 47–57)

The dilemma, however, was sharply posed by Hirsch:

> The direction of this movement conflicts with the functional need of the major economies … To the question of when European monetary union can be expected to be economically and politically feasible, the answer should therefore be something like 'when the economies of the present EEC countries are significantly more integrated with each other than are England and Scotland today'.
>
> (Hirsch 1972: 426)

EMU was a threat to the weaker (regional and state) economies. But it was also firmly on the Community agenda. Either it would succeed to a degree, in which case the Community would be blamed for the ensuing damage or this 'ardent commitment' would be revealed as a mere piece of rhetoric, with consequent damage to the Community's credibility. In the battle to decide which was to happen, forces external to the Community proved more powerful than the Community itself.

France had begun by insisting that the position of sterling must be sorted out prior to accession, contrary to the UK's wishes (*Keesing's* 1971: 24837ff.). France further raised the issue of sterling in relation to EMU, publicly for the first time in a permanent representatives' meeting on 18 March 1971. The sterling row was finally resolved at the 7 June negotiating session (*Keesing's* 1971: 24839); the problem of capital movements was resolved at the 12 July session. Although there is no doubt that the Pompidou–Heath meeting of 20–21 May improved the climate in this regard (*EDB* 812–16, 21–7.5.71), the drawing together of positions appears to have owed not a little to the monetary disruptions of early May (*EDB* 801, 6.5.1971; Strange 1976: 333ff. (May crisis), 336 (August crisis)).

By the spring of 1971 the argument between the USA and the Europeans had reached what Strange called the 'brutal political level of who pays, who bears the pain and discomfort of domestic adjustments, who sets the order of economic priorities' and 'was an admission … that the affluent alliance had come to the end of the road' (Strange 1976: 335). But this alliance was not the only one under strain: it did not prove possible to get a concerted European – in particular Franco-German – response. The Germans were for a joint float – 'a jump, as it were, into Phase 2 of the Werner Plan' (Strange 1976: 335). This approach failed at the deadlocked finance ministers' meeting of 8 May and on 10 May the West Germans floated anyway, taking in parallel measures against non-residents. The whole episode threw doubt over the Community's ability to erect defences around itself, to assert a European monetary identity or to float jointly. Having been made aware that France was itself in an endangered position, it seems that Pompidou was more ready to settle with Heath rather than to keep him outside any longer.

Of course, there was a *quid pro quo*: in the 2–3 September Group of Ten (deputies') meeting in Paris, Britain lined up with the EEC and against the USA for the first time. And, as Strange adds:

> In retrospect it is pretty clear therefore that the knell of European monetary union was rung in 1971 and not in 1974 with the floating of the French franc ... it was the failures of 1971 that had first revealed the lack of political will behind the technical arrangements.
>
> (Strange 1976: 345)

The point is that the Community neither recognised this nor appeared particularly concerned. It carried blithely on, enunciating its former intentions. The record became firmly stuck in the groove. The Vedel Report was still speaking in almost unchanged terms about it in 1972. This was an important but by no means isolated example of the Community 'sounding off' in favour of something that it could not deliver, and making itself look increasingly meddlesome without being able to get itself off the hook, change the agenda and cut its losses.

The Community had gone on as if talking to itself in a dream, rather than daring to face a waking state. There had been the Werner Working Party's interim report of 20 May 1970 (*OJ* C.94, 23 July 1970: 1). The Werner Report itself was delivered to Council and Commission on 13 October 1970 (*OJ* C.136, 11 November 1970: 1) and, just as the waves were about to wash over their heads, the resolution was passed by the Council and representatives of member states on 22 March 1971 (*OJ* C.28, 27 March 1971: 1).

The problem, of course, sprang from several sources. I have noted that, when the moment came, the FRG and France could not agree. Equally, as Vedel reminded its readers: 'A last point to be noted on this vital subject of economic and monetary union is that it is not expressly covered as such by the EEC Treaty', despite the vague references in Articles 105, 103 and 107.

But this was not all. The EP's Political Affairs Committee had, basing itself on the Davignon Report (*Bull. EC* 11–70) adopted by the foreign ministers on 27 October 1970, pointed out that 'the process of economic and monetary union must accelerate political unification'. All this, and enlargement, were to prove more than a little indigestible.

And, as Vedel added, the Council of Ministers, the centre of power (cf. especially Article 145 EEC), found that most of the 'relatively precise provisions' given it, applied to 'most of the objectives set for the transitional period', now ended, while

[I]n other cases, above all now that the transitional period is over, the only restrictions on the Council's power are the requirements of a common policy which it is the Council's own task to define. In this, the definitive period, the Council is therefore the Community's legislator.

(Vedel 1972: 23)

That sounded very grand and positive. Actually, it was menacingly negative in its implications, as the coming period was to show. Three key elements were involved. One was what John Pinder had presciently christened in 1968, the distinction between 'negative integration' and 'positive integration' (Pinder 1968). A second was what Professor Kaptejn was later to call 'the problem of the limits of the Treaty of Rome' (McAllister 1979: 61). The third was that this 'legislator' was, in practice at any rate, since the Luxembourg 'Agreements', required to act in most instances by unanimity. I shall have occasion to return often to each of these three themes in later chapters.

The other major saga that took up much time between 1970 and 1972 was again one that was to cast a long shadow before it. It concerned the reform of the EC's agriculture and the budgetary implications that were associated with it. Again, the two were perceived as inextricably linked; again, the initial noises on both counts from Community institutions were optimistic (structural reform would speed modernisation, moderating prices, thus reducing budgetary demands and releasing resources for other common policies); again, the optimism proved ill founded and instead of a 'virtuous circle' the Community quickly found itself in a vicious one (Rosenthal 1975: esp. Ch. 6).

The British, now acutely interested observers of the process, were perhaps in a good position to avoid eulogies and enthusiasms about The Hague. One assessment not suffering from misty eyes was made by Trevor Parfitt (Parfitt 1970: 1–4). This noted that the summit results represented a slowing down of the Commission's switching over to Community financing of agriculture, but that, crucially, the 'Five have accepted what appears to be an open-ended commitment to pay for French agriculture, and have committed the applicant countries in advance of negotiations being started' (Parfitt 1970: 2). Pointing out that the original Mansholt Plan had wanted a 'central' (i.e. Community) rather than national approach to modernisation of agricultural structures, he added prophetically:

Unless there really is a massive attempt to create new jobs for people displaced from the land, the chance of implementing even an attenuated Mansholt Plan in an orderly fashion during the 1970s must be remote, which means the prospects of reducing the open-ended commitment on agricultural policy must be equally remote.

(Parfitt 1970: 1–4)

On one point, his predictions proved not so accurate: sharing the widely held view that the French were destined to go on being the major beneficiaries, he had said that 'having gained the substance of permanent funding, [they] will not mind how long the Germans spend chasing shadows on the ceiling'. In fact, it was to be the West Germans who in many ways benefited most from the paradoxical workings of monetary compensation amounts (MCAs) during much of the 1970s (Hu 1979).

A more uncritical and enthusiastic response came from 'federalist' John Pinder in the same journal. For him, The Hague 'provided a clear public demonstration that the Community's unhappy Gaullist decade has ended'. The new decade was at least potentially 'much more productive for the unity of Europe'. Yet he too spoke of what was 'euphemistically called "completion"' being in practice the commitment to agree on the 'definitive' regulation of the CAP – 'definitive because there are to be no changes in the principle of the regulation thereafter and changes of detail are to be subject to a unanimous vote, i.e. the veto' (Pinder 1970: 6). Brandt's attempt to 'trade' this for clear limits on the budgetary costs failed, because the Council of Ministers meeting on 22 December 1969 clinched the financing.

He noted that this was the area where the communiqué was hard and precise, in contrast to its vagueness and imprecision when speaking of progress towards economic and political union. Once again, there was the danger that certain items would get in the way of others: 'It would be difficult for the Community to take major steps towards economic or political union during the course of a tense negotiation about agriculture.' A further refrain was heard, by no means for the last time: 'The Community as it stands [is] not much more than a customs union which affords a potential for further integration but whose main achievement so far has been the burdensome CAP' (Pinder 1970: 6). There was a danger to the UK in the Community deciding on other common policies detrimental to it. It could also be envisaged that a functional split would be needed between the institutions: while an economic union might well be the province of the Commission, a political union might have to be implemented by the Council, and this would require treaty amendments.

The Hague was notable also, however, for ideas that did not result in any early action, although they were meant to. One was Chancellor Brandt's proposal, put forward, it appears, at the instance of Monnet's Action Committee for the United States of Europe, for a European reserve fund. Robert Triffin pointed out that it was 'promptly submerged in a more ambitious, but temporising – not to say "stalling" – resolution' – that calling for the establishment of EMU within ten years (Ypersele and Koeune 1985: 4).

Kruse maintained (1980: 2) that 'the 1969 Hague Summit, which formally set EMU as a goal … determined the course of European integration for years to come'. He added that the 'fundamental cause of the failure' was that 'each national government as well as the Commission had its own conception of EMU, reflecting its individual interests'. The grand gesture – of declaring agreement on a grandiose scheme while rejecting the 'modest proposal' of Brandt – surfaced again as a substitute for policy. Perhaps both Triffin and Kruse were right: at all events, this episode was to cost the Community dear in terms of credibility and probably (although by its nature harder to judge) in terms of welfare also.

This saga ran right through the period from 1970 to 1973. The parallels in the events of the latter year to those of the former were interesting. 'In 1973, as in 1970, the nine Governments could not agree on a common strategy. The EMU Project was at a dead stop' (Kruse 1980: 163).

This is to run ahead a little too fast. The weavings of 1970–2 are instructive on several counts. The Werner Committee, mandated by The Hague, had to pick its way through the minefield of 'monetarists' (the Barre approach) and 'economists' (Schiller): it did so by leaning toward Barre. In fact, the opponents of the Werner approach were hardly represented at all in the committee. The 'mistakenness' of its strategy has, however, been vigorously expounded since (see, e.g., Tsoukalis in Wallace et al. 1983: 120). All countries were being asked to surrender crucial powers of economic policymaking just when exogenous shocks were pushing them into more divergent postures and policies. It was already clear in October 1970 that the French government, for one, was not prepared to accept EMU's 'supranational' aspects.

The scheme was also built on shifting sand in being based on the very 'Bretton Woods' mechanisms that were fast foundering. The 'link' between the Community's internal agenda and the world monetary order, so far from proving a 'positive' one, was to be of quite the contrary kind: all the knitting unravelled.

## Turbulence in the Commission

This was a point in its history, if ever there were one, when the Community, and the Commission in particular, could have done with reliable and decisive leadership. But, in fact, these were years of discontinuity in Commission leadership and also in personnel. The Commission was headed by Jean Rey of Belgium until the end of June 1970. Sasse et al. (1977: 193) said that, with the end of the transitional period, 'an epoch of irresolution began, and there was ... an exodus from the framework of the Treaties'. It was as if the Commission motor were 'hunting', failing to find a rhythm. It would not be easy for it to revert to the bold, high strategy of the Hallstein Commission which had led headlong into the clash of 1965–6, the 'empty chair' and the 'rap over the knuckles' which the Luxembourg Agreements represented. But should it slide back into 'mere' bureaucratic torpor? There appeared to be another possibility, perhaps congenial to 'small country' leadership and Rey took it, with consequences that were probably unfortunate. Rey was urging the Commission to 'play a more prophetic role within the Community system, to revive European "faith" and "hope"', as he made clear in speaking to the European Parliament (Sasse et al. 1977: 194–5). 'The Accession negotiations practically paralyzed ambition as far as new Community policies were concerned ... The Community system was going through a "wait and see" stage, a transitional period.' This was when the actual transitional period was supposed to have just ended! The Commission's ambiguous approach to its own identity was clear from its own writings (see, e.g., 4 *GRA*, 1970: 29).

Rey gave over the reins of the Commission presidency to Malfatti of Italy just as enlargement negotiations were getting under way (end of June–beginning of July 1970). There was an interesting contrast in their attitude to institutional matters in the Community. Malfatti criticised the Rey Commission; Malfatti opted for 'align-ment' with the Council and was, in turn, criticised for his pains by the European Parliament!

In March 1972 Malfatti resigned as both president and member and Mansholt was appointed until the end of the year, when the Ortoli Commission was installed including, of course, the commissioners from the new member states. It was felt at the time that all this turbulence had been unhelpful. (One dissatisfied voice close to the throne produced the 'Wieland Europa' articles in *Die Zeit*, 9 and 16 July 1971.)

The problem was not just at the top. A good deal of research (see, e.g., Michelmann 1978) tended to show that these disruptions and the expansion of the Commission consequent on the Merger Treaty (of 1965, but effective 1967), itself instituted in the shadow of the Luxembourg Compromise, had never been properly absorbed.

Of significance for our immediate concerns was Michelmann's finding (based on research carried out mainly in 1973–4) that DG II (economic and financial affairs) attained only a middling rating on most measures of performance. It was hardly as if they had lacked an agenda or, in this period, real problems to get to grips with. Rather, the Directorate-General (DG) was seen to have been both in general somewhat unwilling to poke its head over the parapet and also, when it did, to be rather rigidly attached to 'Werner-type' schemes and quite unable to respond flex-ibly to, let alone actively to influence, the eddy of events that swirled around it. As Michelmann put it (1978: 225), not only did it have 'low autonomy' but also it was 'not ... able to devise an ideology acceptable to major actors in its environment'.

We have already seen that monetary turbulence was one cause of France's recon-sideration of her attitude to UK membership in May 1971. Thus important differ-ences of attitude between the western European states were apparent before the bombshell of the 'Nixon package' of 15 August 1971. 'The May 1971 crisis brought the EMU Project to a halt', opined Kruse (1980: 90). As the Deutschmark and Dutch guilder floated upwards, the French reacted by abandoning joint action in related economic policy fields. Only two months after the 'relaunch', the project was in ruins. Thus the Community faced the greater challenge – of August 1971 – deeply divided and in no sense ready to confront it adequately.

Other views with the benefit of hindsight were not dissimilar. Alexandre Lamfalussy (then of BIS, Basel) suggested that a minimum definition of 'monetary integration' would encompass two aspects: 'a greater stability of exchange rates within the area than between its members and third countries; and a high degree of freedom within the area for current and capital account transactions' (Lamfalussy in Katz 1979: 53). On this definition, he added, 'it is clear that little has survived of earlier attempts at promoting monetary integration within the EEC'. The four large states had been 'moving away from integration rather than toward it'. His diagno-sis of the reasons for this shift, not just from the 'visionary' ideas of the late 1960s but from the 'more modest' ambitions of the early 1970s, are worth underlining. 'We know the reasons ... A *series of external shocks has revealed fundamental differences in the social and political attitudes*, as well as in the economic struc-tures, of the larger member countries' (emphasis added). These, concealed by the 'exceptionally favourable conditions for balanced growth prevailing until about

1968–69', had been highlighted by three major forces: the flight from the dollar, mainly into the Deutschmark; the acceleration in (world) inflation in 1972–3; and the first 'oil shock' of late 1973 (Lamfalussy in Katz 1979: 55). It was not merely the differential impact on the states that mattered, but their varying response – especially policy response.

Oort opined (Katz 1979: 193) that the 'history of the Werner Plan is a fascinating study that deserves careful analysis by students … not least of political science'. We shall see later that much the same may be said of the European Monetary System (EMS) proposals of the late 1970s. The episode showed the Community in a fundamentally reactive light, with instruments (notably the 'Snake' mechanism) originally designed with one objective in mind, being asked to fulfil another.

## The budget and EP powers

In some respects, the easiest part of the Hague communiqué to fulfil was that which spoke of creating a system of 'own resources' (*ressources propres*) for the Community, i.e. a financial system that would no longer consist of contributions made by the member states. The transfer of customs revenue to the Community was the logical corollary of setting up the customs union in the first place. Article 201 EEC had provided for this and the common customs tariff (CCT) had been introduced on 1 July 1968. Agricultural levies were considered in a similar spirit.

The outcome of both the Article 201 commitment and of the Hague communiqué in the 'resources' field was, nevertheless, not without difficulty. The twin agreements of Luxembourg of 21 April 1970 were, first, the Council decision on the progressive replacement of member states' financial contributions by own resources and, second, the treaty ('First Budget Treaty') making consequent amendments to the relevant articles of the founding treaties.

It was clear from the start that there would be problems over the resources. There was first the issue of their adequacy: the Hague communiqué had already anticipated this, with its reference to 'a better control of the market by a policy of agricultural production making it possible to limit the burden on the budgets'. (Altiero Spinelli, indeed, had come up with a scheme similar to UK deficiency payments designed to achieve this, but it was squashed.) The 'adequacy' issue had its other side too: these were neither elastic nor predictable revenue sources, especially as the CCT was liable to be bargained down in multilateral tariff negotiations, and the levies to vary unpredictably, depending as they did on the size of the gap between Community and world prices. In short, the Community had, especially until the advent of the VAT component, a thoroughly 'primitive fiscal system', whose equity, adequacy and control were all controversial.

The decision – subsequently ratified by the national parliaments – meant a certain loss of power by states and loss of control over the resources by national bodies. It was based on two ideas: giving the Community genuine revenue sources to cover its expenditure, and doing so by stages (transferring levies first, CCT proceeds in stages over 5 years and the VAT proportion only later) (Strasser 1980: 5; Commission 1981: 14–16).

The leaching of power from states was taken to imply that EP powers in budgetary matters should be increased. The Treaty of Luxembourg and its annexes sought to resolve this. It made significant changes to A.203 EEC, A.78 ECSC and A. 177 EAEC. It was quickly ratified by the states and entered into force on 1 January 1971. As far as the EP was concerned, in essence the Treaty made it harder for the Council of Ministers to overturn a modification proposed by the EP which did not entail additional *net* expenditure. To reject such an amendment, the Council would have to muster a qualified majority against it. It was still for the president of the Council to declare a budget 'finally adopted', although the question was raised as to the EP's right to reject a budget in toto – a right that the EP, supported by the Commission, maintained that it had. In fact, this 'right' was not invoked until much later, when it was more firmly established; nevertheless, the EP from this point forward regularly proposed modifications to the budgets, but did not at this time try to reject any draft budgets in their entirety.

The other main impulsion given by the Hague Summit was to the development of the rather curiously titled 'political cooperation' field: consultation and, to the extent possible, coordination in external policy.

### 'European political cooperation'

Allen and Wallace (Allen at el. 1982: 21) described the establishment of the political cooperation system as 'a significant landmark in the continuing debate about the character of political integration and the formal or informal nature of European institutions'. As we have seen, it had its basis, as did EMU, in the Hague communiqué; and apart from that, it had neither legal nor institutional basis. In addition, they remind us, 'It was entirely outside the competence of the Treaties ... it had no secretariat ... at best, tenuous links with the existing institutions ... no fixed meeting place' and its objectives were 'couched in the cloudiest rhetoric, thinly disguising the underlying disagreements about its purpose and its future development ... There was no mention of "common policy", even as a distant aim' (Allen et al. 1982: 21) and, unlike EMU, no timetabling by stages either.

The Hague summiteers, having decided on the need to give some new impetus to the *relance*, agreed to establish a procedure rather than a policy. In the light of earlier attempts, even this was something. The 'European army' (EDC) proposal had died in August 1954 when the French national assembly failed to ratify it. Yet periodically, France (and notably de Gaulle) had sought to promote the idea of a 'political secretariat', to be based in Paris, obtaining some support for this from the FRG. Such proposals had run up against an oft repeated set of doubts and objections, the most important being: how would any such proposal affect the existing Community arrangement; how would it relate to NATO; how could the British and other 'candidate' states relate to it? Beyond that, was it to encompass defence specifically, and was it anti- or at any rate specifically non-American? None of this had been resolved in the saga of the Fouchet Committee in the early 1960s.

With this dead weight of the past, perhaps it was surprising that even greater scepticism toward such proposals did not surface at The Hague. It appears that

Pierre Werner, the only summiteer who had 'lived through' the events of 1961 at close quarters, did express doubts, at least concerning the 'ripeness of the time' (Allen et al. 1982: 23; *Bull. EC* 1–1970: 52).

There was a marked contrast also between the high flown rhetoric of the communiqué and the subsequent Luxembourg Report of the foreign ministers, prepared by senior officials who, much more aware of the problems of any 'common foreign policy', spoke instead of 'regular exchanges of information', 'consultations', 'better mutual understanding' and, the key phrase, 'promoting the harmonisation of their views, the coordination of their positions, and, *where it appears possible or desirable*, common actions' (Luxembourg Report 1970: Pt Two, I, emphasis added; also see Bonn 1977). The close connection proposed with Community business proper was underlined by the chairmanship arrangement, which was to coincide with the country having the chair of the EC Council of Ministers, thus rotating on a 6-monthly basis. Ministers themselves were to meet at least every 6 months; the main innovation was to be the political committee to be composed of senior officials ('political directors') of the national foreign ministries, to meet four times a year. Apart from preparing the ministerial meetings or acting under ministerial direction, they were empowered also to set up working groups or groups of experts, or to institute 'any other form of consultation' necessary.

The 'subjects for consultation' were equally wide open: 'all important questions of foreign policy ... any question of their choice for political consultation' (Bonn 1977: 28–9). That was where the trouble began: 'Should the work of the Ministers affect the activities of the ECs, the Commission will be invited to make known its views' and 'The Ministers and members of the Political Commission of the European Parliamentary Assembly will meet ... (biannually) to discuss questions' being dealt with under political cooperation.

This did not prevent the Paris Summit from issuing a generally favourable report on political cooperation. It 'had begun satisfactorily and should be improved still further' (20 *RCW*, 1972: 139). To this end, a second report, the Copenhagen Report, should follow-up from the Luxembourg Report of 1970.

The prospect of accession sharply focused minds in regard to one hitherto troublesome policy area: fisheries. Shackleton commented that 'the prospect of ... new states ... all of them with important fishing industries – applying to join the Community served as an important external spur to agreement' (Shackleton in Wallace et al. 1983: 359). The agreement was reached on 30 June 1970, just one day before negotiations with the applicants began. By laying down the principle of equal access to the waters of all Community countries for vessels of all Community states, it both helped to precipitate the Norwegian 'no' and also ensured that this area would remain one of chronic dispute ever since. It was a classic instance of the connexion between policy scope and geographical scope. It was also a key example of another pattern associated with enlargement: that acceding states were seen by existing members as *demandeurs*, who would have to 'take it or leave it'. The Community drove a hard bargain.

How, then, should the activity of this period be evaluated? The Community institutions were, as often, brightly positive. The Council, for example (20 *RCW*: 1), claimed that 1972 had been 'a most fruitful year for Europe and will remain a landmark in its history'. Yet the summit communiqué itself gave evidence both of unwillingness to realise that pet projects might founder; and also of airy rhetoric, not to say muddle, about the likely results of the actions it proposed. Thus we still find the heady claims for EMU: 'the guarantee of stability and growth', right next to the objective of '*ending* disparities between the regions' (emphasis added) – an aim quite beyond all possibility of fulfilment, as well as being most unlikely to be assisted by the creation of an EMU. Despite the February 1972 Brandt–Pompidou summit in Paris, which had given the go-ahead for closer economic policy coordination (Simonian 1985: 125), despite the 21 March Council Resolution on EMU Stage One (6 *GRA*: 96; *OJ* No. C 38, 18 April 1972), despite the setting up of the 'Snake' (in March; operational from April) and the applicants' joining of it in May, major speculation against sterling in June led to its, and the Irish punt's, withdrawal from the Snake. On the wider stage too, apparent agreement on the reform of the international monetary system did not bear fruit. Despite the London (17–18 July) and Rome (12 September) meetings of the Ten's finance ministers, the acid test was failed at the 25–9 September IMF meeting in Washington.

In France, however, the change of president had undoubtedly ended a logjam, even though Pompidou's 'revisionism' about the Community stopped short of any desire to enhance its autonomy. Indeed, his readiness to contemplate British membership was not least in order to reinforce this view of it, as well as to counter any access of German strength. This latter fear was powerfully voiced by Michel Debré in his dressing down of 'deviant' 'Europeanists' at the Institut des Hautes Études de Défense Nationale in June 1971: he complained bitterly of those officers who, during a recent presidential visitation to the institute, had advocated 'European' solutions (Debré 1971: 1413ff.). One of the great 'certainties' was that the political conceptions of 'European countries' (i.e. especially that of France vis-à-vis those of the FRG and the UK) were deeply divergent, he said.

As to the FRG, two divergences of view were important, one local – German economic influence in Alsace and Lorraine – the other threatening to France's self-esteem in 'greater' Europe – the Ostpolitik. On the latter, in a sense he need not have worried: this tangle took precedence for Brandt and was to occupy the forefront of the FRG's attention during these years. Other than in regard to EMU and enlargement, this period was not marked by any great desire to push ahead with Community schemes.

Indeed, so bad were relations between the two on the defence front during most of this period that this almost overshadowed all else: certainly enough to prevent the kind of entente over Community business which was so often to show itself a sine qua non of progress (McAllister 1972: 10–14).

## Further reading

M. Camps, 'European unification in the seventies', *International Affairs*, 47 (4), 1971: 671–8.

D. Dinan (ed.), *Origins and Evolution of the European Union*. Oxford: Oxford University Press, 2006. (Chapter 8.)

U. Kitzinger, *Diplomacy and Persuasion: How Britain joined the Common Market*. London: Thames & Hudson, 1973.

A. Moravcsik, *The Choice for Europe*. London: UCL Press, 1999. (Chapter 4.)

P. Stirk and D. Weigall (eds), *The Origins and Development of European Integration*. London: Pinter, 1999. (Chapter 8.)

J. Young, *Cold War Europe, 1945–91*. London: Edward Arnold, 1996 (2nd edn).

# 4  A turbulent year
## 1973

The Paris Summit of October 1972 had bequeathed an ambitious programme to the enlarged Community. Its communiqué had declared *inter alia*, 'the time has come for Europe to recognise clearly the unity of its interests', a phrase whose seriousness was soon to be put to the test.

It had repeated the commitment to EMU which to many eyes had already begun to look like a pseudo-commitment. The leaders committed themselves to setting up before 1 April 1973 a European monetary cooperation fund. Regional policy was put in the lee of EMU: 'a high priority ... to correcting ... the structural and regional imbalances *which might affect the realization* of EMU' (*Bull. EC* 10–1972: 18, emphasis added). But they foreshadowed the preparation of the Thomson Report on regional problems, which was to appear in May 1973; and they declared that a European regional development fund (ERDF) would be set up 'before the end of 1973'. It was not: its establishment was delayed until 1975. On social policy, they declared that they 'attached as much importance to' vigorous action in this field as to EMU. This statement too was to prove true in a sense more negative than that intended.

The section on industrial, scientific and technological policy listed obstacles and desiderata: once again, the durability of these items, or in other words the lack of progress on them for a long while, is striking. Environment made its appearance, in the wake of the Stockholm conference establishing the UN environmental programme (UNEP). So too, presciently, did energy policy. A second report on political cooperation was promised for, and achieved by, mid-1973. On reinforcement of institutions, the Commission was to submit by 1 May 1973 a report on the distribution of competences and responsibilities between Community institutions and states that would be required for the proper functioning of an EMU. The parting shot was on European union: it declared that, having set themselves the objective of achieving this by the end of the decade, the institutions should draw up yet another report, this one more slowly, 'before the end of 1975 for submission to a Summit Conference'.

In the meantime, fresh storm clouds had begun to gather. To see how they were perceived, a glance forward a year to early 1974 may be instructive. Both at the time and since, the 'blame' has been attributed to one or more of the following four sources: external shocks; institutional shortcomings; the nature of the policy agenda; attitudes within particular member states. Between them, these cover just about all the logical possibilities!

Commission President Ortoli, in his statement on the state of the EC on 31 January 1974, expressed the general pessimism in speaking of a 'crisis of confidence, of will and of clarity of purpose' (quoted in Scheel 1974: 124). Presenting the Commission's programme to the European Parliament on 12 February 1974, Vice-President Mugnozza echoed him in speaking of a 'series of problems ... a state of crisis' of a 'wave of disillusion and bitterness' which had accompanied this 'accumulation of new problems' and had led the Commission to make a 'public declaration on the state of the Community' (7 *GRA*: xv). The Paris Summit had laid out the 'development charter for this decade', yet the Commission admitted that 1973 had passed 'without ... resolving the difficulties and without settling the main points of divergence between the Member States'. The year 1974:

> [O]pened with reticence or refusal as regards the implementation of the policy guidelines emerging from the ... Summit Conferences: it was impossible to set up the ERDF, there was hesitation over the transition to the second stage of the economic and monetary union, and there was total disagreement on the policy to be followed in dealing with the energy crisis.
>
> (8 *GRA*: 3)

Crucially, the Community had been:

> [S]eriously disrupted by the *increasing impact of external upheavals on its functioning* ... Successive monetary crises, increased commodity prices, the 'soya alert' of the spring, and finally the Middle East and the oil crisis ... have blown the Community off course ... The Community has failed to achieve several of the important objectives set for 1973.
>
> (8 *GRA*)

Scheel himself (1974: 124) commented acidly on the 'state of stagnation we have reached on the way to economic and monetary union, the endless discussions in the Brussels Council of Ministers on details' (institutional), but also on the 'conflicting (national) economic and monetary objectives' (member states) which 'we shall have to live with'. Yet in the next breath it was to the nature of the policy agenda that he appealed: the ambitious target of EMU was 'bound to lead to the moment of truth for at the pinnacle will be integration in spheres which members have so far jealously guarded'. Thus there was the feeling that 1973 was indeed witnessing 'one damned thing after another'; but considerable uncertainty as to whether the 'condition' of EC Europe was curable, and if so, how.

Even Mugnozza's list was not complete. He had not referred directly to the Kissinger–Nixon initiative for a 'New Atlantic Charter', alias the 'Year of Europe' which was to be the subject of so much savage irony by the time he spoke. As Alfred Grosser pointed out (Grosser 1980: 270), 'two texts explicated this idea': one, the speech by Kissinger in New York on 23 April 1973; the other, a long passage in Nixon's report to Congress on US foreign policy, submitted on 3 May, whose inspiration was essentially identical. Taken together, they represented perhaps the most comprehensive restatement (and revision) of US views of its relations with western Europe – and the EC in particular – since the Kennedy 'grand design' of a 'dumbbell alliance' in the early 1960s.

There is something approaching unanimity of view as to the importance of the events that followed, although predictably less when it comes to attributing blame. A seasoned observer, Pierre, was to comment (Pierre 1974: 110–19) that the Year of Europe speech was 'no ordinary speech; next day James Reston in the *New York Times* compared it to General Marshall's' of 1947, launching the Marshall Plan. Yet for such a significant proposal, it appears to have been strangely concocted. In Cromwell's view, it was 'conceived as a rather unproblematic undertaking'; yet, perhaps reflecting the relative isolation of the State Department's European specialists at the time, 'The State Department was not involved in the drafting of the speech, and Secretary of State Rogers had no advance notice of its content' (Cromwell 1992: 81–2). Its tone rankled with many Europeans, and it contained a number of quite explicit hints that were thoroughly unwelcome to some, especially but not only to France. Much later, the interactions of this turbulent year were to be described as 'a significant watershed in the evolution of US–European relations and of US policy with respect to West European unity' (Cromwell 1992: 79).

Kissinger himself was later to comment (Kissinger 1982: 152–3) that he had more or less taken a presidential visit to Europe during 1973 for granted. He added: 'I then used a formula … that I soon came to regret' to describe the differing perspectives of Europeans and Americans: it included these famous lines: 'The United States has global interests and responsibilities. Our European allies have regional interests.' The content of the speech was not the only problem. The timing of what Europeans saw as a claim to moral leadership coincided with the deeper tarnishing of the administration's image over the Watergate revelations.

What compounded the injury was that the 'theory' of the spring texts was perceived to have become the blunt unilateral practice of the autumn. There was not only the US general alert over the Yom Kippur War. As if to underline the divergence of interests and perceptions was the earlier overthrow of the Allende government in Chile on 11 September – less than a month before the Middle East crisis blew up. Still earlier, in June, European fears of 'superpower condominium' had been revived over the Nixon–Brezhnev agreements of 21–22 June on 'offensive' nuclear weapons and on the prevention of nuclear war (*L'Année Politique* 1973: 293ff.; *Aussenpolitik* 1973: 391).

At the time, *EDB* commented: 'the response [to the Kissinger speech] has been ambiguous, reticent, and, in a word, fractious … It could be said that the Europeans are exposing their divisions and their weaknesses with a degree of masochism, and that they are doing it by accusing one another of "conniving with the enemy", and by blaming this so-called enemy for their weakness' (*EDB* 1271, 26 April 1973: 1). Editor Emanuele Gazzo added that it was to be hoped that Europe would give a more reasoned reply: 'Europe's leaders must immediately set out to define between them the objectives of a "European foreign policy".' Next day he wrote of the 'visibly absurd positions' adopted by certain leaders and media (*EDB* 1272: 1). At

*Community* level: 'A first opportunity already seems to have been missed', in the response of the political committee of the Nine on 25 April. He remarked on the 'scepticism and reticence ... of the French delegate in particular'. *EDB* added: 'There was no reaction from European Commission circles (no Commissioner is present).'

Sir Christopher Soames – now a Commission vice-president – did, however, address the EP on 8 May in a speech widely seen as the Commission response (*Bull. EC* 5–1973: 54–6). He said: 'We must acknowledge that for matters which come under the generic heading of foreign policy we can as yet boast little European cohesion.' The USA saw the lack of common policies as a handicap, since it regarded 'the various parts of our overall relationship as integral parts of an integrated whole'. But, he added, he would regard it as 'a serious misunderstanding if our American friends thought that the Community was increasingly stressing its regional interests'.

Just such 'serious misunderstandings' were destined, however, to be the main hallmark of the 'Year of Europe'. The misunderstandings ran deep, and their effects were to prove long lasting, both for 'Atlantic' relations and for the EC itself. For Nixon and Kissinger, a *démarche* seemed timely if not overdue: but one problem was exactly the difference between 'timely' and 'overdue'. As Kissinger was later to suggest, the initiative was either too soon or too late.

US administration perspectives included the following notions: that they had virtually extricated themselves from the Vietnam/Indochina quagmire, and in this exercise French good offices had been helpful; that they had made their point – about the non-convertibility of the dollar into gold – stick long enough to be taken seriously even by France, yet the whole system remained precarious in the light of the monetary turbulence of early 1973; that there had now been significant moves on the *détente* front at both superpower and 'local' – intra-European – levels, whose implications required appraisal and assessment; that the European Community had itself announced a new phase at the Paris Summit. The General Agreement on Tariffs and Trade (GATT) was upcoming; agriculture remained troublesome; the 'strategic nuclear guarantee' was perceived to be wearing thin. It was thus reasonable to think that there was no shortage of things to talk about, even without succumbing to the temptation to relieve 'local difficulties' (Watergate) by diverting attention onto external high politics.

On this view, all that were needed were *interlocuteurs valables* and perhaps an acceptable forum as well. Both were to create enormous problems. How far these might reasonably have been anticipated by an administration with good antennae is not easy to say. Certainly not all the blame for what happened lay on the American side. Yet it is hard to resist the impression that one important subplot in the US scenario was to get the French in several senses 'back into line', to 'tidy up' the European scene.

As to the *interlocuteurs valables*, there were either too many or not enough. Too many, to be sure, if each were to speak for their own state. But only one would not be enough to reflect the divergences of view; in any case, one alone could speak on behalf of only one 'forum' and there were at least two – NATO and the EC.

Further, the silken thread of normally reliable go-betweens proved also too thin: meaning, not least, the British. For both Monnet and Pompidou to praise Heath's 'Europeanness' (Monnet 1978: 504; Pompidou as reported in Kissinger 1982) was ominous: Kissinger mistrusted his 'coolness' profoundly. Brandt was similarly out of favour for his 'neoneutralism'. The omens were not good, and they got worse. Jobert, recently installed as French Foreign Minister, was determined to emerge from the shadows of backroom advice giving and to make a more personal imprint on history. This ambition was unlikely to be diminished by his growing awareness of his chief's state of health. Interpreting and reconciling Jobert's verbal acrobatics became a major industry in American faculty seminars and graduate schools. All told, it was an object lesson in a theme Kissinger had touched on in his PhD written all those years before on the settlement of 1815 (*A World Restored*): the importance of personality in high diplomacy had returned to haunt him.

It was, however, with Pompidou and with Jobert that he chose to proceed, not surprisingly believing France to be the key to the whole operation. After consultations with the UK and the FRG came the Franco-USA summit at Reykjavik from 31 May to 1 June.

The argument over how to proceed became predictably theological: France in particular insisted during the summer that any European response should avoid precisely that 'linkage' of economic to security concerns that the USA was insisting on; thus there should be two declarations, one from the EC and the other from NATO (Pierre 1974: 110–19). On the eve of the September 1973 GATT talks, the Nine agreed a joint text exactly contrary in drift to the US position (Grosser 1980: 272). The EC stress was on the primacy of a stable international monetary order as a precondition for a liberal trading order: the USA replied that it was not possible to have a stable monetary order if trading partners were protectionist. A further irony occurred over the 'NATO' declaration which was produced, according to Pierre, 'on the basis of a French draft' (Pierre 1974: 113).

Pierre exposed the dilemma sharply: 1973 was the year that saw an attempt to create a 'European political identity' but 'two concepts of the future relationship of America and Europe are presently in competition' – one holding that 'Europe' would become an increasingly independent actor in international politics, the other that there was no incompatibility between 'Europe-building' and maintenance of close ties with the USA (Pierre 1974: 117).

From 30 September to 3 October Commission President Ortoli visited Washington at Nixon's invitation. It had originally been intended that Nixon would visit Europe in the autumn, subject to the Europeans producing evidence of an 'adequate' response, i.e. enough togetherness: thus the invitation to Ortoli might already be evidence of trouble. Further, the timing was impeccable: the Yom Kippur War broke on 6 October, just after the visit. The leaders met on 1 October: Ortoli characterised these talks as 'frank, concrete and constructive', hardly diplomatic language for a smooth ride (*Bull. EC* 10–1973: 64).

Some commentators of a Machiavellian turn of mind wondered out loud whether the USA might not have manipulated some of the key events of 1973, with the aim of 'teaching the Europeans a lesson' about the 'truths' of the spring texts: about their degree of dependence in the energy and animal feed sectors; about their 'merely regional' interests as contrasted with US global ones; about their inability to act coherently except in following a 'firm' US lead. The truth of such assertions is beyond our scope. What matters for our purpose is the suspicion and lack of unity with which the original texts were greeted, what they were perceived to portend, and the impact, on both the Community's coherence and its competence, of the events that followed.

There were attempts, in predictable quarters, to speed the process of change. Jean Monnet, now from the sidelines in the Action Committee for the United States of Europe, urged various concrete measures both to follow-up the summit and to respond to the USA. During the summer he had a progress report drawn up on the fulfilment of the summit agenda:

> It was clear that nothing was moving ... the Community institutions alone were powerless to perform the tasks assigned to them, although no one contested their rights ... the institutions had run out of steam. The ... Commission was ... making proposals; but the Council was not taking decisions ... and individual countries were reacting to recession and inflation with purely national measures.

> (Monnet 1978: 502)

What, he wondered, would happen to the Nine's solidarity if a worse crisis arose? 'Monetary ties were lacking; the common market in agriculture was becoming fragmented; the common energy policy, so obviously and urgently necessary, was still at the planning stage' (Monnet 1978: 502). Neither could the problem any longer be blamed on personalities: he spoke warmly of the 'three men whose simultaneous presence at the head of their governments was so fortunate for Europe' – Pompidou, Brandt and Heath. His own proposal, a draft written at the end of August, was for *institutional* changes to which he gave the title 'provisional European government'.

There was widespread agreement that this was where the 'problem' lay: it was one of 'authority'. There was less enthusiasm for the Monnet formula, particularly the name. Monnet told Jobert: 'The point is to place the responsibility for things with the heads of government, since it's they who have the last word' (Monnet 1978: 505). It appears to have been Heath who suggested he could live more easily with 'supreme council' than with 'provisional government'. At all events, all three key actors appeared to give the notion a fair wind: Pompidou in a September press conference; Heath in his speech to the UK Conservative Party Conference on 13 October; Brandt in writing to Pompidou – and, for good measure, Rumor of Italy in writing to Monnet. These moves were seen by the principals as improving the chances of and atmosphere for a Nixon visit in early 1974; thus there must be a heads of government meeting before the end of 1973. Pompidou underlined to the French cabinet that in the light of Middle East events, that timetable was important. Monnet's satisfaction was undisguised: it looked to him like a new triumph for his old preferred methods:

The agreement was total and profound, because it had been arrived at among a small number of men who were able to take decisions. The method that had secured the establishment of the Supreme Council would also ensure that it worked.

(Monnet 1978: 508)

Apart from appealing to heads of government because it promised them enhanced authority, Monnet hoped that it would restore *élan* to his *chef d'oeuvre*, the Commission. To Ortoli he said: 'You will be freer if you can put forward bold proposals which will not be stifled at birth by the technical Ministers of nine countries, as so often happens now' (Monnet 1978: 509). This was a rather partial view, ignoring the danger of generating airy generalities at the level of heads, which would prove quite incapable of translation into action at the technical level; which had also, to echo Monnet's phrase, often happened. At all events, Monnet thought that the only ones likely to be disappointed were those who expected 'that one day the Government of Europe would spring fully armed from the institutions of the Economic Community' (Monnet 1978: 509).

Monnet thought that in November 1973, 'everything favoured the idea of the European Council ... The Community was anxious to present a united front to the Americans, so as to contribute to peace in the Middle East' (Monnet 1978: 510). It was not yet to be, although the idea of the European Council appeared to be lodging more firmly in more minds, including that of Heath. Despite having prepared several concrete proposals, the Copenhagen Summit of 14–15 December 1973 descended into bickering and the search for specific, national advantage in bilateral deals with Arab emissaries for whose very presence no one took responsibility. Monnet wrote: 'The illusory quest for particular advantages revealed ... how weak our European States were if each was left to its own devices ... the failure was too spectacular, and certain changes of attitude were too startling' for any glossing over (Monnet 1978: 510).

Similar 'unseemly scenes' were to occur early in the new year at the Washington 'energy conference' (attended by Ortoli and Soames for the Commission as well as representatives of all the Nine, Scheel being Council president). These led to wry remarks not far from the State Department to the effect that if this was the Europeans acting unitedly, State officials would really like to see them quarrelling.

The outcome was that France withheld its signature from certain paragraphs, following open rows between its representatives and Scheel, in which they accused him of exceeding his mandate on behalf of the Nine. Much was to be heard as the decade progressed of 'national champions' at the level of 'meso-economic' power; but at this point, national governments themselves were doing the trailblazing for them. The rout was completed when the USA pressed home its advantage and summoned a 'follow-up', also in Washington, from 25 February. Since this time France did not attend, there could be no question of the EC as such being represented. It was a clear example of the Community being outflanked as the focus for the views of the Nine. Looking back on the whole experience, Kissinger was to rechristen the 'Year of Europe' as 'the year that never was'.

We have seen how national governments continued to diverge over EMU; they continued to do so also over the CAP. We have seen that in March 1972, the Council, in the name of 'avert[ing] any harmful effects which may result' from the monetary situation (20 *RCW*: 3) had agreed that monetary compensation amounts would be included henceforth in CAP financing, choosing thus to ignore the further 'harmful effects' of a budgetary kind.

The 1973 marathon over common prices was also memorable: 'The compromise ... left much to be desired from the point of view of economic good sense.' Agriculture Commissioner Lardinois admitted: 'The Commission did expect more as far as a return to unity of markets' (i.e. common prices, abolition of MCAs) 'was concerned' (*EDB* 1275: 3). UK Minister Godber, at the end of the 50-hour marathon, criticised not so much the content of the policy as the negotiating method, which he said was 'intolerable'.

Boersma of the Netherlands declared, in a phrase whose validity was to hold good for a decade: 'Ertl [German agriculture minister] is the moral victor of these negotiations.' For this was an area where the constraints of domestic politics enabled one government to speak with two voices: while the German Finance Ministry made respectable noises about budgetary restraint, Agriculture could urge the FDP electoral imperatives of German farmers. The understanding among FDP ministers was of a 'one out, all out' kind: if any one were put under 'intolerable' pressure, they would all leave, thus, Samson-like, bringing down the pillars of the temple around the ears of the hapless SPD (see, e.g., Andrlik 1981; Bulmer 1983). The *EDB* opined: 'We are still far from a real timetable for a return to the unity of the market' (*EDB* 1275: 5). The advantages of the status quo to West Germany went wider than just those of the farmers themselves, to merchants and storers too (Hu 1979). Thus, already the forces that were to delay and limit reform of the CAP were entrenched. The repercussions for the agricultural policy of the monetary disruptions looked like a re-run of the events of 1971 (Simonian 1985: 155–64). And in the defence of the MCA arrangement, and the scope it gave to national governments to reduce domestic inflationary pressures, West Germany was allied with the UK against France.

Neither was the CAP problem limited to disagreements over MCAs. On 5 November the Commission sent the Council its paper, *Improvement of the CAP* (*Bull. Supp.* 17/73), a 'forward look' for the period to 1978. Its opening shot made a familiar claim: that everything was related to everything else and that if governments did not make available the means, and show the will, to complete the job, then they should not be surprised at the outcome: 'The policy (CAP) cannot be properly consolidated and developed unless other common policies, such as the EMU, the regional policy, and the social policy make further progress' (*Bull.Supp.* 17/73: 5). It was a main aim of the Commission 'to cut back expenditure under the Guarantee Section of EAGGF [European agricultural guidance and guarantee fund]' (*Bull. Supp.* 17/73: 6). The logic behind this may have been impeccable, but the realism was lacking, as also in the hope (*Bull. Supp.* 17/73: 9) for the abolition of MCAs and the 'restoration of the single market not later than' the end of 1977.

The Commission said that it sought the *reduction* of the guarantee section of EAGGF, then estimated at 3800m ua for 1973, admitting openly that the price policy 'has the effect of widening still further the income disparities between categories of farms and between the regions of the Community' (*Bull. Supp.* 17/73: 18). Yet this was precisely the period when two developments were combining to produce a result opposite to the Commission's desires. First, the overall proportion of the budget being spent on the CAP was *rising*, not falling; second, within the overall envelope, the proportion being swallowed by the guarantee section was also rising sharply. The figure for agriculture (as percentages of total appropriations for payments) went up from 67.67 for the year 1972 to 72.87 in 1975. Within the total, the amount available for the guidance section (structure reform) had been supposed to be limited to 285m ua until 1973: in practice, in that year it had grown to 757m ua in 1971 and been cut back to 350m in 1973. Thus the guarantee proportion swelled from 78.3% in 1971 to 91.6% in 1973; and thereafter it did not fall below 90% (Bowler 1985: 67, 70; 10 *GRA*: 51).

This was yet another area where almost no progress was made at the Copenhagen Summit and only a little at the summits the following year. As this saga developed, it threw into sharp relief a very central problem concerning the role that the Community system could be expected to play. It was not apparent that Community institutions – specifically the Commission – were demonstrating adequate control or coming up with adequate solutions. Neither was it apparent that proposals could command consensus. Instead, as was to be argued later, what increasingly appeared to national governments was a risk that powers might be removed from them, 'without an adequate alternative being created. With this view the failure to transfer authority can be justified as a responsible, rational stance' (Bowler 1985: 7).

Parallel tensions had appeared over questions of international trade, in preparation for GATT negotiations in April. Once again, the alignment was mainly France with a wish to introduce reverse preferences in the EEC's relations with Mediterranean Basin states (strongly objected to by the USA) versus the FRG, UK and the Netherlands, whose opposition partly reflected sensitivity to US views and to the 'linkage' with security issues (Simonian 1985: 167).

Blame for the Community's problems had been laid at just about every possible door; usually, what was then prescribed for the patient bore some relation to the 'malady' identified. Here it is worth raising two questions. First, how far was there a general agreement about the most important causes of friction? Second, if there was, did that diagnosis allow of *any* effective remedy? It seems that there was indeed a common thread, certainly wherever the 'external agenda' was affected. It was an old theme, not a new one: 'Atlanticism'. And because that was the root of the problem, there was no effective remedy.

FRG Foreign Minister Scheel, in the article already cited, spoke of the American 'Gulliver' in contrast to the European 'Lilliputians' (Scheel 1974: 132). Although such modesty could be described as 'self-serving', coming from the leaders of the self-styled 'economic giant but political dwarf', it was revealing about the dimensions of *ambition* and *self-image*. And this was implicitly recognised by an article in the same journal from a French source: Maurice Delarue of *Le Monde* wrote that there was a feeling abroad, post-Copenhagen and post-Washington, that France was 'to blame': 'Mistrust is directed to a particular degree against France' (Delarue 1974: 134). Quite simply, different conceptions of 'Europe' were held; as Couve de Murville had made plain in a speech at the École Centrale on 23 January 1974, France regarded the notion of 'partnership' advanced by the United States and apparently acceded to by her EEC colleagues as a sham: for it did not translate as a partnership of equals. 'The "American obstacle" makes itself felt at every moment in the life of the Community' (Delarue 1974: 137).

This was a reversion to an old Gaullist theme, a raw nerve just waiting to be touched; a reflex shared by Couve de Murville, Pompidou, Jobert and many others in the French élite, which had chosen this untimely moment to resurface and do maximum damage, just prior to Pompidou's own departure from the scene and replacement by the more Atlanticist Giscard. Yet there is little doubt that, whatever the absurdities, excesses and apparent contradictions of Jobert's policy statements in particular, US policy under Nixon and Kissinger had mightily contributed to this perception of the 'American obstacle'. Although the warning shots had clearly been fired in 1971, it took the western Europeans some time to get used to the profundity of the change in the springs of US policy – partly geographic, partly generational, partly ideological – and to some extent born out of pique and frustration and awareness that the USA itself was not invincible and neither was the 'American century' likely to last half so long unchallenged. If all of this could find voice in one short phrase, it would be the US view: 'Just remember, you're *our* allies: we're not *your* allies' – echoing exactly French suspicions about 'partnership'.

The last quarter of 1973 had thus proved particularly punishing for those who saw the EC as a 'superpower in the making' (to use Galtung's phrase for a concept he deprecated) or as one 'pillar' of a multipolar system. Even the apparent successes did not seem to make much impact. There had been the 'common position of the Nine' – the statement of 13 October on the Middle East. It was not much trumpeted at the time; yet its formulae were essentially those of the Security Council Resolution 9 days later. One reason was that behind the apparent agreement lay much disagreement. France and the UK had been perceived as more sympathetic to the Arabs; Denmark, FRG and the Netherlands to Israel; and in any case, there was no expectation that the EC would do anything about its statement. It expressed the wish to be involved in later mediation and was effectively excluded.

The real action remained with the superpowers: when Sadat asked them to intervene to ensure implementation of the 22 October ceasefire (and save the Egyptian Third Army), the Soviet Union asked the USA to collaborate on the ground but said that, failing this, it reserved the right to do so itself. The US riposte was that this was for the UN minus the Security Council 'permanent Five'; and to put its forces on strategic alert to warn off the Soviet Union. Despite this, it appeared that détente survived well enough at the superpower level: it was the EC that was left on one side.

Brandt in late October had written to Nixon in tones of injured loyalty: the FRG was a good ally, but why had the USA rendered things so difficult both by disclosures about the loading of military supplies for Israel on ships in Bremerhaven and by the announcement without consultation of the strategic alert? On 6 November Schlesinger for the USA 'explained' the alert to the NATO nuclear planning group at The Hague; but it was a case of actions being followed swiftly by television and press interpretation while diplomatic explanations and justifications lagged far behind. Brandt indeed probably hit the nail on the head when he said, concerning the protests over the arms shipments, that in Washington 'It was even intimated to our representatives that the Federal Republic enjoyed only limited sovereignty in American eyes' (Simonian 1985: 199, quoting Brandt 1978). It was not the only European state of which Nixon and Kissinger, not to mention some of their successors, appear to have taken such a view. The view was combined with another: that the EC's main value was of the 'nuisance' kind.

Most crucially, the limits to the extent to which the events served to push the Europeans together could be swiftly discerned. To be sure, the 5 November oil sanctions announcement was followed by the 6 November statement of the Nine, not unfavourable to the Arabs (text: *Année Politique* 1973: 283–4; *Le Monde 7 November 1973*) and the 18 November OPEC meeting in Vienna duly softened the 5 November line. To be sure, also, Pompidou on 31 October had declared to the French *Conseil des Ministres* that it was crucial to have a summit before the end of the year because the Middle East crisis was developing without Europe. Yet none of this prevented major disagreement, at almost the same time, between French and Germans over defence issues, with the classic 'codes' re-emerging: France favoured WEU (it excluded the US); the FRG favoured organising western European security around the Eurogroup (which marginalised France and kept things under the NATO umbrella).

Thus 1973 had revealed several features of considerable importance for the overall shape of the European Community design. It had revealed that, now that the 'limits of the Treaty of Rome' had been reached, the problem of 'what to do next' appeared to have two unexpected correlates: first, such commitments as were produced, appeared to be essentially 'pseudo-commitments' – states would not actually pay *any* price at all to achieve them; second, the motives that led states to a state of *apparent* agreement were often in flat contradiction to each other and if this was not immediately clear at the time, it rapidly became so under the pressure of 'exogenous shocks'. A further feature was the demonstration of the 'wider but weaker' thesis: with enlargement, the interests to be accommodated had become more heterodox and the task of doing so harder. Third, it was acknowledged that 'everything was linked to everything else' – EMU to the CAP and MCAs, but also to regional and social policy and all to the budgetary conundrums. There was little agreement on what to do about this linked agenda and a dangerous policy of drift developed in which the Community was seen as the captive of the best organised and most powerful interests. Further, there was no shortage of scapegoats to be blamed for the mess, but this led to a cacophony at the level of diagnosis and prognosis; there was no agreement about *what* it was that required to be done or about how to go about it. In particular, French policy routinely appeared as diametrically opposed to that of the USA: the only exception, all too revealing from the point of view of 'linkage', was Pompidou's specific request to Nixon that US troops stay in western Europe.

The legacy of 1973 to the Community was not a happy one. In addition, there was a strong tendency to whistle in the economic dark: to fail to realise the importance of the impact of the 'oil crisis' on western Europe's economies and societies and their differential capacity to adjust and the import of the divergence which would result. After the relatively 'fat years' were to come 'the years the locusts ate'.

The verdict on the December 1973 Copenhagen Summit was also generally negative. Annette Morgan (1976: 17–20) described it as 'inconclusive on every single issue'. For many people, the whole period between the Yom Kippur War and about March–April 1974 was the most critical they could remember in the history of the EC to date. Summits had got themselves a bad name. *The Economist* wrote (22 December 1973) that their main effect had been to add a new notch to a system already characterised by indecision and buck passing. Yet, in what was called its 'only solid achievement' (Morgan 1976: 19) the summit decided henceforth to reconvene on a regular basis. The same author commented that, under Pompidou, one of the side-effects of the holding of summits was 'to downgrade' Community institutions by taking from them much power to initiate and to take decisions (Morgan 1976: 6). Whether this view of what many regarded as the most important 'institutional' innovation for some time was justified was, at the end of this traumatic year, still to be tested.

## Further reading

A. Grosser, *The Western Alliance: European–American Relations since 1945*. London: Macmillan, 1980.

H. Kissinger, *The White House Years*. London: Weidenfeld & Nicolson, 1979.

H. Kissinger, *Years of Upheaval*. London: Weidenfeld & Nicolson, 1982.

J. Monnet, *Memoirs*. London: Collins, 1978.

A. Morgan, *From Summits to Council: Evolution in the EEC*. London: Chatham House and PEP, 1976.

A. Shonfield, *Europe: Journey to an Unknown Destination*. London: Allen Lane, 1973.

# 5    The mid-1970s

## Locust years

By general consent, the mid-1970s were 'locust years' for the European Community. At least at the 'macro' level, very little was seen to change and, when things did, it seemed that they did so in an unplanned way and not always for the better. This chapter examines how far this characterisation is accurate; and, to the extent that it is, to what factors it is due.

One interesting phenomenon may be noted at the outset. The 'integration theory' industry, among academic commentators in particular, appeared to grind to a halt at this time. There were notable contributions by Pentland and by Harrison, whose books, in some ways similar in approach, appeared in 1973 and 1974, respectively: after that, the line almost seemed to go dead, as if at least it was recognised that what was happening on the ground, whether it could be dignified with the name of 'integration' or not, did not correspond to the ideas developed up to then. At this very time, another earlier 'father of integration theory', Ernst Haas, produced his work, *The Obsolescence of Regional Integration Theory* (Haas 1975), putting forward the view that none of the earlier theories adequately accounted for what was taking place and instead characterising what the EC was about as 'fragmented issue-linkage': the EC's activity was essentially not about ways of achieving regional *political* integration, but rather about ways of handling 'turbulence' in sectors of the world economy. This view seems broadly correct, at least as far as the mid-1970s are concerned. The Community's preoccupations, and its 'sclerosis', were in no small part the product of forces beyond its control.

In terms of the various 'battles' that we identified at the beginning – over the Community's own institutional arrangements, its internal policy scope, its external projection and its geographical extent – we may note how important all these, too, were at this time. Enlargement had always threatened to create problems not just of adjustment but of digestibility. In the event, what made them far worse (the 1971 British White Paper, in attempting to set out an economic balance sheet, had already been studiously vague about the wide range of uncertainty involved in fore-casts of costs and benefits) was, first and foremost, the differential impact of the economic crisis. Second, the collapse of the Hague 'grand design' in the chaos of monetary turmoil, the 'Year of Europe' fiasco and the 'first oil shock' was not swiftly acknowledged and even less swiftly replaced with any alternative notion or strategy of how to proceed. We explore the reasons for this later. Third, intertwined with the second but worth separate mention, there was growing evidence that the institutional structure was creaking and slowing. The Vedel Report had already pointed this out, but had not pointed to solutions acceptable at the time. Fourth, attention was diverted and a great deal of it absorbed by such issues as the British 'renegotiation' and its budget contribution.

Early 1974 also witnessed a spate of governmental changes and accompanying uncertainties. First was the British 'cliffhanger' election of 28 February, precipitated by the miners' strike, the 3-day week and the 'who governs?' appeal of Heath, an election that produced a hung parliament, a brief period of uncertainty and then a minority Labour government committed to 'renegotiation' of the terms of entry. Next came the death of Pompidou on 2 April; following a closely fought presidential but not legislative election, Giscard was confirmed as his successor in May. On 6 May, Brandt resigned as German chancellor over the Gunter Guillaume 'spy' scandal: Schmidt swiftly and without great controversy succeeded him. Italy was not immune, even though in March it had been a case of Rumor being succeeded by Rumor. This represented the most concentrated set of government changes in the major states since those of 1969 and in many ways should be compared to them. All these changes, it may be recalled, came after the catalogue of woe that Carlo Mugnozza had addressed to the EP in February, and on top of the widely shared sense that USA–western European relations had reached a nadir.

The final touch to that impression was given by yet another round of altercation between Kissinger and Jobert in the weeks immediately preceding Pompidou's death. Kissinger let his dissatisfaction with the 4 March draft declaration of the Nine be known 'unattributably' to journalists on the plane home (*Année Politique* 1974: 209). On 5 March State Department spokesman Vest publicly raised the question '*whether* the EC speaks and acts' in a reasonable manner, as was to be expected among friends. On 7 March Kissinger renewed the claim to moral leadership of the USA. The next day, on Europe-1, Jobert maintained that there was no contradiction between French claims to independence but also support for the continued presence of US troops in western Europe, since 'maintaining US troops is not fundamental for us, but it is for the US'. The same day it became known that Nixon had written to Brandt (as president-in-office of the Council) virtually demanding that henceforth there be routinised consultations with the USA *before* the EC announced any future *démarches* over matters of 'common concern', such as the 'Euro-Arab dialogue'. As usual, the question of who was to decide what such matters were arose immediately. (This was, however, probably the origin of what became known as the 'Gymnich-type' procedures to regularise consultation with the USA.)

To cap it all came Kissinger's famous little speech to congressional wives on 11 March. The gist of his remarks was conveniently historical: his claim was that after World War I (until when was conveniently not made clear) the governments of all European states had lacked full public confidence and legitimacy. This time he did not pretend, as on 5 March, to anonymity himself: rather, to ring the implausible changes, he claimed not to know that the press were there, as he explained to hardened reporters at a State Department press conference a few days later. At all events he did not lack support from his increasingly embattled chief. The day after this, 15

March, Nixon averred that the USA would not have the Nine 'ganging up' on it: they could not have that cooperation from the USA so indispensable to their security if they refused to cooperate in political and economic domains (*Année Politique* 1974: *passim*; Kohler in Allen et al. 1982: 87).

The time had clearly come to lower the temperature. Couve de Murville proffered some thinly coded advice to do so to Jobert at the UDR's (Union pour la Défense de la République) *journées parlementaires* on 18 March; Nixon next day described Jobert's half-amends as 'very appropriate'(!) but sought also to lower the polemic a little. A formula enabling the USA to be brought into EPC discussions was worked out at a meeting of the nine foreign ministers the following month, after an exchange of letters between Brandt as Council president and Nixon. The meeting place, Schloss Gymnich, accordingly gave its name to the agreement, whose essence was that, if all nine agreed, consultations with the USA would be initiated by the EC presidency; if some did not, they could be bilateral. It was, to say the least, a highly convenient moment in the political history of the EC to slip this through: the hiatus in French leadership meant that no one there had to take the 'blame' for capitulation; it was also to prove virtually Brandt's last act, although it does not appear so far to have been suggested that anyone told him that he had better behave himself before the Guillaume story blew (Edwards and Wallace 1976: 38; Feld 1976: 45; Allen et al. 1982: 88).

It is possible to break off from the USA–EC saga there and to turn to other matters, largely because, from that point forward, the US administration found itself too much embroiled in the climax of Watergate (during the summer of 1974) to indulge in any more high-profile rows with the Community even as a 'lightning conductor' ploy – a role in which it had earlier been fairly successful.

Let us begin an appraisal of Community activity in the mid-1970s at the most general level: what kinds of matter presented themselves for attention – either because inherited from the Copenhagen Summit or by forcing themselves onto the agenda? First and foremost, at the 'macro' level, there were the twin issues of monetary turmoil and the 'oil shock' and the deepening economic crisis resulting from these.

The first had, as we have seen, effectively put the EMU scheme into cold storage, although the Community continued to go through the motions of affirming this as a commitment. The pass was sold, however, by a delicate but telling change of terminology – what was to have been 'the' second stage of EMU, from the start of 1974, was rechristened 'a' second stage and soon thereafter the obsequies were pronounced.

Taken together with the oil shock, however, it demonstrated swiftly what was to become a central theme – and a central constraint on the Community during the mid-1970s: the differential capacities of the economies and societies of the EC to adapt and adjust.

It was in particular the *ways* in which they sought to adapt that were most revealing. Above all, they did not seek to do so by joint Community-based action. Instead, beginning with the rush by France and the UK to conclude individual, bilateral deals with Middle East oil producers, they went their separate ways. This applied not just to aspects of external policy, but also to internal economic policy, an area never famous for harmony of views. This was a period that saw, both in the world at large and in the Community, a resurgence of the telltale non-tariff barriers (NTBs) to trade. In the Community, the temptation was particularly great to use them to try to counteract the effects of removal of tariff barriers. It is not easy to quantify this, for NTBs are by their nature various, devious, numerous and unsung: but even a 1969 GATT survey had identified more than 800 (Twitchett 1981: 18).

What was to be the Community's response to this? The answer depended very much on the activity and the miscreant. Outsiders were generally punished; member states were often allowed to do things with questions being asked only afterwards. Insider governments tended to get away with a good deal: any kind of strategy on the Community's part was slow to evolve and usually depended very much on some other member state being able to demonstrate clear harm. Where it could, and where appropriate, it received powerful support from the Court of Justice which, perhaps in this period even more than in others, fulfilled the role of 'political cement' for the Community system.

It was not, however, to be the only 'political cement'. Recognition of the need for a new kind of 'steering' had come slowly, but it came to fruition at the Paris Summit of 9–10 December 1974. As we saw at the end of Chapter 4, it came in the form of an expression of willingness to *institutionalise* and *routinise* the input from the heads of state or government, in the form of what was to be known thereafter as the European Council. As the communiqué of the December 1974 summit put it:

> 2. Recognizing the need for an *overall* approach to the *internal* problems involved in achieving European unity and the *external* problems facing Europe, the Heads of Government consider it essential to ensure progress and overall *consistency* in the activities of the Communities and in the work of Political Co-operation.
>
> 3. [They] have decided to meet, accompanied by the Ministers of Foreign Affairs, three times a year and, whenever necessary, in the Council of the Communities and in the context of Political Co-operation.
>
> The administrative secretariat will be provided for *in an appropriate manner* with due regard for existing practices and procedures. ...
>
> These arrangements do not in any way affect the rules and procedures laid down in the Treaties or the provisions on political co-operation in the Luxembourg and Copenhagen texts.

This development, the formal birth of the European Councils of Heads of State or Government, to give its full but unwieldy title, proved a good deal more reliable as a guide to *immediate* practice than a subsequent paragraph of the same communiqué which read:

> 14. The Heads of State or Government, having noted that internal and international difficulties have *prevented* in 1973 and 1974 the accomplishment of

expected progress on the road to EMU, affirm that in this field their will has not been weakened and that their objective has not changed.

(*Bull. EC* 12–1974: 7–9, emphasis added)

Of the persistence of the crisis there can be no doubt. Council and Commission routinely recognised it: they may to some extent have made of it a favourite excuse. For example, of 1974, the Council said (22 *RCW*: 1): 'During 1974, the Council has had to face a number of major problems'; and the Commission (8 *GRA*: xxxvi): 'Three major problems on a scale unseen since the Common Market was established are behind the difficulties which threaten the Community today' (listing inflation, unemployment and balance of payments), 'the combination ... makes such (economic policy) convergence more difficult'. It added that it had begun policy research on measures required to (ominously) '*adapt*' EMU to the '*new economic and political circumstances*' that had emerged, adding that it should be possible to produce a report on the establishment of EMU during the summer of 1975: the *Marjolin Report*. Perhaps most tellingly of all, the Commission stated: 'Inflation, the energy crisis and the monetary crisis have left us *without a programme and without a doctrine*.' We shall see both how true this was and the consequences it was to have later.

In its review of 1975 the Council said: 'The *considerable* economic recession ... does not yet seem to have become a thing of the past', adding that this 'places many obstacles in the path of European integration' (23 *RCW*: 1). And Ortoli in his swansong as Commission president asserted: 'The [economic policy] gaps between us are wider now than they were when the crisis began' (9 *GRA*: vii); he lamented the 'absence of any decisive progress towards EMU. Circumstances are largely to blame, but there has been a certain lack of conviction too', yet went on to add, in a formulation that indicated the concept's hold: 'Yet it must be made clear that [EMU] is not only essential to European integration: it is also, quite simply, the only remedy for the ills that beset us individually' (9 *GRA*: ix). The Commission president added (9 *GRA*: xxix) that, for 1975 as a whole, industrial production had contracted by about 8%; inflation averaged about 13%, ranging from 6% in the FRG to 21% in the UK. Nevertheless, it was clear that only very modest measures on EMU and related proposals were the order of the day.

The year 1976 was no better. The Council said:

Among the major problems ... during *1976 first place* must go to the serious economic crisis which has persisted ... The situation was one of persistent divergencies [*sic*] and imbalances, and there appeared to be a greater need than ever for a new drive to strengthen the Community's internal economic and monetary cohesion.

(24 *RCW*: 1)

And the incoming Commission President Jenkins said:

It has been an uphill task, and the tug of centrifugal forces seemed at times to increase in proportion to the distance from the goal ... there is no overlooking the fact that Member States' economies are *still diverging* and that none of the efforts to master this crucial problem, *on whose solution hangs all further progress by the Community* has borne fruit in 1976.

(10 *GRA*: 15, emphasis added)

This was of course the year when a UK chancellor had virtually dictated a letter to the IMF telling it what to tell him to do in order to benefit from its help. Jenkins added that there was little progress in coordinating economic policies, and that the crisis situation had entailed a variety of emergency measures at Community level, including frequent adjustments of the MCAs (10 *GRA*: 17–18).

To complete the tale of woe, here is the Commission again on 1977. Of the multifibre arrangement (MFA) it wrote:

> The main purpose of these agreements is to apply a brake on imports so as to give the Community textile industry a breathing-space ... The Community iron and steel industry is likewise in a state of crisis ... European industry in general is going through a process of reorientation ... Measures to restructure ... industries are part of the response to the *continuing* crisis in Europe.

(25 *RCW*: 2–3)

Two indicators of the response, of where Community effort and obsession lay, may be found, first, in the proportion of the budget that continued to be absorbed by agriculture in particular during these years when many other and novel claims were being formulated; second, in the numbers of meetings of the Council devoted to the various major headings during the period (see later).

First, the CAP pre-emption of resources went on unabated. To be sure, inflation and greater than normal uncertainties over prevailing *world* price levels dramatically increased the uncertainties to which the EC 'budget' is always subject, and made any projections subject to frequent change. But during the period, the CAP as a proportion of the total (appropriations for payments basis) tended to rise, as we have seen; and (upward) adjustments in the course of a year became common. For instance, 'The agricultural prices fixed at the ... meeting of 21–3 March were increased by 5% in October in view of the rapid developments in the economic situation and the effects on income' (22 *RCW*: 2). MCAs became built in, and began to have perverse effects; for example, they encouraged storage to be concentrated in high-cost countries; they also distorted production patterns, and, by allowing governments to choose whether and to what extent to realign their 'green' rates, partially 'renationalised' agricultural policy.

The number of Council meetings is also a useful indicator of attention, albeit, of course, not necessarily of 'progress'. Throughout the period, they continued to be dominated by the areas of agriculture, external relations and economics and finance. By contrast, such a crucial area as energy had one Council session in 1974 and none in 1975 (although it did 'better' in the two following years) (see Table 5.1).

The Commission, 'without a programme and without a doctrine' as Ortoli had put it, nevertheless appeared to have a lot to propose. Ortoli announced five objectives in February 1975: a fairly motley bunch.

*Table 5.1* Council meetings

| Topic | Year | | | |
|-------|------|------|------|------|
| | *1974* | *1975* | *1976* | *1977* |
| Agriculture | 14 | 15 | 13 | 12 |
| Budget | – | 2 | 2 | 3 |
| Development coop. | 5 | 3 | 2 | 3 |
| Economics and finance | 7 | 8 | 7 | 12 |
| Energy | 1 | – | 3 | 4 |
| Environment | 1 | 2 | 1 | 2 |
| External relations | 13 | 16 | 14 | 15 |
| Fiscal | – | 1 | 2 | 1 |
| Fisheries | – | – | – | 5 |
| Research | – | 2 | 3 | 2 |
| Social | 2 | 2 | 2 | 2 |
| Transport | 2 | 2 | 2 | 3 |
| **Totals** | **57** | **53** | **61** | **n/a** |

*Source*: *RCW*, 1974–7

*Note*: Totals include other small categories not individually listed.

First came the notion of making Europe 'less dependent', the keys to this being the monetary and energy fronts. The year that 'must be the year of the common energy policy' saw no Council meetings devoted to it, despite the beginnings of the somewhat abortive 'Euro-Arab dialogue' in 1974: the first meeting in Paris on 31 July, followed by the Cairo meeting of 20 October. Ortoli uttered an affirmation which he promptly changed to something that sounded mid-way between a hope and a threat: 'Nor does this programme [of producer-consumer cooperation agreements] conflict with the regular consultations … within the IEA [International Energy Agency]. Or perhaps I should say that *we intend to make it our business* to ensure that it does not conflict' (8 *GRA*: xxff., emphasis added). Instead the intention would be to make full use of the EC's pooled sovereignty, so as to minimise its 'inherent inferiority'.

There had been some success in EPC, to be sure, in 1974, as over the response to the Turkish invasion of Cyprus; but in general it would be hard to claim that much was achieved in the direction of 'reduced dependence': indeed, on the monetary front, the dollar's position as dominant currency was widely thought to have cost the EC some $20bn in 'subsidisation' or 'seigniorial rights' in the period 1958–71 (Commission 1973: 62–3; Kirschen 1974: 355–78).

Much the same quandary applied to the second of Ortoli's 'objectives': the aim of 're-establishing economic and social equilibrium' by trying to use the Community to produce 'complementary' (NB not 'identical') economic policies in the member states. This was rendered difficult by, among other things, the growth of the eurodollar market (estimated at $50bn by 1971) which 'has the peculiarity of not being under the control of any public authority' and, via its inflation transmission effects, created obstacles to policies of short-term economic control (Commission 1973: 62; see also Johnson 1970; Bell 1973: *passim*). We have already seen that this was *par excellence* a period of divergence both of economic *policies* and of *performance* and that the disequilibria were enduring – far into the 1980s, some would argue. At all events, the concern with 'policy compatibility' – if not complementarity – was to prove enduring too: some of its main milestones, which will be examined in more depth later, being the Marjolin Report (1975), the Tindemans Report (end of 1975) and the MacDougall Report (1977).

Third came 'establishing a new relationship with the third world': this 'objective', which at first sight rides a little oddly with the others, was very conveniently included, because it was possible to present what could plausibly be regarded as concrete achievement in regard to it. Early 1975 did, after all, see the conclusion of the Lomé-I agreement with the African, Caribbean and Pacific (ACP) states.

Fourth was 'resuming the progress towards EMU': we have already commented on this, although the formula 'towards' may be noted. It was significant that the Marjolin Report, which was ostensibly about this, in fact finished up discussing very different matters including, significantly, the 'parallel (and redistributive) policies' which would be needed to accompany any such moves.

Fifth and last was 'preparing the way for European Union'; once again, no definition was offered and the Tindemans Report was to explore and modify the concept. It was clear, at least, that little direct harm could be done by announcing it as an objective, since few could object to something that had no clear meaning. Arguably, however, there was an associated loss of credibility and diversion of energy.

Thus, the 'objectives' listed by Ortoli, despite describing the Community as lacking a programme and a road, were an odd bunch. They included one that 'the house' regarded as already just achieved (number 3 – Lomé), and others where many years were to pass before much progress could be reported. We now turn to see what some of the major reports of the mid-1970s had to say about these issues and what reception their diagnoses received.

## The reports

The Paris Summit of 9–10 December 1974 had stated that the heads of the Nine considered that 'the time has come … to agree as soon as possible on an overall conception of European Union' (*Communiqué*, para. 13). The views of the institutions were sought, and Leo Tindemans, Belgian prime minister, was to produce a 'comprehensive report' before the end of 1975.

It was not the only report: the Netherlands Second Chamber produced the first Spierenburg Report at about the same time. Earlier in 1975 came the Marjolin Report: the report of the study group on economic and monetary union 1980, whose contents so much belied its grandiloquent but unrealistic title. Then there was to be the Optica Report – *Towards Economic Equilibrium and Monetary Unification in Europe*, in January 1976; the Maldague Report (which appeared to have been suppressed on suspicion of heresy, although it was reprinted in *Agenor* in December 1976); and finally the MacDougall Report on the role of public finance in European integration (11/10/77 E Final, Brussels, April 1977). The MacDougall Report looked at the fiscal situation in political federations: it was of great importance for specifying and estimating how much would have to be done *if* the EC were to move from what it described as its 'pre-federal' state to that of a 'slim' federation. It was swiftly apparent that the member states were quite unwilling to pay that fiscal price: an approximate trebling of the share (from under 1% to about 2.5%) of GDP going into Community coffers. The crucial implication of this was that the EC would not – could not – then 'be about' the sort of things, the 'social democratic', interventionist ambitions *at the Community level*, being proposed in some of the other reports.

The various reports were addressing two sets of issues. One set concerned the policy issues facing and functional scope of, the EC. The second concerned the institutions: how they had developed and were developing; whether changes in their powers and *modus operandi* were required and, if so, which. Some saw the two as inextricably linked, in the sense that the one could not be resolved without dealing with the other; but others denied this.

It was no surprise that these conundrums should surface during the mid-1970s. But the Community's energy and attention were further taken up with the whole issue of 'British renegotiation' – presented as whether the UK Labour government could achieve terms adequate to recommend continued membership to the electorate in a referendum. The papering over of very large differences had been apparent in the wording of the section of the December 1974 Paris communiqué entitled 'Britain's Membership of the Community' (paras 34–7) (Ferri 1982: 281). This recalled that UK Prime Minister Wilson had 'indicated the basis on which HMG approached the negotiations regarding Britain's continued membership of the Community', chief among which was the size of the UK's budgetary contributions. The heads of government invited Council and Commission 'to set up as soon as possible a correcting mechanism of a general application', which 'could prevent *during the period of convergence of the economies of the Member States*' the development of a situation unacceptable to a member state. But the world they faced was one not of 'convergence', but of *divergence*. In the face of divergent economic performance, itself largely the fruit of monetary chaos and the first oil shock, but compounded by dissonance about the costs and benefits of membership, the Marjolin Report set out, under the heading 'Conditions for an Economic and Monetary Union', a formidable agenda requiring both a degree of consensus and transfers of powers which, it promptly acknowledged, 'cannot be established within a period of five years'. Indeed, 'it appeared to the group impossible and even useless to predict what should be the division of powers necessary for the satisfactory operation of an economic and monetary union' (Ferri 1982: 285–6).

In hindsight, the Marjolin Report's concentration (under the rubric 'the first steps') on problems of industrial structure, unemployment rates and segregation of capital markets following the 'energy crisis', seems entirely appropriate. In other respects, too, the report was ahead of its time. It concentrated on the 'four freedoms', and, in its discussion of the functions that might be fulfilled by an enlarged (but envisageable) Community budget, set the scene for the MacDougall Report of 1977. Its final fling was an augury of things to come – stubbornly high unemployment – although what it proposed: 'A Community unemployment benefit fund', with 'a Community allowance ... clearly visible as such' to recipients – met the refusal of member states to make such fiscal transfers to Community level.

The 'aim' of economic and monetary union by 1980 was clearly recognised as a pseudo-commitment. Instead, the pressing and immediate problems which threatened to pull the Community apart were, it was hoped, to be mitigated by a degree of Community action. Most, even of this modest hope, was to prove misplaced. Early 1975 produced the 'conciliation procedure' to try to deal with wrangles between the institutions over financial matters, but little else (4 March). Other achievements were the conclusion of the first Lomé Convention with, initially, 46 ACP states (28 February) and the declaration, at the March Dublin Summit, that the British renegotiations were 'completed'. (This last process was 'legitimised' by the June 1975 – first ever – UK referendum on continued membership, in which 67.2% of the turnout voted in favour of continued membership. The Second Budget Treaty followed (10 July).)

The Marjolin Report, then, was mainly technical and its concrete proposals modest, albeit unfulfilled. The Optica Report (signifying optimum currency area, OCA) is also revealing in regard to the intellectual fashions and fluxes of the time. The debate about OCAs was very fashionable in the mid- to late 1970s: agreement about what size of area might constitute an OCA was non-existent. Some argued seriously for areas such as Scotland; others for the whole EC. No consensus was forthcoming. In brief, at the supposedly 'technocratic' level, there was no agreement about *what* was to be done in programmatic terms.

### The Tindemans Report

There was little more accord on the institutional front. Leo Tindemans' report followed input from each institution and consultation in the various member states. On the subject of European union, again, the inevitable bifurcation arose between, on the one hand, a 'union' conceived institutionally and, on the other, a 'union' conceived as a certain *process* whereby sharing and/or transfer of functions took place.

Some of the inputs from particular institutions are of considerable interest, as they anticipated or announced debates that were to absorb much attention later. In some ways these contributions are of more interest than the report itself: we shall examine them first, before looking at the final report.

The Commission paper stressed the 'principle of legal unity', as opposed to notions of 'variable geometry' or 'multi-speed' Europe (paras 7–8), and the principle of 'subsidiarity' (para. 12), to be much debated later, whereby the Union should become responsible only for 'matters which the member states are no longer capable of dealing with efficiently'. These competences, it stressed, could be exclusive, concurrent or potential. The Commission admitted that 'the results of these attempts to give economic integration more substance have ... been meagre' (para. 29); and, revealingly of the spirit of the time: 'Both internal and external economic developments mean that the public authorities are *having to intervene more* not only in matters of a general nature but also in specific fields' (emphasis added). It pointed to the risk of mutual damage and the 'exporting' of difficulties liable to arise (para. 30);

this was to become a major theme by the beginning of the 1980s, but its hour, in terms of action, had not yet arrived. Not surprisingly, the Commission paper argued that such 'open economies' needed 'solidarity and joint action' to defend their interests; but this was far from the general tendency of government action at the time.

The 'main Community objective: economic and monetary union', entailed giving the Union competence, powers and means of action in five fields (para. 31): monetary policy, budget expenditure, budget revenue, improvement of economic structures and, finally, social affairs. The discussion of *how* this was to be accomplished (para. 33 especially) was significant: an outline treaty (*traité-cadre*) was preferred to the notion of a law or rules treaty (*traité-loi*). Experience with ECSC in particular, the Commission argued, showed this to be the best way. A delicate balance had to be struck between giving the 'Union' powers of direct intervention that it might need and getting it bogged down in regulating or harmonising matters of detail. This was fine in principle: in practice it was not achieved in the mid- to late 1970s.

The Commission thus argued for the union to have 'centralised decision-making power in the monetary field' (para. 36); 'its own central bank ... [with] a fairly high degree of independence' – a delicate compromise between French and German preferences in these matters (para. 37). The method pursued since 1971 'has not enabled us to make the progress hoped for', admitted para. 39.

The section on the budget looked forward to the MacDougall Report of 1977. The budget should be used to promote economic convergence, but its size and therefore role would for long be far smaller than that of national and local authorities. Yet, anticipating famous later battles, 'the increase in ... the Union's budget ought not in itself to speed up the rate at which public expenditure as a whole is growing' (para. 46). It was a pious hope.

On foreign policy, the Commission asserted that 'recent developments' (the oil shock, etc.) had demonstrated the powerlessness of individual states, and that its inclusion within the competence of European union was justified. Paragraph 63 recited the mixture of formulae in use in the external relations field: existing treaty-related matters being governed by Community procedures and competences; the 'general political aspects of international relations' dealt with via the political cooperation system, established between the nine member states as such; while specifically defence matters were dealt with through WEU and NATO. As the Commission gruffly put it, 'Hitherto, political co-operation has seldom led to anything more than the Community reacting to events' (para. 65). It stressed, too, that the 'narrow' interpretation of the Community's competences meant that 'Community policy proper is confined within bounds which do not permit coherent action'. Such matters as 'co-operation agreements, international investment, credit policy', for instance, were 'contested in certain quarters' (para. 67).

The Commission also put forth a bold claim for bureaucratic tidiness which had the merit of substantially increasing its own powers: 'The Union's field of competence outside ... must cover the same areas and be of the same nature as those it exercises internally.' This was of the greatest importance: it explicitly linked our second and third 'issue clusters' of internal policy scope and external projection. This view had earlier attained the support of the Court, which in the *ERTA* Case (Commission v. Council, Case 22/70) had clearly approved the doctrine of 'parallelism' between the *exercise* of internal legislative power and the transfer in regard to such matters of treaty-making power from states to Community (Hartley 1988: 159–60).

This was already seen as a key area and, of course, remains so. The linkage to defence was also seen by the Commission as inescapable. Its paper added that the gradual development of a foreign policy for the Union would 'have an impact on external relations over and above the aspects already mentioned – particularly in due course in the field of defence' (para. 74). The Commission delicately introduced the issues posed by both NATO and WEU, before adding:

> The working out of common positions in the field of defence will have to be based on a common understanding of international problems and on the achievement of a common foreign policy in certain important areas. [For] a European defence policy to be considered and accepted by the peoples of the Union, the European institution will have to be *recognised as authoritative* and *representative of a sufficiently high degree of solidarity between those peoples.*
> (para. 76, emphasis added)

Those members that had signed the Non-Proliferation Treaty (NPT) had interpreted it to mean 'that their obligations under this Treaty shall not prejudice the rights of a future European Union'. Similarly, the Commission paper spoke of the need for a systematic comparison of the strategic planning by member states, and for a 'common policy on arms and equipment, possibly involving the setting up of a "European Arms Agency"' (paras 80–1). This last was to be taken up less than 2 years later in the European Parliament, when its political committee appointed Egon Klepsch to report on European arms procurement (Klepsch Report 1979). What is striking about all this is how determinedly far reaching and ambitious it all was, at such an early date.

Similarly ambitious was the section on protection of human rights. The Commission was at pains to point out that, despite general agreement on civil and political rights, 'this is not entirely the case with the rights of "groups of individuals" (for example, the status of foreigners) and with "economic and social" rights' (para. 83). Neither could a general lead be supplied from international law. The Commission argued that 'the best assurances' would be provided by incorporating a list of specified rights; but it noted too that the Court took a more 'limited' view, 'to include a general obligation' only (para. 83).

The third section of the Commission's paper struggled with the vexed question of institutional structure. In brief, it argued for 'a *single* institutional structure covering all the fields of competence vested in the union', as opposed to 'partially or totally separate bodies with competence in the various areas'. This anticipated the 'pre-Maastricht' battle over the 'tree' (single trunk) versus 'temple' (separate pillars) structure 15 years later. In para. 88, it listed the many functions that any institutional system would have to fulfil, adding (para. 89) that this showed the need for the system to 'include the fundamental functions of a *state-like political organ-isation*, i.e. a legislative function, a governmental function, a judicial function, pro-cedures for revision of the constitution' (emphasis added).

Again, this discussion was important because it threw long shadows before it: partial resolution of, or compromise on, some of these matters was a feature, for instance, of the Single European Act of 1987 and of the Treaty on European Union (TEU) which finally entered into force in November 1993. Among the key prob-lems which the Commission identified but did not purport to resolve was that of the criteria for delineating the separation of powers between institutions. Rightly, the Commission paper described as 'one of their most difficult tasks' that of the states in 'laying down detailed criteria for the separation of powers' (para. 89). In a European Union, added the paper, these would differ from the problems faced in the customs union phase of the EEC. 'The main task during this period ... has been described as "passive integration"': in the European union phase, however, 'the main aim will be to implement common policies and action – a process of "active integration"' (para. 90) – thus reviving something akin to Pinder's positive/nega-tive integration distinction of 1968. A classic instance of the difficulty of agreeing just such matters was the mainly Anglo-German clash over the European regional development fund (ERDF), which occurred at this time: the fund became enmeshed in the whole British 'renegotiation' process and was both smaller than the British had pressed for and delayed in coming into operation.

These considerations – about 'passive' versus 'active' integration – led on to consideration of the respective role of the institutions, and in particular of Council and Commission, in a 'European Union'. Once again, this is an argument that has, at no time since, either been resolved or gone away and is central to the differing conceptions held of the nature of the EU. It is for this reason, esoteric and a little rar-efied as these debates may have appeared at the time, that some further account of them is worthwhile.

The Commission's view of these questions was predictably guarded. It noted that the basis of the EEC Treaty arrangement was 'the combination of the Commission's right of initiative and the Council's decision-making power'. The Commission also had 'certain executive tasks ... The Council, with a certain ambi-guity, has both legislative and governmental responsibilities ... In the Community system, then, there is *no separation between legislative and governmental func-tions*' (paras 90–1, emphasis added).

Although European union could not dispose of the 'need for dialogue between the institutions responsible for the common interest and institutions representing national interests', the institutions 'must be given a maximum of democratic legit-imacy – with greater powers being vested in a directly elected European Parliament, for instance'. The 'for instance' was important. The EP was not pre-sented as the sole source of democratic legitimacy, but its role vis-à-vis the Council remained unclear. The Commission went on:

> [T]he legislative and governmental functions of the European Union will have
> to be defined in a more rational manner; this would be in line with the more

political character of the Union and increase the effectiveness of the institutions. One reason for the lack of effectiveness of the present institutions is the ambiguity surrounding the role of the Council.

(para. 92)

The Commission also thought that 'evolution by stages' was not feasible in institutional matters: '[I]t will have to have a certain stability and not be subject to frequent change' (para. 94). The institutional debate had revolved around two major problems: direct elections to the EP and the organisation of the executive function. 'European Union means nothing if it does not involve the development of a European governmental executive' (para. 95).

Three formulae for handling the executive–legislative relationship were then proposed and examined (paras 98–109). Each presented difficulties. In the first, a 'European government' would consist of 'European affairs' ministers from the national governments: it would develop out of the existing Council. The constitutional status of each member of such a 'government' would derive from membership of national government. Legislative power would be exercised by a parliament – probably bicameral: a 'chamber of peoples' and a 'chamber of states'. There would be no problem about the relationship of executive to legislature, since each institution would have a totally 'independent constitutional basis' (para. 100).

In a second model, the 'government' would be a collegial body *independent* of national governments. This raised immediately the question of how it was to emerge; of its 'legitimacy, authority and homogeneity' (para. 103). Such a body would effectively 'absorb' the functions of the Commission, which would cease to exist. This 'government' might be appointed by the chamber of peoples, by the chamber of states or by the two acting jointly.

The third model would resemble the second, but in addition there would be a 'Committee of Ministers' composed of national government members, which would retain a role in 'certain decisions of the European government' (para. 105).

The first model, said the Commission, 'would not herald any real improvement on the current situation. The government ... would in substance be an intergovernmental body'; it would thus be 'more suited to a Union which is based primarily on co-operation and the approximation of national policies than to a Union ... based primarily on the pursuit of common policies and the exercise of its own powers' (para. 110). The contrast between a 'union of states' model and a federation could hardly have been more sharply put (see Brewin 1987). By contrast, the second and third models seemed to tune better with the ambitions expressed by the various institutions. The choice between them was 'essentially political', the third being more suited to a 'transitional' period, the second to a 'fully-fledged Union' (paras 110–11).

The Commission went on to analyse 'a number of specific problems raised' by the institutional structure. They cannot all be mentioned here; however, a little needs to be said. The issues included whether the power to initiate legislation should lie with the governmental body alone or be possessed also by other bodies and, if so, under what circumstances. There was the question of how to organise cooperation between member states in the Union. There was the role of the European Council, which had increased 'because of the weakness of the present structures and the need for political agreement at the highest level on ambitious objectives which in many cases go beyond the terms of the Treaties' (para. 122). While the role of the European Council might be crucial during the advance towards a European Union: 'Once new institutions have been set up meetings of Heads of Government should be limited to dealing with the most difficult political problems.'

The Commission next looked at the crucial judicial system of the Community. It began by agreeing with the Court's view that there must continue to be 'binding rules which apply uniformly', and that this was best assured by a 'single supreme court'. Its description of the workings of the system, its balance of advantages and disadvantages, was one widely shared. The main *advantages* of the system of 'judicial co-operation' between the CJEC and national courts or tribunals, leaving most matters of *application* of Community law to the latter, were twofold: it avoided creating a 'vast Community judiciary' and it promoted 'fruitful collaboration between the Court and national courts' (para. 125). Its main weakness was the well-known danger of 'imbalance in the extent to which national courts use the machinery of referring ... to the Court ... for preliminary rulings'; again, it suggested two possible remedies. The Commission then floated a kite of its own: a 'Union' judicial system might administer at least part of the law deriving from union institutions. And the Union constitution could 'provide that the legislature of the Union settles this question itself when legislation is being drafted' (para. 126). As the Commission noted, the Court had not itself made this sweeping proposal.

The Commission also proposed increases in the Court's powers concerning legality and constitutionality. The Court's powers to declare *Community* acts invalid were wider than its powers with respect to the member states (Articles 169–71 and 177 EEC). Both Court and Commission pinpointed this issue, while proposing rather different formulae. The Commission was further concerned to widen the grounds on which private persons had access to the Court.

What was at stake here was (and is) far reaching. It has often been the case, in the history of the Community, that the Commission has relied on support from Court, EP or both in extending 'Community' competence, where that, in turn, entailed an increase in its own powers. These alliances reflected a classic bureaucratic battle for extension of power and function. *Each* institution sought this and often the battle went ahead with scant regard for the issue of the overall legitimacy and acceptability of the system that might be produced. This continues to be the case. This issue received *some* recognition, at least, in the Commission paper. It stated, 'public opinion, while still generally in favour of Europe as a unity, has gradually ceased to regard the Community as a political venture in its own right and has become increasingly sceptical' (para. 131). To mitigate this, it pressed for direct election to the EP (para. 133), and for an 'extension' of the 1975 cooperation procedure (para. 136). Pending such changes, the Commission recognised, it would fall to 'the "European Council"' (always in inverted commas in the paper!) to act as driving and guiding force on major matters.

But on 'reactivation of common policies', the paper was thin gruel indeed. It spoke of concentrating on *existing* common policies, adding an only barely perceptible genuflection about the importance of 'pressing ahead with the task of adapting' the CAP to changed circumstances (para. 138).

Monetary instability, 'uncoordinated industrial policies' and energy policy took first places in the Commission's list of economic and social policy measures: all (needless to say) were declared to require an enhancement of the 'Community dimension'. Similarly in external relations: 'The Community's powers should not be interpreted in a restricted way ... [It] must be permitted to express itself fully ... [It] must also be given new instruments with which to act' (para. 147).

How to proceed was the final issue. Here some prescience was shown. The Commission wanted 'all these changes and commitments ... enshrined in the Act of Constitution, in the form of a new Treaty' (para. 151). The initiative might come either from a 'conference of representatives of the Member States' (para. 153) or 'by institutions representing the Community and our countries' (para. 154) – drafted, for instance, 'on the basis of general guidelines laid down by the "European Council", by an elected European Parliament'. It was a canny prediction of what was to happen, albeit with a lot of pushing and pulling and watering down and delay, in the period 1982–7. Such, then, were the Commission's views: what of those of others?

The *European Parliament* produced two resolutions. That of 17 October 1974 was carefully relative: the process was one of 'constantly moving towards a closer union between the European peoples, while respecting their traditions' (Ferri 1982: 344). Already, however, 'security' figured on its list of 'Community powers'.

The later resolution (10 July 1975) added significantly that the institutional structure should include 'a single decision-making centre which will be in the nature of a real European government, independent of the national governments and responsible to the Parliament of the Union' (para. 3; Ferri 1982: 346). There must be development of policy areas and of institutional structure 'which must take place in parallel' (para. 6). It also urged that the Council abandon unanimity and, in its legislative capacity, meet in public (para. 11); that the Commission's role be extended to include main responsibility for all multilateral relations between member states; and of course it also urged extension of its own involvement in the legislative process. Finally, it said firmly that it 'expects' member states to act on the resolution.

The *Court's* observations were of a suitably judicial asperity. The import of the term 'union' was not clear, it said. Limiting itself to legal aspects, the Court declared that there must be no loosening of the existing structures. The Court stressed the need for *binding* rules, *uniform* rules and protection of the rights of the individual. In particular, it stated:

> [L]egal certainty entails the filling of a legal gap in the Treaty of Rome in that it does not in terms provide for any effective sanction against a state which fails to temper [*sic*] its obligations, to the detriment of states which do.
>
> (Ferri 1982: 350)

To improve this situation, the Court should be able, in its judgment against defaulting states, to *specify* the steps a state must take; next, the *execution* of the judgment must be subject to a systematic control, and finally, advantages sought by offending states should be conditional on their rectification of failures. The Court was equally firm on the second point, the importance of a *uniform* system.

Under the third heading, individual rights, the Court stressed that *if* a European union were to include an elected parliament exercising legislative powers, *then* judicial review would be appropriately exercised by the CJEC. Most significantly, the safeguarding of individual rights required 'the creation for individual persons of an appropriate remedy for infringement of Article 177' (Ferri 1982: 351).

If the Union were conceived as a 'dynamic extension' of the present machinery and not as merely intergovernmental, then it would have to make extended use of the open-ended Article 235, said the Court.

The Court then identified two bottlenecks in the acknowledged 'decision-making problem' which were of growing concern as the 1970s progressed: first, the issue of whether legal instruments needed to be drawn up in great detail; second, the amount of time taken by the national experts to attain unanimity in technical matters, which had the effect of 'putting off their decisions indefinitely'. This was, indeed, a major theme of the 1970s, as dozens of draft Directives and Regulations piled up on the Council's table: many having gathered dust for 8 or 10 years or more. Again, this was an area where the Court itself produced the beginnings of a breakthrough a year or two later. It did so in its judgment in the so-called *Cassis de Dijon* case (120/78) whose essence was that goods legally produced and marketed in one member state must be allowed to enter into free circulation in all.

The Court concluded on a significantly defensive note, trying to hold ground gained against corrupt forces. It was 'of the first importance that there should be one independent Community court'. Further, procedures should be simplified, not made more complex. States should avoid 'informal' undertakings, of uncertain legal form, as a way of conducting business. Finally, the Court urged that national courts be prohibited from treating a Community act as invalid, unless the European Court had considered the matter and specifically so declared it – reminding its readers that this was already the position under the ECSC Treaty.

The Court's view is of some interest as a milestone. It clearly recognised both its own role hitherto as a 'cement' of the system and also pointed to the most important areas of ambiguity or contention which prevented it from policing the system more effectively.

Finally, we come to the Opinion of the *Economic and Social Committee*. It too stressed the need for the Union to 'provide itself with a democratic European authority'. Perhaps anticipating the internal market proposals, it stressed that '[I]t is possible to take large strides on the basis of the present Treaties' – and necessary because of the 'excessive number of setbacks, mistakes and delays' which had damaged the Community's credibility. It stressed the need (para. 3.3) for the institutions to have 'legitimacy ... in other words [to be] democratic ... and effectiveness' (Ferri 1982: 359).

But in policy terms the main thrust of the ESC's opinion was *dirigiste*. It nailed its colours not just to the then moribund economic and monetary union, but also to employment policy, regional policy, energy policy, industrial policy and 'pursuit of' the CAP (Ferri 1982: 361–3). In the whole gamut of 'economic and social policies' it, needless to say, saw an enhanced role for itself.

This *dirigiste* strain was not surprising, but we should pause to consider it, for it represented one of the crucial battlegrounds of the 1970s and opened up important questions about the role and shape of the Community system. *Dirigisme* had much support. The UK Industry Acts (1972 and 1975) are examples. Active regional policy, its rules configured by and aids financed by national governments, was generally viewed positively. Again to take the UK case, authoritative voices spoke of a 'regional policy effect which is encouragingly large' – concentrated, however, in manufacturing rather than in the service sector (Moore and Rhodes 1973: esp. 96–8).

The commonest responses to the icy blasts that blew through the EC economies in the mid-1970s were to enhance the intervention and role of the state. This occurred for several reasons. Community instruments (such as the ERDF) were new, small, sparse and in any case never intended to do more than *complement* national instruments. Community decision making was seen as slow and cumbersome. Quick response was seen as national response. Corporatist pressures ensured this; and the outcomes mainly and for a while reinforced the corporatist pressure.

Protectionism was identified as moving to an upswing at about the same time (see Page 1981). Page stated that '1974 was a clear turning point. The IMF's 1975 *Annual Report on Exchange Restrictions* was the first to find more increases in restrictions than decreases' (Page 1981: 17). Along with the number went change in type: from tariffs to the much more troublesome non-tariff barriers. She further pointed to the effects within the EC as a grouping: in contrast to the traditional view that 'joint trading actions ... restrict the growth of protection because the least protectionist participants restrict the rest ... it appears that the reverse has been true both within the EC and in its role relative to other industrial countries' (Page 1981: 37).

The timing of the Tindemans Report itself was a little unfortunate. It was dated 29 December 1975, thus just meeting the year-end deadline but hardly ensuring a wakeful and alert audience. Comments on it gravitated around notions of tentativeness, the modesty of its proposals, the absence of grand designs. But given the chaotic situation surrounding its birth and the diversity of views put to its author, this was not surprising. Tindemans described the Community as 'unbalanced' (Ferri 1982: 367); as an 'unfinished structure which does not weather well: it must be completed, otherwise it collapses'; he pointed to the 'widespread feeling that we are vulnerable and powerless'. The report gave to the European Council the task of establishing priorities (Ferri 1982: 369). It tried, however, to give them a powerful steer in terms of direction, adding:

> In this vast scheme everything goes together and it is the sum of the progress achieved in parallel which constitutes the qualitative change which is European Union ... These changes cannot occur without a transfer of competences to common institutions ... a transfer of resources from prosperous to less prosperous regions.
>
> (Ferri 1982: 369)

The report, while urging the need for much expanded economic and social policies, at the same time acknowledged that 'there is no agreement on how to achieve
a common economic and monetary policy' (Ferri 1982: 376): instead, a start could
be made on a 'two-tier' basis. There should be common energy and research, social
and regional policies. The dimension of a citizen's Europe was also heavily trailed.
It had two aspects: protection of rights – fundamental rights, consumer rights and
protection of the environment – and 'external signs of our solidarity', especially
regarding free movement of persons, educational mobility and collaboration in the
area of information media. Institutional reform (strengthening) must be based on
the four criteria of 'authority, efficiency, legitimacy and coherence' (Ferri 1982:
382–5).

These debates might have appeared at the time somewhat metaphysical and
unreal. But they powerfully anticipated much later ones and also a number of
concrete developments and directions which were to see the light of day a decade
or so later. Although the Tindemans Report itself and the debates surrounding it
were not seen to have had much immediate influence, they put down markers for
ideas that resurfaced later. Although the report was frequently characterised at the
time as timid, Tindemans, in fact, clearly proposed a stronger executive body
which would be independent of the governments of the member states, whose
functions would be much the same as those of the then Commission and Council of
Ministers combined and which would both be accountable to and elected by a powerful bicameral legislature. This was far from timid, especially given the temper of
the times, dominated by the UK 'renegotiation', the ensuing referendum and a
much wider and more general sense of defensiveness and pessimism (see Mitchell
1976).

In this context, it should be remembered that the Spierenburg Report at the same
time was also graphically describing the causes of decline of Community *élan* and
had stressed the failures and shortcomings of more recent years.

Tindemans was concerned to relate function – what the institutions were there to
do – to form and in this context the whole area of external relations was perceived
to be of the greatest importance. Strong stress was laid on common external policy
especially in relation to energy policy, relations with the USA, security and defence
and crises in the areas close to the EC.

But overall the report was a curious mixture of 'maximalism' and protests of
'minimalism' and the need for realism and recognition of the limits to which states
would go. It did not appear to take full account of the powerful role which the
European Council was busy carving out for itself, especially thanks to Giscard and
Schmidt. Although the Tindemans Report appeared on the agenda of every
European Council for 4 years, it was passed over and not discussed. In due course,
a new report was commissioned, that of the so-called 'three wise men'. It, too, like
the Tindemans Report, was to be 'shadowed' by another Spierenburg Report,
which for convenience may be referred to as 'Spierenburg II'.

But however much emphasis the Tindemans Report had placed on common
external policy, in the 'real world' things looked rather different, and we may now
turn briefly to the EC's actual conduct of external relations in this period.

## EC external relations

The Community's external relations in this period are a mixed bag. On the one hand, the Community was able to congratulate itself on the conclusion, in February 1975, of the first of the Lomé agreements with the ACP states – initially 46 of them; the number was to grow by fits and starts. It also tried to pursue what had become known as the 'global' Mediterranean policy, with mixed results, at best: as it progressed, this exercise became inextricably involved both with 'southern enlargement' and with the animosities of Greek–Turkish relations. The EC proved defensive and cautious over its relations with state trading countries; of very limited efficacy in relations with Japan.

It was, however, being taken seriously by many outside, even while its internal policies languished. The state trading countries (STCs) of Comecon (CMEA) clearly signalled this, prompted to do so, it appears, by the relatively successful coordination of positions and degree of harmony shown by the EC members in the CSCE negotiations, and the role of the Commission in 'basket two'– economic relations. But the Community for its part was unwilling to be drawn into 'bloc-to-bloc' negotiations with Comecon and the story of these years is essentially of a delicate manoeuvring for position and formula, which changed little.

In its relations with Japan, the Community appeared hardly to know what was about to hit it until the 'damage' had been done: there then began, rather late in the day, an increase in the volume of alarm and invective, but very little in the way of solidarity and joint position. For their part, the Japanese proved shrewd in their evaluation of, and adept at exploiting, the extent to which the EC was *not* a common market. They had decided, early in the game and in apparent contrast to the EC, to 'sell their way out' of the first 'oil shock'. In doing so, they would show the western Europeans that the latter's handicap lay not just in the obvious measures of economic performance, but also in being able to be divided, and thus ruled, as well.

### *Relations with the Comecon states*

We begin by looking at relations with the STCs of Comecon. The omens were hardly auspicious: the Soviet Union's refusal to recognise the EC, together with the Rome Treaty requirement that from 1970 all trade agreements involving the members should be handled at Community level, had created an impasse. The initial Community reaction was to 'put off the evil day': a 4-year delay in implementing the transfer was announced.

Two important landmarks occurred in the summer of 1973. First, in August, Fadeyev, as Secretary-General of CMEA, had approached EC Council President Norgaard and 'suggested unofficially that contacts be organised' between Comecon and the EC (8 *GRA*: 261). This was clearly an attempt to break the deadlock over recognition, but to do so in terms of 'bloc-to-bloc' relations. The Community's reply was that it was open to any further moves or suggestions; it reiterated this in May 1974, and the FRG embassy in Moscow was charged with making the point to Fadeyev. The second, the issue of the extent and nature of

*Community* participation in CSCE, was resolved by a Council Decision in September: there would be Commission representation on 'basket two', which dealt with trade, 'cooperation' and science and technology. There would also be what was referred to as 'internal co-ordination of the positions taken by Member States' (8 *GRA*: 260).

A third point was that the end of 1974 would see the expiry of most of the (extended) *bilateral* trade agreements with EC members; it was equally clear, however, that a number of EC members were still unwilling to hand over this area to Community competence if this meant the Commission; and this led the Council to lay down 'autonomous trade arrangements' for 1975 and to send the STCs an *aide-mémoire* containing a model for a possible agreement which, it said pointedly, the Community might conclude *with each of them (Bull. EC* 11–1974, point 1301; 8 *GRA*: 261ff.). It is instructive to compare the account of these moves given by the Commission in the *General Reports* with that given by the Council in the *Review of the Council's Work*. From this it is clear that member states had sidestepped the Commission: if 'trade agreements' are to be Community business and this is undesired, then do whatever you wish under another name and that is not exclusive Community competence; the fig leaf is preserved. Thus the Council reported coyly on its 22 July 1974 Decision on a consultation procedure for *cooperation agreements* with third countries: the 'field of economic and industrial cooperation still comes under the jurisdiction of Member States' but 'it appeared essential to move *towards a certain measure of* Community control' (22 *RCW*: 83ff., emphasis added). Even more to the point: although such consultation involving the Commission would be mandatory for agreements with STCs and oil producers, the select committee in which it took place, although *chaired* by a Commission representative, would have its 'necessary secretarial services [provided] by the General Secretariat of the Council' (22 *RCW*: 84). He who controls the minutes and the agenda, controls all. The same document, however, described this as 'substantial progress' on a common commercial policy (CCP) with respect to the STCs.

While there is not space to give a detailed account of all the exchanges with CMEA, it is an instructive saga. On 16 September 1974, Fadeyev invited the *Commission* president to Moscow for preliminary talks with Comecon: bloc to bloc was Moscow's way here. On 14 November the Commission replied that this was a good idea, but perhaps there should be preliminary talks between officials first to prepare the way. On 4–6 February 1975, Edmund Wellenstein of DG I (external relations) had these talks with the Comecon secretariat (9 *GRA*: 273). They were described in what may be called a meaningful 'low key': they represented only an 'exchange of information'; they were only *part* of the relationship between the Community and the *eastern countries*. CMEA was invited back, but the Community (and that meant the Council) still awaited a reply to its 'model agreement'. Community-to-country bilateralism was the name of the game in Brussels.

It was significant, too, that whatever role the Commission might claim credit for in the CSCE negotiations, when it came to the signing of the final act it was a different story. On 1 August 1975, Aldo Moro signed the document in his dual capacity as Italian prime minister and president of the Council.

Early in 1976 the Council did agree to extend the consultation procedure, now a safely tamed beast and no threat, to all cooperation agreements. But the penny had dropped at CMEA. They tried again: this time, the letter (16 February 1976) came from Herr Weiss of the DDR, as president-in-office of the executive committee of Comecon, to Gaston Thorn, as president-in-office of the *Council* of the EC (24 *RCW*: 134). It appears that there was a lengthy period of 'study' over the reply to be given by the EC. An 'interim reply' was drafted by the Council in March: significantly, the substantive reply had to wait until November, a sure sign of the embarrassment and difficulties caused. This reply again annexed a draft agreement on 'cooperation', while also recalling its earlier reply on 'trade' which, it reiterated, was still open also: on the basis that the *Community* would enter into trade negotiations '*with each of the member countries* of CMEA'. The wording was again carefully chosen: the communiqué concerned relations 'between the Community on the one hand and the STCs and CMEA on the other' (thus fudging the issues of 'bilateralism' and 'recognition'); the Council 'stressed the importance it attached to the development of the Community's relations *not only with* CMEA *but also with each of its member countries*' (10 *GRA*: 284ff., emphasis added).

All of this was almost certainly a blocking tactic. It is worth noting that the *GRA* appears (uncharacteristically) too embarrassed to give either the full text or even a reference to the whereabouts of the full text of the communiqué. No doubt it was also convenient to be able to rub in the point (against Soviet hegemony) by sending all this to Olszewski, Polish deputy prime minister, as chairman of Comecon's executive committee.

On 18 April 1977, a no doubt bemused Comecon replied, this time taking it on themselves to suggest another 'preliminary meeting'. Simonet for the Council replied to accept, but specified that his role would be simply to *welcome* the delegation before handing them over to the tender mercies of Haferkamp, a Commission vice-president, since it 'was responsible for representing the Community at all stages of negotiations' (11 *GRA*: 271). The talks (with a CMEA delegation led by Marinescu of Romania) took place on 21 September 1977 in Brussels, resulting in another communiqué, this time looking forward to 'plan[ning] the start of negotiations for' an agreement 'for early 1978' (11 *GRA*: 271; 25 *RCW*: 155–6). The seasoned connoisseur of Community-ese should have no difficulty in predicting from such wording that agreement was nowhere in sight.

To follow the story forward very briefly, Haferkamp and Fadeyev met in Moscow on 29–30 May 1978; this was then followed by an 'experts' meeting in Brussels from 25–8 July – just before the holidays to give everyone time to cool off and much needed to judge from the evocative report: 'the discussions centred on certain questions' (unspecified) 'about which the two parties have different notions'– in other words, little progress. The Community 'made practical proposals with a view to speeding up'; CMEA was 'not able to give a favourable response'; it agreed to consider and give its reply; the line went dead (12 *GRA*: 301ff.; *Bull. EC* 7/8–1978: 2.2.1). The negotiations later 'continued but were not brought to a successful conclusion' (13 *GRA*: 270ff.).

The point of the saga was this. It illustrates a classic battle royal within the

Community. This battle concerned not just the respective competences of Council and Commission, though that was part of it. Each body was also able to hide behind the other and to pass the buck. They also did this as a way of obfuscating the real issue, which was external–political: namely, the twin beliefs that (a) Comecon did not have/must not be encouraged to develop the kinds of competence that the Community was prepared – when it suited it, as in CSCE – to claim for itself; and (b) nothing must be done that would encourage the growth of Soviet influence over the non-Soviet Comecon members.

### The Mediterranean morass

On the face of it, this period could be seen as a highly successful one for the Community. The EC had first embarked on its 'global' Mediterranean policy in 1972; 'by 1978 the Community had put its trade relations with all the countries of the Mediterranean Basin with the exception of Albania and Libya on a contractual footing' (Rosenthal 1982: 52). At the start of 1974, there were still dictatorships in Greece, Portugal and Spain; by the end of 1977, there was considerable change in all three. Greece applied for membership on 12 June 1975, Portugal and Spain in 1977 (28 March and 28 July respectively). This picture, true as far as it goes, is, however, too simple and too flattering. Chance played a great part in many of the key events; and some had side-effects which, however predictable, were also unpleasant.

At the end of 1973, the Council of Ministers had asked the Permanent Representatives' Committee to continue its examination of the Commission's proposals for 'overall' agreements with what were described as the countries of the 'first wave' in the Mediterranean – Spain, Israel and the Maghreb states – Morocco, Tunisia and Algeria. Again it is worth noting the restricted role of the Commission: detailed Directives were to be thrashed out and then given to the Commission as its negotiating brief (22 *RCW*: 86–7). A similar procedure was followed a year later in regard to the 'second wave', the Mashrek states (Egypt, Jordan, the Lebanon, Syria) (23 *RCW*: 105).

The issues were significant ones. First, according to GATT rules, 'association' arrangements, if they were not to be regarded as openly discriminatory, must be a prelude to full membership of a customs union. Second, the Rome Treaty had two pertinent articles: 238 spoke of association and did not mention the word 'Europe'; 237 spoke about membership, and of course did specify it as being open to 'any European state'. Thus, already at the beginning of the road, thorny issues about the geographical scope, as well as the functional scope, of 'Europe' lurked in the wings. The whole process was likely to be seen as 'creeping neocolonialism', not just by left-inclined critics from within, but by many far from left-inclined critics from outside, most vocally in the USA.

Further, although these articles did not refer explicitly to any necessary democratic credentials for association or for membership, it had always been understood that a 'falling from grace' in this regard represented a reason for 'freezing' an association agreement and still more an impediment to full membership.

Thus, Greece's association had been frozen following the colonels' coup of 1967. By 1974, Greek officers were also in charge of the national guard of supposedly independent Cyprus under the government of Archbishop Makarios; it was they who led a coup on the island in mid-July 1974, deposing Makarios (at first he was declared to be dead) and nominating Sampson as president of the Republic of Cyprus in his stead. The hand of the Athens colonels, widely hated and discredited inside Greece, seeking, it was assumed, some external *panem et circenses* diversion to boost their flagging fortunes at least in some quarters, was immediately seen in this. Inside Greece, centrist, let alone leftist, circles attacked the coup as madness: on 18 July the Commission announced the postponement of the Association Council timed for the following Monday, 22 July.

The coup produced a major invasion of Cyprus by Turkish forces on 21 July. Turkey claimed in justification that it was a co-guarantor of Cyprus's independence. Fast and furious diplomatic activity ensued, producing a tenuous ceasefire from 2 pm on the 22nd. For the EC, Sauvagnargues, who had had a number of telephone contacts with Kissinger, hailed the 'perfect diplomatic coordination' of the Nine (*EDB* 1565: 3); Ortoli was also 'very positive' about it. The whiplash effect inside Greece was every bit as swift as the Turkish invasion, so taut are the sinews always pulled in this relationship: 24 July saw the return of a civilian government under Constantin Karamanlis in Athens; within a couple of days the Community was breathlessly underpinning this development by offering not just the unfreezing of association but the prospect of accession. It was a busy week: 19 July had seen a new government in Portugal; on 20 July, following Franco's illness, came the announcement in Spain that his powers would be assumed by Juan Carlos.

The Greek *démarche* produced its own knock-on effect in the EC's relations with Turkey. Having shown so much favour to the one, favour had to be shown to the other: thus at the 14 October EC–Turkey Association Council, 'it was emphasised that one day Turkey would be called upon to become a full member of the Community': once again, the passive and impersonal are eloquent (22 *RCW*: 92). Turkey, meantime, was more concerned with possible dilution of the real value of association as the EC sought to extend the network of 'special deals' (see *EDB* 1610: 5, 1611: 11). What Rosenthal described as 'the most difficult years of EC–Turkish relations' were to follow the events of 1974, due to delicate coalitions in Ankara which had to pay court to the anti-western views of the minority coalition partner, the National Salvation Party (Rosenthal 1982: 14).

Events in Greece also produced a knock-on effect in a westerly direction. It was clear that liberal–democratic politics was the open sesame to the Community door: the lesson was soon learnt in Portugal and Spain, in the case of the former in particular, with not a little 'outside help'.

### Japan

The Community seemed only slowly to wake up to the extent of its structural problems in its trade relations with Japan. In February 1974, Ortoli met Tanaka to initiate the Commission delegation in Tokyo. It seemed that energy concerns were at the forefront for both and that there was wide agreement. In the Commission's own account of 1974, the tone is of a mild irritant soon to be eradicated: it was noted simply that 'Japan still has a surplus on trade with the Community' (8 *GRA*: 257ff.).

This surplus, about $1.2bn in 1973, grew steadily to about $4.1bn in 1976, when the Commission announced that it 'will exceed' $5bn in 1977. By this stage the tone had sharpened; until then, the impression is of a piecemeal response. December 1975, for instance, saw the initialling of an agreement to limit Japanese textile exports to the Community. That year too, during the regular 6-monthly meetings with the Japanese, the Commission 'restated its concern' at the bilateral deficit, citing in particular Japanese NTBs in the automotive sector.

In 1976, 'The Commission made it clear ... that if measures to improve the trade balance were not taken quickly, the Community would have difficulty in maintaining its liberal trade policies and might be forced to adopt restrictive measures' (10 *GRA*: 279). It would be hard to imagine a clearer message to Japan as to what it should do next, and it is clear that it took the hint. One stratagem was to step up the pressure for bilateral 'voluntary export restraint agreements' (VERAs) with the EC states individually. A second was to 'get in under the wire' and set up 'production' facilities inside the Community, whether of a merely 'screwdriver' kind or not. Japan was swift to do both. Dividing up the Community resulted in large market shares for, for instance, Japanese cars in some EC countries; a very small one in Italy.

Meanwhile, in March 1977, the European Council still 'invited the Community institutions' to step up their efforts to achieve agreements (11 *GRA*: 266). The Council reports, similarly, are almost silent during 1974 and 1975; only in 1976 and 1977 does there seem to be any real concern, culminating in determination to hold 'detailed discussion on all questions' concerning Japan in February 1978 (25 *RCW*: 153). It was hardly an impressive example even of the ability of the Community to show 'foresight' by making the right warning noises and forecasts, even in the absence of agreement as to what to do about them.

## Further reading

D. Dinan (ed.), *Origins and Evolution of the European Union*. Oxford: Oxford University Press, 2006. (Chapter 8.)

S. George and I. Bache, *Politics in the European Union*. Oxford: Oxford University Press, 2001. (Chapter 9.)

J. Gillingham, *European Integration 1950–2003*. Cambridge: Cambridge University Press, 2003. (Part II.)

P. Schnapper, *La Grande-Bretagne et l'Europe*. Paris: Presses de Science Po, 2000.

P. Stirk and D. Weigall (eds), *The Origins and Development of European Integration*. London: Pinter, 1999. (Chapter 8.)

# 6 'Euro-sclerosis'

## The late 1970s and early 1980s

The problems that had so troubled the EC after 1973 did not quickly pass away. In many ways, the late 1970s and early 1980s seemed at the time a period of limited ambitions and limited opportunities: the EC experienced fragile economic recovery for a couple of years (1976–8), only to be hit by the second oil shock and further attempts at national 'defensive' action. For the most part, the economic background continued to be difficult.

Yet this period also saw a number of breakthroughs. Three of our four main 'battles', or issue areas, were to the fore. The establishment of the European Monetary System (EMS) in 1979, although an intergovernmental arrangement and not part of the formal Community system *stricto sensu*, was one aspect of expansion of 'internal' policy competence. However, as we shall see, although it was perhaps the most obvious and one of the most trumpeted, it was not necessarily more important than others that went more unsung at the time: notably, battles over the 'economic order' within the member states. Second, the inter-institutional 'battle' began to take on a new tone and shape, partly but not only under the impetus of the first direct elections to the EP, in 1979. The 'new shape' was also influenced by, third, further moves toward geographical extension: the accession of Greece, from 1981, and the even more protracted negotiations with Spain and Portugal.

This period was marked by other protracted struggles too, in which the UK played a central role: the continuing struggle over the budget and the UK's contribution became enmeshed in a major 'package deal' known as the '30 May Mandate', the battles over which continued to occupy centre stage at least until the Fontainebleau European Council of 1984; this too will be examined.

And yet it was also a period where, so to speak, the 'worm began to turn': notions about the role of the state within the economy, and thus about the role of the EC in helping to 'shape' the economic order, began to change. Intellectual fashions began to shift. A sea change was slowly coming about which was to help to produce the drive, in the mid-1980s, toward the 'single market' and toward the institutional changes seen to be required to achieve it, which will be examined in Chapter 7.

There was first, as we have seen, the EMS. Greeted originally with considerable scepticism, it survived better than its critics had expected. Not least of the surprises was its survival against a background of generally high but also divergent inflation rates, which in most cases peaked shortly after the establishment of the system.

These divergences contributed to a series of 'realignments', most numerous in the early years. (Seven occurred as follows: September 1979; November 1979; March 1981; September 1981; February 1982; June 1982; March 1983.) Once again it was clear how much the EMS owed at the political level to Franco-German agreement: the delays at the very end of 1978 and the beginning of 1979 also reflected lack of it, with the French trying – and failing – to make resolution of the argument over MCAs a precondition. British contributions had also been of the greatest importance, however: those of Roy Jenkins as Commission president, through and following his Florence speech of November 1977, and the less trumpeted work of Michael Emerson and others on the technical level within the Commission.

The other preoccupations were rather different. A second was the continuing institutional debate; but it continued for a while, somewhat as before, to generate more proposals and paper than concrete change. Once again, however, appearances were deceptive. More had changed with the first direct elections to the EP than immediately met the eye. A new menagerie was being born: inside the EP, the Crocodile Club (named after one of Strasbourg's better known restaurants, in which it met) and outside, in business circles, the Kangaroo Group, seeking swifter ways to leap frontiers, both contained the germs of the ideas that were to come to fruition in the mid-1980s with the Cockfield White Paper on completing the internal market and the Single European Act.

Third was the issue of geographical extension. Greece's application, well advanced at the end of the 1970s, resulted in accession from the beginning of 1981. The Portuguese and Spanish applications, entered in 1977, progressed much more slowly, and in the case of Spain, French rearguard action was quite marked: they were members from the start of 1986.

However, another and quite different aspect began to attract attention: it too might be described in terms of task expansion, except that its main thrust was in the direction of *reducing* previous activity, not removing it to a new, Community, level. As so often, at first it appeared a cloud no bigger than one's hand; a nagging worry with no obvious solution. The Commission began to react to the national protectionist economic reflexes of several of the member states in the 1970s. It began to take seriously those treaty provisions averring that the public sector should be subject to essentially the same rules as the private; to object to the previous practices of member states of taking key but ailing enterprises 'under their wing', as it were, and shielding them against the cold winds of competition. That this was to be a major preoccupation became clear when the Commission proposed its Directive on the 'Transparency of financial relations between states and their public sector enterprises' (Transparency Directive, 80/723), and immediately encountered opposition from three members – France, Italy and the UK. These three chose to object in particular to the legal basis of the Commission's proposal.

For its part, the Commission summed up its view of the year 1979 under five main headings. First, it commented favourably on the enhanced democratic legitimacy created by direct elections to the EP. Second was the enhanced economic and monetary cohesion created by the EMS. Third, the Commission spoke of promotion of solidarity on the energy front – this time claiming some success in the face of the second oil shock although, as before, this probably reflected more of aspiration than reality. Fourth, the Commission listed the development of relations with the rest of the world, as evidenced in particular in the conclusion of the second Lomé Agreement with the ACP states. Finally on its list came preparation for enlargement.

Behind this apparently satisfactory balance sheet lay the qualifications. With the second oil price hike, noted the Commission, came also a loss of momentum of the economic recovery. Similarly, inflation had picked up again in all the members, and the spread of rates had widened; there had also been balance of payments deterioration (13 *GRA*: 17–18). By contrast, the EMS was judged, after the first few months, to be working satisfactorily. On the energy front, the Strasbourg European Council of June had agreed to limit consumption during 1980 and imports in the period 1980–5: all of this was in parallel with the thrust of the Tokyo 'western' economic summit.

Probably the most acute sectoral problem lay in steel. The year 1979 saw the crisis plan for the industry renewed. Indeed, in some quarters the crisis was seen as so serious that it might 'lead to the break-up of the Community' (Mény and Wright 1987: 3). The extent of state ownership of the steel industries had been wide in many member states before, or by, the late 1970s; thus, once again, this became a battle about the economic order. There was seen to be a 'contradiction between the essentially liberal model of integration and the view of mixed economies found in all the Member States, where the economic role and share of the State has been constantly on the increase'; while this was 'not so acute in times of rapid economic growth, full employment and balance of payments surplus', it was 'with the advent of economic recession (or should we better call it crisis?) that centrifugal forces became very powerful. Economic divergence increased and so did government intervention at the micro level.' These measures 'often contravened the basic rules of the Common Market' (Tsoukalis and Strauss in Mény and Wright 1987: 186ff.).

That this was recognised at the time to be a major issue (even if one does not share the Commission's view of its own success) is evident from Commission sources too. 'With increasing frequency, the Commission has successfully intervened to curb protectionist pressures which the economic crisis has been arousing in the Member States', asserted the 1979 General Report (13 *GRA*: 21). The Commission was also clear that the integration process had been slowed down by fragmentation of the internal market, due to growing public intervention in the national economies, 'which, if it results in markets being closed off against each other again, could be dangerous for the Community' (13 *GRA*: 25).

'Rustbelt' and 'sunset' industries, public enterprises and state monopolies were all the focus of a good deal of attention. The Commission sent its report on aids to the shipbuilding sector to the Council in November 1979: it 'analysed the problems of the sector and proposed criteria for the appraisal of state aids' (9 *RCP*: 99). Much the same was true of the textiles and clothing, leather and footwear sectors as well as steel. 'On 18 December 1979, the Council gave unanimous assent to a draft decision establishing Community rules for specific aids to the steel industry' (9 *RCP*: 101).

Again the CJEC played its part, establishing basic approaches of which wide use was to be made later. In Case 91/78 (*Hansen GmbH* v. *Hauptzollamt Flensburg*; [1979] *ECR*: 935) the Court's judgment became the basis for raising issues concerning monopolies in France and Italy, notably in the tobacco, alcohol and matches sectors (see 9 *RCP*: 128).

Successive competition policy reports trace the saga of the Transparency Directive already mentioned (8 *RCP*, points 253–4 set out its basis; 9 *RCP*, 131 and 10 *RCP*, 163–5 chart its early progress). In the 11th Report (p. 155), we find France, Italy and the UK arguing in the joined Cases 188–9 and 190/80, against the use by the Commission of Article 90(3) as the legal basis for the Transparency Directive and in favour of Article 94, which gave a role to the Council of Ministers.

For its part, the Commission:

[H]as noted in particular the increasing impact of the public sector on the Community economy. Over recent years this growth has been considerable ... Enlargement of the Community to include countries possessing a developed and sometimes complex system of State financing can only heighten the absolute necessity for the Commission to be adequately informed about the nature of the financial relations involved.

(11 *RCP*: 155)

Adopting its well-known strategy of salami slicing the target, the Commission began by averring that certain sectors were excluded from its purview, to soften opposition and allay fears. Later it moved on to the attack: 'The Commission's services *continued* their examination of the problems involved in *extending* the provisions of the Directive to certain of the sectors so far excluded, notably public credit institutions, energy and transport', it growled (emphasis added).

Thus important political changes and battles were engaged. The national economic responses, we have seen, predated the change of government which brought the socialist-led coalition to power in France; but the losers of 1981 were clearly determined to carry on battle in other fora. Those French elections in turn had a significant impact elsewhere: southern Europe became, in the early 1980s, a socialist/social democrat-led zone, so that in due course (1983) a 'socialist summit' of five premiers – from France, Greece, Italy, Portugal and Spain – could be held. The Commission's moves were a response to the early phases and an anticipation of the later developments. The period indeed saw a 'north–south split' in the EC, the south being broadly 'centre left' in nominal terms, the north centre right. Crucially however, by 1983 France's U-turn meant that it had left the 'southern' camp and joined the north.

Closely linked to these concerns was the more general one over protectionism as a threat to the free movement of goods. 'The resurgence of protectionist measures with which the Community is at present confronted is threatening the principle of free movement of goods, one of the Community's fundamental achievements', stated the Commission (13 *GRA*: 73). This was before the period (1981) when a new French government, with calculated ambiguity, was to speak of the 'reconquest of the internal market'. Once again, the legal basis for the counterattack had been laid by the Court, this time in its judgment in the *Cassis de Dijon* Case (120/78; [1979] *ECR*: 649).

Yet more battles lurked in the wings. On one hand, the Commission was busy congratulating itself on the successes of EMS: 'The EMS has already attained its objective of stabilising exchange rate relationships in Europe', it declared. But, on the other hand, both it and the EP were heading for major problems over the Community budget. Over this, differences in perspective were striking: it was only the timing, perhaps, that had about it something of the inevitable.

The Commission tended to approach issues in a posture of injured innocence. The context was the question of (economic) convergence and coordination. In looking at how far the Community budget could be used similarly to (but on a much smaller scale than) national budgets, the Commission commented that it 'considered that the (Community) budget was the financial expression of common policies for the benefit of the Community as a whole and that its primary function could therefore not be a redistributive one'.

This was fair enough as far as it went. It became also, however, the veil behind which the Commission found it convenient to hide in its refusal to make (or at any rate to reveal the results of) any calculations about gainers and losers – about net contributors to and beneficiaries from the budget.

That brought it smartly up against the determination of the new UK government led by Margaret Thatcher to conduct a further renegotiation – albeit without ever calling it so – on that very issue: 'My billion pounds.' The kernel of the British government's case was that, the Dublin financial mechanism having expired, the UK, in considerable economic difficulty, was again faced with those very same 'unacceptable budgetary situations' to which earlier agreements had referred.

The European Parliament, for its part, was mainly keen to make its mark: in this area, the terrain looked more promising than elsewhere for a move to flex its muscles; to show that a directly elected body was prepared to go as far as possible in asserting its power of the purse. The scene was set for its rejection of the budget; and thus for one skein of the tangle of problems whose resolution came to be known, in another delightful piece of Community-ese, as the '30 May Mandate' (1980).

The European Council, meeting at Luxembourg on 27–8 April 1980, had signally failed to agree on any of several issues. Just over 1 month later, the Council of Foreign Ministers declared a 'success', the nature of which was to package the matters requiring accord and to set about trying to resolve them. The main issues were the British budgetary contribution, the farm price decisions for 1980, the establishment of a regime for the sheepmeat sector and a declaration of the main lines of a common fisheries policy (CFP).

Council and Commission sources are, for once, in agreement in according most of the credit for this 'progress' to Emilio Colombo of the Italian presidency, and to Roy Jenkins as Commission president. The EP and the Economic and Social Committee (meeting on 28–9 May) urgently appealed to the Community to end the crisis. A classic Community marathon of 20 hours' discussion ended during the morning of 30 May. From the British point of view, the episode marked a definite shift away from the Commission's earlier refusal to say anything about net beneficiaries and contributors: a formula was worked out for 1980 and 1981 and, in principle, for 1982 as well.

As usual, all parties made suitable statements for home consumption. In its statement, the FRG urged that agricultural surpluses be reduced to prevent a continuation of these problems. This was too much: the FRG was increasingly identified as, first, speaking with forked tongue (agriculture vs. finance ministries, with agriculture routinely winning out when push came to shove) and, second, as a main beneficiary of the actual working of the MCA system and the storage arrangements. The FRG added that perhaps there should be ceilings on the contributions, and benefits, of *all* member states (4 June statement; see *Bull. EC* 5–1980: 5–13).

For his part, Colombo was at pains to claim that the agreement was 'balanced': sheepmeat for France; the CFP (equal access) for the FRG; the budget formula for the UK. Neither was the Commission slow to take a share of the credit: 'It was the working paper produced by the Commission at the beginning of the General Affairs Council on 29 May that provided the framework for the eventual agreement' (*Bull. EC* 5–1980: 13). Belgium and the Netherlands were a good deal less impressed: this looked like big member ganging up. The Netherlands statement said the 'only alternative was the break-up of the Community' (Deputy Prime Minister Wiegel as quoted in *Bull. EC* 5–1980: 14).

Such local squabbles were but an aspect of the continuing general gloom. With its by now finely honed armoury of exogenous excuses (although this time with rather more justification), the Commission announced, in reviewing developments in 1980, 'The world-wide political and economic situation was marked by increasing instability', especially apparent in tensions and armed conflicts. Following the second oil shock:

> Only limited help can be expected from the State. After the 1973 oil crisis it sucked itself dry by stepping in over and over again to cushion the effects of the quadrupling of oil prices. Now it must put its financial house in order.
>
> (14 *GRA*: 17–18)

This struck a new low in sombre notes. The invasion of Afghanistan, the declaration of martial law in Poland, the Iran hostage crisis and the Iran–Iraq war were the backdrop. Forty-eight per cent of the EC's oil came through the Straits of Hormuz.

Internally, the Community, following the EP's rejection of the draft budget for 1980, lived for 6 months on a diet of 'provisional twelfths' (of the prior year's expenditure). At the end of October 1979 the declaration of 'manifest crisis' in the steel sector received the unanimous assent of the Council of Ministers.

Of the oil shock, the Commission wrote: 'Expressed in real terms the increase in the price of oil between the end of 1978 and mid-1980 was of a similar order of magnitude to that recorded in 1973–4.' Inevitably it led to a slowdown in world trade and in the growth of GDP: the two-and-a-half-year recovery of 1976–8 crunched to a halt (14 *GRA*: 74).

Against this unpromising background, the Commission sought to move forward on several related fronts. Three in particular may be mentioned: the removal of non-tariff barriers (NTBs) to *internal* trade; attempts to remove technical barriers to trade; and attempts to improve information on technical standards.

In this, the Commission was aided in no small measure by the Court. The Commission (see 14 *GRA*: 84) was quick to seize on the importance of the Court's judgment in the *Cassis de Dijon* Case (120/78). The cornerstone of this was that any product lawfully produced and marketed in one member state must in principle be admitted to free circulation on the territory of other member states, subject to very limited exceptions ([1979] *ECR*: 649ff.). The judgment in *Cassis* was confirmed by another of 26 June 1980, *Gilli and Andres* (Case 788/79), providing the Commission with what was rather delightfully called 'interpretative guidance' for monitoring the application of Articles 30–6 on free movement of goods.

On the competition front also, things were moving in a similar direction. Noting that 'there was a tendency in 1980 ... for more massive and more varied forms of state aid to be granted', the Commission (14 *GRA*: 110ff.) strengthened its policy in this area also. Again, its approach was upheld by the Court, this time in the judgment in the *Philip Morris* Case (730/79).

Commenting on this, the 10th Report on competition policy was significant. A corrigendum at the front of the report altered the original formulation in a tougher sense. It said:

> The depth of the economic recession has opened up the possibility of using State aids to assist industries with some degree of viability, in one Member State in particular. Searching discussions have been held on such plans.
>
> Its position strengthened by the Court's judgment of 17 September 1980 in the Philip Morris case, the Commission considers that the grant of such aids is in principle not compatible with the common interest.
>
> (10 *RCP*: point 161)

It then went on to qualify this blanket disapproval, concluding by illustrating examples 'of ways in which state aids, under certain conditions, could help in implementing positive adjustment policies now being discussed in many quarters'.

On another, related, issue, the adjustment of state monopolies of a commercial character, the Commission was also forthright. Its 1980 competition report said bluntly:

> The changes the Commission considers necessary to complete the final stage of the adjustment of the remaining State monopolies of a commercial character ... pursuant to Article 37 of the EEC Treaty are encountering *increasing* national resistance. This is no doubt natural, since the monopolies in question are those which for various reasons the Member States concerned regard as most important.
>
> (10 *RCP*: 159)

They stressed that delays in providing information applied in particular to the French and Italian manufactured tobacco monopolies.

A further related issue of considerable importance for the shape and functioning of the economic order concerned public undertakings. Here the battle, summarised drastically, could be said to concern whether the member states, to whom the treaties had never sought to dictate a particular system of ownership (see Treaty of Rome Article 222 and Paris Article 83) could nevertheless in effect be prevented from achieving the *policy purposes* that they had had in mind in putting the undertakings into public ownership in the first place. 'Form without substance' was thus the nature of the issue.

The Commission was frank in admitting that, on these issues, its 'action breaks new ground both as regards the objective of the directive and the legal basis chosen' (10 *RCP*: 164).

The year 1981 saw significant developments in a number of key issues and battles. As the Commission itself foresaw (15 *GRA*: 17): 'The discussions that began on how to reform the Community's policies and institutions may prove to be a turning-point in its history.' Some significant contributions to this debate include the Commission's own report to the Council pursuant to the 30 May 1980 mandate; initiatives from the EP, and from the German and Italian governments (the so-called 'Genscher–Colombo proposals'); and a memorandum from France.

But the Commission was equally stark about the background to these initiatives: it spoke of 'the development of the Common Market now at a standstill – and even in some danger of moving backwards'. It was not a happy prospect and the explanation (excuse) that came most readily to hand was the generally unsettled state of international relations, 'the feeling of inability to make any easy headway on the most pressing questions, whether they be political, economic or security matters, has made it even more difficult to decide *which direction to take*' (15 *GRA*: 17, emphasis added).

## Domestic politics and the economic order

Neither did the constraints imposed by domestic politics, always important, offer any help to the beleaguered Community. It badly needed 'windows of opportunity' in terms of the electoral constraints and domestic pressures and agendas of the member states, but at this time such were definitely not available: 'There was little room on the political scenes in the Member States for thoughts about how to revitalise the Community' (15 *GRA*: 18).

In 1981, parliamentary elections were held in six of the 10 members; there were seven changes of government, several requiring lengthy coalition formation negotiations; and ruling parties were voted out in several states. Perhaps nowhere was this more important than in France, where Mitterrand's defeat of Giscard in the presidential elections in May and June, followed by the victory of the left in the national assembly elections, had a number of important consequences for the Community (and for European politics more widely). It ended the close relationship of Giscard and Schmidt. It ushered in a period of 'dash-for-growth'

Keynesianism in one country, accompanied by talk of the 'reconquest of the internal market'. While this was short lived and ended in a decisive U-turn of economic policy in March 1983, and while it was reputed to be a failure and hence held up as a warning of the limitations on freedom of manoeuvre of an economy in the EC, it nevertheless led, on the way, to strains especially within the EMS and with the Germans. Initially however, it had a powerful 'demonstration effect' in *southern* Europe; Pasok was later to win in Greece; in Italy the socialists did well in regional and local elections; on the margin, Spain and Portugal moved in a somewhat similar direction (from dissimilar starting points). Later was to come the 'summit of the Mediterranean socialist five'.

These developments in southern Europe contrasted with the political currents to the north, led by the return of the Conservative Party in the UK in 1979, and followed by other swings to the right. It was, thus, perhaps no wonder that the Commission spoke of the difficulties of deciding 'what direction to take': but that was where the French volte face of 1983 was crucial in making clear the direction to be taken. It was to be the requirements of 'Europe' that would triumph over 'socialism' (Ludlow in Dinan (ed.) 2006: 226, quoting Lacouture 1998).

It became very clear at this time, however, that major battles had been joined over the economic order in the EC. An interesting dialectic was at work. The very existence of the EC had, arguably, sharpened the economic difficulties of the weaker members, and tended to push them into greater protectionism and special deals. The next question to arise was the Community's response to what it had helped to create: would it allow such developments or effectively impede and countermand them? And if it sought to countermand, what would be the effects on its own legitimacy?

Predictably, the answer to this was neither simple nor always consistent. Broadly, protection on the external dimension was used to 'compensate' potential losers from the increasing liberalisation of the internal dimensions. Examples of this latter 'liberal' tendency include the moves over the financial relations between states and public undertakings already mentioned, and also a significant shift in the Commission's approach over the 'general aid' schemes proposed by certain governments. For instance, France's system of low-interest loans for exports could no longer be applied for exports to Greece from the date of the latter's accession, said the Commission (15 *GRA*: 106).

Other aids too were to be modified, or abolished. The new aid code for the steel industry, introduced on 7 August 1981 to replace that of February 1980, tried to insist on the link to 'restructuring' to reduce capacity and restore viability (*OJL* 228, 13 August 1981). There must be a fixed timetable, ending in 1985 at the latest (15 *GRA*: 107; 29 *RCW*: 33). Even this proved not enough to fend off US pressures: its steel producers threatened to file anti-subsidy suits against Community producers and the Department of Commerce on its own initiative in November opened five inquiries into subsidies, including one each into exports from Belgium and France (15 *GRA*: 258; 29 *RCW*: 112). The crisis escalated as the Council, on 8 December 1981, decided to continue the existing *external* measures in 1981 (29 *RCW*: 104). Shipbuilding and textiles were the other main sectors to witness a clear tightening, at least in principle, of aid criteria. These occurred in the Fifth Directive on aid to shipbuilding, adopted by the Council on 28 April 1981 (29 *RCW*: 107; *OJL* 137, 23 May 1981) and in the Commission's Communication to the Council of 27 July on textiles (*Bull. EC* 7/8–1981, points 1.4.1–1.4.9).

The main weapon in the UK's general system of regional aids, the regional development grant (RDG) was another straw in the wind. As the Commission delicately put it, the UK agreed to progressive modification and elimination by 1984 of the operating aid elements 'following protracted discussions' between UK and Commission departments (15 *GRA*: 107). The Commission also opened Article 93(2) procedures against Belgium and the FRG in 1981 in respect of aspects of their regional aid schemes (15 *GRA*: 108). These were prominent examples of a change of mood; but they were frequently countered by indications of the Community endeavouring to act as a 'defensive cartel' in its external trade relations.

The links between the internal policy agenda and the Community's conduct of its external relations were especially clear at this time in regard to relations with the USA and Japan. The Reagan administration's main economic impact arose via high interest rates and the associated appreciation of the dollar continuing from the end of the Carter presidency through much of 1981. Along with these policies, with their predictable effects on US competitiveness internationally, went what the Commission described as 'aggressive assertion of US rights' (15 *GRA*: 258). Frequent shuttling of delegations from both sides during the year (usually led by Davignon or Thorn for the Commission, and by combinations of Messrs Baldridge, Block, Brock and Haig for the USA) pointed up the acuteness of the strains (see also Woolcock 1982).

With Japan too, the story was the familiar one: all the talk was of 'restraint' of Japanese exports; of sensitive sectors and of opening up Japanese markets; of the need for yen appreciation as well as of an enhanced international role for the currency. These themes, already familiar from the 1970s, were to remain the well-worn refrains throughout the 1980s. From a Japanese point of view, however – in terms of those products on which Japan had decided to concentrate via its 'laser-and-cascade' approach – the notion of a *common* market remained obscure, to say the least. A regime of separate, national quotas or VRAs (voluntary restraint agreements) remained the rule in the automotive sector. This was the time also of France's *cause célèbre* of the channelling of imports of all Japanese VCRs through the single customs post at Poitiers.

The situation was otherwise in regard to the renewal of the multifibre arrangement (MFA). Although the process of negotiating the new MFA began formally in December 1980, it was not until the end of 1981 that the negotiations entered a decisive phase, in which, to quote the Council: 'It was clear that the Community was in a particularly delicate position and that the negotiations would be difficult' (29 *RCW*: 107). The overall protocol was agreed by the end of 1981, but subject to the negotiation of satisfactory bilateral agreements with exporting developing countries which were not completed until late 1982. On 23 December, only a week before the existing arrangements finally came to an end, the Council adopted the Regulation on common rules for imports of certain textile products from non-member countries

(Reg. 3589/82; *OJL* 374, 31 December 1982). This agreement, too, was widely regarded as protectionist.

One key issue concerned people's perceptions of the extent and nature of the economic restructuring required in the EC and the capacity for adaptation and change of its component parts. The Commission certainly became loud in its advocacy of the need for re-equilibration of certain national economies. Prominently, it issued stern homilies to Italy and to Belgium (1 and 23 July 1981 respectively) on the policy steps considered necessary. In the Italian case, the main bone of contention was the scheme adopted by the Italian authorities on 27 May for 90-day frozen non-interest-bearing deposits to be lodged in respect of all foreign currency purchases over a 4-month period. Italy had appealed, citing Article 109 EEC as grounds for this.

The Commission's response was distinctly chilly. In its Recommendation of 1 July (*OJL* 189, 11 July 1981) it stated, *inter alia*, that it 'considers nevertheless that the difficulties stem primarily from insufficient control over the domestic economy', citing in particular the need for 'interest rates on public securities, together with the discount rate … set at a level sufficient to maintain market interest': in other words, a tighter monetary policy. The predominant orthodoxy was apparent. The Commission repeated its well-worn warnings about the dangers of 'unilateral action' and 'protectionist chain reactions'. The roots of the problem, it asserted, were poor budgetary control, wage indexation and associated labour market rigidities. It went on to put a figure on the ceiling of desirable public sector borrowing and to suggest changes in the habits both of local and regional authorities and the central bank. A little later (23 September), it nevertheless allowed the Italian authorities to maintain the deposit scheme, subject to certain conditions, with clear time limits (Commission Decision 23 September 1981; 81/803/EEC; *OJL* 296, 15 October 1981: 50).

The Recommendation addressed to Belgium (*OJL* 228, 13 August 1981; 15 *GRA*: 71) also focused on the balance of payments and budgetary situation. Again the Commission put figures on what it deemed desirable budgetary ceilings, indicating also the precise policies that should be emphasised to achieve this; again it focused on wage indexation, citing its communication of 22 July to all member states; again it urged continuation of tight monetary policy.

The European Council, at its Maastricht meeting on 23–24 March 1981, had focused on the issue of wage and salary indexation opining that an 'adjustment', in its euphemism, of such mechanisms must be considered. On 28 July the Commission submitted a paper to the Council of Ministers, suggesting, *inter alia*: the exclusion of certain factors from indexation; delays in and limits on the processes of wage adjustments; a ceiling on indexation where inflation rates were appreciably above the Community average; and foregoing certain indexation adjustments entirely. Once again, the Commission, albeit mainly as an advocate, was playing its role of banging heads together, and trying to achieve a degree of 'best practice' by shaming those whose practices it deemed inadequate; a role not unlike, of course, that of the IMF (15 *GRA*: 72).

It was not surprising in such circumstances that the EMS should come under strain (15 *GRA*: 73). The Commission noted that divergences in economic development were not reduced. Two realignments took place in 1981: on 22 March and 4 October. At least the Commission could report with relief that 'the decisions were consistent with the design of the system, whose flexibility and adaptability they demonstrated' (15 *GRA*: 73).

## The '30 May Mandate' saga

Economic issues had clear political effects in another *cause célèbre* at about this time. The events surrounding the so-called '30 May Mandate' (1980) are instructive both in terms of how the issues came together to be processed and also for how they were handled once that agenda was defined. The importance of the episode went beyond that, however. While major participants were not slow to congratulate themselves and each other on the 'successes' entailed, it was equally clear that one result was to reinforce the UK's relative isolation in the Community; to reinforce the impression already given by the EMS saga that the UK was essentially arguing from the sidelines, more of an irritant to processes and less central to the development of the Community system: or, to put it another way, that thoughts of a trilateral *directoire* of France, the FRG and the UK were a delusion and aberrant and, consequently, a reversion to seeing the bilateral Franco-German relationship as the core of the Community and the locomotive of further progress.

We look first at the events themselves, before moving on to some analysis of them. The problems of economic convergence and of the British contribution to the Community budget dominated the first European Council meeting of 1980 – at Luxembourg, 27–8 April (14 *GRA*: 28). The Council of Ministers on 29–30 May reached agreement in principle on the issue of the UK's contribution to the budget. The Commission, having hyperbolised this as 'the outstanding event of 1980'(!), then added more soberly that, in a series of decisions, 'the Council produced a *temporary, pragmatic* solution to the problem – and gave the Commission a mandate to find a more satisfactory solution from 1982 onwards' (14 *GRA*: 59, emphasis added). Thus what was agreed was, first, a 2-year arrangement, and second, the hope of long-term CAP and budgetary reform.

The essence of the problem lay in the size of the UK's *net*, rather than, as previously addressed, its *gross* contribution to the budget, which in turn reflected its agricultural structures, its relative lack of receipts under the then existing system, its status as an oil exporter and the extent to which its per capita income and balance of payments were *not* likely to be such as to trigger the recompense mechanisms agreed under the earlier (Dublin) formulae. At all events, most observers are agreed on the saliency and centrality of the issue. Shackleton goes so far as to say: 'The attempt to rectify this situation dominated the Community agenda in the first years of the 1980s until the Fontainebleau Summit in 1984' (Shackleton 1990: 3).

The two aspects, reduction of net contribution and supplementary help to reduce regional disparities (by increasing UK receipts), were dealt with in two proposals from the Commission, sent to the Council of Ministers on 12 June (*OJC* 169, 9 July 1980; *OJC* 171, 11 July 1980); these were adopted on 27 October (*OJL* 284, 29 October 1980). The temporary solution was expected to reduce the UK's net contribution by about two-thirds in 1980 and in 1981. There was also a formula for apportioning the financing of any excess over these anticipated sums (figures and formula in 14 *GRA*: 60). From 1982 onwards, the Community pledged itself to resolve the problem by means of 'structural changes', and this formed part of the Council's charge to the Commission to produce, by the end of June 1981, a study of the development of Community policies aimed at preventing a recurrence of such 'unacceptable situations for any Member State' (14 *GRA*: 60).

In truth, the going had been far from smooth, and these issues were firmly enmeshed with others. In the Commission's own words:

> After *long and difficult* negotiations which began early in March (1980), the Council, at its 28–30 May meeting, reached agreement on the common agricultural prices, on the basis of a *much more general compromise* which also included decisions on agricultural structures, the market in sheepmeat, fisheries policy and the question of the UK's contribution to the Community budget.
>
> (14 *GRA*: 164, emphasis added)

Here lies the main point. For all the announcements about durable solutions and firm deadlines for agreement across a defined package of issues, what actually happened was much messier, cobbled together and more akin to putting a patch on a boil. Thus, while the UK at the London European Council of 26–27 November 1981 continued to demand a durable solution to the problem, throughout 1982 the contentions remained. In May 1982 the Falklands crisis preoccupied the main actors; little progress was made. As the Commission put it:

> [S]everal variants of a transitional budgetary mechanism in favour of the UK were examined ... the Foreign Ministers ... meeting on 25–26 October 1982 produced an arrangement for 1982 whereby, pending agreement on a multiannual plan, the old *ad hoc* solution would again apply.
>
> (16 *GRA*: 52)

These disputes meant that 'other Community business had to be pushed aside' (Simonian 1985: 292); once again, however, it appeared that resolution depended on French and German views above all. Perhaps fortunately for the UK, Schmidt felt under pressure not to let these problems fester, and to try to present a united Community image in the face of a threatening international configuration of renewed cold war; in Simonian's words: 'Once again, in spite of its economic predominance and the development of its political standing, the Federal Republic felt more exposed than most of its European partners to wider instabilities in international relations' (Simonian 1985: 293).

One telling aspect of the problem had concerned linkage: whether or not the budget issues should be considered in isolation or a clear link established with the contentious issues of the CAP. States were not, however, consistent in their positions on this. In 1980 the UK had begun by arguing for separating out the budget, the French for linkage (Parfitt 1980a, 1980b; Simonian 1985: 293). Two years later, the British espoused linkage between budgetary contributions and agreeing to agricultural prices in the 1982 round. 'Unfortunately, in neither case were the British entirely successful. The incidents offer an illustration of a deeper misguidedness that has often marred every British Government's European negotiating strategy since Heath' (Simonian 1985: 293). Simonian appears correct that the agreement was 'a traditional package deal, involving British concessions to France over lamb and farm prices, and to Germany on fishing, in return for their accord over the budget' (Simonian 1985: 293).

The other notable sources of strain between the UK, on the one hand, and the FRG and France in particular, on the other, were energy and fisheries. In the aftermath of the second oil shock, the UK failed to signal a willingness to be an emergency energy provider to the Community at large. Agreement on a common fisheries policy had been expected by the end of 1980, but continued to be a bone of contention also:

> Four years after [Community members] extended their fishing zones to 200 miles, their efforts to develop a CFP to meet this new situation has still not met with success. The Council remained divided on essential points such as conditions of access to fishing zones and its allocation among the member states of the Community's catch quotas.
>
> (14 *GRA*: 182)

There had been progress in principle on important matters, including 'technical conservation measures' – net mesh sizes, no-fishing zones and so on. The problems of fisheries were (are) not least about the viability and effectiveness of measures proposed, and the trust reposed in those who are to police for compliance (a pervasive Community issue to which we shall return in other contexts). On this last point, the Commission's velvet phrases scarcely concealed the problems:

> On 28 October the Council agreed *in principle* on Community rules for the supervision of fishing *by vessels of Member States*. The rules establish common procedures for *inspection by the national authorities* of fishing vessels both at sea and in port and supervision of *landings of species for which a TAC (total allowable catch) has been fixed.*
>
> (14 *GRA*: 183, emphasis added)

Here, too, the UK felt particularly threatened: not only had the 200-mile zone changed the whole picture and not only were the structures of its industry and their interests substantially different from those of several other member states, but British attempts to 'do something' in the late 1970s to counteract the new forces at work ran foul of the CJEC. On 10 July 1980 the Court ruled that the UK had failed in its treaty obligations in respect of three national measures to conserve fish stocks (14 *GRA*: 183, 326; Case 32/79 *Commission* v. *UK*).

Once again, as with the other disputes, much determined sounding noise resulted in little agreement. In 1982, the Commission reported: 'Long and difficult negotiations ended with the failure of the efforts to establish a new CFP' (16 *GRA*: 179). This time, all member states except Denmark had been prepared to agree to a set of Commission proposals on access, TACs and quotas and conservation: these thus failed to be adopted before the expiry date of the 1972 'exceptional' fishing arrangements. Proclaimed success on 25 January 1983 was immediately qualified. The agreement on 'Blue Europe', after 6 years of negotiations, 'was having some difficulty in settling down' (17 *GRA*: 193). Nevertheless, and despite vital gaps in the policy only agreed later (e.g. over North Sea herring), the Council of Ministers was at pains to point out the 'very particular importance' of achieving an agreement valid for 10 years, over access to fishing zones and allocation of resources (31 *RCW*: 217).

However, the problems of agreement over the CAP in relation to the '30 May Mandate' were no less and were to lead to the famous British attempt to use its veto over price fixing, overruled by other member states on the ground, essentially, that the veto could only be used over new policy proposals, not over timetabled deadlines which members were legally bound to meet. The Council was laconic:

> At the meeting on 10 and 11 May 1982 nine delegations were able to agree Finally the decisions ... were adopted ... on 17 and 18 May 1982, using the (qualified majority) voting procedure provided for in Article 43. This was an important event since it was the first time that the decisions on prices were not adopted unanimously.
>
> (30 *RCW*: 175)

The dissenters were Denmark, Greece and the UK.

Again, the background was important. The negotiations, which resulted in substantial price increases, followed 3 years of decline in real farm incomes, according to the Commission (16 *GRA*: 159). The average increase, expressed in national currencies, amounted for the Community as a whole to 12.2%; in European currency units (ECUs) 10.4% (30 *RCW*: 175; 16 *GRA*: 160). Again, monetary turbulence resulted in several changes to MCA arrangements. Perhaps most important was again an 'exogenous' factor. The dollar surge, whatever its effects in reducing the gap between world (dollar-denominated) prices and Community prices, meant that 'the CAP, especially its export refunds, was repeatedly the target of sharp criticism from a number of non-Community countries, among them the United States' and the invocation on several occasions of GATT dispute settlement procedures (16 *GRA*: 156).

In formulating the agenda: 'The Commission decided against a purely budgetary approach, preferring to undertake an overall review centred on three elements; revitalization of the common policies, reform of agricultural policy and budgetary matters' (15 *GRA*: 24). On 24 June 1981, it adopted its report and presented it to the European Council (*Bull. Supp.* 1/81 EC). Significantly, in his covering letter to the heads of state and government, Commission President Gaston Thorn proposed to invoke the mechanism of a 'wise men' committee: 'I doubt if cohesion would survive the complexity of normal procedures A better solution ... would be ... to refer the report ... to a select group of individuals chaired by a member of the Council' (*Bull. Supp.* 1/81: 22). The group should report back by the end of 1981, its findings should be examined in detail at an extraordinary extended meeting of the General Affairs Council, 'with an eye to the first European Council in 1982'.

This was not quite what happened. Instead, the London European Council of 26–7 November 1981 considered the Commission's May Mandate report and supporting documents direct (*Bull. EC* 11–1981: 7). The European Council instructed the foreign ministers to meet before the end of the year to discuss still unresolved issues. At the end of the European Council meeting, Prime Minister Thatcher's statement as president was revealing:

> We had a very thorough discussion of all three chapters [common policies; CAP changes; temporary budgetary correction] agreeing at the outset that agreement on any one chapter ... *would depend upon agreement on the other chapters.* We went through it ... *section by section, in a detailed way which I have never seen in the European Council before.*
> 
> (*Bull. EC* 11–1981: 7, emphasis added)

These revealing comments perhaps indicate why no agreement was forthcoming; they also illustrate well a characterisation by former UK Prime Minister Callaghan and a theme in Bulmer's analysis of the Council: 'strong on discussion, not so strong on decisions' (Bulmer and Wessels 1987: 100).

Four areas of disagreement were identified – milk, agricultural expenditure guidelines, Mediterranean agriculture and the budget problem itself – and it was at length agreed that a special meeting of foreign ministers should be convened. If this route did not work, the problems 'would have to be referred to the next Council' (*Bull. EC* 11–1981: 7). Thatcher concluded: 'It was therefore a very, very busy European Council ... The Heads of State or Government [were] very, very much aware that we were perhaps negotiating in detail on matters which would normally have been left to the specialist Councils' (*Bull. EC* 11–1981: 8).

The vital factor was that exogenous events had removed the pressure from the Community. The 'surprising developments' of 1980 and even more of 1981 were the radical alteration in the agricultural situation (temporary, to be sure) involving higher world food prices (as the dollar rose) and thus less export restitutions from Community funds, thus relieving the pressure on the Community's budgetary ceilings. This took the pressure off the Community to look beyond its nose. Further, the unexpectedly favourable outcome for the UK of the budgetary refunds took the edge off the UK's crusade. Thus, 'there was little progress towards the fundamental structural changes envisaged in the Mandate' (Denton et al. 1983: i). Three years of virtually continuous negotiation had got almost nowhere; had, at best, produced a pause for breath.

A paper analysing how this situation came about, and how it looked in September 1982, from the pen of Pauline Neville-Jones, the former chef de cabinet to Budget Commissioner Christopher Tugendhat, writing in a personal capacity, appeared shortly afterwards. It is instructive and will detain us for a little. Neville-Jones began bleakly: 'It cannot be disguised that the promise held out by the Commission's report on the Mandate has been largely vitiated' (Neville-Jones in Denton et al. 1983: 98). The very terms of the mandate had created certain problems. They committed the Commission to maintain the 'principles' of policy, especially of the CAP and its common financing. This set 'strict limits on the degree of radicalism which could result' (Denton et al. 1983: 98). Second was the issue of the relationship between structural changes of policy and the prevention of the 'unacceptable (budgetary) situations'. Was budgetary rectification to be limited to what might be brought about by *new* Community policies, which would in any case have to be 'justifiable and politically acceptable in their own right' (Denton et al. 1983: 98) or should there be budgetary rectification over and above this? Member states differed sharply on this issue and also on that of the technique to be espoused for any 'rectification'.

A further limitation had lain in the antipathy of several member states (including the UK) to any increase in the Community's revenue, which in practice meant the 1% limit on the VAT base. With no revenue enhancement, any 'solution' would have to be achieved entirely on the expenditure side. Thus constrained both to maintain policy 'principles' *and* not to increase revenue, 'the Commission was limited ... to [solutions] based on the idea of *ex post facto* correction of the results of the interaction of the revenue and expenditure sides of the budget' (Denton et al. 1983: 99); this did not leave it much room for manoeuvre.

Although the 'individuality' of the 30 May Mandate agenda was now looking fictional, obeisance continued to be made to it. The Commission described the preliminary draft budget for 1983 as 'the first step towards achievement of the objectives of the mandate of 30 May' (16 *GRA*: 44), while at the same time emphasising that it 'took into account the constraints on public expenditure at all levels'. Most striking was that the Commission proposed very substantial increases in the non-compulsory expenditure (NCE) heads (33.19% in commitments, 24.6% in payments, over 1982), which the Council savaged (to only 6.6% and 8.18% respectively). The by now familiar ritual ensured that the EP, at its first reading in October, 'restored virtually all the appropriations entered by the Commission' (16 *GRA*: 47) and proclaimed that once again there were differences of opinion as regards calculation of the base for NCE for 1983. Next, the Council made slight concessions at its second reading but 'did not accept any of Parliament's proposed modifications to compulsory expenditure' (16 *GRA*: 47). Parliament at its second reading restored certain of the amendments; the Council finally accepted these and on 21 December the EP president declared the 1983 budget adopted. It was no surprise that the Commission should describe the budgetary procedure as a 'battlefield between the two arms of the budgetary authority – the Council and Parliament' or that the dispute over the CE/NCE breakdown should finally have gone to the Court (16 *GRA*: 21). Nevertheless, the adoption of the 1983 draft budget approved by both Council and EP was the first time that this had happened in 5 years, even if 'against this positive achievement' had to be set the rejection of the draft supplementary and amending budget No. 1/82, which concerned the UK and FRG (30 *RCW*: 239).

There were arguments first of all about compensation mechanisms and about the length of time for which they should apply. The UK had originally argued for a

7-year period, on the grounds that only something durable could justify the enormous effort and time put into negotiation. The Commission originally favoured a period of 4 to 5 years. Most other member states, however, were unwilling to agree to any time period until two other problems had been resolved: first, that of the 'excessive' rebates which the UK had received, over and above what Commission figures had suggested, in 1981 and 1982 on the basis of the 30 May 1980 agreement (the so-called *trop payé* problem); and, second, the issue of progressive reduction in the amount of compensation *henceforth* to be paid to the UK ('degressivity').

The two became linked by the UK's partners. Once they decided that it would be difficult, if not impossible, politically and/or legally to 'claw back' cash already paid to the UK, they set out to adjust the future flow of resources to achieve a similar result. Degressivity was discussed by ministers, but the *trop payé* issue, although identified and an irksome irritant, was not openly on the table. In a soured negotiating atmosphere, the Commission was unable to find any basis for compromise satisfactory to all (see Neville-Jones in Denton et al. 1983: 109–12; Denton 1984: *passim*). It made a final effort to do so, at the Brussels Summit of 29–30 March 1982, but this was rejected by the French.

More exogenous factors promptly intruded: the Falklands War and the replacement of Carrington by Pym as British foreign secretary, 'inevitably unfamiliar with the details of the negotiations' (Denton et al. 1983: 113). A final bone of contention could no longer be avoided: discussion of the actual figures (rather than mechanisms and duration). This occurred in late April and predictably revealed a large gap between UK notions and those of its partners, a gap not remotely bridged by the foreign ministers on 8–9 May. The last straw was what was happening simultaneously in the annual farm price negotiations. Here agriculture ministers, backed powerfully on the streets by protesting farmers, took advantage of the 'windfall' resulting from dollar appreciation, to propose substantial price increases. The UK thought (or, rather, hoped) that it could resist here, making its agreement to the agricultural prices dependent on a satisfactory budget settlement. The Commission was now completely boxed in, and finally did on 16 May 1982 what it had hitherto resisted – it abandoned the notion of a durable pluri-annual settlement and made a budget proposal confined to 1 year only.

The crucial meetings at which everything eventually 'unravelled' were the foreign ministers council of 17 May 1982 and the agriculture council the following day. Successive headlines of the *Europe Daily Bulletin* read:

| | |
|---|---|
| 17–18 May | Falklands, budget, agricultural prices: A terrible 'package' |
| 19 May | Falklands, budget, agricultural prices: A package which exploded |
| 20 May | Majority vote: Ignorance of the Law not admissible? |

In a way, this said it all. The Commission had abandoned any hope of getting a pluri-annual or robust budgetary arrangement for the UK. Already Schmidt and Mitterrand (having met on 15–16 May in Hamburg) had rejected any link between the budget regulation and fixing the agricultural prices (*EDB* 3373, 17–18 May 1982: 3). The Commission instead fell back on the last sentence of the mandate terms, which had rather feebly said that, failing agreement, 'the Commission will make proposals along the lines of the 1980 and 1981 solution and the Council will act accordingly'.

The Commission's proposal was a highly 'safe' one from its point of view – i.e. one that it knew would be acceptable to most member states. It signalled, however, a clear retreat: that 'The Commission ceased to hold the ring' (Denton et al. 1983: 113). It ceased to be in charge of events. Even on the thus minimal proposal, negotiations between the foreign ministers failed to achieve anything on 17 May.

On 19 May and in retrospect, many commentaries were damning. The consensus was that not only should the extension of sanctions against Argentina over the Falklands never have got mixed up with budget arguments, but there should never have been a sanctions time limit in the first place: conformity by Argentina with international law alone ought to bring an end to sanctions. Further, the pathetic extension of only 7 days would push the UK further down the military path and it dramatised the EC's lack of resolve. Worse still was Italy's breaking of ranks, on the basis of a 'blood relationship', 'as if this could justify violation of international law' (*EDB* 3374, 19 May 1982: 1).

The final straw was the decision over agricultural prices on 18 May. On this, as we have seen, for the first time in the Community's history, the Council adopted the agricultural price fixing and related decisions by majority vote (Denmark, Greece and the UK refusing to participate). The other states did this by voting one after the other for the 69 regulations required. This procedure was adopted because only regulations (and not an overall consensus 'package' needing unanimity) could be voted by majority approval and thus be held legally valid.

The UK invoked the 'Luxembourg compromise' on the grounds of vital national interests. Denmark and Greece considered that this invocation should cause the Council not to vote. The other member states refused to become embroiled in any discussion of the validity or interpretation of the 'Luxembourg compromise': their argument was that the Council was duty bound to fix the agricultural prices and must do so. The Netherlands went further, declaring that it had always been opposed to the Luxembourg compromise (despite Luns' role in working out the wording!). Article 43 EEC was the relevant basis and it permitted majority decisions.

The arithmetic was precise. The required majority at the time was 45 votes out of 63: the seven states that participated in the vote mustered exactly those 45 votes. The 'credit' for this move was attributed to 'the determination of the Belgian presidency supported by the … Commission' (*EDB* 3374, 19 May 1982: 6).

The British response was to try to avoid raising the dramatic temperature, while retaining all options to call the outcome into question. Both Peter Walker and Mrs Thatcher took this line, Walker referring to a new situation which the British government would have to think about, and Thatcher calling it 'unprecedented'. While the French (Edith Cresson) maintained that these were annual decisions required by the treaties, Walker held that it violated all the conventions and practices since 1966; and that there was no obligation to adopt agricultural prices by a certain date (*EDB* 3374, 19 May 1982: 6).

Thus the linkage that had been created between the various issues produced a great deal of bad blood. The telephones had been running hot between the Italians over Argentine sanctions, but to no avail: Craxi would not budge and the Italians, along with Denmark and Ireland, thus limited themselves to 'national measures' based on Article 224 EEC (*EDB* 3374, 19 May 1982: 5).

A few days later (24 May) a temporary budget settlement for 1982 was voted, thus fulfilling the minimum commitment to the UK. This marked not so much the end as merely a stage, in a process that continued in fits and starts until the Fontainebleau Summit of June 1984. Nevertheless, it is worth pausing at this point to examine the rival interpretations of events.

One strand is the pressure on public expenditure generally that was apparent. But against this went the temporary *reduction* of pressure on the agricultural portion of the EC's own budget. It was – and is – argued that only crisis forces the Community not just *to* the water, but to drink and that the removal of the absolute imperative to agree was fatal. But there was a further dimension too. The whole episode revealed no agreement on any guidelines and 'this in turn reflected the underlying lack of consensus on long term objectives' (Neville-Jones in Denton et al. 1983: 115) on what kind of Community the member states wished to see. She concluded that long-term budgetary arrangements would only be agreed, or make sense 'if ... set in a wider agreement about the way forward' for the Community (Denton et al. 1983: 116). Altogether it had not been an edifying sight, but it was one that lent point to further attempts at institutional and constitutional reform afoot at about the same time, to which we must now turn.

## The Genscher–Colombo Plan

It was at the London European Council meeting of 26–7 November 1981 that the joint Italian–German initiative known as the Genscher–Colombo plan for an act of European Union came onto the agenda at the highest level. Its concerns, not surprisingly given the flow of events that we have discussed, were very closely related: they were principally policy development, institutional improvement and tidying up the relationship between the EC *stricto sensu* and EPC.

Earlier in November 1981, Genscher and Colombo had presented their draft European Act and draft statement on European integration to the EP. *EDB*'s federalist editorial preview (18 November) declared, 'It's weak, but it's there' (*EDB* 3251, 18 November 1981: 1). It was deemed to be the necessary 'political' counterpart of the 'economic' impetus of the 30 May Mandate. Colombo stressed the need for common policies in all the important sectors, as well as development of European Political Cooperation (EPC), declared to be a success but in need of strengthening at a time of instability. The Italian government was convinced, said Colombo in his letter to other governments, that European union could not be achieved on the basis of the founding treaties alone or of the *acquis communautaire*. There were two documents. First was the 'European Act', a politically binding declaration containing both concrete objectives and various institutional measures. Second was the 'Declaration on the themes of economic integration'.

Interestingly, it appears that the two states had worked more or less independently of each other, but produced proposals with so much in common that it was possible to pool their efforts (*EDB* 3244, 6 November 1981: 3). Genscher put his proposals to the EP on 9 November.

In presenting the documents on 17 November, Colombo stressed that no progress had been made since 1972; the treaties alone seemed insufficient. The initiative was fairly well received except for Denmark, which characteristically entered a reserve straightaway (*EDB* 3251, 18 November 1981: 1). Right through this phase, the Genscher–Colombo initiative was 'in parallel' with ongoing Mandate discussions and probably seen by its authors as a way of raising everyone's eyes above immediate intractables.

But theirs was not the only handiwork. Indeed, part of what marked out 1980–1 on the institutional front as 'something of a coincidence in the history of federalism and European Union' (Burgess 1989: 120) was that this point marked 'both the beginning of a new federalist initiative by Altiero Spinelli in June 1980 and the culmination of a series of reports and debates emanating from [the EP] during 1974–81' (Burgess 1989: 120).

It is important to stress the *varied* sources of pressure that appeared for change. To be sure, the results, as we shall see later in our consideration of the Single European Act (SEA) and the Single European Market (SEM) proposals, were on the surface fairly modest. But such is (was) the force of inertia in the EC that it is probable that only sustained and multiple pressures (perhaps amounting to an 'ambush' of the opponents) could produce even that degree of change.

At least four kinds of pressure may be identified. One was the access of confidence, and the expectations, produced by direct elections to the EP. A second was that institutional issues had, as we have seen, got swept up with others in the '30 May Mandate' deliberations, and thus thrust themselves firmly onto the agenda of Council and Commission, and of Council–Commission dialogue, in a very central way. A third pressure came from particular governments – in this case led by the German and Italian, in the form of the Genscher–Colombo proposals. Fourth was the continued battering of Spinelli, with his rival and much more 'federalist' schemes.

Direct elections to the EP created one source of pressure, as we have seen also in relation to the budget. Again, the EP was not acting in a void: to bolster its new found sense of its own legitimacy, it could draw on earlier EP work, going back several years to the 1974 Kirk Report. Earlier, it had been thought prudent to 'go slow' on proposals to enhance the EP's powers, lest states take fright and further postpone direct elections. Now that trap was sprung. (See Kirk-Reay Report 1978; Cardozo and Corbett in Lodge 1986a: 19; earlier versions: May 1974 draft, PE, 37.065; first draft resolution to Political Affairs Committee (PAC), PE, 44.076, March 1976; *Journal of European Integration* 1983.)

The Kirk-Reay Report showed its worth following the establishment in October 1979 by the EP's Political Affairs Committee of a new subcommittee on institutional problems. No fewer than eight reports followed on aspects of inter-institutional relations. (See Palmer 1983: 187–9; Bieber 1984: 283–304; Cardozo and Corbett in

Lodge 1986a: 19–22; Burgess 1989: 121.) The first of these to be debated was the Rey Report in April 1980. Five others were debated and approved in the major EP debate on institutional issues in July 1981. The seventh (Antoniozzi) was debated in December 1981 and the eighth (Blumenfeld) in February 1982.

Bieber claims that for once it is fairly easy to discern the genealogy of the ideas – the connection between influence (opinion of the EP) and action (final text of a decision of the Council). (See, especially, Palmer 1983: 192–3, which lists the 'successful' EP proposals, i.e. those accepted by the Council by February 1983; but see also Bieber 1984: 284; Burgess 1989: 121.)

Certain related initiatives of a more daring kind were less successful at the time, in particular those concerned with security aspects of 'foreign policy'. Nevertheless, the markers were put down at around this time, following the Klepsch Report, adopted by the EP in June 1978, which had been concerned with cooperation in European arms procurement (1979; EP Document 83–78), and in December 1980 the Commission transmitted to the EP the interim report by David Greenwood of Aberdeen University, on issues involved in promoting cooperation in defence technology by western European countries (PE, 71/650/Ann.II, cited in Palmer 1983: 194–5). These were thought too sensitive to produce action immediately, as they dealt with areas where Danish, Irish and other raw nerves might be touched.

As to the second source of pressure, that resulting from the 30 May Mandate, little needs to be added to our earlier discussion. What Burgess has described as a sense of the Community's 'impotence', and of its processes as an intergovernmental 'war of attrition' (Burgess 1989: 123) meant that it was certain that the machinery itself should come under increasingly critical scrutiny. Although the Commission's Mandate report to Council on 24 June 1981 read like a shopping list, Gaston Thorn was keen to extend the debate. In the months that followed, the Commission's involvement with the EP deepened: it was one classic instance of the 'alliance' of Commission and EP to goad the Council into some kind of action. The 'shopping list' items were addressed in such documents as those on the Mediterranean programmes and the EC policy for industry as required by the Mandate (e.g. COM (81) 637, 638, 639; 23 October to 3 November 1981); but the Commission also chose to latch on to another opportunity, to address inter-institutional issues. The opportunity was the EP's debate in February on the Commission's programme for the year, when the Commission undertook to 'produce a comprehensive paper on inter-institutional relations' of which it said pointedly: 'The Commission regards this paper as a logical addition to its report on the May Mandate' (COM (81) 581, October 1981: 1). Equally, it declared openly that the paper 'echoes the institutional debate held in Parliament last July'.

In particular, what was to become a major issue emerged clearly: to stay *within* the existing treaties or to amend them? The Commission said that the time was ripe for it to present its views of 'possible developments outside the framework of the present Treaties'. It rehearsed priorities by now familiar: 'restoration' of the founding fathers' notion of institutional balance, majority voting in Council, and yet a bigger role for the EP. It also spoke of 'citizen appeal' (COM (81) 581: 2) in a clear anticipation of the Adonnino 'citizens' Europe' initiative.

The battle for elbow room in the inter-institutional warfare was, as always, a sensitive one. It was presented as essentially zero sum: expansion of someone's competences must imply diminution of someone else's. Here the Commission was treading on delicate ground; and as if this were not enough, it is once again literally visible in the document, where (*inter alia*) a section of the sensitive paragraph 13 was redrafted: the changed typeface and 'paste-in' marks are clear. The final version of the delicate compromise reads:

> While it is accordingly keen that Parliament should engage in moves of its own, and fully intends to give these every possible support ... the Commission feels it must also state forthrightly that Parliamentary participation in the actual decision-making process cannot be other than at the expense of the Council's quasimonopoly of this.
>
> (COM (81) 581 final: 8)

It suggested as an initial step an 'extension of the conciliation procedure'. It would be interesting to be able to compare this final version, for public consumption with what it superseded.

The Commission acknowledged that the (1975) conciliation procedure had not satisfied the EP (COM (81) 581: 11). It also signalled that it had 'received and understood' the meaning of the EP's recent changes to its rules of procedure, this time to facilitate conciliation between *Commission* and EP. All of this was within the framework of the treaties as they then stood. But the Commission finally allowed itself a glimpse above the clouds in section IV, 'Beyond the Treaties'.

Here, describing European Union as a 'dynamic process', it said 'the basis for this could be a new Treaty' and referred to the earlier Tindemans' genealogy, to Genscher's ideas and the FRG proposal for the adoption of a 'European Act' to cover the EC, political cooperation and the European Council. This, of course, is exactly what the SEA was later to do. Finally, the Commission endorsed the EP's desire to draft a new treaty itself (COM (81) 581: 16–17). It sought to add to the EP's legitimacy and sap that of the Council, by adding, 'European Union is not a matter for the member states' governments alone ... The Commission feels sure that Parliament, as the voice of the spirit of Europe, will do all in its power' (COM (81) 581: 17).

The third source of pressure, as we have seen, was from Genscher and Colombo, and more widely from the German and Italian governments. Again, the question of what motivated them is of interest and while a full discussion cannot be given here (see Weiler 1983: 129–53; Bulmer and Paterson 1987: esp. 134–5; Pryce 1987: esp. Ch. 8), some of the pertinent considerations seem to have been the following.

Genscher launched the plan in public on 6 January 1981 at the FDP's Stuttgart Congress. Its first draft seems to have been made inside the German foreign ministry. But it is not clear whether Genscher 'was responding to governmental or party cues' (Bulmer and Paterson 1987: 134) as there were pressures inside the party to take such a stand, without which it might 'have continued to be dormant within the *Auswärtiges Amt*' (Bulmer and Paterson 1987: 135). Be that as it may, one of his most senior officials, Von Niels Hansen, head of the planning staff, produced his own exegesis of the motives (Hansen 1981: 141–8). This laid greatest stress on the wider global, not only the purely local, gloom: the 'second cold war' and renewed superpower tension (Bonvicini in Pryce 1987: esp. 176). Yet it is probable that domestic political reasons were also crucial: Genscher's need both to assert his position within the party and also to distance himself from Schmidt's SPD (visibly cooling over the EC), from which the FDP was to break at the end of 1982. Indeed, some of the main obstacles to the plan's more ambitious aspects were in the SPD-led finance ministry, where general irritation over budgetary demands was further fuelled by particular annoyance at French economic policies as 1981 and 1982 progressed.

Genscher's next move, however, was to ventilate the idea further in a speech in Rome on 21 January. Support was immediately forthcoming: Italian Foreign Minister Emilio Colombo expressed his readiness to take the idea further. Collaboration was not smooth, with the Germans pressing for a legally binding treaty, while the Italians preferred a looser arrangement. Next came content, where the Italians stressed deepening and strengthening internal cohesion and thus the enhancement of the EC's external profile. The problem from a German point of view was that economic and other policy cohesion had an expensive ring to it; Schmidt was disenchanted and Genscher had little support (Bonvicini in Pryce 1987: 177–8). Despite its lukewarm reception at the London European Council on 26 November, it achieved one main result: the agreement of the foreign ministers, on 4 January 1982, to set up a high-level officials' group to discuss the proposal. One more source of pressure, and commitment to consider change, was in place.

The fourth was the irrepressible Altiero Spinelli, his activities not confined to the EP, but, as we have seen, moving out into what was called the 'Crocodile Initiative' (see Cardozo and Corbett in Lodge 1986a: 15–46). Prophetically, if also improbably, as it seemed at the time, Spinelli had asserted the potential of the EP in a 'constituent' role. Back in 1977–8, he had written: 'if the final draft is accepted by a massive majority in the Assembly [EP], it will arrive at the national Parliaments for the final ratification with a political force behind it which no diplomatic intergovernmental conference could provide' (Spinelli 1978: 88; also quoted in Lodge 1986a: 23). He had been a Commissioner, he was a national parliamentarian when he wrote this and he became an MEP: a useful series of vantage points, as well as building blocks for alliances.

Indeed, as with other famous figures, he cannot be accused of concealing his thoughts from his critics. The 1978 discussion is a fair prospectus and came after several years of trying to make 'Monnet's Europe' work as a Commissioner. Spinelli's initiative marked the sharpest challenge to that legacy; it also threw into high and unambiguous relief the issues at stake.

The challenge and the issues have been well discussed by Burgess (Burgess 1989: esp. 43–60). The 'Monnet model' had had the merit that in its day it had achieved acceptance, including, crucially, that of national governments. Its demerit was that it remained at their mercy, as had been graphically shown in the Luxembourg crisis of 1965–6. Its key 'merit' of having a quasi-constitutional status was also a key demerit: to alter it meant getting not merely agreement to go back to the drawing board, but also agreement on what was to replace, or supplement or complement, the status quo. It was a tall order, but it was a challenge that Spinelli was willing to take on, goaded by his conviction that 'Monnet has the great merit of having built Europe and the great responsibility to have built it badly' (Spinelli interview; Burgess 1989: 55–6).

If these, then, were the main sources of pressure for change, two issues rapidly became apparent. First, the sources of change did not point in the same direction: would what emerged be simply some kind of patchwork quilt or would it have any coherence and logic? Second, which forces would prove to be the key promoters and which the key resisters of change? Once again, this debate was a hardy perennial: there were apparent 'resolutions' of it and agreements, but each time they presaged further salvoes and further skirmishes around the never resolved questions concerning the processes, the modalities, the functional scope and the 'destination'.

What, then, did 'Genscher–Colombo' propose? Their draft European Act was presented as another stage on the way to European Union. The contents of the draft Act were in most respects hardly radical (see later: text in Ferri 1982: 490–9). But it proposed that the 'Heads of State and Government shall subject this "European Act" to a general review five years after its signing with a view to incorporating the progress achieved in European unification in a Treaty on the EUROPEAN UNION'. The reader who is thinking ahead may reflect that what was eventually agreed in 1986, ratified in 1987, was entitled the Single European Act; and that some 5 years later the states were engaged in the battle over ratification of a Treaty on European Union. Some will be impressed at the 'perfect foresight' – albeit with delays – that this might be thought to imply. Others will note, more agnostically, that 'Maastricht' was the result of accident as well as (more than?) design. Some evidence on these rival evaluations of the role of 'design' and of 'contingency' will be presented in later chapters. For the moment, the remarkable coincidence at least deserves to be noted.

The proposals included a strengthening and development of the EC to include cultural cooperation, a juridical union and a 'legal judicial area' (echoes of Giscard's éspace juridique?) and political cooperation. It sought to spell out more clearly the role of the European Council. It spoke of increased powers for the EP, but in practice these were very modest. It discussed the modification of voting procedures in the Council: again it was modest.

The 'Act' was laid before the London European Council of 26–27 November 1981, which received it 'with satisfaction', i.e. without warmth (Bull. EC 12–1981). The Council handed the somewhat unwanted gift on to the Council of foreign ministers to consider and report back. Ostensibly it appeared to be on the way to a quiet burial, rather as with earlier proposals. But before the watering-down process that produced the Stuttgart 'Solemn Declaration' was complete, others were to have their say.

Certainly, no love was lost between the main protagonists over these proposals: Spinelli thought the Genscher–Colombo proposals 'futile' (Burgess 1989: 131). Mauro Ferri, chairman of the EP's Institutional Affairs Committee, was also categorical in his view of the gulf separating the EP's efforts from the Genscher–Colombo initiative: the latter was 'part of a different philosophy: that of "small steps" to be taken by the governments' (*DEP* No. 1 289/261, 14 October 1982).

The EP debate of 14 October 1982 was a particularly memorable one: the occasion was debate of the interim report by Lambert Croux on behalf of the Political Affairs Committee, on the Genscher–Colombo draft European Act. Colombo (an ex-president of the EP) and Genscher themselves addressed the EP. Croux himself was conciliatory, claiming to see 'no contradiction' between the draft European Act and the EP's own longer term objectives (*DEP* No. 1 289/236, 14 October 1982). Colombo in reply argued that: 'History has taught us that European Union cannot be attained by moving too fast or trying to force the pace.' Genscher expressed 'the hope that we can count on your support' (*DEP* No. 1 289/237 and 242, 14 October 1982), adding that European unification had always been crucial for Kohl, now the new German chancellor. But its authors had 'deliberately restricted the draft Act to proposals on which we are convinced that the Member States can now reach a consensus' (*DEP* No. 1 289/246, 14 October 1982).

For the Commission, Frans Andriessen did not disguise the watering-down process that had already taken place. 'In diplomatic discussions, a number of interesting elements have been removed from the original draft, particularly those elements which could be regarded as revolutionary' (*DEP* No. 1 289/247).

Mauro Ferri was far more damning: 'A year has passed, and not the slightest progress has been made. The atmosphere on the government level has continued to deteriorate, however, and your Act is being lost on the diplomatic and bureaucratic shoals of expert opinion' (*DEP* No. 1 289/261). 'The approach they [Genscher and Colombo] advocate is unfeasible; it cannot produce the desired results' (*DEP* No. 1 289/262).

Spinelli recalled that, 10 years previously, the Community had declared that EMU and political union would be 'a fact of life by 1980 and it instigated procedures that any simpleton could have predicted would lead to neither monetary nor political union'. Similarly Genscher and Colombo, a year previously, had spoken of:

> [R]ealistic, pragmatic proposals to start the building of Europe and to do so they would use the same procedures of ten years previously, in other words, brief and superficial consultations with the genuine European authorities, namely the European Parliament, and secret negotiations in national diplomatic circles.
>
> (*DEP* No. 1 289/263)

The EP had already in July voted by a large majority in favour of basic guidelines on institutional change. At the beginning of 1984, he promised, it would submit its own draft treaty, not to the Council but to each government with the request for ratification by the relevant national authorities (*DEP* No. 1 289/263). Thus they would hope to bypass the smoke-filled rooms of the Council, bring the recalcitrant straight into the blazing light of publicity and shame them into repentance.

Spinelli believed in the exploitation of moments of crisis and talked up the notion that this was such a moment (Burgess 1989: 134–5). Further, he was aware that the

EP's mission to be a 'constituent' body fell to it also by default from the Commission. If the Commission wanted to move beyond the ground it could firmly claim – the 30 May mandate and the treaties – it must do so circumspectly. Nevertheless, it may be that the early 1980s represented something of a high watermark of cooperation between Commission and EP; that Thorn's attitude was more positive than that of Delors from the start of 1985 onwards (see Burgess 1989: 139). But by that point, the scene had been set.

The FRG held the Council presidency for the first half of 1983 and, on 11 January, Genscher presented the programme for that period to the EP. He did not pursue the question of the European Act, on which he had agreed to report separately to the EP. The internal market did, however, figure on his list, and became an increasingly common theme in the early 1980s. Genscher's own position, however, did not escape criticism. The awkward domestic political situation in the FRG was sharply commented on by German socialist Arndt. Neither did Spinelli spare the rod: 'You well know,' he said to Genscher, 'that the Genscher–Colombo plan is making little progress if it has not already been shunted onto a siding.' And he regretted that Genscher said nothing about the EP's own rival plan for a draft treaty (*DEP* No. 1 293, 64 and 69, 11 January 1983).

Influential academic voices were raised in a similar sense. Weiler, for instance, averred:

> The Genscher–Colombo draft Act does not amount either to a comprehensive or to a coherent diagnosis or strategy for a relaunching of institutionalised Europe ... the proposed Act can, at best, be regarded as an exercise in substitute politics, at worst as serving some internal political ends.
>
> (Weiler 1983: 153)

What, then, of its actual fate? The Solemn Declaration on European Union was signed at the end of the Stuttgart European Council on 19 June 1983. Its name was probably its most portentous (and pompous) feature. It consolidated existing practice to a large extent, 'reaffirming' certain commitments, modestly expanding the scope, with references to cultural cooperation and approximation of laws as well as to foreign policy (*Bull. EC* 6–1983: 24–9). In no sense did it present solutions to the various deficiencies that the authors had themselves portrayed; but this itself was not surprising, since it was *par excellence* a product of those very 'intergovernmental' processes, operating at every level in the decision process – working groups, committees, COREPER – which, most observers agreed, bore the main responsibility for slowing the development of the specifically *Community* dimension. (See Weiler 1983: *passim*; Bonvicini in Pryce 1987.) The solemn declaration is fairly described as the 'pale legacy' of the draft European Act (Burgess 1989: 129). Perhaps the most that can be said for it is that some of the matters it mentioned, such as political cooperation, were later fully incorporated in the 1987 Single European Act.

The Genscher–Colombo process and the EP's own initiative coexisted in full knowledge of each other. But whereas Genscher–Colombo presented itself as 'first steps' and a 'starting point' for more thorough reform, the EP was, from the start, dismissive of the tactics and efficacy of the authors of the draft European Act. Mauro Ferri declared that for the EP 'no form of consultation with the Council of Ministers and the Commission is possible'. They would proceed on the basis of the EP's vote of 6 July 1982 and in 'complete autonomy' (*DEP* No. 1/289: 261–2, 14 October 1982; Burgess 1989: 131). Spinelli and his friends were convinced that only different *methods* would suffice. They had already achieved a substantial degree of support within the EP; their resolve was almost certainly strengthened by the European Council meetings at Stuttgart (June 1983) and more especially Athens (December 1983).

It had been a strange period. Beneath an unpromising surface, things were beginning to move. On the surface, the 'ground rules' appeared rather stagnant. 'Windows of opportunity' still appeared to dominate the political calculus. National political imperatives – especially those of national elections – continued to act as a serious restraint. The rotation of Council presidencies continued to be important: presidencies, it remained clear, continued to have pet projects that were dear to them and it remained important to 'aim' proposals at a particular presidency 'window of opportunity' if it were to have much chance of passing. This was especially so, given the tendency for proposals lacking a 'fair wind' to accumulate dust on the Council table.

Particular Commissions, too, continued to have a certain 'style'. They behaved in characteristically different ways. Strings were sometimes 'pulled', cabals formed, in ways not immediately apparent. It was bruited around Brussels that, in the Thorn Commission, the 'centre right', Christian Democrat led, tended to go into a huddle and set its own agenda; and that it did so a good deal more effectively than social democrats and socialists. That Commission was sometimes referred to as 'Stevie Davignon's Commission', as a backhanded compliment to the influence that gentleman was thought to wield in a 'college' formally led by another.

'Euro-sclerosis' was not an easy condition to cure. Yet during this period, quite a lot of spadework had been done by those with ambitious agendas. A certain momentum was very slowly established: imperceptibly at first, pebbles began to move.

**Further reading**

M. Burgess, *Federalism and European Union: Political Ideas, Influence and Strategy*. London: Routledge, 1989.

D. Dinan (ed.), *Origins and Evolution of the European Union*. Oxford: Oxford University Press, 2006. (Chapter 8.)

S. George, *An Awkward Partner: Britain in the European Community*. Oxford: Oxford University Press, 1998.

P. Ludlow, *The Making of the EMS*. London: Butterworths, 1982.

A. Moravcsik, *The Choice for Europe*. London: UCL Press, 1999. (Chapter 4.)

H. Simonian, *The Privileged Partnership: Franco-German Relations in the European Community*. Oxford: Clarendon Press, 1985.

P. Stirk and D. Weigall, *The Origins and Development of European Integration*. London: Pinter, 1999. (Chapters 8 and 9.)

# 7 The mid-1980s

## 'Single market' and 'single act'

The main developments of the later 1980s became headline topics with surprising swiftness, yet their roots were deep, as we have seen. It is significant that they followed hard on the heels of the appointment of the new Commission at the start of 1985, under the presidency of French socialist – or more accurately 'left-of-centre technocrat', Jacques Delors.

Because Delors was to be so central to developments in the Commission for a whole decade (1985–95), we shall introduce him here.

Jacques Delors, born in 1925 in the Paris suburb of Ménilmontant, 'Jansenist' progressive catholic, was much influenced by Emmanuel Mounier's 'personalist' movement (Laughland 1997: 57): his view was that 'society could not be reduced to a market writ large or a utilitarian agglutination of isolated individuals' (Ross 1995: 17). He followed his father into the Banque de France rather than the 'normal' high fliers' *cursus honorum* through the *grandes écoles*. His work ethic was widely reported as extraordinary. He was involved with the mainly catholic trade union CFTC; in the 1960s that took him to the French (consultative) Economic and Social Council; that in turn to involvement with the (Monnet brainchild) planning commission. Then he had a period in the *cabinet* of Gaullist prime minister Jacques Chaban-Delmas. Significantly, then, he was almost always an 'outsider', a loner and frequently mistrusted among the tribes of French politics generally and in regard to his adopted Socialist Party more particularly. Grant reminds us that:

> He spent the 1960s moving away from the left ... in May 1968 he lay low. Then he spent three years working for a Gaullist prime minister ... In the 1970s [the left's] revival would draw him back – just in time to hold office in the socialist governments of the 1980s.
>
> (Grant 1994: 31)

Markets were important to him, but not the 'be all and end all'. Just as important was his good fortune: not least, in being elected to the EP in the first direct elections of 1979, a perfect vantage point from which to master the dossiers and form a view: and where, again portentously, he became chair of the Monetary Affairs Committee. From there he became Mitterrand's minister of economy and finance, first as a 'counterweight' to leftists within the 1981 government, then as architect of the policy 'U-turn' of 1982–3 that enabled both the realignment and the survival of the EMS.

Ambiguity seems to be a hallmark of the man: there is widespread disagreement about his role and his achievements (Drake 2000: x and *passim*; see also Grant 1994; Ross 1995; Endo 1999; Moravcsik 1999: Chs 5, 6; Gillingham 2003, esp. 149–299). For Drake, his combination of pragmatism and utopianism, of thought and action, made 'the European Commission Presidency … in many respects Delors' ideal professional and political home' (Drake 2000: 27). But several things are clear. There is first no doubt that Delors as Commission president *had* a 'grand strategy', even though 'accident' also played its part. Second, this strategy reflected those long-held personal convictions concerning the relationship between the role of markets and his view of 'social justice' just discussed. Third, he enjoyed loyal support in his *cabinet* in pushing forward with these plans. Fourth, the outcomes were to prove mixed.

First, as to the 'grand strategy'. It contained both 'market-building' elements and 'state-building' elements: but his initial investigations had shown him that the 'market' measures would be the only ones initially likely to generate sufficient support. Thereafter the 'politics of implication' would have to carry the project forward. But the politics of implication required a friendly shove: hence the secretive strategy of the 'Russian dolls': revealing one after the other his further plans: but *only* one at a time and with the subsequent ones hidden.

The metaphor of 'Russian dolls' is attributed to François Lamoureux, second in command in Delors' *cabinet*: '"You take the first doll apart," he said, "and then inside it is another one, which leads you to another … until it is too late to turn back"' (Ross 1995: 39). For Ross, it implied 'iterated episodes of strategic action to seize upon openings in the political opportunity structure, resource accumulation through success, and reinvestment of these resources to capitalize [*sic*] on new opportunities' (ibid.: 39). The dolls were moves towards 'state building'. There were six. First was the SEA – 'means to the end' of the single market: this will be discussed in this chapter. Second was the 'Delors I package' of 1986, largely budgetary. Third, and most controversial, was the 'social dimension'. Fourth was EMU – 'the highest-stake Russian doll' (Ross 1995: 42). Fifth, the 'political union' proposal; sixth, the 'Delors II' package. (Ross 1995: 39–50; Gillingham 2003: 259–89). These are looked at in Chapters 8 and 9.

Verdicts about the strategy as well as about the man differ sharply. For Ross, close in both time and place (and not unsympathetic ideologically?), the strategy was 'motivated by urgent concerns to make sure that the European Community became something more than a simple market' (Ross 1995: 47). For neoliberal Gillingham, Delors' 'scheme was every bit as unworkable as the scam of the fast-talking auto man' [John Delorean]: the 'state-building' strategy, in contrast to that of market-building, was a costly and confused error (Gillingham 2003: 259).

The turnover in personnel among Commissioners at the start of 1985 was almost total, with 14 new faces out of the 17. The new Commission also included a strong contingent of former finance ministers, for whom it might be thought that EMU as a project would have considerable saliency (though perhaps varying appeal). It is thus noteworthy that EMU at this time did not achieve unstoppable momentum: although Delors had slated it along with other possible 'new directions' for the Community, his tour of national capitals prior to taking up office had rapidly convinced him that consensus on this would not be forthcoming.

The Thorn Commission had, as we have seen, bequeathed the substance and some of the institutional arrangements for the 'internal market' heart of what became the new agenda, even if the passing of that Commission was not widely lamented. Considerable hopes were, however, held out for its successor, arising in part from Delors's soundings in late 1984. These had clearly shown that, of the various possible 'ways forward' – defence and security, monetary, or 'internal market' – among the substantive policy priorities or institutional reform, the internal market commanded widest support.

The internal market Council had, by that time, been active for some 2 years. But the SEM initiative had, as already noted, steadily gathered other sources of support too: the pressure of the 'Kangaroo Group' from as far back as 1979 but getting into its stride in the early 1980s; the Commission's work on strengthening the internal market; and the declarations of the European Council on several occasions (as Lord Cockfield was to be quick to remind them).

Even the 'wasteland' of the mid-1970s up to and including the early 1980s had produced certain elements which were to prove helpful in pushing forward the internal market initiative. One was the EMS, which increasingly seemed to operate as a 'quasi-fixed exchange rate' regime, especially from the 1983 Franco-German confrontation onwards. Another was the 'steering' function of the European Council, providing a forum for reassembling matters hitherto dealt with in unrelated ways. In addition, sections of business, alarmed at the effects of fragmentation, retardation and poor performance, began to take on board the relevance of the Kangaroo message. And a new wind was beginning to blow in certain national governments, beginning, as we have seen, with the UK in 1979, but successively reinforced by governmental changes in Belgium, Denmark, the Netherlands and, most importantly, Germany in the period to the end of 1982 (see Brewin and McAllister 1983; Cameron in Sbragia 1992: *passim*). Together with the U-turn in French economic policy in 1982–3, this represented a significant change in the political centre of gravity of a majority of member states; and it was no accident that this was the period that saw the birth of the internal market Council. This followed logically on the European Council's request (London, 26–7 November 1981) for a Commission report on the internal market, duly delivered in time for the Copenhagen European Council in December 1982 (17 *GRA*: 81). This had outlined the obstacles: in the report for 1984, the Commission was able to claim with some justice that it 'has made the strengthening of the internal market one of the main girders of Community policy' (18 *GRA*: 79) and to point to concrete (if undramatic and bulky) achievements such as the single administrative document (with its singularly unhappy acronym SAD) in December 1984. Thus, while few cheered, the groundwork had been laid by that time.

Plainly, the European Council was insisting on being reported to: equally plainly, it was not just reactive but proactive in the development of policy concerning the internal market. This was true in the early 1980s; it was even more so in the period of the development of the 'double-barrelled gun' – single act and single market – in 1985–6.

This complex of forces at work was a very mixed bag: some of the 'push' factors came from positively 'federalist' sources; others were at the opposite, 'intergovernmental' end of the spectrum. This in turn means that the initiatives should not be interpreted as a step toward an inexorable 'integrated and federal' outcome. Indeed, the strategic role of the European Council is evidence of a quite opposite tendency: the 'colonisation' of the Community arena by the domestic priorities of member states (Bulmer and Wessels 1987; Cameron in Sbragia 1992). It was but one example of the blurring of the distinction between domestic policy and foreign policy.

The first public indication of the lines that the Delors Commission was to pursue, was in his 14 January 1985 statement to the EP on the 'thrust of Commission policy' (*Bull. Supp.* 1/85: 5). The Commission president was appearing in Strasbourg before a relatively recently elected EP. His statement was notable for its upbeat and even optimistic tone. First, disenchantment, he claimed, was receding. The EC was, 'I hope – on the point of settling the family feuds which have literally paralysed it in recent years' – feuds that 'future historians will find laughable in the harsh light of contemporary challenges' (*Bull. Supp.* 1/85: 5).

He astutely picked up a theme touched on in the preceding chapter: the engineers of integration were 'fumbling not over "what has to be done" but rather over "how to go about it"'. A chord was struck with those of Spinelli's persuasion. He indicated that the 'approach' he was about to outline would be complemented by the detailed discussion of the Commission's programme for 1985, duly presented to the EP on 12 March (*Bull. Supp.* 4/85). These two statements need to be considered in relation to three other key documents: in order of appearance, they are the ('Cockfield') White Paper on the completion of the internal market by 1992 (Commission to European Council, June 1985; Office for Official Publications, Luxembourg); the Final Report of the *Ad Hoc* Committee on a People's Europe ('Adonnino') (*Bull. Supp.* 7/85) and the Single European Act (*Bull. Supp.* 2/86). This last, in turn, was in the main the eventual outcome of the work of the Dooge Committee.

These were the main key documents. It now needs to be asked: first, how were the proposals contained within them selected, while others, although tabled at some point or other, were eliminated? And second, how were the various documents seen to relate to each other: was there a logic at work or just a jumble of compromises?

On the issue of agenda shaping, two points perhaps need to be made. The first is to recall that the completion of the internal market was but one of four main 'priority directions' for EC development canvassed by Delors and those close to him, the others being: first, the area of economic and monetary union (again!); second, EC identity in the area of security and defence-related matters; third, institutional reform. It would seem that the internal market was chosen partly according to the principle of 'least resistance': it was a firm treaty commitment, thus not evoking any *arrières-pensées* or kneejerk negatives. It was a matter of bad conscience for all the member states. It could be presented as already enshrined in a whole host of declarations of European Councils, back as far as Copenhagen (December 1982), via Fontainebleau (June 1984) and Dublin (December 1984), all to be reinforced at the Brussels (March 1985) European Council. Further, it particularly suited both the Commissioner in charge of the internal market, Lord Cockfield, and the prime minister via whom his nomination had had to pass, Margaret Thatcher, who had also, of course, declared that treaty revision and institutional tinkering were a lowly priority, compared to the unfinished business to which the Community was supposed to be so fundamentally committed. The programme for consolidation of the internal market had, as Delors reminded the EP in January, been 'presented by the outgoing Commission': one more example, like that of the EP in respect of the draft treaty, of an outgoing body passing on a chalice to its successor. Delors's stress on putting this programme into effect 'as quickly as possible' was for once to be fulfilled at least as far as the proposal stage was concerned (*Bull. Supp.* 1/85: 6).

Already in Delors's January 1985 statement, the clues were there to be read. He declared, for instance:

> Achievement of the internal market has been held up by the rule of unanimity, deriving either from the Treaty itself ... in particular of Article 100 ... or from the misuse of the concept of vital interests ... the new Commission will make full use of all the possibilities offered by the Treaty to overcome these obstacles A *programme*, a *timetable* and a *method* for these areas will be proposed to Council and Parliament.
>
> (*Bull. Supp.* 1/85: 10)

Pursuing the social democratic theme of 'efficiency and social justice', Delors used an interesting and revealing analogy, declaring that just as (he claimed) the EMS had prevented 'monetary dumping', so 'There should be no social dumping either': hence a 'minimal [*sic*] harmonization of social rules' (*Bull. Supp.* 1/85: 11).

In contrast, he made clear, 'and this may surprise you', that the idea of a 'real Community currency' would not be one of the immediate objectives (*Bull. Supp.* 1/85: 12). He declared that he was too well aware of the complexities and technical problems involved, especially for central banks, to make rash promises on this front. (In fact, he was keeping his powder dry: by specifically associating the central bankers with the preparation of the Delors Plan in 1989, he would hope to neutralise them.) He might have added that early 1985, in the middle of another monetary maelstrom, was not, for those with vivid memories of 1973–4, a propitious time. But he did not forget to raise in passing the issue of whether 'the burden of the dollar is too heavy'; equally, in anticipation of the 1989 report, he asked his hearers whether a stronger monetary system might not 'reopen the path to economic and monetary union mapped out by the Werner Report almost 15 years ago' (*Bull. Supp.* 1/85: 12). Those who thought that these musings could be safely ignored did so at their peril.

Averring that 'all things are interconnected', whether in dynamism or decline, he turned to the institutional conundrums. The 'what' was easier than the 'how'. 'But as soon as we start discussing "how" to achieve them – let's face it – the difficulties start' (*Bull. Supp.* 1/85: 14) – as his visits to national capitals while president-designate had confirmed. Europe was no longer capable of taking decisions. Unfortunately, the only thing on which people were agreed was its impotence: there was no agreement on a path of reform. It was imperative to prevent the institutional quarrel becoming in the future what the 30 May Mandate had been in the past. The preliminaries to Iberian enlargement had furnished further examples of 'tit-for-tat diplomacy'. Thus he suggested a 'simple two-pronged approach … let us identify the improvements to be made within the framework of the existing rules and then decide what can be done beyond the Treaty of Rome'. Both tactics were essential. 'The Treaty of Rome must not be regarded as the be-all and end-all' (*Bull. Supp.* 1/85: 14–16).

Immediate problems continued to press in: enlargement, budgetary discipline, the integrated Mediterranean programmes (IMPs), farm price decisions, environmental issues and steel. Delors was also concerned not to be seen to overstep the Commission's role; in his reply to the debate (on 15 January), he addressed one difficulty thus:

> If the Commission wanted to act quickly on the … budget … it would have to … get more and more involved in what is the work of the Council's Secretariat, that is to say, reconciling viewpoints and doing the legwork. And even if we were to pull it off, we would be repudiating the origins, the very essence, of our institutions.
>
> (*Bull. Supp.* 1/85: 17)

Temptations to get around this risked 'moving even further away from the purity of the original design, a design which reveals more than a touch of genius on close inspection' (*Bull. Supp.* 1/85: 17).

It may be that Delors was here revealing a characteristic studied ambiguity. The remark quoted may at one level be a reprimand to Spinelli-type federalists and in favour of Monnet's 'grand design'. Yet it also indicates a certain despair about the efficacy of the machinery, modulated by a plea not to shoot the bearer of the bad tidings.

He looked further forward, to the situation 'beyond the Treaty of Rome' and again his remarks are worth quoting in the light of the events we are to examine:

> Some favour a small treaty within the present one; others want a separate treaty, still others want a totally new treaty … [S]ay, by some miracle, that an intergovernmental conference is convened in June 1986 and agrees on a new treaty to supersede the old one. When would this new treaty come into force? Three years later at the earliest. So what do we do for those three years? … We have to find the happy mean. There is no need to abandon 'the great beyond' but we must go on working here and now within the existing treaty, all of the treaty.
>
> (*DEP* No. 2 321/39, 15 January 1985)

This indicated rather clearly an aversion to attempting to 'supersede' the existing treaty by an entirely new one, thus once again opposition to the 'Spinelli' and

DTEU (Draft Treaty on European Union) strategy. These had had a gadfly function; they had provoked action and reaction; but theirs was not to be the future plan. Indeed, Spinelli had taken the precaution of setting out his views in an open letter to Delors some days before, urging that the EP be a partner, and not merely consulted, in the preparation of the Intergovernmental Conference (IGC) on the European Union Treaty; and that Delors disavow what he called 'the Council ploy of so-called budgetary discipline'. Delors had said nothing: so Spinelli would abstain on the motion for investiture of the new Commission. This first ever investiture vote was, however, carried by 201 to 34 with 37 abstentions (*DEP* No. 2 321/41, 15 October 1985; *EDB* 4007, 16 January 1985: 5).

Optimism had been in the air since the Fontainebleau Summit, which had both tidied up the past and also launched the Adonnino Committee on a people's Europe and the Dooge Committee of personal representatives of the heads of government to consider the more clearly institutional and political dimensions of change. But as so often in the past, the Community's moods proved spectacularly unreliable and dependent. Burgess cautions that what happened between Dublin (December 1984) and Milan (June 1985) is largely conjecture, but that 'the intergovernmental arena, always prey to sudden unexpected shifts in member-state positions, produced a new climate much less favourable to the progress of European Union' (Burgess 1989: 190). Yet despite these difficulties, what emerged from Milan did include precisely that agreement to hold an IGC against which Mrs Thatcher, along with others, had earlier set her face.

Ireland held the presidency for the second half of 1984 in succession to France, and premier Garret FitzGerald appointed senator James Dooge as his 'personal representative' to the second of the committees set up by Fontainebleau. After some delay and jockeying for position, Dooge became chairman of this committee. The Dooge Committee produced an interim report for the Dublin European Council of December 1984 and a final report for that at Brussels in March 1985. It is worth emphasising that both stressed the importance of a 'homogeneous economic area' and, under this general heading, of *completion* of the treaty 'by creating a genuine internal market' (*Ad Hoc* Committee on Institutional Affairs ('Dooge'): Interim Report to the European Council, December 1984 ('Interim Report'); Report to the European Council, March 1985 ('Report')). Thus 'Dooge' prepared the ground also for the Cockfield White Paper, which was being worked on at a furious pace meantime, as well as for the SEA.

But it did a good deal more. The 'Report' declared, a little ambiguously, that it set out the objectives, policies and institutional reforms needed 'without purporting to draft a new Treaty in legal form' ('Report': 12). It nevertheless declared that it proposed the convening of a conference of the representatives of the governments of the member states to negotiate a draft European Union Treaty ('Report': 32).

The vicissitudes and triumphs of 'Dooge' have been well examined elsewhere (Burgess 1989: 188–98). Here, some of the important factors at work may be mentioned briefly. First, the make-up of the Dooge Committee was probably about as favourable as the Spinelli-ites could hope for in the circumstances. Ferri, ex-MEP and ex-convenor of the EP's Committee on Institutional Affairs, carried the flag for

Italy. Fernand Herman for Belgium had a similar profile. Initially, the Commission's man on the committee was the enthusiast Andriessen, later replaced by Ripa di Meana – but by that time much of the work was done. For Burgess, the key figure was Maurice Faure of France, another ex-MEP and, crucially, the only representative of a head of state (Mitterrand) not a head of government, and thus able to escape 'from the clutches of the Quai d'Orsay' (Burgess 1989: 187; see also Moravcsik 1991: 39).

It is noteworthy that both the 'Interim' and 'Final' versions of 'Dooge' refer specifically to western Europe's longstanding poor economic performance as one of the factors pushing the internal market programme: 'Furthermore, after 10 years of crisis, Europe, *unlike* Japan and the US, has not achieved a growth-rate sufficient to reduce the disturbing figure of almost 14 million unemployed' ('Dooge', Interim and Final, Preface: 11).

Following this, under 'II. Priority Objectives', the *first* one was:

> A homogeneous economic area –
> (a) Through completion of the Treaty
> 1. By creating a genuine internal market.

There was, however, a significant difference of wording between the 'Interim' and 'Final' versions. Whereas 'Interim' said that the aim was 'to bring about economic and monetary *union and* to create the fully integrated internal market', 'Final' states: 'The aim is to create a homogeneous internal economic area, by bringing about the fully integrated internal market envisaged in the Treaty of Rome *as an essential step towards* the objective of economic and monetary union': a significant modification of theology ('Interim': 13; 'Final': 14, emphasis added).

Other significant differences, markers of shifting priorities amounting to a subtly different philosophy, can be detected between the 'Interim' and 'Final' reports. For instance, 'Interim' continues with, as its *second* priority, 'the creation of economic convergence', with the by then traditional, interventionist and disparity-reducing litany of 'the promotion of solidarity among the member states aimed at reducing structural imbalances, *which prevent* the convergence of living standards'. This is number 3 in the 'Final' report, and follows the much more 'bracing' second section now called 'Through the increased competitiveness of the European economy'. This is unequivocal: 'European economic life must be made fully competitive through a return to the fundamental principle embodied in the Treaties of promoting efficient producers' and for good measure stresses that this is to be via the 'removal of all measures distorting competition' and involves 'introduction of the necessary transparency in nationalized industries' ('Final': 15). The writing was firmly on the wall and becoming rapidly firmer.

Similarly, the section of 'Interim' entitled 'Through the *realization* of the European Monetary System' is more weakly rechristened in 'Final', 'Through the strengthening of EMS' ('Interim': 14; 'Final': 17). Here, 'Final' adds a reference to 'liberalization of capital movements and the removal of exchange controls' and a Delphic but Thatcherite reference to participation in the ERM 'provided that the necessary economic and monetary conditions are met' ('Final': 17; compare 'Interim': 14–15). Further, there is a reordering of the Interim Report's statement on 'the means'. Significantly, the Final Report promotes to greater prominence the following statement:

> The trend towards the European Council's becoming simply another body dealing with the day-to-day business of the Community must be reversed. Heads of State or Government should play a strategic role and give direction and political impetus to the Community. For this purpose two European Council meetings a year should suffice.
>
> ('Final': 25)

Equally, reservations about the use and extent of, and resort to, majority decisions in the Council of Ministers, are spelled out much more explicitly in the Final Report. Last, the section on the Court of Justice contains in the Final Report a clause presaging the creation of the Court of First Instance: the Court 'must be relieved in an appropriate manner of responsibilities incumbent upon it as regards disputes between officials and the institutions' ('Final': 31).

These differences between versions do not, however, conclude the list. Equally interesting is to note that certain reserves even over the strictly 'internal market' agenda, which were to emerge in the autumn of 1985, did not appear at all in the early months of the year (Brewin and McAllister 1986: *passim*; Pryce 1987: 226). Economic 'convergence' shifted (as in other contexts in the early 1980s) from referring to *result* (outcomes or 'life chances' as between regions) to referring instead to convergence of *policy* ('rigour', as emphasised by the FRG, with varying support from the Dutch and the Belgians).

EPC again reared its head: partly *because* the Irish understandably demoted the 'defence and security' aspect and partly because it was one of the few matters on which the British and the original 'Six' could agree, as they also showed in WEU at the time (Pryce 1987: 226). But then WEU, as *both* a convenience and a potential rival at the same time, led a charmed life which involved moving out of, and back into, the shadows.

At this point it is important to note that there was not an exact 'one-to-one' relationship between the 'input' documents – 'Dooge' and Adonnino' – and the 'outputs' – the 'Cockfield' White Paper (SEM) and the SEA. 'Dooge' moved beyond its internal market starting point and, perhaps with more enthusiasm, took up again the question of institutional means: these were also adumbrated on by 'Adonnino'. On the crucial 'Council' issue – majority voting, the 'veto' and the Luxembourg Agreement – Denmark, Greece and the UK maintained that there should be no change. The Republic of Ireland and Luxembourg nuanced their positions. Disagreements over Commission and EP were less important and over the Court they were virtually non-existent.

The 'Dooge' final section on 'the method' was, too, hotly fought over. This was to lead forward to the summoning of the Intergovernmental Conference (IGC), which again Denmark, Greece and the UK resisted, but over which, when push came to shove, they did not feel able to go to the barricades.

It has been said before that the whole 'Dooge' process illustrates the importance of 'footnote diplomacy': the 'reserves', or reservations, entered by member states were crucial to the achievement of any kind of result; they were *possible* because of the 'pre-negotiation' format. It was, of course, no accident that the original Six took one standpoint on most (not all) issues, while three of the 'latecomers' produced most of the footnotes. It probably was an accident of timing, however, that Ireland, the most willing of the latecomers to push the maximalist cause forward, conveniently held the chair of the Dooge Committee.

Along the road from pre-decision to decision, it was common for a number of proposals and items to be on the table and to be presented as (often) inextricably linked. This was especially true of the internal market SEM initiative, to which the Brussels European Council in March 1985 had reaffirmed its commitment and agreed a target date of 1992.

The Brussels European Council was a strange affair, held against a very mixed background – monetary instability and instability of superpower relations – yet achieving, finally, basic agreement on Portuguese and Spanish accession, dependent only on settling a 'price' for Greek agreement – the so-called IMPs or integrated Mediterranean programmes. So the Iberian enlargement was finally achieved, but the enormous difficulties involved were apparent in two ways: first, the time taken – from 1977 until agreement was finalised in March 1985; second, the length of the documentation, which ran to 500 pages in the *Official Journal* – the opinion of the Commission, decision of the Council, 403 articles of the Treaty, 36 annexes, 25 protocols, 47 declarations (Brewin and McAllister 1986: 314). Beyond that, the heads set out the procedure to be followed over institutional questions, on the basis of 'Dooge' and agreed in principle to base themselves on the Adonnino Report in proceeding toward 'a people's Europe' (*Bull. EC* 3–1985: 11). The internal market proposal now headed the European Council's list of specifics: '(i) action to achieve a single large market by 1992 … it called upon the Commission to draw up a *detailed* programme with a *specific* timetable *before its next meeting* (*Bull. EC* 3–1985: 12, emphasis added).

It could hardly have been so bold had it not known that thinking along these lines was already advanced, and capable of being brought to fruition. Other topics that were to find a place in the Single European Act also appeared, notably a 'technological community' and environment. The conclusions also stressed the importance of ensuring that 'the achievement of the objective of abolishing frontier formalities must remain compatible with the need to combat terrorism and drug-trafficking' (*Bull. EC* 3–1985: 13) about which much was to be heard, and a lot more publicly unheard, but discussed in the interstices of the Trevi Group of EC justice and interior ministers, established back in 1975. But any systematic discussion of 'Dooge' was delayed until Milan, with a promise that detailed examination would continue on a *bilateral* basis in the months between. Delors immediately characterised the institutional aspect as 'a very difficult problem' and looked forward to full discussion at Milan to 'enable the Community to go beyond the Treaty of Rome and in particular to improve and accelerate its decision-making process' (*Bull. EC* 3–1985: 15).

The link was not just between economic *programme* and 'better decision-making', but also from enlargement to the latter, as Tindemans for one immediately opined as the Brussels meeting opened (*EDB* 4060, 30 March 1985: 3). Maintaining the veto meant the risk of paralysis, he said; and Commissioner Ripa di Meana added his voice, urging that this time things must not become bogged down in diplomatic procedures. President Mitterrand, who had spoken of a 'surprise initiative' by France, unsurprisingly declined to say what it was: it duly appeared, as the rather oddly named 'European Union' proposal, presented jointly with the FRG just in time for the Milan Summit. It was strongly suspected of trying to take the wind from the sails of the so-called 'Howe Plan', also on the subject of European Union, presented by the UK (Howe 1996: 23; *EDB* 4061, 31 March 1985: 8). For his part, Delors did not disguise the pressure amounting to blackmail which had taken place over IMPs/enlargement; he described the former as 'inside market penalties'.

Once again, what stands out is the way that the various components were linked ('Adonnino', 'Dooge', enlargement, the internal market deadline) and the mutual pressures being exercised which would eventually keep everyone on board, some reluctantly. The Brussels European Council had (albeit only just) cleared away obstacles; this meant that the Milan Summit might hope for a clear run at the agenda.

However, again the path was far from smooth. Notably, the German veto on cereals prices (its first on such an issue) was greeted with despair. (It came just as the Portuguese and Spanish acts of accession were being signed.) It was certainly regarded as underlining the futility of 'solemn declarations'. This despair was the more marked because the FRG seemed on several issues to speak with uncertain voice: rivalries between the chancellor's office and the foreign ministry, a wary eye on *Land* elections and the suggestion, retracted, that a German should chair 'Dooge' were examples (Pryce 1987: 231; Burgess 1989: 191 for details). On the opposite side of the balance was Lord Cockfield, who weighed in in support of the view that changes in decision making were vital if the internal market White Paper were to be carried through.

France also seemed to speak with Delphic tones. Mitterrand's optimism of the May 1984 EP speech seemed to have waned. The 'U-turn' in French economic policy, urged on by German exhortations bordering on threats, had accelerated the government's crumbling popularity; the 1986 legislative elections began to loom. Several articles in France's leading foreign affairs review reflected broadly the twin view: the centrality of the Franco-German relationship for 'getting anything done' in the EC, yet ambivalences and ambiguities in that relationship (Moreau Defarges 1985: 359–76; Moreau Defarges 1986: 199–218; Grosser 1986: 247–55; Weisenfeld 1986: 131–41).

The Italians, however, seemed well placed to set the pace: indeed here, in contrast to the FRG, political competition – especially between Craxi and Andreotti – seemed to have as its objective the demonstration of enthusiasm (Pryce 1987: 232). In particular, it was important to extract agreement to hold the IGC from the confusion of the Milan Summit.

This confusion arose in part from the plurality of proposals on the table. Everyone seemed anxious to put a piece of paper there in token of goodwill. Some amounted to very little: *Europe Daily Bulletin* predictably editorialised, 'The "Howe Plan": a lot of fuss about nothing' (*EDB* 4116, 24–5 June 1985: 1). On the very eve of the meeting came the 'new draft treaty on European Union' from Mitterrand and Kohl. If this was the 'surprise' that the former had promised, that element translated itself mainly as disappointment (Burgess 1989: 192).

Again, while both the British and the Franco-German proposals were to be 'bases' for further work, it is of interest to note certain straws in the wind (EP Doc. PE 100.343, 10 September 1985; *Bull. EC* 6–1986: 14).

First, it is clear that the British wanted to 'make the running' with something concrete and could after all claim some 'form' on political cooperation, with the London (Carrington) Report of October 1981. Second, equally clear was the determination of the Paris–Bonn duo not to allow this to happen, at all costs. Third, their scrambled effort amounted to plagiarism for the most part: the contents corresponded, to a high degree, article by article and could not have been thus composed without the rival at their elbow.

But this having been said, there remain some revealing differences of formula. For instance, the preamble to the Franco-German proposal spoke of renaming the European Council 'Council of European Union' and creating a general secretariat to act alongside it. Their Article 1 set as objective 'the gradual implementation of a European foreign policy'; the British spoke of ensuring 'a broad identity of views on the main problems of international relations' and of ensuring 'that their combined influence is deployed in the most effective way': phrases that cast long shadows before them to the Gulf crisis and the 1991 Political Union IGC. The British had a paragraph 2 to Article 5, urging that:

> In particular a member state shall not support a resolution [in international organs or major conferences] which directly criticizes or might gravely affect the vital interests of another member state. The member states shall also work to avoid a situation where one or more of them co-sponsor a resolution which another or others of them vote against.
>
> (EP Doc. PE 100.343, 10 September 1985)

There was no parallel provision in the Franco-German proposal: here the British one was more rigorous. Similarly, the British listed, in Annex 3 to Article 7, specific measures for strengthening cooperation in third countries. Again, the British Article 8 made unequivocal mention of NATO in a way that the French would find theologically unacceptable and the Franco-German draft was again predictably vague.

The main genuflection the other way was in the Franco-German draft's reference to the EP's 'participation' in political cooperation, where the British spoke of its being 'informed of developments' there. But the British proposal, once again, set out in some detail, in Annexes II and III, the functions of the PoCo secretariat and the ground rules.

A glance ahead shows that quite a number of details found their way from each of these drafts into the SEA's Title III on political cooperation. We may also note how far *both* were from the approximately corresponding Articles of the EP's draft treaty. (The three drafts – British, DTEU and Franco-German – are 'tabulated', as far as this is possible, in EP Doc. PE 100.343/Ann.; 10 September 1985; see also *FT* 10 September 1985.)

Craxi, it appears, met Margaret Thatcher before business began on the opening morning, 28 June, 'to put forward the "pragmatic" reasons for making a "qualitative leap forward"', ones which would appeal to her, viz. that the non-achievement of the internal market after 28 years showed clearly that the decision-making processes would have to be changed (*EDB* 4120, 29 June 1985: 3).

The Franco-German draft may have put Delors in some difficulty. It was clearly not what he had been urging. Yet it is not clear how far he had been kept informed, or when; and it might not have been politic for him to say. Instead, he contented himself with the view that it had one virtue at least: two large member states had declared themselves in favour of European union! The draft limited itself almost entirely to political cooperation matters – i.e. foreign policy – and was extremely brief (*EDB* 4120, 29 June 1985: 4–6).

Wilfried Martens of Belgium seems to have adopted a particularly strong line against the Franco-German draft. Belgium indeed seems to have led the 'Benelux voice', predictably maximalist and helpful to Craxi's own position. Mrs Thatcher reportedly allowed that the European Council could set itself up as an IGC without the need for a special conference; this was taken to mean no UK objection in principle and was probably the open sesame for later events (*EDB* 4120, 29 June 1985: 6).

The crucial point was that the decision *was* taken at Milan to proceed to an IGC, in terms of Article 236. Its remit was broad enough to placate maximalists and minimalists; and just about everyone had been supportive of the internal market initiative. Delors, who had all along been careful to 'balance off' the (liberal) internal market with the (euro-protectionist/promotionist) 'technology community', declared, 'This European Council will stand in the history of Europe as a ... turning point' (*Bull. EC* 6–1985: 13).

The Milan Council conclusions made clear that the IGC would deal both with political cooperation and with amendments to the EEC Treaty to deal with institutional changes and extensions of spheres of activity in accordance with the 'Dooge' and 'Adonnino' proposals. As to the internal market proposals, it required a precise action programme to be initiated:

> [W]ith a view to achieving completely and effectively the conditions for a single market in the Community by 1992 at the latest, in accordance with stages fixed in relation to previously determined priorities and a binding timetable; [the European Council] therefore requested the Commission to submit its proposals swiftly and the Council to ensure that they were adopted within the deadlines established in the timetable.
>
> (*Bull. EC* 6–1985: 15)

The Conclusions went on to prioritise: removal of physical barriers to free movement of goods; removal of technical barriers to same; creation of a free market in the financial services and transport sectors; full freedom of establishment for the professions; liberalisation of capital movements. Further, after discussion of 'the method' (general equivalence of member states' legislative objectives, etc.) and of VAT and excise, the document asked the Council of Ministers 'to study the institutional conditions in which the completion of the internal market could be achieved within the desired time limits' (*Bull. EC* 6–1985).

The precision and detail here set forward were remarkable and it is surprising that the reception given to the Milan conclusions was as subdued as it was in certain quarters. Craxi was very low key and non-triumphalist: 'We would have preferred a general consensus and unanimity, but these were not to be had … In Milan, new initiatives were born and new impulses are pushing out' (*Bull. EC* 6–1985: 16). Delors lamented that the Commission's original proposal had not been taken up by the European Council, but added, 'That is why Mr Craxi decided to call an IGC … The Commission endorsed Mr Craxi's initiative entirely … At least we now know where we stand' (*Bull. EC* 6–1985: 17).

The British, Danes and Greeks had been outvoted and the IGC would go ahead – with or without them. In the event, it was to be with them, despite Mrs Thatcher's protestations of 'disappointment' and reaffirmation of the importance of the Luxembourg Agreement. Nevertheless, in the *Europe Daily Bulletin's* opinion, 'there was a change – probably irreversible – in the nature of the European Council which took a decision without being paralysed by the habitual consensus'; all this despite the '"guerilla" tactics employed by an irritated Mr Papandreou (like Mrs Thatcher) with his real offensive against the Presidency, in a manner never seen before' (*EDB* 4122, 1–2 July 1985: 1).

The disappointed were the Spinelli-ites, those who hoped that the mandate that emerged would refer explicitly to the EP's draft treaty and/or who anticipated that the Article 236 (unanimity) basis for amendment would lead to the IGC's early collapse. It appeared that the Italian presidency, by dropping explicit reference to the EP's document, had achieved a strong majority even though not unanimity. Perhaps it was all worth it. On her return to Britain, Mrs Thatcher assured parliament that the UK would attend the conference and make a constructive contribution. The *Europe Daily Bulletin* growled: 'It would be a good thing if the aim of British participation was the success of the Conference rather than its failure' and it added that a great responsibility lay with the Luxembourg presidency just begun, which would have to confirm its reputation 'as being at the "hard core" of Europe' (*EDB* 4124, 4 July 1985: 1).

As required by Article 236 EEC, both Commission and EP were consulted on the IGC question. On 9 July, the EP adopted by 192–71–21 the resolution submitted to it by the Institutional Affairs Committee (*EDB* 4128 and 4129, 10 and 11 July 1985; Lodge 1986b: 208). Those voting against included the French Communists; 11 Conservatives; British, Greek and Danish Socialists; and the Rainbow Group. The Commission's opinion also supported majority voting in Council along with, predictably, a strengthening of its own as well as the EP's powers. On 22–23 July, the

Council agreed that the IGC should be convened at the level of foreign ministers. Two working groups were established, anticipating Titles II and III of the Single Act: the Dondelinger Group on Treaty revision and the group of (foreign ministry) political directors on EPC (Lodge 1986b: 208). This pleased Greece and Denmark; it also allowed the possibility of an EPC treaty signed by some but not all (Corbett in Pryce 1987: 239).

The process of negotiation proved extremely tricky. It rapidly appeared that, although the 'maximalist'/'minimalist' distinctions remained, within each group of states there were considerable differences of priority and emphasis. However, it was clear that 'at last the status quo was not an option' (Burgess 1989: 202). But *change* still required unanimity, whereas the *calling* of the IGC had not. The impending enlargement meant, however, that the three 'footnote' states were aware that the numbers were in reality not seven but nine to three against them; this constrained them further.

Convened on 22 July 1985, the IGC's first ministerial meeting took place on 9 September. The IGC was to be the real locus of negotiations over treaty revision, in contrast to earlier episodes (the 'Merger' and the two 'Budget' Treaties – 1965, 1970, 1975) when it had merely provided assent (Corbett in Pryce 1987: 239). The 'minimalists' were being unwillingly dragged along: unwilling to be excluded by staying away (*les absents ont toujours tort*) they yet participated without any commitment as to how they would act at the end.

The EP, too, was determined to keep its foot firmly in the door even if it were not being offered a seat. The conference agreed to 'submit' its results to the EP, which *seemed* to imply something more than merely to 'consult'; but after a lengthy row, was declared to mean only informing it and allowing it to express its opinion (*DEP* No. 2 331/87, 23 October 1985; Corbett in Pryce 1987: 241). Italy later tried to strengthen the EP's hand by declaring that it would only ratify a new treaty if the EP accepted it (Brewin and McAllister 1986: 338). But parliament's strategies had very limited success. As Spinelli (who along with Pflimlin made up the EP's delegation) commented in the EP debate of 23 October, Jacques Delors's explanations 'of the extent to which the Commission has taken Parliament into account' were 'persuasive … but not always very convincing'; *a fortiori* the extent to which the IGC as a whole took account of the EP (*DEP* No. 2 331/102, 23 October 1985). Spinelli also averred that 'Parliament is cut out of the whole constituent procedure and looks rather like a vast, busy café where people express opinions with no political weight behind them' (*DEP* No. 2 331/90, 23 October 1985).

For its part, the IGC concentrated first and foremost on the *policy* component and only in the light of that did it entertain the idea of what institutional reforms might be necessary in order to arrive at the policy outcomes. This was far from the EP's draft treaty; and Luxembourg's prime minister was fairly frank early on in his 9 July speech to the EP, as was Jacques Poos the next day (*DEP* No. 2 328/ 36–41 and 113–21). Santer referred to the 'unsuspected virtues' of Article 236 EEC, the ability to convene at the behest of *some* member states only, which would then have to convince the others of their proposals. He added disarmingly that this 'should not be seen as a conspiracy or attempt to exert pressure – as some have claimed it is – on the part of notably the founder Members of the Community' (*DEP* No. 2328/41,9 July 1985).

Following him, Delors suggested that 'there are not seven countries on one side and three on the other, but four main schools of thought, with some countries straddling two of them' (*DEP* No. 2 328/42, 9 July 1985). Between the advocates of complete economic and social integration with unified institutions and those of a free trade area with political cooperation as an external adjunct, were two other schools: the advocates of two-speed Europe and those who, seeing the community as too bureaucratic, had 'suddenly succumbed to the attractions of the intergovernmental process' (*DEP* No. 2 328/42). This situation, he argued, had also dictated the choice of priority policies: only over the internal market, and over technology, was there some prospect of agreement; over economic convergence, and strengthening the EMS, 'believe me … the differences were too great, and remain too great, for progress to be possible'. Further, in being bluntly 'liberal' in its internal market proposals and not seeking to introduce 'compensatory' policies, the Commission, he claimed, was deliberately seeking 'to call the bluff of governments which had constantly proclaimed that they were in favour of liberalism and the enlarged market' (*DEP* No. 2 328/42, 9 July 1985). Not all member states had been prepared to commit themselves to the complete Cockfield package.

From the beginning of September, activity at many levels was intense, the timetable tight. The two working parties met on a virtually weekly basis; they reported to the foreign ministers who met six times before the summit, with an additional gathering immediately prior to it. Even after 21 hours of discussions at the European Council – 11 more than planned – there were unresolved issues, which then had to be finalised at a further foreign ministers' meeting on 16 and 17 December (Corbett in Pryce 1987: 244).

The main national priorities, concerns and reservations have been more fully explored elsewhere and here may be summarised briefly (Brewin and McAllister 1986: 313–44; Corbett in Pryce 1987: 244–69). Two aspects are important for our purposes. Agenda shaping took place in two ways. First, there was the 'positive' aspect: what areas to include or changes to agree. No less important, second, was the negative: certain proposals were resisted and reservations entered. Although other battles, too, were to emerge, these reserves provided early clues as to later sticking points on the road to '1992', on the part of certain states in particular.

We have already seen that the internal market was in many ways the keystone of the arch: indeed, it was the Cockfield White Paper that had put treaty reform onto centre stage. Three issues quickly arose. First was how to *define* the internal market. Second was the status of the 1992 deadline. Third was the question of whether all the single market measures should be taken by a 'blanket' majority vote procedure or whether there should be a series of specific treaty amendments.

The Commission draft pushed for the most far reaching definition of the internal market: an area 'in which persons, goods and capital shall move freely under conditions identical to those obtaining within a member state' (Corbett in Pryce 1987: 245). France, the FRG and the UK all appear to have found this too sweeping. What emerged in Article 8A of the SEA was much more subtle. The Community was to adopt measures 'with the *aim of progressively establishing* the internal market' in accordance with a number of specified provisions. And the definition: 'The internal market shall comprise an area without internal frontiers in which the free movement of goods, persons, services and capital is ensured in accordance with the provisions of this Treaty' (*Bull. Supp.* 2/86: 11). This last clause was felt to give some states wishing to hold the line, especially on such grounds as public security, public policy and public health, some weapons with which to fight.

The deadline was thought, notably by France, Greece and Ireland, to be too rigid. This was 'softened', as we have just seen: to 'the *aim* of *progressively establishing*' was attached, as the third of a long list of declarations, one stating that it was the 'firm political will to take before 1 January 1993 the decisions necessary to complete the internal market defined in those provisions, and more particularly the decisions necessary to implement the Commission's programme described in the White Paper'. Nevertheless, 'Setting the date of 31 December 1992 does not create an automatic legal effect' (*Bull. Supp.* 2/86: 24).

Over majority voting, telling divisions cast long shadows before them. Denmark and Greece maintained their outright opposition. The fiscal and tax field was the ground of opposition for the FRG, Ireland, Netherlands and the UK. The FRG also sought to maintain unanimity for social security for migrant workers and for the organisation and regulation of the professions. The FRG and Denmark were concerned to defend their higher standards of environmental protection; Ireland to underline the 'sensitivity' of its insurance and banking industries; and, together with Greece and acceding Portugal, to link agreement on the internal market to a solid Community commitment to compensatory policies, 'cohesion' and so on (see Brewin and McAllister 1986; Corbett in Pryce 1987: 245) Belgium, indeed, thought that the UK's insistence on unanimity on matters of plant health would amount to scrapping about one-third of the White Paper (*EDB* 4216, 2–3 December 1985: 3a).

Some of these reservations found their way into the single act and its list of 'declarations'; some were bargained away or compromised on. Ironing this out was a main purpose of the 11th-hour foreign ministers' meeting *before* the summit. There was a considerable struggle to have the 'last word'. Ironically, this seemed to have had a double result: both a crowding in of final efforts to influence events in the days and hours before the European Council and also a 'tidying-up' operation required afterwards, notably in time for the foreign ministers again on 16–17 December.

Thus Jacques Santer of Luxembourg, as Council President, in a letter to his colleagues stressed the importance of the monetary dimension (echoes of Werner over 15 years before!). He in particular urged that during the conference the foreign ministers be invited to convene 2 or 3 weeks later, to sign all the acts that constituted the outcome (*EDB* 4215, 30 November 1985: 3).

The main business was conducted on Luxembourg's chilly Kirchberg Plateau on 2 and 3 December. The *immediate* outcome was the adoption of a series of texts, several accompanied by the 'reservations' that remained. By the first evening, those that had fought their way out concerned the monetary dimension (an Italian reserve said this represented a step back, not forward), 'cohesion', technology, social dimension (British reservation) and the executive powers of the Commission. Interestingly, although the internal market centrepiece had had an early airing, agreement was not swift; it had to be returned to.

The most troublesome areas were to prove to be the internal market, the powers of the European Parliament and two of those just mentioned – 'cohesion' and monetary capacity. Again, examples of the bargaining and bickering must suffice. On the monetary dimension, the UK thought that it had 'squared' the FRG at the London Anglo-German meeting the previous week: there should be *no* mention of the monetary aspect. However, on Monday two proposals were tabled: the Commission wanted EMU to be mentioned in the preamble, the Netherlands wanted a briefer mention in Article 2 (*EDB* 4216, 2–3 December 1985: 5).

The latter was adopted as the basis; it was too ambitious for the British; the Germans suggested a compromise; this in turn was revised to include reference to the ECU, at Delors's request. The result was a weak formulation in the preamble, and a weak Article 20 SEA on monetary capacity, still attracting an Italian reserve as too feeble. The delicacy can even be seen in the 'double heading' of the new 'Chapter 1' of Part Three, Title II, which in the final SEA reads 'Co-operation in economic and monetary policy (Economic and Monetary Union)', thus providing both formulae, but the stronger only in parentheses (*EDB* 4217: 4 December 1985: 4; SEA, *Bull. Supp.* 2/86: 13).

The 'internal market' draft, too, proved extremely troublesome. The difficulties centred around the 'three ds' of 'definition, deadlines, derogations' (*EDB* 4217, 4 December 1985: 4). Here too, voices cried that the Community was going backwards, for example Netherlands minister Wim Van Eekelen. The British delegation seems to have insisted that the terminology speak of the adoption of 'measures' rather than of 'directives' in what was to become SEA Article 8A. Neither did they or the Irish like the implications of free movement of persons for the fight against terrorism (Lodge 1986b: 210; *Europe Documents* 1383–4, 5 December 1985).

At the end of the European Council, Denmark entered a blanket reservation on everything; Italy made its acceptance conditional on examination by the Italian parliament, but not by the EP. These and specific reservations were to be examined by the foreign ministers, who would also consider submission of the two texts – treaty amendment and EPC – as a 'single act'.

Each leader congratulated himself on the outcome – a remarkable testimony to its ambiguity or to compromise. For some, such as Denmark's Poul Schlüter, the satisfaction was because the drafts did not represent 'the slightest loss of sovereignty'. Some, such as Kohl, said they would have gone further; Craxi, much more so.

What had brought them to this point was a far from tidy process. Let us recall some of the pressures which produced the rather awkward package of the single act. First, it is fair to describe the IGC exercise as a 'pantechnicon into which the accumulated frustrations of the 1970s and 1980s would be stuffed from all sides' (Colchester and Buchan 1990: 21). Particular countries and institutions fed pet projects into the process during the hectic autumn of 1985. Something of the frenzy of the loading operation can be gleaned by comparing the several documents prepared to keep the European Parliament informed of the whole process. The dates they bear are very closely bunched. First came the comparative table on political cooperation: the DTEU, Franco-German and UK proposals put at Milan (EP Doc. PE 100.343, 10 September 1985). Then came the series directly on the intergovernmental conference: Bulletin 39 on 26 September; there followed Addendum 1, 7 October; Addendum 2, 10 October; Addendum 3, 25 October; with Addendum 5, 5 December, immediately after the Luxembourg European Council (EP Doc. PE 100.805 and Addenda).

These contain successive proposals and redrafts for inclusion. Several of them appeared quite suddenly, at the behest of some member state(s) or institution(s); others are equally suddenly redrafted, to square potential vetoes or skate round objections. An intriguing example is what finally became Article 10 of the SEA, on the powers of the Commission in regard to implementation ('comitology' in the jargon). The original proposal had been to *add* a section to Article 155 EEC, an article under the 'Commission' heading. This later became, with altered wording, an addition to Article 145, whereby the *Council of Ministers* 'may confer on the Commission ... powers for the implementation of the rules which the Council lays down'. (Compare successive draft proposals, PE 100.805/Add.: 12; Add. 3:15–16; and PE 103.151: 29; and SEA Article 10.)

Similarly, with varying degrees of support from member states, the Commission was active in promoting environment policy, technology policy and 'cohesion' – or enhanced assistance to poor regions. There was some pulling and pushing, as Denmark, for example, sought to defend the right to have higher environmental standards.

The SEA had, then, many of the characteristics of a 'mega-package deal'. As the 'pantechnicon' rolled along, additional items were thrown on board. This was largely a one-way process; very little fell off, at least in the short term. What was thrown on board, however, tended to be matters to which there were no significant objections by member states, especially major ones. Whenever there were such objections, the trend was to 'a process of limiting the scope and intensity of reform' – a 'victory for the minimalists' (Moravcsik 1991: 42, 41).

Neither were the contents totally clear. Some were plainly ambiguous or formulated in an 'all things to all people' fashion, as with the section on monetary capacity; or even the very definition of the internal market itself. But it 'had the required "something for everyone" character' (Nicoll and Salmon 1990: 40). Greece and Ireland got commitment to 'cohesion' (extra funds); Denmark got commitment to the right to higher environmental standards; the UK got treaty effect for the White Paper. But the overall picture was one of lowest common denominator bargaining. This meant that the UK, despite its apparently exposed unpopularity, achieved most of what it wanted, both in matters included and excluded: most of the rhetorical support for maximalism remained just that; and in particular, the areas of convergence of interests of three most important states – France, the FRG and the UK – delineated the outcome closely (Moravcsik 1991: *passim*).

## Further reading

D. Dinan (ed.) *Origins and Evolution of the European Union*. Oxford: Oxford University Press, 2006. (Chapter 10.)

J. Gillingham, *European Integration 1950–2003*. Cambridge: Cambridge University Press, 2003. (Chapter 7.)

A. Moravcsik, *The Choice for Europe*. London: UCL Press, 1999. (Chapter 5.)

J. Pelkmans and A. Winters, *Europe's Domestic Market*. London: Routledge for RIIA, 1988.

H. Wallace and W. Wallace (eds), *Policy-Making in the European Union*. Oxford: Oxford University Press, 2000 (4th edn). (Chapter 4.)

There is a vast literature on Jacques Delors. Here, mention may be made of:

C. Grant, *Delors: Inside the House that Jacques Built*. London: Nicholas Brealey, 1994.

G. Ross, *Jacques Delors and European Integration*. Cambridge: Polity Press, 1995.

# 8 The late 1980s and the road to '1992'

Armed with its main new programme, the Internal Market White Paper, and with the SEA spelling out other areas for task expansion and the institutional means, the EC appeared to have regained its *élan*. The questions to be confronted were, however, significant. First, how coherent were the proposals? Second, what of the problems, not so much of preparing the draft legislation in the Commission (considerable though these were) but of the subsequent stages – agreeing it, implementing and policing it? Third, would the Community be able to stick to the task it had set itself or would it once again be 'blown off course'? Together, these three related questions amount to asking how ambitious the programme was. No less important, it was to prove, was a fourth: what of the *external* implications of the programme, both 'locally' – for relations with EFTA, eastern and southern Europe – and globally – GATT, the USA and Japan in particular?

How ambitious the programme appeared depended, not surprisingly, on where one stood and one's bases of comparison. Those, including perhaps Mrs Thatcher, who had chided about 'unfulfilled Treaty commitments', might consider that the Community was 'merely' agreeing to do now what commonsense linguistic usage ought to have meant by 'completion' in 1969: in this sense it was hardly ambitious. A second perspective is to enquire what it was that the 300 or so measures of the White Paper replaced. The answer was, over 1000 draft proposals, many of which, as we have seen, had been gathering dust on the Council of Ministers' table. Seen in this light, the White Paper represented a substantial *reduction* in the *legislative* ambitions of the Community (von Sydow in Bieber et al. 1988: 98), albeit accompanied by a greater chance of realising what remained.

A third perspective was graver. '"Completing" the internal product market is a *highly ambitious* objective, requiring an interdependent programme of economic integration in a number of important policies' (Pelkmans 1986: 22); and the proposals went far beyond *product* markets. They included some of the areas deemed to be among the most difficult to achieve, notably the fiscal and technical ones. In the area of physical barriers, too, what happened bore eloquent testimony to another aphorism: that as some areas of national control are eroded, so reasons are advanced for clinging ever more tenaciously to those that remain.

Although the 'Cockfield logic' was hard to argue against in terms of treaty commitment and considering the historical record of the 1970s and early 1980s, yet there were various grounds of objection which could be, and to some extent were, raised against it. They were of rather different kinds. At least four strands may be identified. First and most obvious was that the whole supporting exercise on the 'cost of non-Europe' was flawed. The 'arithmetic' was wrong because the logic and the methodology were far from unassailable. Thus the supposed 'gains' would not, it was argued, be as claimed (see, for example, Davis et al. 1989).

A second, to some extent related, line of sceptical criticism was advanced by Susan Strange. This held that in global and strategic terms, the EC as an animal was ill adapted to negotiate its corner with others because, *even if* the SEM programme were carried out, the EC would lack the state-like single defence/procurement dimension and thus be unable to deny market access to others in the way that a unified political and security authority could (Strange in Bieber et al. 1988: 73–6).

A third kind of objection was that the SEM implied other (not only economic) costs that made the whole undertaking much more questionable. Prominent among these concerns was the threat that the SEM appeared to pose to the existing 'vital' or at least 'useful' functions of state frontiers. These included the familiar litany of drugs; terrorism; illegal immigration; threats to human, plant and animal health; and so forth.

A fourth kind of objection was related to the third: namely that behind the single market 'carrot' there lurked an undesirable hidden agenda. Other issues, it would be argued, would be claimed to flow necessarily and ineluctably from, to be implied correlates or consequences of, the SEM programme. Prominent here were, for instance, arguments about a 'single currency for a single market'. The third and fourth kinds of objection tended to run together, and to be conveniently telescoped as 'the sovereignty issue'.

Thus, fairly quickly, the SEM programme defined a new set of battlegrounds, both internal and external. The external ones concerned the ramifications of the 'internal liberalisation'. It was by no means inevitable that this would be 'externalised' in terms of the EC's outward profile, hence first the 'Fortress Europe' rumblings; second, the saga of the GATT Uruguay Round; third, the issue of the EC as at once a 'pole of attraction' and a difficult neighbour for the rest of Europe, the European Free Trade Association (EFTA), east and south.

The internal battles were no less acute. They continued to concern both the matter of inter-institutional competence and the 'political design' of the EC and also the issue of scope and task expansion. Again, both of these tended to be linked by leading protagonists, notably by the 'Punch and Judy show' of Delors and Thatcher in 1988: he declaring before the UK TUC that 80% of economic and social legislation might shortly pass to Brussels; she in the Bruges speech of September, declaring that the frontiers of the state had not been rolled back in Britain to be re-extended by the Brussels back door.

This, however, lay some time ahead. For the Council, the major achievements of 1985 were enlargement and treaty revision. Yet the way it described the latter was ominous for 'maximalists': the revision, said the Council, 'gave tangible form to the wishes of the Heads of State or Government in the Solemn Declaration' (33 *RCW*: 7). Additionally, the Council cited some economic improvement (though not on the unemployment front): the new budget Decision replacing that of 1970 on own resources (raising the maximum VAT precept from 1% to 1.4%) (see also Nicoll 1986: 31ff.); and modest strengthening of the EMS and the role of the ECU, by authorising the European Monetary Cooperation Fund (EMCF) to issue ECUs against deposits made by the central banks of third states and by international monetary institutions. (See 33 *RCW*: 7; 19 *GRA*: 84–5; *Bull. EC* 3–1985: 21; 4–1985: 14.)

The Commission was also generally bullish: the EMS had 'worked very satisfactorily during the year, performing its function as a regional zone of monetary stability in Europe. Despite sharp upward and downward movements in the dollar, there was no serious strain between the currencies participating in the ... ERM' (19 *GRA*: 84). Even the one realignment on 20 July, 'after more than two years of no change', had occurred 'under exemplary conditions of speed and discretion, thus ensuring ... no serious speculation against the lira' (19 *GRA*: 84). This was too much: what for some was 'discretion' was for others 'pulling a fast one' (Brewin and McAllister 1986: 339).

Other clouds had reappeared. The European Council had in June invited the Commission to submit by December a report in detail on 'current inadequacies as regards growth and employment in the European economy compared to its major competitors – and on the new strategies that could be implemented to remedy the situation'. Also, in discussing the White Paper priorities, it had been unequivocal about removal of *physical* barriers, but had, in relation to *technical* barriers to free movement of goods, picked out 'standards for major new technologies'. It had been positively coy beyond that, concentrating on the creation of a free market in financial services and transport, full freedom of establishment for professions and liberalisation of capital movements; but was particularly careful about indirect taxation:

> As regards the approximation of VAT and excise duties, the European Council invited the Council of Ministers for Financial Affairs to examine *on the basis of* the white paper *any measures which might be necessary* for the achievement of ... a single market and the *possible* timetable for the application of those measures.
>
> (*Bull. EC* 6–1985: 14–15, emphasis added)

The burst of *élan* was already running into banks of fog.

Japan remained a specific further cloud, the emphasis being on increasing 'significantly and continuously its imports of manufactured products and processed agricultural products' and on 'liberalising Japanese financial markets and internationalising the yen' *(Bull. EC* 6–1985: 16).

The Soviet scene was at the time deemed more positive. Indeed, Soviet interest in the whole '1992' process was not slow to emerge. This extended to Comecon: the European Council had exchanged views on the recent letter from that body to the Commission:

> [P]roposing the resumption of their mutual relations ... More generally, [the European Council] also discussed the interest in the political role of [the EC]

recently demonstrated in statements by the secretary-general of the CPSU. They noted these developments with interest.

(*Bull. EC* 6–1985: 16)

Well they might.


## Ambitions and implications of the White Paper

There was no doubting the pride of place that had been given to the White Paper. It was 'the first priority of the present Commission, and ... perhaps the major achievement required of the Commission during its term of office; if the programme succeeded, it would fundamentally alter the face of Europe' (*Bull. EC* 6–1985: 18). Again, this was (perhaps understandable) hype as regards its internal, though not its external, effects.

More interesting was the Commission's gloss on its task. There would be:

> [N]o more attempts to harmonise or standardise at any price – a method originating in too rigid an interpretation of the Treaty; in most cases, an 'approximation' of the parameters is sufficient to reduce differences in [tax] rates or technical specifications to an acceptable level.
>
> (*Bull. EC* 6–1985: 18)

It was soon to become clear that over such very matters as these – technical standards, tax rates – the wheels ground exceedingly slowly.

The White Paper distinguished between the 'new strategy' and a 'new approach' which it proposed. The 'strategy' referred to choosing between harmonisation on the one hand and mutual recognition on the other (Cockfield White Paper: 18–23, esp. paras 61, 65, 77, 79; von Sydow in Bieber et al. 1988: 92). It was asking, basically, whether there was a *need* for harmonisation. The 'new approach', by contrast, asked *how* such harmonisation might be achieved. The Commission's suggestions on this were adopted by the Council of Ministers: Commission and Council would no longer be involved in the detail of harmonisation Directives, but would instead concentrate on the objectives to be attained. The task of working out the actual details would be carried out by the various (private) European standards bodies – CEN (the European Committee for Standardisation) and CENELEC (the European Committee for Electrotechnical Standardisation) (see Swann (ed.) 1992: 56–9). 'Mutual recognition' applied if and when harmonisation was not thought essential.

Mutual recognition built unashamedly on the CJEC's *Cassis de Dijon* judgment: the White Paper urged (para. 58) that 'if a product is lawfully manufactured and marketed in one Member State, there is no reason why it should not be sold throughout the Community' and it went on to extend the point radically: 'What is true for goods, is also true for services and for people.'

The language may have been regarded as blunt and 'revolutionary' by critics (von Sydow in Bieber et al. 1988: 93) but it only repeated what had been said in other, earlier internal market declarations. One result of the shift was the abandonment of hundreds of drafts and proposals on harmonisation. A second was the extension, from goods to other areas, of the principle of mutual recognition. Again, this ground had been prepared before, at the Fontainebleau European Council of June 1984, in regard to the mutual recognition of degrees and diplomas (*Bull. EC* 6–1984).

Mutual recognition was thought of as a temporary expedient, until European standards could be developed: it did not, however, *replace* harmonisation: the latter might remain necessary on such grounds as public health, technical safety or consumer protection and/or on grounds of achieving economies of scale or of compatibility of products in a unified market. Again, the ground had been prepared before the White Paper, but the notion appeared capable of extension. (See Council Resolution of 7 May 1985, 'New Approach to Technical Harmonisation and Standards'; *OJ* 1985, C136/1; von Sydow in Bieber et al. 1988: 95.)

Grand principles were not the only issue, however. In this minefield, the question of who was to define the technical specifications needed and of who was to oversee the *implementation* of Council decisions, were of equal importance. Setting specifications, as we have seen, was to be done by CEN and CENELEC. And on implementation, the White Paper, while carefully not advocating specific institutional reforms, drew attention to the Council's powers to delegate to the Commission under Article 155 EEC (*White Paper*: 20; von Sydow in Bieber et al. 1988: 95).

One further crucial point had been raised in the Council's May 1985 resolution and in the White Paper. This concerned the legal basis for harmonisation. The Commission noted, in the field of veterinary and phytosanitary controls, the Council's tendency to insist on reference to Article 100 EEC requiring unanimity, as well as Article 43 which allowed qualified majority. 'The Commission', said the White Paper (para. 61) 'does not think this position is justified.' Bringing the real difficulties into the open was far better than the bureaucratic blockage of relying on an automatic veto. Indeed, a fine paradox had emerged: 'The principle of majority voting leads to unanimous decisions, while the principle of unanimity leads to no decisions at all' (von Sydow in Bieber et al. 1988: 98).

Similarly, it was important to prevent the emergence of *new* barriers to free movement. Here too, the groundwork had been done, this time in Directive 83/189/EEC (the so-called Mutual Information Directive), requiring member states to notify draft regulations and standards concerned with technical specifications which they proposed to introduce.

The White Paper approach depended largely on simplification and reduction of the burden of legislation. It also held out the promise of seeing the whole process as a positive-sum rather than zero-sum game. It sought to incite Commission, Council and EP to work together. Yet it also provided sticks as well as carrots and notably a large stick in the Commission's own hands: in paragraph 156, the White Paper declared that:

> [I]n the event of approximation lagging behind the agreed schedules, the Council's inaction cannot relieve the Commission of its obligation to take *whatever measures are necessary* to ensure free movement of goods … consistent with the aims of the Treaty and the deadline of 1992.
>
> (Cockfield White Paper: 39, emphasis added)

In other words, agree among yourselves, or we shall determine on your behalf.

Over physical barriers, the Commission appeared categorical, but again, there seemed at first a slight ambiguity: the programme would propose no measures which 'in fact maintain checks at internal frontiers and therefore the frontiers themselves ... their disappearance will have immense psychological and practical importance'. Did 'their' refer mainly to the checks or also to the frontiers themselves? But the Commission went on: 'The objective is total removal of barriers – not just their reduction. The Commission's intention is that the internal frontier posts will disappear completely' (*Bull. EC* 6–1985: 18). Some functions presently carried out at frontiers ought logically to cease in an internal market: for the rest, other means would have to be developed to carry them out elsewhere (such as veterinary and health checks at point of destination, it was suggested). Right from the start, it was recognised that this involved 'straying into sensitive areas such as tax policy and the fight against drugs and terrorism. It recognises frankly that these are difficult areas, which will pose real problems' (*Bull. EC* 6–1985: 19).

The quotation also serves to show that the division between physical, technical and fiscal barriers in the White Paper was 'somewhat artificial' (Pelkmans and Robson 1987: 185): here, physical immediately entailed fiscal; elsewhere, whatever did not fit into these two categories was labelled 'technical', which produced a very mixed bag.

At the same time, the White Paper contained a long list of 'unfinished business' – draft technical harmonisation Directives to be implemented under the slow and cumbersome 'old approach'. Public procurement also featured prominently in the technical barriers discussion: the so-called 'excluded sectors' – energy, water, transport and telecoms supply – were now to be covered. Similarly, free movement for labour and the professions and the markets for services, both 'traditional' and 'new' (e.g. information), particularly financial and transport services, were to be opened up. Capital controls would have to go; cooperation between undertakings would have to be facilitated; there was also talk of a 'Community-wide broadcasting area'.

On fiscal barriers, the Commission began from the abolition of frontiers, to propose far-reaching fiscal harmonisation. 'This "reasoning backward" ... is, in political terms, audacious' (Pelkmans and Robson 1987: 186), implying as it did that there would be no possibility of sustaining markedly different levels of indirect taxes. This led the Commission into yet deeper water: if VAT and excise continued to be levied on the 'destination' basis that it proposed, might there not have to be a Community clearing-house system for VAT, to ensure that VAT collected by an exporting member state and deducted by an importing one were reimbursed to the latter (see Swann 1992: 91; Cockfield White Paper: 43, para. 172); a linked system of bonded warehouses for excisable products; and only small variations from state to state in the tax rates?

Just how ambitious and audacious the White Paper was, is clear from further implications: strict surveillance of national public aids; a head-on approach in such matters as transport and trade policy where 'given the cumbersome decision-making system of the Community, progress ... is likely to be very difficult'

(Pelkmans and Robson 1987: 191). Further, scepticism about the claimed benefits was in order, given that these would not arise if the 'single' market were to be as ossified as the previous national ones.

Another important dimension was the domestic (national) political consequences of the programme. Adjustment costs would fall heavily on some member states: it would be necessary to operate compensation at Community level, but distinctly difficult given the Community's structures and the attitudes of the states. It was no exaggeration to say that 'if the White Paper is taken seriously it will have pervasive implications for the Member States' capacity for autonomous economic policy-making and for their "sovereignty"' (Pelkmans and Robson 1987: 191–2). Already one could discern the ground on which the Bruges Group, and others of like mind, would choose to stand and fight. Already, too, another battle was joined: for Lord Cockfield and others of his persuasion, the White Paper had to stand entire: it was to be eaten as a complete menu; it could not be sampled *à la carte*.

Yet despite the grim determination of Cockfield's 'take it or leave it' approach, the White Paper programme was not set in tablets of stone. Even the *number* of measures was not fixed: it slithered up and down in the range of the upper 200s as repackaging and reordering took place.

What it did provide was not just a rather comprehensive statement of 'what is to be done', albeit with certain gaps. There was also a timetable (and hence sequence), at least at the two levels of Commission *proposal* and Council *adoption.* Effective *implementation* and *enforcement* would prove something else, and became major preoccupations as the single market programme developed (see Cini 2003: esp. Chs 9, 22 ; Macrory 1992 [*CMLRev* 29 (2): 349–69]).

There continued to be vigorous argument about the precise content of, and manner of bringing into being, the internal market. Once again that, too, although ostensibly about policy scope and competences, proved to be very closely linked to the other battles. It was clearly linked to the inter-institutional battle, over competences, 'comitology' and 'who does what'. It was linked to the battle over the Community's external stance, via the issues of 'Fortress Europe'; of how far scope for national derogations would remain; of how far internal liberalisation entailed external liberalisation. Last, it was to prove, before the decade was out, linked to the issue of *geographical* scope, both because '1992' was to prove a magnet and a worry to other parts of Europe and also because enlargement up to that point (i.e. the inclusion of Spain and Portugal from 1986) had increased the heterogeneity of those very economic orders of the member states which it was a main purpose of the White Paper to render not merely more 'open' to one another but also more similar to each other. The apparently technical was once again to prove, for neither the first nor the last time, to be highly political.

On the single market, the Commission's report for 1986 was equivocal. After noting a marked speeding up of Commission proposals and of Council deliberation, it added: 'None the less, there have been delays which, if not soon made up, could jeopardise the completion of the full programme by 1992.' The Commission's slow start in 1985 had to some extent been improved upon in 1986. The same could not be said of the Council, however, where the backlog amounted to almost two-thirds of the proposals due to have been adopted by that stage. Sectorally, the most troublesome areas in 1985 and 1986 proved to be plant and animal health, and taxation questions (20 *GRA*: 91–2).

Not surprisingly, the delay in the entry into force of the SEA was invoked the following year to explain the hold-ups: this was 'bound to affect the timetable contained in the White Paper'. Once more, 'there can be no question but that most headway has been made by the Commission', with proposals notably on public procurement, indirect taxation, capital movements and standardisation. The Council's progress was a good deal less swift: nevertheless, the Commission at this stage characterised the process as 'virtually irreversible' (21 *GRA*: 86).

For 1988 again a mixed verdict was returned, with some of the by now familiar troublesome dossiers again highlighted. While the Council had decided to adopt, by qualified majority if necessary, certain decisions in the areas of road transport, insurance, public procurement and diplomas, nevertheless 'the disappointing progress on all matters concerning the removal of frontier barriers for both people and goods is to be deplored' (22 *GRA*: 98).

Since issues of coherence and 'tidiness' were to play such a prominent part, it is convenient here to remind ourselves of an exceedingly important dimension of aggravation and confusion. This concerned the EC's relations with by far its largest trading partner at the time, EFTA, which, from this point on, generated a good deal of recrimination, friction and reassessment.

## Implications for the 'wider western Europe'

In April 1984 observers could have been forgiven for thinking that a milestone of mutual understanding had been reached, in the so-called Luxembourg Declaration. On 9 April, foreign ministers of the 'Community Ten' and the 'EFTA Seven' had met in Luxembourg for perhaps the most important such gathering since the signing of the 1972 free trade agreements between the EC and the individual EFTA members. Significantly, the closing joint declaration spoke of deepening and extending cooperation 'within the framework of *and beyond* the Free Trade Agreements'. With free trade arrangements completed, it went on to speak of 'the aim of creating a dynamic European economic space': thus the concept of the 'EES' came into the light of day. The list of *desiderata* and priority areas read like a foreshadowing of the White Paper 14 months later and specifically stated: 'In this regard the Community's efforts to strengthen its internal market are of particular relevance' (*Bull. EC* 4–1984: 9–10; see also 18 *GRA*: 251–4). The very next month, reference was made to 'demonstrating the new spirit of EEC–EFTA relations following … Luxembourg' (*Bull. EC* 5–1984: 76).

The Iberian enlargement had, from this standpoint, a double effect: first, the 'transfer' of Portugal from EFTA to the EC; second, the question of the arrangements to be made in regard to both Spain and Portugal.

For a while, the Luxembourg Declaration was regarded by most parties as an adequate, and politically significant, basis for EC–EFTA relations. However, EFTA's 25th anniversary celebrations in mid-May 1985, where again optimistic and positive sounds were heard, proved also to inaugurate a period of strange silence, a kind of 'phoney war'. The silence was shattered when both sides, but particularly EFTA, had had proper time to mull over and begin to understand the implications of the *detail* of the Cockfield White Paper.

It was a full year before 'radio silence' was broken. In June 1986 at the conclusion of Delors's visit to Sweden, it was said that 'the implementation of the Luxembourg declaration met with certain problems of institutional, legal and technical nature and certain delays were noted' (*EDB* 4332, 5 June 1986: 12). Commissioner De Clercq's Reykjavik meeting with EFTA ministers a couple of days later ended with an expression by EFTA of 'keen interest' (i.e. concern) over the EEC's intentions concerning unified financial markets. The conclusions of the EC Council of Ministers in September were also neutral in tone (text: see *EDB* 4389, 17 September 1986: 7–8). By the late October meeting of EFTA's consultative committee, the change of emphasis, although subtle, was unmistakable: 'The main point on the agenda was the consequences for EFTA–EEC co-operation of work currently underway to complete the EEC's internal market' (*EDB* 4419, 29 October 1986: 15).

The EFTA states had slowly been forced to confront several uncomfortable truths. First, the White Paper was so absorbing EC attention that there was little to spare for EFTA. Second, the implications for the interests of EFTA states of what was proposed were profound. Third, since agreement among EC states was likely to prove extremely difficult, there would be strictly limited willingness to expose private grief or to open up the family to dissent from the margins. Thus, fourth, decisions deeply affecting the EFTA states were going to be taken without their active participation, and mainly without their consent. Fifth, it was quite unclear whether it would prove possible, or preferable, for EFTA states to try to work together, or to be obliged to work separately, given their non-identical interests. Here, rather as with successive enlargements, it began to look as if EFTA *governments*, at least, might be left shifting uneasily from foot to foot in the cold, waiting to see what might be done for or to them. Whether the main economic actors – corporations – would be so marginalised was yet another issue: increasingly, many sought to 'position' themselves, to act as best they could 'as if' they were themselves simply already within the EC.

Once again, the EC found itself in the realm of unintended consequences; but once again, it had scant spare decisional capacity to devote to trying to deal with this. The EFTA states experienced the phenomenon of the 'elephants and the grass', as indeed did the non-member Mediterranean Basin states: Portugal felt that it had jumped just in time.

As for Comecon, the timing of its approach was assuredly no accident. On 14 June 1985 Delors received a letter from Vyacheslav Sychov, CMEA Secretary, again proposing establishment of relations between the EC and CMEA. For the Commission, De Clercq replied on 29 July, indicating the Community's willingness to take up again the dialogue broken off in 1981 and asking what CMEA thought a joint declaration by the two should contain. As before, the EC sought to stress its relations *qua* EC with the individual CMEA states. It was striking evidence of the gathering thaw in relations with the Soviet Union in particular, consequent upon the 'Gorbachev effect', even if, when *this* 'mutual recognition' finally came 3 years later, it was a meagre creature indeed (*Bull. EC* 7/8–1985: 90–1, 10–1985: 65–6, 85; 33 *RCW*: 115–16).

Not to be outdone, Turkey presented its formal request for accession in April 1987: Greece predictably renewed its opposition. Other reserves followed. In June Thatcher stated that this must be linked to a Cyprus solution. Not a few were keen to find ways to delay: but it seemed that nobody had the frankness to declare openly that they simply did not regard Turkey as within the pale. Once the pass had been sold ('a European state'), then the fallback had to be on features of the 'internal order' – the economy and human rights notably. So the EP sent observers to the Turkish elections late in the year; in November the Germans indicated that no rapid decision was going to be possible; following the elections, the Turkish government confirmed its wish to join.

All of these issues and more – whether of accession or of the form that future relationships with the EC were to take – were to return to haunt the Community at the end of the 1980s. They were to do so in a context of both euphoria and trouble, for which the EC was markedly, if not surprisingly, unprepared. The issues of geographical scope and of 'what kind of Europe' – issues raised not least by Margaret Thatcher in her Bruges speech – were soon again to prove their centrality. They were to add to the growing strains on the 'Monnet model' Europe – itself slowly changing, to be sure; but with the question marks about the adequacy and appropriateness of the institutional/constitutional arrangements steadily growing.

It is now time to return to these and to the main strands of the 'internal' action in 1985–7. Little could be done about implementing the White Paper unless and until the SEA was in place: this very fact acted as a spur to the unwilling, but they remained unwilling. The SEA was eventually signed in Luxembourg on 17 February 1986 by Belgium, France, Germany, Ireland, Luxembourg, the Netherlands, Portugal, Spain and the UK. On 28 February the official 'awkward squad' – Italy from the 'maximalist', Denmark and Greece from the 'minimalist' positions – fell into line after more or less gallant (according to taste) rearguard actions and signed in The Hague (34 *RCW*: 16).

The British had already seen their room for manoeuvre closely constrained (Burgess 1989; Colchester and Buchan 1990: 23). The Danish Folketing rejected the SEA, thus forcing the government to a swiftly held referendum. Again, this was fought essentially as a membership issue, not narrowly on the merits. It resulted in the underwhelming figure of 56% in favour; and it was only then that, from their conveniently opposite perspectives, Italy and Greece succumbed.

That was not, however, the end of the untidy business and sighs of relief were premature. Signature was one thing: ratification, beyond challenge in each state, another. To the surprise of some and sheer disbelief of others, the last battle was fought in Ireland, by means of the claim of the campaigner Raymond Crotty that the SEA contravened the Irish Constitution: a claim upheld in the Irish Supreme Court, which again had the effect of forcing a referendum, again with a result in favour of the SEA (Brewin and McAllister 1988: 463–4; Colchester and Buchan 1990: 23–4). And so 'the single market begat the Single Act'.

## The 'Delors package' and 'the inter-institutional agreement'

The delay in achieving the ratification and coming into force of the SEA may have been frustrating for Delors and others at the Commission, but he did not let up the pressure. The Council was to be given no chance to rest on its laurels in 1987. On 18 February Delors not only presented the Commission's annual work programme to the EP but accompanied it with the document *Making a Success of the Single Act: A New Frontier for Europe* (COM (87) 100, of 15 February; 21 *GRA*: pt 2; *Bull. Supp.* 1/87). Hard on its heels came the next salvo: on 28 February was published the Commission Report to Council and EP *On the Financing of the Community Budget* (COM (87) 101), which opened by asserting: 'The Community is at present … on the brink of bankruptcy.' This was followed up by a letter to the heads of state and government on 10 April, not only drawing attention to the critical state of the budget, but rejecting any recourse to past 'expedients' in resolving the problems (*Bull. EC* 4–1987, pt 2.3.1). Thus was launched yet another Delors memorial – this time to be known as the 'Delors package'.

With the Irish referendum out of the way and the SEA about to come into force, the minds of government leaders were focused at the Brussels European Council of 29–30 June 1987. Aspects of the *New Frontier* paper were considered there and most governments appeared ready to go along with it. Not so the British: the Conservative victory in the 11 June General Election reinforced the reflex to oppose. There were, of course, aspects of which the UK approved, notably the discussion of budgetary discipline and aspects of budgetary management.

By now the Commission papermill was whirling fast. There followed, notably: the proposal for Council Regulation COM (87) 400, on 24 July; a provisional text on reform of the structural funds (COM (87) 376) and the own resources decision (COM (87) 420) – both on 31 July; and the communication on budgetary discipline (COM (87) 430) of 4 August. This high workrate at the approach of the holiday season cleared desks at the Commission: it also, no doubt, gave others plenty to think about over August.

More papers followed after the summer, from both EP and Commission. The EP's Committee on Budgets produced, notably, the Baron Crespo Report on 6 and 7 November (EP Doc. A 2–200/87). In September, Émile Noël retired as Commission Secretary-General, the post he had held right from the inception of the Community. That he was succeeded by David Williamson of the UK, previously adviser to Mrs Thatcher on Community affairs, was to prove of more than passing importance when the moment arrived (in February 1988) to compromise and agree. The 'package' approach had worked before: it was to be clear this time too that, if the UK wanted budgetary discipline and other benefits, it would have to give way on additional expenditure for 'cohesion'. Inter-institutional relations, too, remained fraught: perhaps partly to get their own back for the CJEC's 1986 judgment declaring that the EP's president had exceeded his powers in declaring the budget adopted when it did not have the blessing of the Council of Ministers (see *FT* 4 July 1986), the EP now made common cause with the Commission against the Council because of the latter's failure to adopt the draft budget for 1988 on time (21 *GRA*: pt 65)! *This* time it was to be EP and Commission vs. Council before the CJEC!

Yet even by year's end, it was not all over. The Copenhagen European Council had to agree to continue discussion of the Delors package into the early months of 1988. It was another classic British 'cliffhanger', in the lineage of the saga culminating at Fontainebleau in 1984 and the saga over the SEA. This time four related issues held centre stage; some familiar from the 'British rebate' saga. They were CAP expenditure, budget 'discipline', the need to agree new revenue sources and the issue of aid to the two new southern members in particular (see Taylor in Lodge (ed.) 1989: 14).

By common consent, the UK gained nothing concrete or visible by prolonging the agony and indeed made most of the concessions. In the most obvious areas – the CAP, funds for Spain and Portugal and 'own resources' – the UK caved in, albeit at the last moment (Taylor in Lodge (ed.) 1989: 15–17; Nugent 1991: *passim*). It can be argued that what the British did do, however, was to limit and dictate a good deal of the pace and nature of change, in terms of both 'concealed' and 'emergent' agendas. In doing so, of course, they did not make themselves loved.

Explanations of the British 'retreat' have tended to be of several kinds. For some observers, the UK was deserted by those it had thought to be its allies, at least of convenience: in turn, the FRG, the Netherlands and Spain. The UK may also have feared very concrete losses: of part at least of the 'rebate' so painfully agreed. Others noted that Mrs Thatcher was also 'sandwiched' by her compatriots: under strong pressure from her close, if little loved, Foreign and Commonwealth Office (FCO) advisers and also from new Commission Secretary-General, David Williamson, until so recently her adviser on EC affairs. Whatever the pressures, Taylor suggests that during mid-afternoon on 12 February, 'according to officials, Mrs Thatcher did something which for her was quite extraordinary: during the conference she retreated by herself to a room for an hour's contemplation. Afterwards her position was conciliatory' (Taylor in Lodge (ed.) 1989: 17).

The public presentation of these events was, as always, interesting. Some things could be said out loud, notably how 'good the deal was for the taxpayer'. Other things had to be left unsaid or at most hinted at: that the UK 'victory' over budget discipline was actually a way of restraining interventionist propensities in Brussels and concentrating minds on the *kostenfrei* aspects of the single market. 'Budgetary discipline' was a very handy lever. 'It allowed prior judgements about finance to constrain the choice of policy, rather than the other way round' (Taylor in Lodge (ed.) 1989: 18).

The measures agreed constituted a 5-year programme to shift the balance of EC spend away from the CAP in favour of the structural funds and of the new members in particular. In June 1988 the presidents of the Council, Commission and EP formalised this by signing the Inter-Institutional Agreement on Budgetary Discipline and Improvement of the Budgetary Procedure (*OJL* 185: 15 July 1988). An important limitation was placed on the overall growth of the budget: expressed as a percentage of the total GNP of the Community, it was to grow only from 1.15% in 1988 to 1.20% in 1992.

## Padoa-Schioppa, EMU and the Delors Report

The importance of the internal market White Paper was not just that it had set out 'what was required' in a linked and timetabled way. A mechanism was provided for monitoring progress at least as far as Commission proposals and Council of Ministers passage of legislation was concerned. This was to take the form of periodic reports by the Commission: in addition to annual reports, there were to be milestone 'stocktaking' reports in 1988, 1990 and 1992. They provide useful insights into sticking points and difficulties in particular (COM (86) 300, 26 May 1986; (87) 203, 11 May 1987; (88) 134, 21 March 1988; (89) 311, 20 June 1989; (90) 90, 28 March 1990; (91) 237, 17 June 1991; see also COM (88) 650, 17 November 1988 and (89) 422, 7 September 1989).

Of the highest importance for the next round of battles over the EC's evolution was a further burst of activity concerning the implications of the internal market. Hardly was the ink dry on the Single Act than the Commission requested a report from a committee of experts, on what might now be expected. Once again, an interesting political process was at work. Delors himself had long argued in favour of EMU: the ambiguous outcome of the SEA in that regard was a disappointment to him. Conveniently to hand lay work done fairly recently for the Commission: the report *Money, Economic Policy and Europe* by Tommaso Padoa-Schioppa, the preface for which had been written by Commission Vice-President F.-X. Ortoli in 1985. This had argued strongly in favour of EMU.

Now Padoa-Schioppa was again called into service, aided, as *rapporteur*, by one of the key EMS authors whom we have already encountered, Michael Emerson of the Commission, and six other collaborators (one of whom did not share its final conclusions). There was a strong 'Massachusetts mafia' at work: no fewer than four out of the eight had spent some time at MIT – King, Papademos, Padoa-Schioppa himself and Pastor – with a contribution from the new trade theorist along the river, Paul Krugman of Harvard. (Anyone tempted to describe the Community in terms of 'networks' should be aware of those of *this* kind.)

This report, *Efficiency, Stability and Equity* (Padoa-Schioppa 1987), argued that the Community now faced an 'inconsistent quartet' in policy terms: the combination of free trade, capital mobility, fixed exchange rates and national control over monetary policy meant that 'something had to give'. Its solution was – to no one's surprise – a single Community-wide monetary policy (21 *GRA*: 81; *Bull. EC* 4–1987: 7–9).

A central proposition of the report echoed work at least as far back as the 1977 MacDougall Report. 'Essential interactions exist between the Community's resource allocation function (completion of the internal market), stabilisation function (the EMS and macroeconomic co-ordination) and distribution function (regional policies, structural Funds and the Community budget)' (*Bull. EC* 4–1987: 7). To overlook these interactions might well mean the internal market programme running into trouble, with a significant loss of economic welfare. To prevent this, the internal market programme should be made part of an overall strategy involving those three functions as well. Once again, for Delors, author of the preface to this report, interventionist up to a point as well as integrationist, this was manna indeed.

Further, the 'inconsistent quartet', implying that national monetary policies would have to be much more closely unified, 'raises questions as to how coordination is to be organised and institutionalised' and the group unveiled what it called a 'stage two EMS', with a range of accompanying proposals.

Not only should 'monetary policy co-ordination and the mechanisms of the EMS ... be significantly strengthened' to cope with free movement of capital plus exchange rate 'discipline', but much more powerful redistributive policies were called for (not least because of enlargement), as was a 'co-operative growth strategy': echoes of the French pleas of the early 1980s (*Bull. EC* 4–1987: 9; Padoa-Schioppa 1987: 5–16).

The authors were at pains to stress that although enlargement and the internal market, 'the two decisions of 1985', might not appear at first sight to have '"systemic" implications, as they represent a geographical widening and an economic deepening', nevertheless the two had wide-ranging implications. In the new, more heterogeneous Community, free movement of capital might be 'inconsistent with the present combination of exchange rate stability and considerable national autonomy in ... monetary policy'; by the same token, market opening 'will have distributive effects that are likely to be stronger and more disruptive than those experienced in the sixties when trade integration proceeded among less heterogeneous countries and in a context of faster economic growth' (Padoa-Schioppa 1987: x).

Complementary programmes were, therefore, essential and would have to address the three policy functions of market integration, economic stabilisation and equitable distribution of gains, 'without which the success of the "allocative programme", i.e. the completion of the internal market, would be jeopardised'. The report's comments on the limitations on Community redistributive policies and its 'barely significant' stabilisation role also echo the MacDougall Report. 'The danger now comes from potentially disruptive imbalances between different policy dimensions in the Community' and the solutions proposed had (once again) 'an unavoidable institutional content', its author's covering letter concluded (Padoa-Schioppa 1987: xi–xii).

We may break off briefly from consideration of this lineage, simply to observe that the Commission appeared to want to have its cake and eat it. On the one hand, it had promoted the internal market on the grounds of welfare *gains* and economic growth and, indeed, went on to defend this viewpoint in the (much controverted) Cecchini Report, *The European Challenge: 1992* (Cecchini 1988). (Emerson was associated with work on this report also.) The 'cost of non-Europe' was the *leitmotif* for propounding the SEM. Yet, on the other hand, said the Padoa-Schioppa Report, there would be welfare *losses* unless other things were done as well. The Commission also sought to bolster scope expansion at Community level in another report, *La Dimension sociale du marché intérieur* (Degimbe 1988).

What, then, of the connections between the Padoa-Schioppa and Delors reports? One answer is direct and personal. In the Delors Report, Padoa-Schioppa, with Gunter Baer, were the two *rapporteurs*. They also co-authored two of the collection of papers submitted to the Delors Committee, significantly that on 'The Werner Report revisited' and that on 'The ECU, the common currency and monetary union' (*Report on Economic and Monetary Union in the EC* (Delors Report 1989)). One obvious difference was that, whereas the Padoa-Schioppa Report was the product of an invitation from Delors and the Commission, the Delors Report was an invitation *to* him as Commission president, from the Hanover European Council of 27–8 June 1988. Nevertheless, the circle was complete and, to no one's surprise, a lot of the original expertise was recalled to serve again.

A second obvious difference promised to affect the prospects of the whole exercise. Delors was careful to include on the committee all the central bank governors, the very people who would have to make any such system work or at least hand it over in mid-stream to their successors. In associating them with the work right from the start, Delors was endeavouring to ensure backing and political commitment to whatever emerged, at the highest level. Although it was made clear that 'the Heads of State or Government [had] agreed to invite the Presidents or Governors of their Central Banks to take part *in a personal capacity* in the proceedings of the Committee' (emphasis added), they also agreed to invite, by common agreement, three 'outside' experts and one other Commissioner. These were, for the Commission, Frans Andriessen, and as the 'outside three': Niels Thygesen, Professor of Economics at Copenhagen; Alexandre Lamfalussy, Director-General of the Bank for International Settlements in Basel; and Miguel Boyer, President of the Banco Exterior de España (*Bull. EC* 6–1988: 166).

At another level, it is worth looking at the intellectual debts and the connections between the two reports. They are apparent, first, in the authorship of the background papers, on 'Werner' and on the ECU. Traces can also be found in the footnotes to other papers, for example Delors's citation of Padoa-Schioppa (p. 84); even of MacDougall (p. 88). Lamfalussy, too, acknowledges Padoa-Schioppa's collaborators; the 'new' trade theory of Paul Krugman in Annex A to that report (Delors Report 1989: 99n.). It is not too far fetched, then, to see at work the same kind of process that we saw in the 1983–6 period with respect to the 'piggybacking' between Genscher-Colombo and Stuttgart; the DTEU, Dooge and Adonnino; and the SEM and SEA. Once again, the IGC method was to be invoked – initially, there was to be but one, with EMU as its core concern. Under the pressure of more exogenous shocks, soon to be discussed, there would be two, the second concerned with political union.

June 1988 was marked by a number of significant events. The Council adopted a Regulation on interstate carriage of goods by road, an important single market measure. On the 24th, it adopted all the legislation resulting from the February 'Delors package' agreement – on own resources, the budget and so forth. The Commission sent the EP its 'People's Europe' assessment and outlook. It sent the Council a proposal for a Directive on voting rights in local and euro-elections in the state of residence. And just before the Hanover European Council came the EC–CMEA joint declaration.

Delors had good reason to be pleased. The Hanover 'summit' not only recalled that 'in adopting the Single Act, the Member States of the Community confirmed the objective of progressive realisation of economic and monetary union'; it set a date a year ahead, in Madrid in June 1989, to examine the means of achieving this, and entrusted to the committee chaired by Delors 'the task of studying and proposing concrete stages leading towards this union' (Foreword to the Delors Report). Conveniently, it was also agreed at Hanover to reappoint Delors as Commission president. It is not clear whether there was any *open* opposition to that. Those tempted to oppose might live to rue their lack of nerve. Delors rubbed salt in the wound with his speech to – horror of horrors – the British TUC, where he promised a good deal via 'social Europe' and delivered rather little. Others were not to survive. Lord Cockfield for one was to depart at the end of the year, having unforgivably 'gone native'.

If Delors had reason to be pleased, Thatcher had reason to be displeased. The mutual antipathy was visceral and by now an automatic reflex. What her Bruges speech of 20 September did reflect was a profoundly different view of the nature of the Community and its place in Europe as a whole. At the time, its author was the butt of a good deal of adverse press comment. How far she accurately 'sniffed the wind' will be discussed later. In the meantime, there is no doubt that the UK – and ultimately Thatcher herself – paid heavily for it.

*The Economist*, for one, did not follow the chorus of excoriation. The speech had not been:

> [A] predictable diatribe against European unity … Predictable the speech was not: it was a thoughtful, elegant essay on the Europe Britain would like to see … Mrs Thatcher set out a more achievable prospect for the mid-1990s than Mr Delors has done.
>
> (*The Economist*, 24–30 September 1988: 16)

Delors's own 'rash comment' that within 10 years 80% of relevant legislation would be 'made in Brussels' 'gave the British prime minister the ideal clay pigeon to shoot down', the paper opined (*The Economist*, 24–30 September 1988: 61). Whether from convenience or from a different 'visionary gleam', Mrs Thatcher had chosen to remind her audience at the College of Europe, that 'den of federalism if ever there was one' (as *The Economist*'s anonymous columnist had it): 'We shall always look on Warsaw, Prague and Budapest as great European cities.' Her speech, it said, was one that 'no other European leader could have made, precisely because Britain has for so long looked beyond western Europe' (ibid.: 61).

Here indeed lay the rub. She had dared to voice something other than belief in those doctrines of logical entailment, of one thing leading ineluctably to another, which were precisely the stock in trade of most of the Brussels establishment. She denied, said *The Economist*, that the Community had any *exclusive* claim on European loyalties, and she praised 'that Atlantic Community – that Europe on both sides of the Atlantic – which is our greatest inheritance and greatest strength'. The elements of her version were essentially fivefold: voluntary cooperation among independent 'sovereign' states; a 'practical' approach to EC problems; a boost to enterprise through deregulation; a single market open to the world, not a Fortress Europe; and finally, more action by Europeans on behalf of their own defence, but through NATO *(The Economist*, 24–30 September 1988: 61).

Battle was well and truly joined. Was it already too late for such views – had things already gone beyond, or 'too far'? Many claimed that notions of sovereignty had long been illusory. Others stressed the extent to which the pursuit of EMU would entail (again) severe limits on the fiscal powers of states, thus reducing considerably further the scope for national economic 'intervention'; others claimed that the slow but notable growth of the EC's external persona would make the absence of a security dimension look extremely odd. Some argued all three. But others were beginning to note changes in the landscape especially to the east and to wonder what these might portend. Was Thatcher's reference to Warsaw, Prague and Budapest just a useful diversionary tactic or a sign of real change?

But in the short term at least, it was Delors, secure in his new mandate, who continued to make the running. A few days before the Bruges speech, the Commission adopted its working paper on the social dimension of the internal market. On 19 October was to follow a Commission discussion on the *external* dimension. 'Entailment' was again at work, hooked on to what the British had played for – the internal market. Other extensions were pressed forward: institutional, as with the Council's decision to establish the Court of First Instance, on 24 October; or of policy, as when the EC ratified the Vienna Convention on the protection of the ozone layer on 17 October. A harbinger of the New Europe, however, was the trade and economic cooperation agreement signed with Hungary on 26 September. In mid-October too, negotiations began for renewal of the ACP–EEC Convention.

The main dark cloud as year-end approached was the Rhodes European Council, 'culminating', if that is not too lyrical a term, the Greek presidency – a dismal failure by most accounts. To be sure, the Greek presidency was not helped either by Papandreou's health or that of his government; it was also bound to find the successful German presidency a hard act to follow. But the Greeks did not help themselves. Their announced priorities were mainly external: although a few of these, such as the fraught GATT Uruguay Round, were inevitable topics, some of the others were not and would have been better avoided, as they were never going to produce agreement: notably, a Greek attempt at Rhodes to press a formula for virtual recognition of a Palestinian state ran into the sand. What promised to be a pretty vacuous set of noises on external policy matters was supplemented, and to some extent replaced, by an equally vacuous parading of environmental concerns unaccompanied by much concrete action (Brewin and McAllister 1989: 350–1).

The first half of what was to prove a year of high drama, 1989, saw Spain assume the presidency. Whatever the presidency's own priorities, it became clear that the agenda for 1989 was to be dominated by two aspects above all: one, to an extent under the Community's control, the discussions over EMU and the Delors Report; the other, the radical changes in central and eastern Europe whose implications will be examined in the next chapter.

Of more immediate significance were relations with the EC's nearest neighbours. The EFTA countries had begun to duck and weave. Their difficulties were manifold. How far could they work *as EFTA* any more? Who was going to break ranks, under what conditions and with what consequences? It was Austria that seemed to move first. Austrian industrialists, indeed, generally favoured accession. Neutrality was seen as the main stumbling block; neither was this simply about external (mainly Soviet) reactions – in October 1988, Franz Vranitzky had said that he considered EC membership to be a threat to Austrian neutrality. But there was also pressure from within the EP: German European People's Party members of the EP in January 1989 called for Austria to be made a member. In March, Vranitzky was still emphasising that he thought it difficult to envisage an accession bid soon; but in April the SPÖ said that it favoured membership 'with a neutrality guarantee'. In June, the Austrian parliament voted for accession and in July Austria's formal bid was submitted.

Events on another of Austria's borders were no less significant. On 2 May, Hungary had begun to dismantle the barbed wire on the Austro-Hungarian border. A decisive change in the whole pattern had begun, even though the Soviet Union still felt it appropriate to voice 'concern' about the membership application, just as Austria had itself in July rejected any 'negotiation' with the Soviet Union over membership.

As events in central and eastern Europe rolled on at a heady pace in the second half of 1989, so there was a clear knock-on effect, accelerating reflection and reconsideration of position in the EFTA states. In Sweden, it was announced in September that the parties would soon consider the position: in October, King Carl Gustav spoke of the country being a member of the EC within 6 or 7 years.

In Switzerland, late September was the moment that saw the creation of the 'expert group' on the EC in Bern. The country had been forced to move beyond a clear notion of its own preferences ('EFTA, a purely intergovernmental structure, suits Swiss neutrality and independence better than the more integrational mechanisms of the EC' – Saint-Ouen 1988: 275) to a much more painful recognition of the pressures on it and the dilemmas it faced (see, for example, the Swiss Federal Council's 1988 report on Switzerland's position in regard to European integration; compare with the evaluation of the 'dilemma', 'Das schweizerische Europa-Dilemma' by Fred Luchsinger, *Neue Zürcher Zeitung*, 23 August 1991: 25).

On the SEM front, progress could be reported, even though it had been far from smooth. By March 1990 the Commission was able to announce that 'all the proposals announced in 1985 have now been transmitted to the Council'. As time went on, however, it had felt obliged to give more of its attention to the process of transposing proposals into national law (COM (90) 90, 28 March 1990: 1).

The Commission report heavily underscored the remaining bottlenecks and areas of difficulty. 'No such speeding-up [in decision-taking] has been seen where unanimity is imposed either by the legal basis (trade mark law, taxation) or the Council's refusal to implement the principles of the Single Act concerning the powers of implementation of the Commission; [which] … has requested a debate at the General Affairs Council on … "comitology".' Or again, 'matters requiring the Council to be unanimous are falling behind schedule' (COM (90) 90: 3, 4).

Intergovernmental measures were being taken instead of agreeing the delegation of implementation powers to the Commission. Italy was fingered as being the member state with the greatest backlog in transposition and implementation, while the situation in Spain and Portugal had improved: the Commission hoped that Italy's La Pergola law (speeding implementation) would improve matters.

Classic Commission ploys were again invoked to urge matters forward. First was the 'interdependence' ploy: it was once again argued that everything depended on everything else. Time and again, the SEM proposals revealed how each part depended on the others: for instance, reduction of frontier formalities required 'substantial measures on indirect taxation' (COM (90) 90: 4).

Second was the cry of the 'crucial stage': 'In short, the Community is now at a crucial stage in the implementation of the Single Act. *This year will determine*' whether the White Paper objectives would be attained.

Third was the strategy of 'permanent revolution': insist not only on winning this crucial stage, but also that this 'victory' can only be consolidated by further Herculean efforts on a related front. For instance: 'It is *in this context* that ... EMU offers the prospect of reinforcing the effects of the internal market.'

And finally there was the ploy of 'risk of diversion' or even, in a stronger and usually unarticulated version, 'the enemy without':

> [I]n this same crucial year the Community faces a new challenge *resulting from ... the Community's lodestone effects on its neighbours*. Such success cannot be allowed to compromise what has been achieved. The internal market must lose none of the momentum carrying it towards economic and political integration.

> (COM (90) 90: 5, emphasis added)

No longer, the Commission seemed to be arguing, was it to be a question of 'widening versus deepening': now, again, the one required, *entailed*, the other. What was now portrayed was a race against time: something that, in the past, the Community has seldom been good at – so much so that one seasoned observer, who shall remain anonymous, said that the Community would have to 'learn to walk and chew gum at the same time'. But would it prove able to do so? The initial responses to the events of 1989–90 are the subject of the next chapter.

## Further reading

D. Dinan (ed.), *Origins and Evolution of the European Union*. Oxford: Oxford University Press, 2006. (Chapters 10 and 11.)

J. Gillingham, *European Integration 1950–2003*. Cambridge: Cambridge University Press, 2003. (Part III.)

T. Padoa-Schioppa, *Efficiency, Stability and Equity: A Strategy for the Evolution of the Economic System of the EC*. Oxford: Oxford University Press, 1987.

P. Stirk and D. Weigall, *The Origins and Development of European Integration*. London: Pinter, 1999. (Chapter 9.)

D. Swann (ed.), *The Single Market and Beyond: A Study of the Wider Implications of the Single European Act*. London: Routledge, 1992.

# 9 Europe transformed again
## 1989–1993

There have been many little arithmetical wrinkles worth noting about the EC, which have sometimes been important to the way things happen. One such fact is that, up to this time (until the TEU changed the situation), in only very few years had there been both a new Commission and a newly elected EP; 1989 was such a year. However, since these elections were not due until mid-year, it was to the old EP that Delors made his 17 January speech setting out the perspectives and programme of the incoming Commission.

The speech is of interest not only as marking the halfway point in time of the single market programme and not just as the agenda for the new Commission. It is of interest also for the things that it said and for the things that it did not – perhaps could not – anticipate. For the most part, the tone was upbeat: the Spanish–Portuguese enlargement had, Delors claimed, shown 'enlargement versus deepening' to be a false dichotomy; progress on the single market had been good, though much remained to be done on the fourth of the freedoms – significantly, free movement of persons.

There were flashes of mercantilism:

> At a time of profound change, research and education are the *sinews of economic war*. In the interests of competitiveness and the preservation of Europe's cultural identity, the Community does not intend to allow the Japanese to monopolise audiovisual technology or the Americans to monopolise programmes.
>
> (*Bull. Supp.* 1–89: 8, emphasis added)

The EP itself was promised more powers; the establishment of EMU was pushed. He stressed that EMU 'can only be achieved by means of a further change within the institutions' and that EMU by stages meant that 'it will be necessary, as in 1985, to open the way for another inter-governmental conference ... to amend the Treaty of Rome' (*Bull. Supp.* 1–85: 16). But at this stage it was to be an IGC on EMU alone: only later, when German unification had come fully to occupy centre stage, was the proposal made, and accepted, to add a Political Union IGC as well.

On the external front, the speech contained remarks more than usually Delphic or contradictory. On the one hand (*Bull. Supp.* 1–85: 11): 'Europe must begin to develop what might be called "flexible proximity policies" tailored to a wide variety' of other countries. On the other, the Commission's position was that 'internal development takes priority over enlargement' (*Bull. Supp.* 1–85: 17). More ominously, as regards EFTA, 'with each step we take the slope is getting steeper ... The climber wants to stop and get his breath, to check that he is going in the right direction.' This amounted to a repudiation of the past strategy, reinforced when he added that there were two options: one could either 'stick to our present relationship, essentially bilateral ... a free trade area', or alternatively, 'one could look for a *new, more structured* relationship with *common decision-making and administrative institutions ... to highlight the political dimension* of our co-operation'; adding tantalisingly that, while he had ideas of his own, it would be premature to go into the details of this, and (Delphic again) 'It should be noted that the options would change if EFTA were to strengthen its own structures' so that there could be a two-pillar negotiation (*Bull. Supp.* 1–85: 17–18, emphasis added).

Carefully leaving the institutions there and moving to substance, 'several delicate questions arise', not least of which was: 'Can our EFTA friends be allowed to pick and choose? I have some misgivings here.' In other words, take it or leave it: the *acquis communautaire* or nothing. He spelt out these 'misgivings': would they abide by the common commercial policy? Did they share 'our [i.e. his and the maximalists'] basic conceptions?' Would they accept harmonisation, the transposition of common rules 'and, in consequence, accept the supervision of the Court of Justice'? He stressed that the Community was much more than a large market; it was a:

> [F]rontier free economic and social area on the way to becoming a political union ... The marriage contract is, as it were, indissoluble ... Only that *affectio societatis* which binds our twelve countries enables us to rise above the difficulties and contradictions ... It is *extremely difficult, within this all-embracing union, to provide a choice of menus*.
>
> (*Bull. Supp.* 1–89: 18, emphasis added)

It was at one and the same time an eloquent exposition of the 'counter-Thatcher thesis' and, from EFTA's point of view, a most unwelcome bombshell. In effect, he could be seen to cast doubt on the whole 'Luxembourg process' – the regular meetings that had been taking place since the Luxembourg Declaration on the EES of 1984. By the end of 1988 the evidence is that many political actors 'had started to wonder whether the dialogue would produce the needed results' (Laursen 1990: 311). Indeed, even prior to the May 1987 Interlaken meeting at which the first two conventions with EFTA were signed – concerned with the single administrative document (SAD) and with goods in transit – Commissioner Willi de Clerq had laid down three principles that should govern relations between the EC and EFTA. These three were ominous from EFTA's point of view. They were priority for internal EEC integration, preservation of the EC's autonomous powers of decision and the need for what were called 'balanced' results – i.e. a balance between benefits and obligations. 'This meant that the EC would neither wait on the EFTA countries nor allow them any kind of co-decision' (Laursen 1990: 315; *EDB* 20 May 1987).

Although further progress was made during 1988 (e.g. in the important Lugano Convention on Jurisdiction and Enforcement of Judgments in Civil and Commercial Matters adopted in September), there was a very long list of unresolved problems at the end of 1988. 'In reality the EC was negotiating with six countries, not EFTA as such, which was not constructed for such negotiations' (Laursen 1990: 317).

Delors further claimed in the 17 January speech: 'The Twelve must be prepared for a full and frank discussion of the scope for further co-operation with the EFTA countries.' And for good measure, he reacted to the Gorbachev image of a 'common European house' in a way that sent a clear signal to all the EC's neighbours. He would rather speak of a common European 'village' and 'in it a house called the "European Community". We are its sole architects; we are the keepers of its keys; but we are prepared to open its doors and *talk to* our neighbours' (*Bull. Supp.* 1–89: 18, emphasis added). He ended with an obeisance to the principle of subsidiarity.

Of no less interest was his reply to the debate the next day (18 January). He wanted to stress four points. The first concerned 'the method': the SEM programme contained severe difficulties especially over taxation and abolition of physical frontiers. Over the latter: 'I gave the governments a plan, not of a primrose path but of an assault course.' This 'assault course' had taken them through, notably: common immigration policies; right of abode; and drugs, crime, terror and delinquency. Second, the Community 'has to address the consolidation/enlargement debate'. Third, 'the Commission has not lost sight of the fact that the objective is political Europe'. In this context, 'Mr de la Malène asked a pertinent question: what is to become of the States?' And the pertinent answer? Meaninglessly, Delors said: 'I do not wish to go into all aspects of this subject, but continue to say, Europe will help those who help themselves.' Fourth, he purred supportively about the *compagnonnage* of EP and Commission.

Yet he also balanced it. On EMU he claimed: 'I am taking enormous precautions to be realistic and to allow scope for the States to exercise a major share of responsibility over macroeconomic policies.' But, on the other hand, there lay opportunities for the EP: 'I said this was going to be the last elected EP with the current limited powers, and that the debate on EMU, *to which there is an institutional aspect that you should not underestimate,* would give you the opportunity to state your views.' Finally, to underline the wearying burdens of negotiating with 'one Member State', 'It is not possible for me … to resign myself to leaving a country on the sidelines, *as we have come close to doing over the past four years.* I shall devote all my energies to keeping them together as 12' (*Bull. Supp.* 1–89: 24, emphasis added).

Nothing was said on east central Europe, for most people at this juncture another cloud no bigger than a hand: but one that, once it burst, was to challenge almost all the assumptions – spoken but more especially unspoken – on which 'Community Europe' *à la* Monnet had been painfully constructed.

The first cracks in the 'iron curtain' appeared when Hungary began dismantling the barbed wire on its border with Austria at the beginning of May. (See, e.g., *Le Monde* 4 May 1989: 5.) This did not seem to make any great impact on the Madrid European Council at the end of June, itself held just after the third direct elections to the EP. Indeed, the 'Austro-Hungarian events' were rather seen, in Vienna particularly, as an aggravation, portending further flows of migrants from Romania in particular.

The Madrid Summit concentrated on the Delors Report (EMU) and on further struggles over the key 'internal market' dossiers – aspects of fiscal and physical barriers – which had proved, and were to continue to be, so troublesome. The 'logic' of Delors had already been attacked, notably in the UK, where Professors Alan Budd and Charles Goodhart put 'Delors under the Microscope' (*FT* 12 June 1989: 21). The same paper the same day predicted that the 'course will get rougher' for the internal market programme (p. 6) and that 'storm clouds' were gathering over the social charter, which had assumed 'disproportional symbolic status' (p. 18). This was the more likely, since the elections had produced an EP whose overall political centre of gravity had moved slightly to the left (despite some gains by the extreme right).

As to the tough parts of the SEM, heads of government seemed content to breathe a sigh of relief at (they 'welcomed') the Commission's 'new approach' to indirect taxation and excise duty (*Bull. EC* 6–1989: 8; 5–1989: 8). It is doubtful whether they should have done so: the thing was a fudge and went on causing trouble. A year and a half later, laments were still arising: the pattern was the same: reasonable progress over technical barriers; little or none on physical and fiscal, especially over indirect taxation. On this, 'the Commission regrets that its initial proposal for VAT payment in the producing country was not adopted' (*EDB* 5376, 23 November 1990: 9).

The same lack of progress occurred over free movement of persons: the 'Palma Document' was produced, drawing up a 'positive' list of countries whose nationals would not need visas to enter the EC and the area was worked on by a 'coordinators' group' at the instigation of the General Affairs Council; but it was slow going. This was in part because different fora tripped each other up (the Schengen Agreement on Borders intended to involve, initially, Benelux France and Germany; and the Trevi Group of interior ministers of the Twelve); in part because there was considerable reluctance to let the EC as such in on the act and a determined exercise of *cacher les dossiers* by national authorities in such a 'sensitive' area (and these had an automatic tendency to 'level up' to the most restrictive and repressive set of national practices available on each matter); and in part because, in a classic 'linkage', the exogenous shocks from the east did obtrude themselves and caused a certain amount of panic and division within the west. Worse still, what started off as 'exogenous' moved directly into the heart of the camp and caused far more heart searching and bad blood in and around the Community than those involved thought politic to reveal at the time: the 'German question', the ghost at the feast, had come back to haunt some and to trouble almost all.

## Hegemony versus equality? New strains on the system

In and from 1989 Germany moved ineluctably to centre stage. Future historians will no doubt try to arrive at a mature and careful judgment as to just who tried to plan what, or for what contingency; who knew what when; who was simply swept or blown along, in regard to the unification of Germany. While I have my own views on this matter, it is not our central concern here. What does matter is how it was all perceived – for the perceptions influenced the tone and nature of responses, and these in turn were interpreted, and scores were kept.

More than that: a central but never quite explicit assumption of the original Community scheme had been that the relationships established should be on a basis that traditional diplomatic usage tends to call 'reciprocity', but that Monnet, much earlier, had tantalisingly gone a stage further to call 'equality' – indeed, in his memoirs, he had explicitly stated 'I have always realized that equality is absolutely essential in relations between nations, as it is between people' (Monnet 1978: 97). To which Churchill had earlier asserted that the principles of the Sermon on the Mount, admirable in interpersonal terms, were nevertheless not those that govern the intercourse of states. Stated baldly, the notion of a 'rough equality' between and among the largest states of the Community had been highly convenient and for some reassuring; but it was increasingly mythical and threadbare and German unification was about to blow it to smithereens. A barely credible 'equality' was about to be replaced by a perceived near hegemony and it was far from clear that the structure could take the strain. Some openly felt that they had been conned: the rules of the game had been changed on them while they watched helplessly. The 'contract' had been broken. They had not signed up to be towed along in the wake of German hegemony and accompanying worries and risks.

As soon as such reactions surfaced, so did German resentment that mistrust remained so near the surface; that oft repeated 'allied' commitments to the goal of German unification were revealed as entire hypocrisy; that almost two generations of *Modell Deutschland* appeared still not to have laid ghosts to rest.

For the summer of 1989 may be seen as more important for what happened at the margins of the EC than strictly within it. It was President Reagan who had urged Gorbachev to 'pull down that wall'. Gorbachev and Kohl met in June 1989 and discussed, among other things, what flesh might be put on the bones of the 'Common European house (or home)' idea. German opinion, in turn, had been well prepared long before. An interesting instance was the speech of 24 January 1989 of Federal Minister for Inner German Relations Dr Dorothee Wilms. The interest lay not least in the fact that the audience to which she had been invited was the main 'opposition' body, the Friedrich-Ebert-Stiftung in Bonn. She began by averring that this was a sphere in which the widest possible consensus was desirable between 'democrats of all opinions' (*Bull. der PIB*, 8/S.61, 26 January 1989). East–west relations were in flux because of internal developments in the Soviet Union and throughout the Warsaw Pact states, even if to date the DDR leadership had tended to set its face against change, she said. As if to prove her point, some 100 were arrested in Leipzig on 7 May for protesting at the rigging of local elections. On the eve of German Unity Day (17 June), she forcefully stressed the theme of the 'self-determination of peoples' (*Bull. der PIB* 1989, 64: 571).

By the end of June, then, the tone had markedly stiffened: Genscher, speaking to the German–Polish seminar on military doctrine in Ebenhausen on the 23rd, spoke of 'profound change' and a shattering of the old order (*Bull. der PIB*, 30 June 1989, 68: 597). The 'Europe of the Twelve' was becoming increasingly the core of an all-European 'peace order'. The day before, Head of the Chancellor's Office Rudolf Seiters had stressed the FRG's high hopes of the third directly elected EP.

On 8 August Bonn closed its DDR mission after 130 East Germans took refuge inside. Occupations of embassies in Budapest, Prague and Warsaw forced their closure; on 10 September Hungary opened its border with Austria to allow the departure of East German refugees and 30,000 took their opportunity. The crisis mounted throughout September and October. On 7 October Gorbachev, attending the DDR's 40th (and, it was amazingly to prove, last) birthday celebrations, made his famous remark to Honecker about not missing the tide of history. Eleven days later, Honecker stepped down, officially for health reasons, to be replaced by Egon Krenz: and on the 24th, 52 members of the Volkskammer refused to vote for Krenz as head of state. Events were now galloping out of any kind of control. Despite Krenz's expression of support for *perestroika* in Moscow on 1 November, five Politburo members resigned on the 3rd; on the 4th, Czechoslovakia opened its border for thousands of 'Ossis' to travel west, and perhaps half a million demonstrated in east Berlin; on the 5th–6th, new travel laws were no sooner announced than denounced as inadequate and free elections were demanded as well. On the 7th the DDR government resigned; on the 9th the Wall became permeable; Kohl immediately cut short his visit to Poland and next day addressed the people of Berlin.

It was some 3 weeks later that Kohl put his '10-point programme' before the Bundestag (28 November: see *Bull. der PIB*, 29 November 1989, 134: 1141–8). Its title was of the greatest significance – 'for overcoming the division of Germany and of Europe' – in that order, but with a clear link made between the two. (The following day, Krenz told a leading journalist that reunification was 'not on the agenda' [Marsh 1992: 35].) This, of course, once the dust had settled, was to precipitate also the demand for the calling of a Political Union IGC. Kohl insisted, in the sixth of his 10 points, that the 'development of inner-German relations remains embedded in the all-European process', i.e. in east–west relations, and he cited the joint communiqué of his June meeting with Gorbachev. In his seventh point he stressed the power of attraction and the 'radiating power' of the EC: it must be strengthened further. Then the ground began to move. The BRD supported the rapid conclusion of a commercial and cooperation agreement with the DDR, which should help to pave the way for the approach of the DDR to the single market. Not, it transpired, as a separate entity in its own right, however. In his 10th point he stressed that he was talking about the 'reunification' (*Wiedervereinigung* was, alarmingly to some of his hearers, the term used) though he added, 'That is, the restoration of state unity to Germany' which remained the political aim of the FRG.

December was no less hectic, and undoubtedly it was around this time that Delors began to take a position that was to please the Federal government – Kohl in particular – every bit as much as it was to alarm several other EC members. On 1 December, the Volkskammer struck the SED's (Sozialistische Einheitspartei Deutschlands) power monopoly from the DDR constitution. On 3 and 6 December, Krenz resigned from all party and government posts. At the NATO summit on the

4th, Bush reported on meetings with Gorbachev at which the 'German question' was discussed. On the 7th, the brief career of the so-called 'Round Table' discussions in the DDR began, between governing and opposition groups: free elections were announced. On the 19th and 20th, Kohl met the new DDR leader Hans Modrow in Dresden and the discussions centred on the 'developing relations' between the two German states. On the 22nd, the Brandenburg Gate in Berlin was opened. It fell to Delors to set out the 'Community dimension' of all this in his speech to the EP on 17 January 1990, outlining the Commission's programme for 1990.

## 1990: the year of German unity and its EC repercussions

Remarking on the 'astounding series of events which have unfolded virtually on our doorstep' since he had spoken to the EP a year before, Delors claimed in his 17 January 1990 speech that the EC had 'served as a lodestone, a lodestar' to its neighbours. He quoted Tocqueville on the aftermath of the 1848 revolution: 'It has ceased to be an adventure and is taking on the dimensions of a new era' (*Bull. Supp.* 1/90: 6). He was at pains to damp down expectations of rapid full membership for the east central European 'three', but was equally clear that the pace of events posed 'enormous risks' for the Community:

> I have heard it argued in some quarters that the Community, as a product of the Cold War, should die with the Cold War, completely disregarding the experience accumulated over 40 years on our difficult but exciting journey to pooled sovereignty. I interpret this variously as a return to facile nationalism or a temptation to play the Metternich card. It is as if a changing world had created openings for those driven by vanity or for would-be statesmen seeking to play yesterday's hand.
>
> (*Bull. Supp.* 1/90: 7)

A little later, President Mitterrand was to find himself characterised by a writer in the *Financial Times* as 'Metternich in the Elysée' (*FT* 30 August 1991).

Delors said that he would tackle the German question 'head on'. Although *rapprochement*, 'or even reunification, of the German people', was 'clearly a matter for the Germans themselves', yet the Community had an interest too, based on several provisions of the founding documents. Then he added the famous line, 'This makes East Germany a special case', although 'the form that it will take is, I repeat, a matter for the Germans themselves'. Several possibilities were open:

> [P]rovided, as the Strasbourg European Council made quite clear, the German nation regains its unity through free self-determination, peacefully and democratically, in accordance with the principles of the Helsinki Final Act, in the context of an East-West dialogue and with an eye to European integration.
>
> (*Bull. Supp.* 1/90: 6)

In fact, a great deal was to turn on matters of form and process; and in influencing those, the importance of the EC and perhaps of Delors in particular was quite

considerable, as German leaders acknowledged. They reserved less flattering epi-
thets for their other British and French 'partners'. In particular, there were basically
three rival formulae as to how to proceed and the differences between them were far
from merely cosmetic. These were described at the time as 'four plus zero', 'four
plus two' and 'two plus four'.

'Four plus zero' implied still a '1945' world: the ex-'victor powers'
(*Siegermächten*) would get together and agree the fate of Germany among themselves, at first without the Germans. This was the initial real preference of the
French, the British and the Soviet Union. At the other end of the spectrum was 'two
plus four': after the East German elections (originally scheduled for May, but
advanced under the frenzy of events to 18 March) were out of the way, the two
Germanies would get together and discuss their economic, political and legal unification. Then, the four would meet with the two Germanies to discuss security and
'external' aspects: the size of the armed forces a unified state might have, its relationship to NATO and security guarantees to its neighbours (*IHT*, 17 February
1990: 1, 5). This left out the issues for which the EC itself was competent. Initially,
it appears that this approach was favoured by the USA and the Federal German government: but it is less than clear when in truth (as opposed to as publicly presented)
they concerted their views. Shifting slightly from foot to foot in the middle was
'four plus two' – with the first moves being taken by the 'four' but bringing in the
two in a substantive although not initial phase. Genscher, unsurprisingly, was keen
to avoid this. What, it seemed, no one in this charmed circle was prepared to consider, was bringing in other states at anything other than the very last minute,
whether other NATO states or Germany's worried eastern neighbours.

Carefully crafted formulae were used to convey positions. Thus, in his New Year
message to the French nation, Mitterrand spoke of a 'confederation' as the way
things should tend, defined as a common permanent organisation for trade, peace
and security of all the states of the Old World. A few days later, at a joint meeting
with Kohl and the press, he was more than usually Delphic. When asked about the
'confederation' formula, he replied: 'The German problem is of a different nature.
There is at the same time a specific German problem and the problem of Europe. On
Europe we have similar views' – implying that on Germany they did not? (French
Embassy, London: *Speeches & Statements*, 7/90).

Delors's riposte was rapid: whatever might be thought about a 'confederation',
the EC should be the essentially federal 'core' of the new Europe. In an effort to
keep the initiative, Mitterrand in February argued both for advancing the date of the
EMU IGC and for adding consideration of political union also. He received considerable support for this from Belgium, Italy, Spain and Ireland – which held the
presidency.

The story of the onward rush of German unity in 1990 is well enough known, and
here it will suffice to give a brief outline. (On the EC aspects, an excellent detailed
account is to be found in *Zeitschrift für ausländisches öffentliches Recht und
Völkerrecht* 1991, 51/2; especially, in this context, the papers by Frowein and
Giegerich.) February 1990 was in many ways the crucial month. On 10 February
Kohl and Genscher met Gorbachev in Moscow, Gorbachev assuring them that he

was willing to contemplate the prospect of a single German state. On the 13th and 14th, when Modrow came to Bonn, Kohl proposed an economic and monetary union. 'German monetary union' was thus now on the table: and the interactions between GMU and the already proposed EMU were to be a central preoccupation for the next decade. On the 14th also, the 'two-plus-four' (for thus it was) talks got under way. The next day, Kohl briefed Mitterrand in Paris on his talks with Gorbachev and on the 24th and 25th he met Bush at Camp David to assure him, among other things, of the importance to Germany of the continued security connection.

On 18 March the free elections in the GDR produced a sweeping victory for the three parties that together made up the 'Alliance for Germany' headed by the Christian Democratic Union (CDU). The Alliance had swamped the GDR with money, people and resources throughout the campaign. It was a campaign driven by and from the FRG and without the slightest thought in that quarter that any other outcome would be countenanced but state unity. Although the negotiations over a GDR 'Grand Coalition' – needed to pass much of the envisaged legislation – were tricky and protracted, on 12 April Lothar de Maizière was chosen as prime minister and on the 19th he declared that his government's aim was German unity.

Further Franco-German consultations were held at the end of April, immediately prior to the 'Extraordinary' Dublin European Council on the 28th. This gathering 'welcomed' the inevitable and unstoppable, and set as target the 'adaptation' of the 'eastern part' to the Community to coincide with German unification. The EC and its member states did not merely feel that they were being bounced: they had been. The EC's existence had provided the context in which all this could happen. But thereafter neither it nor the other member states had much effective part in determining, scarcely in influencing, the speed and shape of change. As at least three Commissioners jostled for a piece of the action, Martin Bangemann headed the working group to consider EC–German questions, thus ensuring that Germany controlled the agenda.

It was to be in essence a two-stage process. First would come the monetary, economic and social union with the FRG on the basis of the *Staatsvertrag* (state treaty) from 1 July. Then would come the formal integration of the GDR with the FRG through the treaty of union, the *Einigungsvertrag*, to take effect on 3 October. All-German elections would follow in December. Thus the die was cast on the crucial question of the 'choice' of approach – the 'Article 23' route triumphed over the possible use of Article 146 of the German Basic Law: what would happen in October would be the accession of the GDR to the territory of application of the German Basic Law. Consequently, in terms of the EC, what would happen would be, not the *state accession* of the GDR, but the extension of the territorial scope of application of the treaties to the ex-GDR by virtue of its becoming part of the FRG. The 'price' Kohl was seen to agree to – hardly a high one, since he had announced it as his firm wish in any case – was the summoning of the political union IGC alongside the EMU one.

Events roared along in these directions. On 18 May, the 'State Treaty' on Monetary, Economic and Social Union was concluded between the FRG and the east, to come into effect on 1 July. On 27 June agreement was reached on the elimination of border checks along the intra-German frontier as of the same date. The regular European Council in Dublin at the end of June welcomed the conclusion of the treaty between the two German states, which would speed the formal integration of the GDR territory into the EC.

July was taken up rather with the external aspects: the London NATO Summit on the 5th–6th declared that unified Germany would be a vital factor for stability in the Atlantic Alliance. The pressure on Gorbachev which had been building for many months now came to a head. On the 14th–16th, Kohl met him in Moscow: they agreed that united Germany should be fully sovereign, decide its future alliance membership and reduce the strength of its armed forces to 370,000. The Soviet Union agreed to withdraw its forces from the GDR within the next 4 years. On the 17th, in the 'two plus four' context but with the Polish foreign minister also, agreement was reached on principles for establishing the definitive borders of united Germany. It was further agreed that, instead of a peace treaty, a document on Germany covering all questions concerned with the establishment of full sovereignty would be signed by the participants and submitted to the November CSCE Conference for approval (see *Auf dem Weg zur deutschen Einheit* 1991: Chronologie).

This was also the point at which the EC timetable attempted to accelerate from the merely frenetic to the frankly unmanageable. The April Dublin Summit had charged the Commission with drawing up proposals for the transitional arrangements to come into force at the moment of unification and to aim at full integration as quickly as possible (EC Commission, London: ISEC/B26/90). Most of the plethora of transitional arrangements – the main exceptions being over environmental matters – would extend only until the end of 1992.

For those involved, this was to be anything but a summer of ease. The EP set up the Donnelly Committee – the 'Temporary committee to consider the impact of the process of German unification on the EC'. It issued its interim report – in three volumes – on 9 July (EP Doc. A 3–183/990/C); the final report followed later (EP Doc. A3–240/90). The Commission's detailed documentation – also in three volumes (COM (90) 400 – *The Community and German Unification*) – appeared on 21 August. Volume 2 contained the proposals for legislation. The overwhelming impression, quite clear in the documentation, is of breakneck speed, German pressure, solutions cobbled together, and a great deal of irritation and argument over the procedures used. The Commission produced its amended proposal (COM (90) 495) on 25 October, over 3 weeks after the Day of German Unity. On 2 October, a Commission briefing had stated:

> The package of transitional measures cannot progress through two readings in the Council and Parliament until November. *The German decision to bring forward the date of unification has made it necessary to propose provisional measures* – a Directive and a Regulation – to cover the short period between unification and adoption of the transitional arrangements. These enable the FRG to authorise legislation in the GDR which is not compatible with EC law, but which will be covered later by the transitional arrangements.
>
> (EC Commission, London: ISEC/B26/90, emphasis added)

For all the haste, the problems went well beyond those of deadlines and procedures. An August special document by *European Report* said of the integration of
the GDR: 'It will be a major exercise ... The symbolic protocol signing ceremonies
will soon be forgotten with the arrival of major practical problems to resolve' (*ER,*
Supplement to No. 1608, 4 August 1990). So it was to prove. Resource transfers
began on a massive scale. In May 1991, Kohl estimated that 'In the 18 months from
mid-1990 to the end of this year, a total of DM 100,000 million ... will have been
made available' (Kohl 1991: 10). Despite earlier promises, taxes had to rise. So did
inflation. So did interest rates – to the acute discomfort of those obliged to follow
the lead of the 'anchor currency'.

There was certainly a takeover boom – amounting indeed to a kind of 'merger
mania' in the middle of 1990. The great bulk of the activity was 'German–German'.
From the Commission, Leon Brittan fired off a number of warning shots. But as the
east was not subject to EC competition rules until unification, there was little he could
do. There were some fine ironies here: traditionally Germany has been thought of as
'unfriendly' to takeovers – especially to being taken over by others. Yet the spate of
west–east activity provoked several cries of 'foul' and dark mutterings about economic Anschluss and asset stripping (Brewin and McAllister 1991: 410).

For a while there was a 'unification boom' too, but by 1992 there were clear signs
of recession accompanied by a high level of wage claims throughout unified
Germany. In the view of most observers, the potential long-term benefits appeared
considerable: it was fashionable to say that the problem was just that the costs were
massive, 'frontloaded' and rather pressing.

Institutionally, the addition of over 16 million 'easterners' made – surprisingly –
no difference to the various EC bodies, except for the EP. Here, in a resolution
adopted on 12 July 1990, MEPs agreed that it was only right to increase German
representation in the parliament. Otherwise, there was no change in the composition of the Commission or in the way that the qualified majority voting 'weight'
was calculated in the Council. Neither – in the short term at least – did Germany
press for any change in the permanent membership of the UN Security Council.
Despite this, much attention was given over to 'Bonn watching', to see to what
extent the voice of the new Germany would change. Those in Brussels certainly
detected a change of mood and attitude. It appeared increasingly difficult to get
decisions, movement or agreement out of the Germans once unification was on the
agenda: hardly surprising, to be sure, but noted and commented on at the time
(Brewin and McAllister 1991: 409).

Perhaps too much attention was paid to watching Bonn. For the 'implications of
the new Germany' most vehemently did not stop at its borders. Perhaps most crucial, if not widely foreseen at the time, was the extent to which the events surrounding the emergence of 'new Germany' themselves helped – they were of
course by no means the only factor – to precipitate the break-up of the Soviet Union.
Once that had happened, the whole balance in Europe had changed. Then people
began to ask anxiously whether they should be talking about 'balance' at all;
whether this was dangerous and outdated; whether the language of 'anchoring' or
'embedding' was more appropriate, or merely self-deluding. Some even dared to

ask whether the European Community – undeniably a child of the Cold War – could survive its 'end'. But at the very time that some were declaring 'the Cold War's over: we won', other instabilities appeared and posed grave questions to the EC.

But if the EC faced new challenges, it also continued to pose them to national politicians. The most dramatic instance was, of course, in the UK, where Thatcher's departure in late November 1990 owed not a little to the sense that her style in the conduct of policy toward the Community, and perhaps the content, were costing the UK dear.

## 'Widening and deepening' again: the road to Maastricht

We have seen that the EC was now committed to 'twin' IGCs – one on EMU and one on political union: Kohl in April had agreed to the proposal for the latter originally made by Mitterrand in February 1990. The decision of the European Council which emerged at Dublin in April said:

> A detailed examination will be put in hand forthwith on the need for possible Treaty changes with the aim of strengthening the democratic legitimacy of the union, enabling the Community and its institutions to respond efficiently and effectively to the demands of the new situation, and assuring unity and coherence in the Community's international action.
>
> (*Bull. EC* 4–1990)

Foreign ministers were charged with preparing proposals for discussion at the June 1990 Dublin European Council, the intention being to agree on the holding of a second IGC to work 'in parallel with the Conference on Economic and Monetary Union with a view to ratification ... in the same time frame' (quoted in Commission 1990: 7).

The trajectory of the ERM had become more stable as the 1980s proceeded. The numerous parity changes and chaotic conditions of its first 5 years (1979–83) were followed by relative stability from 1983 to 1987; between 1987 and the autumn storms of 1992 there were no realignments. Indeed, in the latter period, '[t]he EMS had contributed to the undervaluation of the DM, which ... created large trade surpluses' (Moravcsik 1999: 391): there was no urgency on the part of business at least, to rush headlong from that satisfactory state to the 'unknowns' that EMU might entail.

And the Bundesbank (Buba) was not lightly to be persuaded to abandon its proud guardianship of Germany's 'national treasure', the mark. Early on in the Delors Committee's negotiations, all of Pöhl's main demands were conceded by the others: but Pöhl in turn made one crucial move: against objections of several of his Buba colleagues. He agreed to a single currency. The seismic backdrop to all this was German unification, with all its attendant uncertainties – about the speed, terms and implications of German monetary union (GMU) – the centrality of which was bound to preoccupy German policymakers and the Buba above all.

So the support base for EMU remained shallow, with scepticism widespread and some outright opposition. Most key players within the Buba – Pöhl, Tietmeyer, Schlesinger – as well as some German ministers, continued to regard the whole thing as a 'French plot'. They were aware that ever since Delors' 1983 U-turn, French enthusiasm had been 'founded on a desire to shackle the D-Mark – and, eventually, to bring about its demise' (Marsh 1992: 15). France's painful *franc fort* (irony of ironies!) policy had been 'the route to wresting monetary leadership from Germany' (Connolly 1995: 32). From at least 1988 French international monetary policy was marked by 'extraordinary continuity in the face of deep and persistent domestic conflict'; by support for EMU 'maintained to the present day, regardless of which party is in power' (Moravcsik 1999: 404). But, as with Werner in 1970, it remained support for EMU 'on monetarist terms ... with looser convergence criteria, greater political control over the ECB, a relatively large number of members, an explicit mandate to target employment and growth, and a weaker European currency than that favored by Germany' (Moravcsik 1999: 411). Compared to the EMS 'straitjacket', EMU was expected to loosen the constraints on France.

The British clung on with 'modest proposals': first with Lawson's 'competing currencies' scheme of 1989, then with Sir Michael Butler's 'hard ECU/parallel currency' proposal of early 1990 (Dyson 1994: 141–42; Stephens 1996: 160–62; Moravcsik 1999: 424). With the mammoth preoccupations elsewhere, neither made many waves outside the UK. The timing of sterling's eventual ERM entry, in October 1990, was 'exquisitely unfortunate. The Treasury tied sterling to the D-Mark just as the Bundesbank was propelling German interest rates upwards to cope with inflationary pressures caused by unification' (Marsh 1992: 12). Its entry coincided – another fine irony – with Thatcher's exit. Its exit, in turn, would take place only 2 years later – with the 'humiliation' (Stephens 1996: 226) of 'Black Wednesday', 16 September 1992, just prior to the French referendum on Maastricht on the 20th.

The following year, up to autumn 1993, was one of crisis for the ERM. It was clear that unless the 'rules' were changed, financial markets would always win their one-way bets on devaluation. The solution adopted, a 'beautiful compromise' (Verdun in Cini (ed.) 2003: 319) was to widen the ERM band to plus/minus 15%. The paradox was that thereafter, member states usually succeeded in staying within the *original* bands and by the end of the 1993 EMU – to the surprise of many – could move on from 'stage 1' – free movement of capital, greater economic policy 'coordination' and central bank cooperation – to 'stage 2'. It had been a close run thing: '[T]he EMU project almost died before being brought back to life by a combination of time, bureaucratic perseverance, political support of the elites, and institutional path dependence' (Verdun in Cini (ed.) 2003: 319).

'Political union was seen by both parties as a concession to Germany in exchange for EMU' (Moravcsik 1999: 413). Just as the inception of the political union IGC did not happen in a void, but was in no small measure a response to events in central Europe and in Germany, so the course of the negotiations could not fail to take account also of contemporaneous events. Three sets of events were of great importance. First was the Gulf War: the invasion of Kuwait in August 1990 led on to the conflict in January and February 1991. Second was the gathering crisis in

Yugoslavia, right on the Community's flank and giving rise to differing initial partisan responses and to lasting tensions over policy. Third was the dissolution of the Soviet Union, which proceeded apace after the failure of the August 1991 coup attempt. All were to produce a fairly raised temperature when it came to deciding about the 'unconditional reliability' of partners.

It will come as no surprise that the Commission espoused broadly 'maximalist' positions on European political union (EPU) as on EMU or that the EP, particularly in the shape of the Martin reports, also put forward essentially maximalist views (EP Docs. A3–0047/90; 166/90; 0270/90). Rather more intriguing were the positions put forward by the two presidencies of the main negotiating period, 1991: Luxembourg and the Netherlands. Both might have been expected, in terms of reputation and previous positions, to have supported strongly 'maximalist' positions. Thus it is to be noted that Luxembourg did not do so. In April 1991, the Luxembourg presidency produced a 'non-paper'. (Such drafts are not uncommon: but there were to be several in this process.) This meant that it did not purport to be a formal set of proposals representing agreed conclusions of the political union IGC working parties. The presidency, however, tried to claim that it represented, if not an agreement, at any rate a 'consensus view': that too was swiftly disputed by several member states. The Commission in particular thought it so weak that it proceeded to produce another paper of its own in May, known as the 'composite paper' (Lodge in Paterson 1991: 39).

A second Luxembourg presidency draft was discussed at the 28–29 June summit. This resolved none of the main contentious issues. For instance, proposals to give the EP enhanced power to block decisions in areas such as the environment and R&D, went too far for Ireland, Portugal and the UK but not far enough for such as Germany and Italy. Nevertheless, it was agreed that the will existed to continue the negotiations with a view to concluding them at Maastricht.

The Netherlands took over the presidency in July and battle was again joined. A first Netherlands draft was so 'pragmatic' that it pleased the UK, which, probably foolishly, praised it publicly. This was enough to guarantee that it would be assailed by the Commission and various other members and late in September a second draft had undergone major 'strengthening' amendments. For example, unlike the Luxembourg draft, which had favoured a 'three-pillared' approach (often referred to as the 'temple') with separate agreements outside the EC Treaty-based structure for judicial cooperation and for common foreign and security policy (CFSP), the Dutch draft spoke of a single 'trunk' (the 'tree' model) having several branches. Many states were critical of the September draft and on 30 September the foreign ministers decided not to use it as their basis for negotiation at Maastricht. Again, it was clear that agreement not to use it was as far as agreement went: states differed on whether it went too far or not far enough, on a whole range of issues. Thus the IGC's basis of deliberations became again the June Luxembourg draft.

A second Netherlands draft was published on 8 November. On CFSP, it did not provide for majority voting on issues of principle, although it did provide for qualified majority voting on matters of 'implementation'. It also envisaged quite distinct institutional arrangements for CFSP from those of the Rome Treaty and the SEA.

Once again, these negotiations did not take place in isolation. For these were areas of vital inter-organisational competition, in which WEU and NATO have played the main part. At the NATO summit of 7–8 November, President Bush pointedly asked the western Europeans to say if they wanted the USA to leave Europe. The final communiqué spoke of the European defence arrangement as a strengthened pillar of NATO, which was the 'essential forum' for European defence.

In brief, the agreement at Maastricht left CFSP as an area of enhanced but clearly still intergovernmental cooperation. Technically, it still lay outside the EC Treaty. It left several ragged edges, notably with regard to WEU, whose members (those of them also numbered among the Twelve) issued a declaration to coincide with the Maastricht Summit. This stated that they welcomed:

> [T]he development of the European security and defence identity. They are determined, taking into account the role of WEU as the defence component of the European Union and as the means to strengthen the European pillar of the Atlantic Alliance, to put the relationship between WEU and the other European states on a new basis for the sake of security and stability in Europe.
>
> (TEU: 245; Declaration on Western European Union)

Thus they invited the remaining three to join or to become observers; and simultaneously 'other European member states of NATO are invited to become associate members of WEU'. They declared that 'the objective is to build up WEU in stages as the defence component of the European Union'.

Maastricht, of course, contained a good deal more. Its definition of 'subsidiarity' in the new Article 3b was one that tended strongly to preserve the competence of states. Its Article A dropped the term 'federal goal' and instead used the original Treaty of Rome formula, 'an ever closer union among the peoples of Europe'. Yet at the same time the EP gained new powers, albeit of a mainly negative kind, allowing it to reject a proposal by an overall majority of its members if agreement could not be reached between itself and the Council of Ministers in the joint Conciliation Committee. Rather confusingly, this was sometimes referred to as the 'co-decision procedure'. The Commission's term of office was to be of 5 years beginning in 1995, coinciding with the EP term, and subject to the EP's approval at the start of their mandate. One wonders who could have thought of this as an adequate effort at the 'creation of legitimacy'.

The treaty said that the Union should have a single institutional framework, yet it left CFSP and judicial affairs, each with its own ways of working, as separate 'pillars' standing beside the EC treaties.

Maastricht was like Janus. It faced both ways: towards intergovernmentalism and towards some kind of 'federal vocation'. It was as ambiguous as the oracle of Delphi; as the Community itself. It reflected the extent to which the states were, and were not, able to agree. It relied heavily, as the Community had always done, on 'one thing leading inevitably to another'. Yet the 'compelling logic' was again to face some fairly stiff challenges. The irony was that the Community's very 'success', its 'lodestar quality', helped to produce the 'New Europe' which was now again to test severely its abilities and capacities.

## The ratification process

The Treaty on European Union (TEU) was finally signed on 7 February 1992. That was to prove the beginning and not, as expected, the end of a series of problems.

The process of ratification proved at least as troublesome and protracted as had that of the Single European Act. The process was supposed to be completed during 1992, so that the TEU could enter into effect at the start of 1993; in the event, it was not until 1 November 1993 that the European Union was officially born. Further, the difficulties were apparent in most member states. The causes of the rapid evaporation of optimism were several and varied: from deeply entrenched national resistance to this or that policy, to the recriminations over the agony of Former Yugoslavia. The year 1992 ended with the Community a great deal more bruised and battered than at the beginning.

In Denmark, failure to achieve the required five-sixths majority in the Folketing vote on 13 May 1992 was followed by the 2 June referendum: the 'no' majority was some 46,000. This plunged the Community into legal and political uncertainty (Lodge 1993: 387). Opinion was divided as to whether Denmark could stay within the EC if it failed to ratify the EU Treaty. The sense that a small state might be bullied and blackmailed had negative effects on public opinion in Finland, Norway and Sweden. The UK, the presidency state for the second half of 1992, announced that it would not itself proceed to ratification until the situation over Denmark had been resolved.

It fell to the European Council at Edinburgh in December 1992 to agree a solution. The formula was instructive. The Council described the governments as 'signatories of the Treaty of European Union, which involves *independent and sovereign* States having freely decided, in accordance with the existing Treaties, to exercise in common some of their competences' (*Bull. EC* 12–1992, emphasis added).

In Ireland, the campaign on the ratification referendum was complicated by arguments over abortion. But finally, on a thoroughly underwhelming 57% participation rate in June, nearly 69% voted for and about 31% against. On 23 November Ireland declared its ratification completed.

Mitterrand's announcement, the day after the original Danish 'no', of a referendum in France seemed a reversal of his earlier position and a risky gamble for an unpopular government. The extremely close result showed just how risky: on 20 September, nearly 30% abstained; of those voting, 51% approved, 49% voted against. The French referendum took place just days after the exchange rate mechanism (ERM) crisis which saw the lira devalued on the 13th, and on 16th–17th sterling and the lira suspend their membership and the peseta devalued. Thus it was already less than clear just what remained of the content for which people were voting. What was quite clear was that the French referendum had split the country not just arithmetically but in terms of a 'rich, urban yes' versus a 'rural and working class No' (*Le Monde*, 22 September 1992: 2–3). The campaign was also marked by some 'less than pleasant remarks about Germany' (Nugent 1993: 31), which provoked resentment.

The UK's problems were no less acute for seeming in part self-inflicted and not involving a referendum. What is more, they were played out in the full glare of publicity arising from its own tenure of the presidency in the second half of 1992. The 'Maastricht' issue had hardly figured in the April 1992 general election, yet caused endless trouble for the next 18 months. Opposition within the Conservative Party grew after the first Danish referendum, at the party conference and through the autumn when the vote on the so-called 'paving motion' produced a majority in favour of only three, even after government promises to delay a final vote until after a new Danish referendum.

But the difficulties by no means ended with the ratification process itself. Equally evident throughout 1992, and not least at the Edinburgh Summit, was a marked resurgence of tough, assertive stances by the governments of several states, including France over GATT, Germany over monetary policy as well as over Yugoslavia, Spain over 'cohesion' and the UK mainly over the timetable.

In the light of this, it was regarded as something of a triumph, not least for John Major, that agreement was reached at all at the Edinburgh European Council of December 1992. 'Maximalists', however, were quick to say that agreement had been bought at too high a price. The main elements in the package were the following. First was a set of conclusions including a Council 'decision' – for which there is no treaty provision – and declarations on 'Denmark and the TEU'. Second came guidelines on the implementation of subsidiarity. Third were measures purportedly to increase transparency and openness in the Community's decision-making procedures. Then there was a medley of 'other measures' also intended to help the ratification process – including agreement on the enlargement process, but also Spain's hard bargain on 'cohesion' (see *Bull. EC* 12–1992; Nugent 1993: 34–8). Then and only then came the completion of the ratification process during 1993.

The central question is the interpretation to be put on all this. Although there were some nuanced positions, two diametrically opposite views should be considered. On the first view, what was witnessed was just a rather acute bout of difficulties and indigestion. The proponents of Maastricht, on this view, had just been unlucky with their timing. The Community had hit one of its periodic squalls which had rather blown it off course. When the weather calmed, the voyage would be more enjoyable.

The second view was much less reassuring. On this reading, as with the original EMU design of the 1970s, the whole design was fundamentally flawed. The Maastricht 'design' had been 'gestated a decade or more back and ... intended for a different world from the one that now exists after the collapse of Soviet power'. The Community was 'offering the remedies of the 1970s and 1980s for the problems of the 1990s' (Hartley 1993: 203).

'Maastricht' proved only the first of a series of attempts at reform or revision – of policy scope and of decision-making arrangements. The following chapters explore its 'successors': Amsterdam 1996; Nice 2000; the 'Constitutional Treaty' abandoned in 2006; and the Lisbon 'Reform' Treaty.

## Further reading

D. Dinan (ed.), *Origins and Evolution of the European Union*. Oxford: Oxford University Press, 2006. (Chapter 12.)

A. Duff, J. Pinder and R. Pryce (eds), *Maastricht and Beyond*. London: Routledge, 1994.

R. Fritsch-Bournazel, *Europe and German Unification*. Providence, RI, and Oxford: Berg, 1992.

B. Lippert, R. Stevens-Ströhmann, D. Günther, G. Viertel and S. Woolcock, *German Unification and EC Integration*. London: Pinter, 1993.

D. Marsh, *The Bundesbank*. London: Heinemann, 1992.

C. Preston, *Enlargement and Integration in the European Union*. London: Routledge, 1997. (Chapter 5.)

P. Stephens, *Politics and the Pound*. London and Basingstoke: Macmillan, 1996.

P. Stirk and D. Weigall (eds), *The Origins and Development of European Integration*. London: Pinter, 1999. (Chapter 11.)

# 10 Paradoxes of the New Europe
## 1994–2000

The atmosphere at the time of Maastricht was as we have seen, a strange and heady mixture: the EU felt summoned, inevitably, to assume new and weighty roles, but both it and its member states were timorous and unself-trusting in the contemplation of those urgent tasks. In the mid- and later 1990s, it seemed that the magnitude of the tasks and the paucity of leadership combined to accentuate a sense of failure. Delors might have little cause to regret passing on 'the torch' to Santer.

The issues which dominated this period were few but major and often intractable. The 'internal' agenda continued to be dominated by EMU. The key linkages between 'inside' and 'outside' were enlargement and 'concomitant' institutional reform. The 'institutional reform' attempts had become an exhausting habit, ratification of Amsterdam hardly complete when Nice negotiations got under way, but the results remained Lilliputian. The biggest 'external' preoccupation was with the EU's 'near abroad': the multiple crises in the Balkans were the tragic backdrop, from Bosnia in the mid-1990s to Kosovo at their end.

The year 1999 saw the definitive move of the German government to Berlin and Germany holding the EU and WEU presidencies in the first half-year. It also saw this new 'Berlin Republic', under a 'Red–Green' coalition, with Joschka Fischer of the Greens as foreign minister, at war – without a clear UN mandate (see Hyde-Price 1999: 13–15). Europe retained its capacity to surprise and horrify – itself not least.

## Windows of opportunity

Throughout the rest of the decade, the EU's trajectory seemed more than ever dominated by its 'windows of opportunity' and these were few. In the history of the EC/EU, these have come in several different shapes and sizes. Sometimes they have been recognised and taken; sometimes recognised but not taken; sometimes not recognised at all.

One of the most significant, recognised by some, but rejected as a possible way forward, occurred very near the start of the whole enterprise, and was considered in Chapter 1: the first attempt to associate the fledgling Community in a clear way with tasks of defence and security, in the Pleven Plan and the European Defence Community (EDC) proposals consigned into oblivion by the French national assembly in 1954. It was another fine irony that, when this dimension again surfaced, it should do so as the result of a direct Franco-British agreement – at St Malo in December 1998, itself presaged by a rare accord between Major and Mitterrand on defence in 1994 (see later).

There have been several other kinds of 'window'. One which continued to matter a great deal, concerned the windows of opportunity presented by the calendar of national political agendas. Elections set one kind of constraint. Particular member state governments were put under pressure, deemed incapable of acceding to demands or on occasion even helped, because of electoral imperatives. The UK, in the period up to 1997, provided something of a classic case, as we shall see. A second aspect of the 'national' calendars was a country's tenure of the presidency. National priorities and preferences were often as clear as national taboos: certain topics and dossiers could be 'aimed' at a particular presidency, as surely as others were best and wisely avoided.

Equally, there were limits to such calculations. As the membership grew, conclusions had to be drawn. One was that more members meant more national political constraints, more things that had to be allowed for or avoided. But beyond that lay a quite opposite conclusion: 'avoiding' these national sensitive spots had become a full-time, and debilitating, occupation: the only way around it was to cease to allow such national 'vetoes' to dominate, to have greater resort to qualified majority.

Neither was the question of Council presidencies simple. Small country and/or maximalist presidencies in succession had proved powerful in 1985 and, more debatably, in 1991. But in the period discussed here, successions of 'weak' presidencies were implicated in poor or little output: it is fairly clear that this happened in 1994–6.

The year 1994 was another important 'electoral' year, both at member state and EU level. It saw a most significant sea change in Italy where, at the end of March, Berlusconi's *Forza Italia* eclipsed the hitherto dominant Christian Democrats. In the Netherlands in May, a 'purple coalition' of left and right triumphed. Above all, it was a 'bumper year' for elections in Germany, ending with Bundestag elections in October which saw Kohl's coalition returned with a small majority. It saw a new EP: elected (once again) on a lower turnout yet determined to flex its muscles over everything in sight; but also with explicitly sceptical forces strengthened, notably in the Other Europe Group. The overall size of the major groups – PES and EPP – was little altered, as was the balance between them (PES, 198; EPP 157); but the right of centre grouping was now less cohesive and more heterodox. Nine political groups in all were constituted. Austrian elections in October saw substantial gains for Haider's far right Freedom Party, but at this stage not its inclusion in government: hence this did not excite the wrath that was to descend on Austria in 2000.

That same year (1994) also saw the formal launch of Europol (16 February); the inaugural meeting of the Committee of the Regions (9 March); and the formal signing of the GATT Uruguay Round (heralding GATT's replacement by the WTO) in Marrakech (15 April).

Another kind of 'window', and other kinds of reputation, concerned the Commission, as the main 'initiator'. Here Delors proved a hard act to follow, even though his 'Russian dolls'' strategy had come increasingly unstuck in its attempted 'state-building' phase (Grant 1994: *passim*; Ross 1995: 166–247; Endo 1999: Chs 9–11; Drake 2000: 113–56; Gillingham 2003: Part IV). The first shot at replacing him was acrimonious: the nomination of a new Commission president was slated as the main business of the Corfu Summit concluding the Greek presidency in June 1994. The Belgian Jean-Luc Dehaene had a clear lead in the first voting, but was vetoed – as 'too federalist' – by the UK. With Germany's presidency upcoming, Kohl announced a special Council in July to resolve the matter, which nominated Luxembourg's Jacques Santer. But the EP confirmation vote turned into a cliffhanger: he was endorsed only by 260 votes to 238 with 23 abstentions. Santer's leadership was to prove less than vigorous and ended ignominiously. Some individual Commissioners continued to make names for themselves, not all of them flattering.

The EP squeezed more power for itself in the confirmation process for the new Commission. The EP's revised rules of procedure required individual Commissioners-designate to appear before the EP committees corresponding to their portfolio for a confirmation hearing and insisted on this despite misgivings expressed by the outgoing Commission. Clearly that required that agreement be reached *beforehand* on the distribution of Commissioners' responsibilities – another innovation: and the hearings themselves were postponed to January 1995 to enable MEPs from the acceding states to participate. Santer thus held the key to the distribution that took place, one notable feature of which was the division of external relations competences among three Commissioners – Brittan, Marin and van den Broek – under his chairmanship (Corbett in Nugent (ed.) 1995: 40–2).

The issues that dominated the rest of the decade and Santer's Commission presidency were deeply intertwined. They were principally – preparations for the 'achievement' of the highly ambitious EMU; the 'fourth' enlargement (to 15) and the snail-like progress toward the fifth (to 25); treaty reform – first Amsterdam, then Nice; a largely unpromising economic background, in terms of unemployment and low growth; ongoing difficulties in the EU's relations with its 'near abroad'; and finally a growing mood of public disillusion with the European 'project'. The last was strengthened by the forced resignation of the Santer Commission in March 1999.

## Pains and strains on the road to EMU

The pursuit of EMU remained at the heart of the policy agenda and of public controversy. In Chapter 1, it was suggested that 'Community progress' often depended much on the wider macroeconomic situation. Now, however, the pains and strains involved in trying to get to EMU – in particular the fulfilment of the motley Madrid 'convergence criteria' – were seen as very much part of what made the whole situation worse. They reinforced the already substantial problems of the downswing in the economic cycle and those resulting from German unification.

The 'road to EMU' proved no smoother from 1994 onward than previously. Stage 2 began on 1 January 1994 – hardly propitious, in the direct aftermath of the monetary hurricanes of September 1992 (when the Danish and French Maastricht referendum had been the triggers for massive speculation) to August 1993. While Britain and now Denmark were headed for 'opt-out', Germany and France for full steam ahead, other member states had to prioritise restrictive policies if they were to qualify, under the rules, for 'first wave' membership. So central a priority was this that 'progress on most other EU business essentially stopped in 1993–7 as domestic manoeuvring to meet the Maastricht criteria took centre stage' (Heisenberg in Dinan (ed.) 2006: 243–4).

The strains showed in virtually all member states. In France, Jacques Chirac spoke with forked tongue during the 1995 presidential election campaign; and immediately afterwards, he and his lieutenants spent much time in scurried mending of fences while an autumn and winter of unrest, strikes and attempts at reform ensued, one finance minister departed and a Juppé Mark I government was replaced by Juppé Mark II.

In Germany, the tendency (outside the *Kanzleramt*) still to see the whole thing as a 'French plot' persisted. The Buba's reservations, scarcely concealed, expressed themselves in ever fiercer insistence on no fudging of the conditions; on sanctions for 'backsliding' so tough as to deter all but the least faint-hearted 'partners'; in the view that if anything had to give, it should be the timetable, not the rigour. To the Buba's voice was added that of Theo Waigel suggesting that Germany itself might not fulfil the public sector borrowing requirement criterion. Indeed, at one stage, it seemed that only Luxembourg did!

Majority suspicion or hostility in Germany found an echo in the UK electorate; open warfare in the Conservative Party (and cabinet) was only staunched by the 'opt-out' and the mantra that whether, when and how to 'put the issue to the British people' was something that could be safely left until well into the future.

The 'crunch' nature of the EMU issue was well summed up by Kenneth Dyson, whose recital of the unpleasantness that 'ought' to stop its happening was capped only by the conviction that, despite all, in some form it was likely to happen (Dyson 1994: 295, 342).

The major problem was always going to be whether, when and how to get to stage 3. As to 'whether' – at several points, serious doubts recurred as to whether sufficient member states would be both qualified and willing to enter. 'When' paradoxically proved easiest: it rapidly became apparent that the earlier of the two dates stipulated, 1997, was not realistic: thus states focused on gaining admission in a 1999 first wave. (The decision on which states would constitute the original membership was taken in May 1998.) 'How' posed several problems. Of the several fudges, the biggest was the creative accounting over budget deficits resorted to by several states. A classic instance related to the treatment of France Télécom's accounts in the French budget, a move which had to be cleared by the EU statistical office Eurostat, whose director, Yves Franchet, just happened to be French (*ER* 2171: 1 November 1996: II.4). But there were many more (see Clift, *BJPIR* 8, 3, 2006: 388–409). The '60% ratio' of public debt to GDP was clearly, if rigorously maintained, going to exclude both Italy and Belgium (each over 100%): it would look odd indeed if 'Europe's capital' were not part of 'Europe's money'! A great deal of 'flexibility' was shown to enable 11 of the 'willing' 12 to join.

But the notion of 'flexibility' in another context, also proved controversial – and ironical. Germany in particular feared that countries would 'aim' their deficit targeting at 1997 and then resume their profligate ways: this led, in early 1995, to discussions between Buba and the German finance ministry about a 'stability pact' under which states running deficits above the 3% would suffer *immediate and automatic* financial penalties. This was opposed by most other states, arguing first that the deficits should be *persistent* before incurring penalty; then that there should be 'political peer review' rather than automaticity. Undoubtedly, to penalise a deficit country would merely push it further into trouble: but there was logic in both positions. At the Dublin European Council (December 1996) Kohl, isolated, had to choose between no pact at all or one he did not like. Sanctions, a Belgian compromise had it, would be on a 'case-by-case' basis (*ER* 2183: 14 December 1996: II 3). To provide more balm for France and others, it was also renamed: *stability and growth pact* – SGP: but it was still far from their real preference, which was for an 'economic government', rather than a banker's 'cross of gold'.

What emerged, and was inscribed in the Amsterdam Treaty, was a most unbalanced arrangement, the very 'irreversibility' of which (so insisted on by France) continued to be in doubt. 'EMU' was not now in reality, as it had originally been, '*Economic* and monetary union': but rather 'European monetary union': there was precious little economic, certainly not fiscal, union about it: and the 'political union', as already noted, was a creature of vanishing slenderness. It was an arrangement, furthermore, which paid little attention to, and said little about, relations between the 'ins' and the 'outs'.

As we have seen, it was above all one of the great Franco-German battles, even if it resulted in one of the great 'Franco-German compromises/bargains' eventually. Was it one where it is possible to discern a 'winner'? This is more difficult. In origin, it was largely a 'French plot'. In most of its constraints and stringencies (in principle at least), in the name of the currency and the reassuring location of the ECB in Frankfurt, Germany's hand may be seen. But it would not have come about at all if Kohl had not been prepared to 'do a deal' with Mitterrand, giving up, contrary to the opinions of most of Germany's elite and a majority of its citizenry, his country's proudest mark of identity. With equal irony, the relaunch and ultimately the birth of EMU owed much to the author of the French U-turn of 1982–3, setting that country on the road to the *franc fort* – with heavy symbolism, also French for Frankfurt – the Commission president and policy entrepreneur Delors. It appeared, however, that there were few 'winners', in welfare terms, among the general population: growth rates, low for much of the 1990s due not least to the pains of 'convergence', remained low for years after the proclamation of stage 3. There were other casualties, including involved and concerned insiders: notably the Briton, Bernard Connolly, head of the Commission unit responsible for EMS and monetary policies until 1995 and author of *The Rotten Heart of Europe* (1995). Connolly noted early on that when the *economic* case for EMU was shown to be seriously holed, it was declared by true believers to have been a political project all along.

And the economic case *was* seriously holed. 'The consequence was a "lock-in" to a politics of deflation in the first half of 1990s, which caused output loss and contributed to escalating unemployment and *rising* budget deficits as tax revenues fell and public spending rose in a context of recession' (Dyson and Featherstone 1999: 800, emphasis added). EU-11 government debt *grew* from 55% in 1990 to nearly 75% of GDP in 1997, they noted. John Grahl, writing in 1997, stressed 'how closely the project of European construction has become engaged with a *very narrow and dogmatic* project for monetary stabilisation. This linkage is *both damaging and inextricable*' (Grahl 1997: 224, emphases added).

## The 4th enlargement …

EFTA states moved from the EEA to applying for accession to the EU for two basic reasons. As we saw in Chapter 8, the first was essentially to gain decisional influence over economic concerns; the second was the diminished significance of 'neutrality' (in its several forms) in the post-Cold War context. However, they were also 'pushed': as negotiations proceeded, they found an EU increasingly unwilling to contemplate 'quasi-membership'. Pedersen argued that such a possibility was viewed as threatening by many members of a body whose own cohesion was weak and who believed that 'partial privileged membership arrangements risk reopening sensitive debates inside the regional unit' (Pedersen 1994, quoted Preston 1997: 167).

We also saw, however, that despite all the EFTA advantages (high GDP, few problems in agreeing the *acquis*, given what had already been accomplished through the EEA), negotiations, begun in early 1993 and lasting a little over a year, were still far from easy. Many existing members would have preferred Maastricht to be in force prior to enlargement, but following the Danish 'no' of May 1992, looked for some compensatory 'success'. The list of awkward issues was quite long: alpine transit; fisheries; 'marginal' agriculture; the right to insist on higher environmental standards; and inevitably budget contributions. The 'dog that did not bark' in the event was neutrality: the applicants were not required to renounce it; and they in turn could accept without difficulty the vague formulations of Maastricht on CFSP. As Cameron noted at the time: '[T]he most lengthy and arduous part of the negotiations was not between the Union and the applicants, but between the Member States themselves' (Cameron in Nugent (ed.) 1995: 21). A case in point was the 'Ioannina compromise' concerning what should constitute a qualified majority in the Council following enlargement and what should be done following a Council vote that fell just short. ('[T]he Council will do all within its power to reach, within a reasonable time … a satisfactory solution that can be adopted by at least 68 [65, following Norway's No] votes' (see Nugent (ed.) 1995: 174).)

This should have served as something of a warning for the CEEs and Mediterranean two. These states, which were to *become* the 'fifth wave' were, in the process of very lengthy negotiations, grouped and regrouped, demoted and promoted like teams in a multi-division sports league.

Referenda were held in all four pre-accession EFTA states. The sequence was significant and deliberate: the 'first to go' would be the countries where a 'yes' was most confidently anticipated, in the hope of achieving a 'domino effect' on the least willing. The pattern of votes entirely confirmed this expectation. Austria said 'yes' by about 67% to 33% (turnout 81%); Finland 'yes' by 57% to 43% (74% turnout). The Swedish result was seen as crucial to that in Norway and the result very close: 52% 'yes', about 47% 'no' (turnout 82%). It should thus have come as no surprise that the Norwegians again voted 'no' by 52.2% to 47.8% on 27–8 November 1994. Austria, Finland and Sweden entered the EU at the start of 1995: this meant the 'rump' EEA consisted only of Norway and Iceland until joined by Liechtenstein on 1 May 1995.

Swedish and Finnish accession did not abruptly terminate all habits of 'Nordic' cooperation: however, as time went by Sweden and Finland increasingly used the EU as their 'channel' in dealing with Norway over such tricky issues as free movement of persons.

## ... and moves towards 5th enlargement

As the 'new Europe' began to obtrude, complications appeared. The debate was couched in terms of the 'security architecture' of the New Europe. The most obvious complication concerned the *dual* enlargement of the EU and of NATO: what kind of conceptual linkage should there be between them and, more particularly, the questions of *who* and *when*. 'Who' also implied 'who not', and the reactions of Russia in particular. There were widely varying views about how far Russian concerns should be a determining factor, should be 'taken on board', be assuaged or (notably in some US circles) be effectively ignored. Even as late as 1997 an EP background note stated that although the EU 'who' question had been settled in principle at Copenhagen in June 1993, 'The question whether NATO enlargement should on the whole precede the enlargement of the EU or vice versa is still unresolved'. It noted that the German preference was for EU accession to take preference over that to NATO: but that, given the expectation of NATO enlargement in 1999, 'the EU has a major problem as regards the time framework of its enlargement' (*EP* 1997: 3). The trickle of further EU accession applications had become a flood. It had begun with Hungary's on 31 March 1994, swiftly followed by that of Poland on 5 April. In June 1995, the implausible Romania and authoritarian Slovakia joined the queue: there seemed little logic or self-awareness in who tried to muscle in through the door first. Then followed Latvia (27 October), Estonia (28 November), Lithuania and Bulgaria (8 and 16 December). Finally in January 1996, two 'easy' states (as many then thought) completed the queue: the Czech Republic and Slovenia.

Most observers found the EU's response to all this defensive, ungenerous and incoherent. For a start, there seemed little shared view or vision of 'Europe' – whether as to geography, priorities, values or modalities.

The main stages in EU negotiation/adaptation were several. First had been the 'Europe agreements', originally proposed as far back as August 1990 by the

Commission as 'second generation association agreements' (COM90/398: 27 August 1990). Here, despite the rhetoric, 'protectionist interests held sway' (Edwards in Hill and Smith (eds) 2005: 46). The EU gave with one hand ('market access' for the CEEs to the EU without reciprocity) but decidedly took away with the other – *except* in the so-called 'sensitive sectors' – coal and steel, textiles and agriculture – precisely those where the CEEs enjoyed comparative advantage. There followed the 'Copenhagen Criteria' of 1993, again insisting that the CEEs had to converge on EU norms before accession was permitted. The criteria were refined and developed in the Essen (1994) Cannes and Madrid (1995) European Councils: and then the Commission's *Agenda 2000: For a Stronger and Wider Europe* in July 1997. (For detailed accounts of enlargement, see Maresceau (ed.) 1997; Preston 1997; Croft et al. 1999.)

And so the NATO enlargement process, which early on had lagged behind that of the EU, overtook it. Only in December 1994 had NATO foreign ministers initiated a study of the issues involved in alliance enlargement. The NATO process was marked by three stages and three summits: Madrid, 1997; Washington 1999; and (looking ahead) Prague 2002. The identification of countries as potential full members began in earnest, as with the EU, in 1997. The Brussels NATO ministerial of December 1996 set the Madrid Summit of July 1997 the task of beginning formal negotiations with (yet to be specified) CEEs, with the aim of completing their membership by NATO's 50th anniversary in 1999. That Madrid NATO Summit was followed only days later by the EU's *Agenda 2000*; and then followed immediately the 'face-saving' visit of Russian Prime Minister Viktor Chernomyrdin to the EU in Brussels – designed to soothe the bear but not to let him nose into the house. (Dannreuther 1997: 6 and *passim*; Allen and Smith in Edwards and Wiessala (eds) 1998: 80).

At the 1999 Washington NATO Summit the Czech Republic, Hungary and Poland were admitted. This event, intended as a 'full-scale celebration of half a century of security success in Europe' (Rogers in *WT* August–September 1999: 4–6) was completely overshadowed by the Kosovo crisis. Although the Washington Summit issued no further new membership invitations, it did provide a 'membership action plan' (MAP) – a roadmap for potential candidates to follow.

It also endorsed the EU's ESDI concept: it 'picked up much of the language of the [St Malo] Declaration'; likewise the appointment of former British Defence Minister George (later Lord) Robertson as NATO Secretary-General 'may facilitate the task of ensuring that this European development will not be seen as being in competition with NATO' (Roper in Edwards and Wiessala (eds) 2000: 10–11).

*Agenda 2000* spelled out the EU accession criteria as: stability of institutions guaranteeing democracy and the rule of law, human rights and respect for and protection of minorities; a functioning market economy and the capacity to cope with competitive pressure and market forces within the EU; the ability to take on the obligations of membership, including adherence to the aims of political, economic and monetary union. To these came to be added the 'absorptive' capacity of the EU itself. It was to prove a tall order and much frustration, as well as some dire threats about 'euro-exhaustion', costs and delays in the applicant countries was to accompany the process. *Agenda 2000* proposed dividing the candidates into two groups, with six – Cyprus, the Czech Republic, Estonia, Hungary, Poland and Slovenia – forming the 'lead' group. Crucially, there was to be no financial generosity: the budget stayed capped at the 'Delors II' 1.4%; accession states would not benefit from the direct farm payments agreed in the 1992 CAP reform; there would not be a wholesale redirection of structural funds in their favour; and there would be a ceiling of 4% of GDP pa on the transfers any could receive from the EU. It was a disheartening reality check for the pre-accession states. The European Council took the decision to open negotiations with the 'first wave six' in December 1997 – although actual negotiations began only in November 1998. At the end of 1999, the EU abandoned the 'two waves' approach and assessed each applicant's fulfilment of the criteria individually.

Not until May 2004 were the 'next wave' states to clamber on board. Even then, it was untidy, particularly as regards Cyprus; Bulgaria, Croatia and Romania were unsurprisingly still waiting: while Turkey, so critical in US calculations and so divisive in European, was still held outside. Although it had been declared a 'candidate' in 1999, it was only at the Brussels European Council of December 2004 that the opening of accession negotiations was announced with Turkey and with Croatia, for 2005.

EU applications thus slowed for a whole variety of reasons, including the Balkan/ Former Yugoslav chaos; they also became enmeshed in the complex dance involving relations with both WEU and NATO. Again, the issues were who, how fast, by what criteria and with what – intended or unintended – consequences. In the case of NATO, the agenda was being substantially driven by the views and preferences of the USA which, whether by design or just carelessly, was thus again involved in 'shaping Europe' and in predictable quarters resented for so doing.

## Treaty of Amsterdam

This time, there was plenty of time to prepare for reform. Unlike the earlier IGCs of 1985 and 1991, that of 1996 was mandated: in Article 2 of the TEU. The June 1994 Corfu Summit set up a 'reflection group', under Spanish Secretary of State for European Affairs Carlos Westendorp. It did not, however, begin its work until June 1995, reporting in December – by which time others, sensing that there would be little agreement of substance, had made pre-emptive moves. Notably, the German Schäuble-Lamers paper of 1 September 1994 had 'unabashedly raised the "F" word': this time, F for 'flexibility' or permitting, even encouraging, a 'hard core' of states that so wished, to proceed deeper and faster without the possibility of being blocked by 'slow' ships. It was a 'deliberately provocative' offering (Duff 1997: 187). The Germans stressed that it was a 'party' not a 'government' document: but Kohl was far from abjuring it. The paper 'with unusual honesty for a quasi-diplomatic document' (Dinan in Cram et al. 1999: 296) proceeded to *identify* the 'core' countries as the original 'six' minus Italy: it thus also raised, predictably, alarm in the UK, concerned about being 'marginalised', having second-class status. John Major's riposte was immediate: in his Leiden speech of 7 September 1994, he signalled agreement with 'flexibility' but rejected both the 'inner core' and the 'two speed' approaches. Verbal barrages continued. French premier Balladur proposed a 'concentric circles' approach (*Le Monde*, 30 November 1994); other French voices – Juppé, Lamassoure and Giscard – followed; finally came the joint Kohl–Chirac letter of 6 December 1995, the day after publication of the reflection group's report, which had acknowledged the breadth of the UK's dissent. The letter, aimed at the UK, stated that they intended to propose to the IGC the notion of an 'enhanced cooperation' (*coopération renforcée*) mechanism (Nugent (ed.) 1996: 183; Duff (ed) 1997: 188–9).

The IGC was launched in Turin in March 1996. Some 15 months later, on 16–17 June 1997, the European Council in Amsterdam reached agreement on the draft treaty: it was formally signed on 2 October. The general verdict on it was at best damning with faint praise: the treaty fell well short of the declared aspirations of most, while going farther than the just defeated British Conservatives would have allowed. Throughout, the UK had fought a determined rearguard on almost all fronts and mostly alone: other states resigned themselves to await the defeat of the Major government, by which time the game was up.

Ex-Commissioner Peter Sutherland reminded people that at the Turin launch, its three main objectives had been: to enhance the EU's capacity for external action; to prepare for eastern enlargement; and to make it more relevant to its populations. '[T]he first two objectives were not achieved and the third only partly' (EPC 1997: 29). Although the treaty 'was never likely to amount to much', lack of progress in the external field was particularly dangerous in light of the Bosnian crisis. Even WEU's mooted integration with the EU had become 'a vague possibility rather than an objective'. There had been complete failure to resolve the issues of reform of Commission and Council of Ministers: inconclusive argument over large states' right to a second Commissioner versus the weighting of votes in the Council meant that next time – and inevitably there would have to be a next time – not only would institutional reform become entangled with enlargement but there was a risk of undermining the essential institutional construction of the EU: Commissioners were not meant to be 'national' representatives; therefore not for states to 'give up'.

By common consent, it was at best a modest 'tidying' operation. It was also a case, for the institutions severally, of 'all have won so all must have prizes'. Briefly, the role and right of initiative of the Commission president were strengthened. For the Council of Ministers, it prescribed further extension of QMV and of co-decision with the EP. The European Council's role in EMU was confirmed and in regard to CFSP strengthened. On CFSP, there was otherwise little change: whereas the TEU had had the external 'stimulus' of the Gulf War behind it, 'Amsterdam had nothing comparable' thought Duff (1997: 124): apparently, Bosnia was not enough. The EP, in addition to co-decision, saw its power to approve the appointment of the Commission president and the Commission as a whole strengthened. The 'cooperation procedure' was abolished except for some EMU matters. A ceiling of 700 was put on the number of MEPs. The Court obtained increased jurisdiction in 'third-pillar' (JHA) matters (see Bomberg and Stubb 2003: 46–7). Schengen was incorporated in the treaty; asylum and immigration had been transferred from JHA Pillar III

to the 'Community' Pillar I. 'Flexibility', alias enhanced cooperation, was in –
although 'so qualified [as] to make … deployment in practice against the wishes of
the UK virtually impossible' (Duff (ed.) 1997: xxxv). 'Integrationists' could point
to a few limited achievements, but very few.

'Agreement was reached … by the … well-tried method of agreeing to the highest common rhetoric and the lowest common substance' (Edwards and Wiessala
(eds) 1998: 2). Others were less charitable: Amsterdam 'is a caricature of all that is
wrong with the EU … intended to bring Europe closer to its citizens' it was instead
'more than 50 pages long, littered with arcane language and unexplained references
to existing treaty provisions … the Treaty is unlikely to endear either itself or the
EU to a sceptical public' (Cram et al. 1999: 305). It might potentially strengthen the
Union's effectiveness, but at the cost of continued or increased complexity. For the
rest of the year, there was a deafening silence: ratification would take some
time yet; and all involved would have to become familiar with the new article
numberings!

'Amsterdam' was an especially sensitive matter in Germany, where care had to
be taken not further to alienate German institutions (especially the Constitutional
Court – *BVG*) and a neuralgic public worried about the euro. If this further constrained ambition, it also meant that very little was done in the IGC or the treaty to
address the issue of legitimacy.

Just as important, then, were the 'Amsterdam leftovers', illustrating how modest
and incomplete the result had been. During that IGC, difficult institutional issues
relating to enlargement had been mainly swept under the carpet: they lay attached
to the treaty as the 'protocol on the institutions with the prospect of enlargement':
'a fig leaf for the fact that nothing could be decided', declared the EPC's commentary (EPC 1997: 33–4; see also Duff (ed.) 1997: 133; Galloway 2001: 26–7). It had
been chicken and egg: it was argued that these issues assumed less urgency *because*
enlargement was not imminent: but it was also the case that further enlargement
was slowed down *because of* these related issues.

The spring (May–June 1997) saw electoral disasters for the centre right in both
Britain and France, but of quite different kinds: long anticipated in the UK; much
less anticipated, and the result of a presidential miscalculation, in France. Major
and Juppé were out, but the consequences of 'reform' majorities proved, for the
EU, very different. Tony Blair's personal preference for joining EMU when feasible was quickly squelched by the Treasury coup in which Gordon Brown set out
five notional 'tests' for the UK to join the single currency – and the unmentioned
sixth: would any proposal to do so, based on supposed 'fulfilment' of those five,
pass in referendum? Meantime, Jospin and the French left, victorious not least on a
backlash against the pains and strains of EMU preparation, set out their own 'four
conditions' for joining and had a programme promising the usual heady mixture,
difficult of fulfilment: shorter hours, more jobs, while qualifying for EMU.
Something had to give, though some hoped that a pickup in economic growth –
apparent in 1997 – might save the day.

When Jacques Santer's native Luxembourg took over the presidency in July,
it was time for the Commission to promote its *Agenda 2000* programme,

designed – again – to address the ongoing challenges of enlargement and internal reform.

## EMU arrives, 1998–9

The Commission's list of those 'qualified' for EMU stage 3 was published in March 1998. Community founders Italy and Belgium amazingly were deemed to qualify, despite government debt to GDP ratios far above those stipulated in the criteria: they were saved by the clause allowing for 'significant progress towards' the 60% ratio specified.

There was another surprise to come, this time concerning what had been assumed to be a formality: the appointment of the ECB's first president. The head of the EMI, its forerunner, was the Dutchman Wim Duisenberg, who had taken the job in 1996 on, he thought, the clear understanding and agreement of the governments that he would continue. But Chirac had not given his formal assent and at the last moment proposed instead the head of the Banque de France, Jean-Claude Trichet. When this failed to gain traction, there were more machinations about dividing the 8-year term of office – designedly lengthy as a guarantee of no political interference! In the end this too was fudged: on 'age' grounds, Duisenberg would leave 'before' the 8 years were up: but the date not specified. (see Verdun in Cini (ed.) 2003: 320–1; Heisenberg in Dinan (ed.) 2006: 246).

And so the 'virtual' euro came into being at the start of 1999: notes and coins would only circulate 3 years later. This launch managed, perhaps fortunately, to avoid any high drama.

Guessing at exchange rates proved, for the euro following launch as in most other instances, a mug's game. It had been widely predicted that, once safely launched, the euro would appreciate against dollar and yen, borne along on a tide of price transparency, general 'efficiency' gains, growth, overseas portfolio diversification, Uncle Tom Cobley and all. The opposite proved the case, although due in part to the very circumstances – high initial exchange rate, dollar pessimism and so on – attending its birth. It was launched 'just as the European recovery was failing to live up to expectations, and the US to live down to them' (Cottrell in Edwards and Wiessala (eds) 2000: 77). Euro weakness continued for a while: in October 2000 the dollar reached a peak against the euro; from that point, it was to fall – by about 35% by August 2006 (*FT*, 7 August 2006: 14).

Nevertheless, its arrival was greeted as 'the single most important event in European and transatlantic politics since the Soviet Union's demise', albeit also 'a tremendous gamble' (Calleo 1999: 5); 'a *global political and* economic event of the first order' (Buiter 1999: 182, emphasis added). The turmoil surrounding the recent Asian crises meant that the euro's introduction was 'quite by chance, very well timed indeed' (Buiter 1999: 184). But right from the start, criticism of the cobbled together compromises that constituted its 'governance' were rife. Its differences from earlier monetary unions far outweighed the similarities; it was 'a bold step into the unknown'; 'Great idea, shame about the execution', was Willem Buiter's 'main message' in December 1998 (Buiter 1999: 182, 181).

## Defence and security: from ESDI to ESDP

Howorth argues that both exogenous and endogenous factors combined to produce 'a forceful drive towards ESDP' (Howorth in Hill and Smith (eds) 2005: 183). Chaos in the Balkans in the 1990s, the early phases of which were traced in Chapter 8, went hand in hand with tentative steps toward an enhanced specifically EU military capability. It was a most painful path. The EC had earlier been in disarray and recrimination over the recognition of Croatia and Slovenia. It was no better over Bosnia and only a US shove produced the fragile 1995 Dayton 'peace accords'.

Underlying all this was a whole host of debates and reforms, especially in French and British defence circles in the 1990s. Here, mention of just a few must suffice. One lesson the French took from Gulf War I was to begin to move – slowly – to the abolition of conscription. But in late October 1991 came the announcement – kept quiet for a while – of the Franco-German 'Eurocorps' proposal, inciting US ire (*FAZ* 17 October 1991: 1, also 2, 5, 14). The Rome NATO Summit of 7 November 1991 is often described as the 'nadir' of French relations with NATO: an aggrieved French delegation stalked off to its tents, leaving its 'nine point' aide mémoire smouldering on the table (text: French Embassy London: *Speeches & Statements* 144/91; McAllister 2000: 3–5). From there, things could only go one way: in the direction of fence mending. And they did. Despite the sending, on the *same* day in July 1992, by the *same* group of ministers, of *two* flotillas to the Adriatic – one under NATO Southern, the other nominal WEU Command, the 'Eurocorps' row was diffused in December 1992–January 1993 by the 'three-way agreement' between NATO, France and Germany, providing for the French forces within it to come under NATO operational command in crisis (Grant 1996: 61). At the Brussels NATO Summit in January 1994, fences appeared mended: Mitterrand spoke of 'the Alliance ... taking account of the new European identity ... *That shows how far we have progressed since the Rome NATO Summit*' (French Embassy London: *S & S*: 94/3: 6, emphasis added).

There were further signs of change, against the Balkan background. If the French *Defence White Paper* of February 1994 was – in part for reasons of domestic political weakness – something of a damp squib, the 'defence review' launched by Chirac on becoming president in 1995 proved much more significant. French insistence on a 'final' round of nuclear tests in 1995 had put them in bad odour; or 'at the centre of an international debate', as Juppé preferred (French Embassy London: *SAC* 95/198: 2). Yet Juppé stated that France's future would increasingly 'be shaped in concert with all the countries of Europe and ... relations between Europe and the United States will ... be better balanced than they were [during superpower confrontation]'. Juppé at that point concentrated on nuclear questions; the president, in February, announced the progressive phasing out of conscription, as well as the restructuring and reduction of nuclear forces. Given their apparent radicalism, it is interesting that the proposals were accepted so easily by the political system as a whole: timely use had been made of a 'non-cohabitation' interlude to push things through.

Chirac spelled out the changes on 22 and 23 February 1996 – first in a broadcast, then in a speech before the *École Militaire* – interestingly, that way round. To the latter, he spoke of professional forces as essential 'to satisfy our ambition to build a credible European defence, capable of becoming *both the defence component of the European Union and the European pillar of the Atlantic Alliance*'.

As always in French defence questions, every word, every formula, each sequence requires Kremlinological attention. There are real similarities between these episodes and the debates of 1967–69 discussed in Chapters 1 and 2: indeed, a sense of a real sequel. But these announcements left many asking whether France was being 'more Atlanticist today in order to be more European tomorrow'. And the answer to that remained unclear. In February Germany had been the first mentioned on Chirac's list: then, 'in liaison with ... especially the British, who share with us a long tradition of action abroad', in the 'engine of European defence'. (French Embassy London: *SAC* 96/56: 25–9).

This key speech was followed 9 months later by the conclusion in Nuremberg of a 'common security and defence concept' with, again, Germany. Although concluded on 8–9 December 1996, there was a 7 weeks' delay before making it public (*Le Monde* 30.1.1997; 12–13; French Embassy London, *SAC* 97/32: 1–13; McAllister 2000: 14–15). '[O]ur two countries are determined to press on with developing a European security and defence identity in the Alliance as part of the latter's reform', ran the key sentence. 'Common armaments policy' figured prominently but ambiguously. The two said that they 'intend to reform the [Atlantic] Alliance', the stakes over which were indeed raised during that very period of silence about the 'common concept'. On 3 January 1997, a spat began over the NATO Southern Command – AFSOUTH – with France proposing, as a touchstone of 'good intent' over alliance reform, that this command should be held by a 'European' (read French national) – this as a condition for a French return to a 'renovated' (adapted) NATO. The Americans flatly refused: this was the home of the US Sixth Fleet; Congress 'would never accede to ... a European taking charge of this command' (Petras and Morley 2000: 56–7, cited in McAllister 2000).

Out of all this eventually emerged St Malo. Although both French and British claimed it as their own, it seems likely that its origins lay in the 'intense frustration felt by Tony Blair in 1998 ... to formulate a policy on the Balkans' (Howorth, *Survival* 42, 2 Summer 2000: 33): but the French were delighted to 'capture' the British in the name of 'autonomous' capability. The breakthrough began at the informal meeting in Pörtschach, Austria, in October, then St Malo in December. Stripped of all the bunting, key elements of St Malo were: the reference to 'capacity for autonomous action' – *not* later rescinded, despite US concerns; balanced by that to NATO and WEU collective defence commitments, and by stating that 'The different situations of countries in relation to NATO must be respected' (French Embassy London, *SAC* 98/350: 7). Howorth opined, 'It is difficult to overstate the significance of recent developments in European security and defence policy' (Howorth 2000: 33). However, he wisely followed his recital of the 'historic significance' of the agreement with a series of 'cautionary notes'. Franco-British honeymoons 'have a cyclical dimension to them'; differences in security culture 'remain considerable'; there remained 'important asymmetries ... in the context of Atlantic security' (Howorth 2000: 35).

Late 1998 and early 1999 pointed up the paradoxes sharply. The ink was not dry on the St Malo agreement when Kosovo again came to the fore: the Rambouillet Conference, 'co-chaired' by the British and French in February 1999, was generally regarded as deeply unsatisfactory – and the Paris 'follow-on' talks a few weeks later as not much better (see Guicherd 1999; Judah 1999; Roberts 1999: 102–23; Weller 1999: 211–51; Buckley and Cummings (eds) 2001: *passim*). Friction with the USA, over tactics and strategy, bombing from 15,000 feet versus 'boots on the ground', was apparent over Kosovo, and showed some convergence of views between the French and British.

'The lesson of Kosovo merely strengthened the developments that were triggered in autumn 1998 *by the British government's U-turn* that led to St Malo and ... culminated in Nice (December 2000)' (Rutten [compiler] 2001: ix, emphasis added). The director of WEU's Institute for Security Studies, Nicole Gnesotto, averred: 'In the two years between St Malo and Nice, the character of the EU changed': what had previously been 'unthinkable' – the inclusion in the Union's legitimate competencies of a common security and defence policy – became agreed. She stressed that there was nothing inevitable about this: it 'required all the European traumatisation of the decade in which Yugoslavia broke up' (Gnesotto in Rutten 2001: vii). Although Nice had sanctioned this development, much remained to be done, on two fronts: operational capabilities and coherent decision making. The truth of that was soon evident.

Although much of the action over Kosovo/Former Yugoslavia was ostensibly NATO and 'contact group', rather than EU, business, nonetheless defence and security, along with enlargement, EMU and institutional reform, embedded itself in the agenda in the run-up to the next IGC and the Nice Treaty. So did issues of human rights generally, of racism and xenophobia, minority rights and citizenship, 50 years after the Council of Europe's landmark Convention on Human Rights. The EU's own Charter of Fundamental Rights, arguments about its precise legal status notwithstanding, was to be 'solemnly proclaimed' at Nice.

## Nice Treaty, 2000: more leftovers, more hangovers

Amsterdam having been unable to reach agreement on its original remit – reform of the institutions to accommodate enlargement – it fell to the Nice Treaty to try to remedy the situation. Even its exact genesis was not clear: 'one could argue that the decisions of IGC 2000 had been an eternal leftover' (Gray and Stubb in Edwards and Wiessala (eds) 2001: 8). Official discussions began in May 1999, at the levels of Coreper and the General Affairs Council (GAC). Neither was its exact scope clear: 'agreement' that 'only' those reforms necessary for enlargement to work should be discussed, was as far as agreement went: member states had very different views on that. 'The agenda became an obsession': although the June 1999 Cologne European Council decided that attention should concentrate on the 'institutional leftovers', the Prodi Commission, keen to fly kites on a wider front, appointed another 'wise men's' group – consisting of Dehaene, von Weizäcker and Simon – which reported in October 1999 (Dehaene et al. 1999). This conveniently provided the Commission with 'ammunition' for its own input, without committing it to all details (Galloway 2001: 29–30).

In May 2000, 50 years on from the Schuman Declaration, German Foreign Minister Joschka Fischer, speaking, he implausibly claimed, in an individual capacity, initiated yet another debate about the 'future of Europe'. His title was 'From Confederacy to Federation: thoughts on the finality of European integration'. We shall return to it, in Chapter 11, in the context of the origins of the convention on the future of Europe; but for now, it should be noted that he proposed to transform the EU from a 'union of states' (*Staatenbund*) to a 'lean federation', a *fully sovereign body* in which member states would have 'a much larger role' than the *Länder* in Germany (Norman 2003: 11; German foreign ministry website – www.auswaertiges-amt.de). Late in his speech came the suggestion for a constitution, to both secure democracy in the Union and to delineate clearly matters to be regulated at European and at state level.

Soon, everyone was putting in their twopence worth. Chirac spoke to the Bundestag on 27 June, just before the start of the French EU presidency (French Embassy London: *SAC/00/675*). Although he too spoke of Franco-German 'pioneers', his ideas were 'far from Joschka Fischer's federal-leaning plan' of a few weeks earlier; and his reception, tellingly, was described as 'polite' (unenthusiastic) (*ER* 2514: 5 July 2000). Blair, who declared himself 'neither surprised nor concerned' by these ideas, in turn set out his own views in Poland in October. We discuss these three contributions in more detail in Chapter 11. And several foreign ministers including Cook, Lipponen and Amato, also contributed: Amato backing the UK against Chirac on the 'two speed' issue (*ER* 2516, 12 July 2000: I, 1).

Once the negotiations proper began in February 2000, it was to be another marathon: 'a total of 370 official negotiating hours in 30 representatives' meetings, 10 ministerial meetings and three European Councils' (Gray and Stubb in Edwards and Wiessala (eds) 2001: 5).

What, briefly, was achieved? The EU would retain a 'one Commissioner per Member State' arrangement until the Union reached 27 states. The thorny issue of weighting of votes in the Council was resolved by agreeing that both a majority of votes and a majority of member states would be required, plus, if requested, a check that the vote represented not less than 62% of the Union's population. There was a further growth in the *number* of issues covered by QMV: but the most sensitive were still subject to unanimity. The articles dealing with 'enhanced cooperation' were amended in anticipation of more frequent recourse to it later. The statutes of, and articles referring to, both ECJ and CFI were significantly amended.

How were these agreements arrived at? During the summer and early autumn of 2000, 'the supporters of a narrow agenda … won the battle but lost the war' (Gray and Stubb in Edwards and Wiessala (eds) 2001: 10). The Portuguese presidency's handling of the IGC negotiations (first half 2000) was widely praised: its report at the Feira European Council 'bequeathed the French presidency a good starting base on which to build' (Galloway 2001: 36). Such compliments were rarely paid to the French presidency in the second half. It 'did not demonstrate that it was going to be an impartial Presidency, but rather one that would advocate a shift in the balance of power ... decisively towards the larger Member States'; perhaps in the same vein, the most important issue for large member states, Council voting weights, was one on which precious little time had been spent until the last days before Nice (Gray and Stubb in Edwards and Wiessala (eds) 2001: 11, 15). The French also wanted progress on security policy and relations with NATO (*ER* 2513: 1 July 2000).

The EP as usual sought to push things in a 'maximalist' direction. In October, it pressed for the co-decision procedure to be used in all matters decided by QMV. Its Duhamel Report pressed for a 'constitutionalisation' of the treaties: there should be two stages – a single, brief, readable treaty dealing 'simply'(!) with the goals of the EU – (far from agreed, of course); and then a 'Constitution of the EU' to be initiated at Nice and pursued – presciently, here – via a 'Convention', along the lines of that which had produced the charter of fundamental rights (CFR). The Gil-Robles Report concentrated on 'enhanced cooperation/flexibility', insisting that this *not* be used for areas covered by QMV; and that CFSP and defence policy *should* be included within the scope of closer cooperation. (*ER* 2537: 21 October 2000: I, 1). Yet another EP report (Lalumière) sought to distinguish the core role of NATO (territorial, collective defence) from that of the EU.

Defence and security was one of many background 'rumblings' for the IGC. It figured prominently in Cyprus/Greece/Turkey issues in November 2000. It figured also in the absorption of (most of) WEU's functions; and in the row over access to documentation relating to defence matters, where Solana had to insist that most of this, coming as it did either from NATO or member states, had to remain confidential, or else ESDP could not function.

Relations with NATO and especially the touchstone term, for the French, the 'autonomy' of European arrangements, remained a most sensitive topic in late 2000. UK Foreign Secretary Robin Cook angered several EU partners in early December by saying that 'enhanced cooperation'/flexibility was not suitable for defence and military matters (*FT* 5 December 2000: 1). In the end, this was the line that was agreed.

But neither the NATO row nor US concerns would go away. Reflecting on Kosovo: 'Many [American commanders] swore that they never wanted to be part of another alliance operation ... British critics are right when they say that creating the European force will pose the question of NATO's purpose. If the European force handles crises in Europe, what is NATO for?' asked William Pfaff (*IHT* 5 December 2000: at iht.com/articles/3375.htm). Answers to this were to come swiftly: often for crises *outside* Europe! US Defence Secretary William Cohen next day, in his swansong and that of the Clinton administration, underlined the point in an impassioned speech to NATO defence ministers in Brussels. He warned that NATO would become a 'relic' unless the EU's 'autonomous capability' plans were much more closely linked to it (*FT* 6 December 2000: 10). On the same day, 5 December, both Solana and Robertson stressed that the detail of the EU–NATO relationship was both crucial but also still 'work in progress'. Stressing the importance of getting NATO–EU institutional linkages right, Robertson said 'but a great deal of detailed work remains to be done ... We are looking forward to the outcome of the EU Summit in Nice later this week' and to the next NATO foreign ministers meeting in Brussels in the middle of December (*ER* 2251: 9 December 2000: I, 2: see later). This was an understatement: by way of 'local' example, the Turks were quick to indicate that they opposed any 'automatic' provision of NATO assets to the EU: it should be on a 'case-by-case' basis. There was a far bigger, 'global' issue: getting to formal agreement on the (June 1996 NATO) 'Berlin Plus' procedures was to take 'over 4 years'; and they 'remain tightly classified' (Howorth in Hill and Smith (eds) 2005: 185). The eventual formal basis for EU–NATO strategic partnership was only to emerge in the joint declaration on ESDP on 16 December 2002!

All this, then, was going on *on the very days preceding* the start of the IGC negotiations – another horrendous marathon. Was there any 'logic' to the outcomes? Here, the consensus is that classic EU compromises were the order of the day: but that the results frequently lacked logic. 'The leaders emerged *bleary-eyed at dawn* on 11 December at the *end of their scrappy five-day* IGC with a convoluted deal' (*ER* 2552: 13 December 2000 I: 4, emphasis added); the result another 'watered-down compromise', which Belgium's foreign minister called 'a bad treaty'; Prodi (predictably) regretted that 'we did not manage to go further'; a whole procession of EP party group leaders equally predictably expressed disappointment. Of course, the 'much-criticised host, Jacques Chirac, said that Nice would be remembered as a great summit' (*ER* 2552: 13 Dec 2000: I, 1–9). Perhaps the wisest of Chirac's remarks was to remind the EP's members that they should not gallop ahead of public opinion.

On defence and security, the European Council agreed the (French) presidency's draft report on ESDP. The aim was to give the EU the means of playing its international role fully, 'by *adding* an *autonomous capacity to take decisions and action*'. It was precisely this autonomy in decision and planning that irked the Americans: 'duplication' they were against. The *scope* was to be 'the full range of Petersberg tasks as defined in the TEU' and, doubtless to assuage British sensitivities, 'This does not involve the establishment of a European army'. However, on progress concerning permanent political and military structures it added: 'The strength of the resources needed … in particular [for] the Military Staff, will have to be increased without delay' (*ER* 2552: I, 1). By another nice irony, the poisoned chalice of carrying this forward passed next to a Swedish presidency. Robin Cook was at pains to point out that the document stressed that Europe would only launch an operation 'where NATO as a whole has already decided not to' – such operations being crisis management, peacekeeping or humanitarian intervention.

If the basic CESDP text of the Nice conclusions was quite brief, as always the devil was in the detail. And of that there was no lack: some 40 annexed pages. Not merely were there six 'annexes', but several annexes to the annexes (*sic*) and a couple of appendices to the annexes to the annexes! A separate monograph would be needed to do full justice to it. But essential changes included the establishment of three bodies: a political and security committee (PSC– Annex III to Annex VI); a military committee of the EU (EUMC – see Annex IV to Annex VI); and a military staff of the EU (EUMS – see Annex V to Annex VI). Two further annexes to Annex VI – (numbers VI and VII) – were significant. These concerned, respectively: 'Arrangements concerning non-EU European NATO members and other countries which are candidates for accession to the EU' and 'Standing Arrangements for consultation and cooperation between the EU and NATO'.

NATO foreign ministers had their promised further bite at the apple on 14–15 December: the meeting went on far beyond schedule, but still had to record that the ad hoc working groups had produced no agreement on the 'permanent links' (standing arrangements) with the EU (*ER* 2554, 20 December 2000: I, 1). It would be another full 2 years before agreement was reached.

Meanwhile, on EU enlargement, loud rumbles were heard from the pre-accession states: some in the 'vanguard' said they risked being made 'hostages' to the laggardliness of others: Estonia was thinking about its fellow Baltic states, Latvia and Lithuania; the Czechs and Hungarians fretted about their fate depending on slow Poland.

For the rest, Nice looked a little like another Amsterdam. The compromise kept everyone on board 'by limiting the scope of overall concessions'. Much of what was agreed would not come into effect until at least 2005 – some provisions later. Voting 'solutions' – in Council and EP – lacked coherence but were deeply revealing about what member states thought important. The QMV deal appeared to favour the larger member states. French (adamant) insistence on maintaining Council voting parity with Germany was 'balanced' by a sharp increase in Germany's 'advantage' in number of MEPs (it retained 99, while the three next biggest – France, Italy and the UK – saw their number drop to 72 each). Spain and Poland held out for almost as many Council votes – 27 – as the 'biggest four' (29), which meant that each, with half of Germany's population, had almost as much Council weight; they 'lost', relatively speaking, in MEPs, where their 50 each was almost exactly pro rata to Germany's 99. In dealing out the EP 'rations', Nice ignored Amsterdam's '700 ceiling': once the anticipated accession of Bulgaria and Romania took place (in the event, in 2007), the body would have 732 members. The Commission president obtained more power and, from 2005, was to be appointed also by QMV (no more UK veto of Dehaene). But until 2005, all states retained the right to 'one or more' Commissioners; thereafter one per member state to a maximum of 27. France and the UK had agreed in wanting a smaller, more 'streamlined' body – and lost: several smaller states saw themselves as being 'streamlined' out of the picture too much! Roughly 90% of all EU legislation was henceforth to be by QMV: this included sensitive areas such as border controls and visa rules and foreign trade in services (*ER* 2552: I, 4). The veto was thus to be removed over 29 treaty articles. But the UK refused to budge over taxation (backed by Ireland, Luxembourg and Sweden) or social security. In the end, Chirac was not quite alone in diplomatically finding something to praise. Schröder said, 'without us highlighting it, Germany's weight has grown', adding tactfully that more Council votes 'would not have helped Europe and would have hurt French–German ties in a way we simply did not want' (*ER* 2552: 8). And the CEEs at least felt that their accession would not yet again be put on hold pending yet another IGC.

And then came the inevitable: *'We have to meet again!'* Another IGC was agreed, for 2004, to consider 'a more specific determination of responsibilities' – i.e. division of labour – between the EU and the member states; the exact status of the charter of fundamental rights; simplifying the treaty – 'without changing its meaning'; and the role of *national* parliaments. Germany, the Bundesrat specifically, drove this, having resolved that it would refuse to ratify unless there were a real attempt to resolve the 'subsidiarity' issues that were its core concerns.

Nice was described by Dinan as 'by any measure ... a shoddy piece of work' and the Irish were later (June 2001) narrowly to vote 'no' to it – until, as is the way with the EU when democracy produces unwelcome outcomes, persuaded to 'think again' (Edwards and Wiessala (eds) 2002: 2, 32).

This had been a period of great uncertainty, but one in which some shifts of actual or potential significance had taken place. These shifts were often despite, rather than because of, the Commission, which hardly distinguished itself. But there was now no doubt about the salience of the 'external agenda', which now often forced itself upon the attention of EU leaders. Its trade aspects had been clear in the Uruguay Round/WTO negotiations; but the ACP dimension too was important – in the 'mid-term' Lomé IV review of 1995; and then in what became the Cotonou Convention of 2000. From now on, 'WTO compatibility' was to be the key issue here. But beyond trade, the security agenda was transformed – in the Balkans, much more by failures than by success: but in the case of the CEEs with some promise of, for them, eventual success in the dual 'return to Europe'.

Yet thick fog continued to envelop Brussels (as it so often did the airport), in the non-resolution of NATO–EU issues. For long indeed, it seemed that the two bodies – literally 'just down the road' from each other, 'so near and yet so far' – oscillated between not communicating at all, and bursts of 'megaphone diplomacy'. On both sides of the Atlantic, new leadership was in the offing: a new US president, a new EU Commission president. It remained to be seen how relations would now develop.

## Further reading

A. Blair, *Saving the Pound?* Harlow: Pearson Educational, 2002.

B. Connolly, *The Rotten Heart of Europe*. London: Faber & Faber, 1995.

C. Crouch (ed.), *After the Euro*. Oxford: Oxford University Press, 2000.

K. Dyson, *The Politics of the Euro-Zone*. Oxford: Oxford University Press, 2000.

K. Dyson and K. Featherstone, *The Road to Maastricht. Negotiating Economic and Monetary Union*. Oxford: Oxford University Press, 1999.

D. Galloway, *The Treaty of Nice and Beyond*. Sheffield: Sheffield Academic Press, 2001.

D. Gros and N. Thygesen, *European Monetary Integration: From the European Monetary System towards Monetary Union*. London: Longman, 1998 (2nd edn).

M. Maresceau (ed.), *Enlarging the European Union. Relations between the EU and Central and Eastern Europe*. London: Longman, 1997.

P. Stirk and D. Weigall (eds), *The Origins and Development of European Integration*. London: Pinter, 1999. (Chapters 10 and 11.)

H. Wallace and W. Wallace (eds), *Policy-Making in the European Union*. Oxford: Oxford University Press, 2005 (5th edn). (Chapters 6 and 16.)

J. Zielonka, *Explaining Euro-Paralysis*. Basingstoke: Macmillan, 1998.

# 11  The new millennium
## 2000–2005

This was a period which showed, with a vengeance, the interconnections between our four 'battles'. Four themes and issues of great importance were now to the fore. The first two could be put, with some exaggeration, in Roman Imperial terms: 'a currency and an army', even if not, officially, a European army. The economic fate of the EU would not, to be sure, depend mainly on the performance of the euro: but that would be significant. And if the EU were to cut more of a figure on the larger stage, it would need at least *some* capability to project 'hard power'. But crucial were the third and fourth issues, inextricably linked it seemed: that of (again) who was to come on board and under what terms and conditions (enlargement), and the never answered question: 'What kind of animal is it?' – in 'constitutional' terms: or is it to be in perpetual undefined flux?

The period of the Prodi Commission witnessed a number of other important developments. Monetary union moved from the virtual to the highly visible, as from the start of 2002 notes and coins circulated – and in 12 member states as Greece, amazingly, joined. This did nothing, however, to help the EMU 'governance' issues or those concerning rule breaking – which Prodi himself was memorably to describe as stupid; neither was the eurozone's reputation in matters of employment, growth and competitiveness enhanced, although the 'Lisbon Agenda' tried to address precisely these. Another initiative to 'loosen up' the market, the 'Bolkestein' (services) Directive, got bogged down, then watered down. Economic–ideological heat continued to be generated within the Commission's ranks, though it was widely judged (*pace* Gillingham) that economic 'liberalisers', at least relative to the European context, had the weight and usually the upper hand.

The year 2000 began badly. Chapter 10 referred to 'democracy producing unwelcome outcomes'. It did so in January, in Austria, when Wolfgang Schüssel's Christian Democrats (ÖVP) opened coalition negotiations with Jörg Haider's far right Freedom Party (FPÖ). An attempt was made, led by France and Belgium, to use certain Amsterdam Treaty provisions to 'bite' Austria: although one might ask just who was actually bitten. The Amsterdam revision of Article 6 TEU, first paragraph, states that: 'The Union is founded on the principles of liberty, democracy, respect for fundamental rights and human freedoms, and the rule of law, principles which are common to the member states' – clearly intended as a 'score card' for the pre-accession CEEs. It does not spell out how *member states* are to be deemed non-compliant or sanctioned. However, on 31 January, the other fourteen, led by Belgium and France, issued a joint declaration threatening action against Austria if the FPÖ were included in the coalition. It amounted, argued Gillingham, to the 'de facto expulsion of a member state because of its voting preferences' (Gillingham 2003: 324–5). The threats (for which there was no clear legal basis if, as was clearly the case, they were acting qua EU, rather than as 14 concerted sets of 'bilateral' actions) did not work: the government was formed on 4 February anyway and the 14's bluff was called. Not many weeks later, most states had quietly abandoned their sanctions, finding them impracticable. But they did not do so publicly!

Eventually, ways were found to 'defuse', then end, the crisis: Austrian Commissioner Franz Fischler proved to be an important conduit and a 'wise men's' report struggled to conclude, face savingly, both that sanctions had 'improved' Austrian awareness of the corollaries of Article 6 and that ending sanctions was thus justified. Most observers were united in judging the 14's initial reaction precipitate, inept or worse. France and Belgium's motives included concern about their domestic far right: others, notably Denmark, wondered out loud whether a large state would have received the same treatment. It had all been most unedifying. It was the biggest negative during the Portuguese presidency. It also showed how difficult it would be to try to use sanctions to guarantee the ongoing 'good behaviour' of a state once admitted to membership. (See Dinan in Edwards and Wiessala (eds) 2001: 36–41; Gillingham 2003: 324–5.)

*External* events too, beginning with the fallout from 9/11, seemed to conspire to test to destruction the strength of the EU's 'actorhood', especially over the whole of the 'broader Middle East' and Bush's 'axis of evil'. The fifth enlargement finally occurred, but not smoothly and with growing signs of popular disillusion in several states. The EU also had to deal with a new and uncertain 'near abroad', as Putin's disgruntled Russia flexed its energy muscles; Ukraine lurched from seeming crisis to 'orange (non-)revolution' to awkward compromise; and much of central Asia became a seething cauldron. If there had been a 'WTO honeymoon', it appeared now to be over, as that body's dispute resolution mechanisms were stretched to the limit and a Doha Round seemed at least as difficult and protracted as Uruguay had been. By no means least, a chorus of concern with sustainability, environmental impact, climate change and biodiversity was becoming a cry of alarm in Europe much at odds with most noises from White House and Capitol Hill.

Yet grand schemes – especially 'institutional' ones – did not go away: most notably the one whose very name was redolent of the hard to classify nature of the European project, the 'Constitutional Treaty'. All in all, in the 'new millennium', the EU seemed marked by the old Chinese curse: 'May you (be condemned to) live in interesting times'.

## The 'Lisbon Agenda'

We have earlier discussed the role of the Portuguese presidency in the fields of defence and security and preparation for the 'Nice' IGC (Feira, June 2000). It was significant on another front too. In grandiose language, the HOSG at their earlier special European Council meeting in Lisbon on 23–24 March 2000 announced the strategic aim of making the EU by 2010 'the world's most competitive and dynamic knowledge-based economy'. The Council's title was 'Employment, Economic Reform and Social Cohesion – Towards a Europe of Innovation and Knowledge'.

It focused a good deal on new technologies, the information society, e-commerce and the 'knowledge economy'. It was notable for introducing the so-called 'open method of coordination' (OMC) in these areas (essentially, non-binding 'guidelines', avoiding the need for EU legislation). As usual, the Commission provided much of the detailed paperwork, including such documents as COM (2000) 130 – *eEurope: an Information Society for All*; COM (2000) 567: *Innovation in a Knowledge-based Economy*; and COM (2000) 48: *Strategies for Jobs in the Information Society*. By another fine irony, this 'dot.com summit' occurred just before that stock market bubble burst. With EU unemployment at about 15 million, it was particularly ambitious on employment targets, urging the creation of 20 million jobs in the decade to 2010.

Progress, however, was at snail's pace. Two years on in 2002, when the 15–16 March Barcelona European Council reviewed the Lisbon Strategy, the HOSG 'expressed disappointment that progress had been slow'; in July, the Commission reported that although the EU labour market had shown structural improvement, there remained considerable legal and administrative barriers to mobility (Kassim in Miles (ed.) 2003: 53–5).

## Enlargement: 'the biggest yet' – and its sequels

This was the great event of the period: the expansion of the EU from 15 to 25, finally agreed at the Copenhagen European Council of December 2002 and taking effect from 1 May 2004. It was also the essential catalyst for the further attempt at institutional reform and 'constitutionalisation' discussed later: the conventional wisdom had it that an EU of 25 would be unworkable without at least the kinds of reform that had been 'ducked' in the Amsterdam and Nice Treaties.

This 'achievement' had been very long delayed; the process had been full of disappointments for the candidates and of acrimony; and even at the last, in Copenhagen in December 2002, Poland in particular made the financial negotiation something of a cliffhanger. Finally, in purely financial terms, the EU earmarked 40.8 billion euros for enlargement.

The Helsinki Summit of December 1999 had agreed to open negotiations in mid-February 2000 with six further states: Bulgaria, Latvia, Lithuania, Malta, Romania and Slovakia; they were to follow in the wake of the 'Luxembourg six' (Cyprus, the Czech Republic, Estonia, Hungary, Poland and Slovenia) with whom negotiations had begun in March 1998: but, crucially, sufficient progress in the 31 'chapters' of the negotiations could permit them to 'catch up' with any or all of the first six – the so-called 'regatta approach' (Smith in Edwards and Wiessala (eds) 2001: 115–16). In practice, four did, so that in December 2002 the European Council deemed all but Bulgaria and Romania to be on track for accession by 2004 and these last two to be helped to achieve their aim of accession from 2007.

The enlargement saga also became entwined with other unfinished wars. In 2002 the British had pinned their hopes on Franco-German discord over financing and the CAP, believing that German concern to restrain enlargement costs would mean they would pressure the French on budgetary matters generally, inevitably including the CAP. This proved yet another miscalculation. Indeed, the affair appeared to revive the Franco-German relationship, and to re-emphasise its importance.

The two European Councils – Brussels in October, Copenhagen in December 2002 – were the venues for spat and spite. Schröder and Chirac announced their 'private' agreement on financing as they left their hotel, en route to the Council meeting on the morning of 23 October. In essence, it provided for no change in the CAP before the end of 2006 and a freeze on CAP spending in real terms subsequently (2007 to 2013). Payments to the accession states, meanwhile, would be phased in from 2004 to 2013. Controlling Community expenditure after 2006 (always a British concern) ought, said the pair, neatly turning the knife, to call the British rebate into question – thus deflecting any animus away from themselves (*ER* 2722: 26 October 2002: I.6–7). Blair had clearly been jumped: he prayed the agricultural *volet* of the Doha negotiations in aid to try to hack back the CAP. He was not alone: the Dutch, who said they were 'flabbergasted' took much the same line (Horsley 2002: 3 – http://news.bbc.co.uk/1/hi/world/europe/2362681.stm).

The final negotiation with the '10' was thus described as 'from Copenhagen to Copenhagen' (Friis in Miles (ed.) 2003: 49–50): from the setting of the original 'Copenhagen criteria' in that city in 1993 to the conclusion of negotiations there in December 2002. Still it did not settle the 'battle' over geographical extent. In October, Turkey was still left in the dark about dates, although the warmer tone of the Conclusions, welcoming the progress made, helped prepare the ground for Copenhagen in December. Turkey was now told that its application would be revisited at the end of 2004 and that only if, at that time, it were deemed able to fulfil the criteria, would negotiations begin 'without delay'. Bulgaria and Romania's negotiations were not concluded and early 2007 was confirmed as the most likely entry date.

This fifth enlargement coincided with further NATO enlargement – although the membership lists still did not. A great deal of American huffing and puffing had been heard throughout the whole 'dual enlargement' and continued. The enlargement left a series of problems in its wake. Apart from the 'poor vs. rich' issue, the whole large vs. small member state balance was profoundly changed; and the failure to resolve the Cyprus issue prior to and as a condition of entry was, as we shall see, to return to haunt the EU.

Predictably but crucially, it left a major set of issues about relations with the new and shifting 'near abroad'. Southeastern Europe – including the western Balkans – was one thing. But beyond – in the rest of eastern Europe, in the Middle East and the southern Mediterranean – developing relations acquired the title of 'European neighbourhood policy' (ENP), agreed in 2004.

## The democracy debate: the 'home front'

The reflection group that had prepared the Amsterdam IGC as far back as 1996 had urged member states to reform the EU in ways which promoted the principles of 'efficiency, democracy, transparency and solidarity'. The EP's resolution on Amsterdam had indicated its dissatisfaction with IGCs as a method, arguing for a more 'political' and less 'diplomatic' approach. Nice had, in the eyes of most, reinforced that evaluation: in July 2001 Jack Straw for the UK joined the chorus, while insisting that such a Convention should not try to 'tell the citizens of Europe what is good for them' (Norman 2003: 24–5).

But the 'democratic deficit' debate remained insistent, not just in the 'Brussels village' but among academic commentators and analysts (see, for example, Beetham and Lord 1998; Lord 1998; Chryssochoou 2000; Siedentop 2000).

'Stealth politics' was again at work here. Those who most readily resorted to the 'democratic deficit' phrase in Brussels and Strasbourg usually had in mind as 'redress', not just an increase in the powers of the EP over the Commission, but a *reduction* in the powers of the Council of Ministers and of national governments (Urwin 1996: 124). Frequently, thus, especially if conceived of in 'zero-sum' terms, it was an attempted power grab thinly disguised. It was also a disingenuous argument, ignoring (or seeking by another sly coup to transform) the very nature of the EU – moving from a body based on the principle of *conferral* – the Union's having (only) those powers specifically given to it by member states – to a radical 'implied powers' concept where there might be no limit to what could be claimed as 'implied' (see Stuart 2003: 45).

The Council co-legislator is also the *second* – along with the EP – source of 'democratic' legitimation. And the EU system has needed it there, to be exactly that. But the 'democratic deficiters' had an easy rhetorical target here: what other legislature, they asked, decided in secret? There was never an acknowledgement that this might be *advantageous* – in actually getting a decision instead of not, or in sealing a package deal. Even most 'eurofederalists' hardly advocate a 'withering away of the state': most of the few who do are sub-state 'nationalist' secessionists, for whom that argument has an inevitable appeal.

## A step too far? Three visions, hubris and retreat on the Constitutional Treaty

Even Tony Blair had declared at the end of Nice (December 2000) that one could not go on like that. There was wide support for the 'something must be done' school. Amsterdam and Nice were portrayed as '3000 mile oil changes for an automobile with rapidly accumulating mileage', whereas the novel 'Giscard' Convention represented 'a comprehensive service examination and engine overhaul', suggested Burghardt (Foreword in Serfaty 2003). The 'Convention on the Future of Europe', later Constitutional Convention, borrowed from the precedent of the body that promulgated the charter of fundamental rights.

As backdrop was the spectrum of 'thoughts out loud' in 2000 by Joschka Fischer,

Jacques Chirac and Tony Blair mentioned in Chapter 10. The first two contributions in particular led to the appending of Declaration No. 23 to the Nice Treaty Final Act – on the future of the EU. In many ways the positions taken by the three were predictable and they bore the hallmarks of very different national political cultures and traditions. But just as significant is that they illustrated another of the 'unutterable truths': tectonic plates were shifting: the real French preference in matters of *finalité politique* and hence of 'constitutional' arrangements was drifting away from the Germans and in some ways toward the British. That could *never* be confessed!

The French, unlike the British, were at least afforded the courtesy of some advance warning of Fischer's speech: but while he had the support of Belgium and the Commission, the French were 'less forthcoming although the Minister of the Interior [*sic*] did indicate that Fischer's project was "legitimate"' (*ER 2501*, 17 May 2000, I, 3). Significantly, the only real support in France came from the ageing Giscard and the UDF. British Foreign Secretary Robin Cook was undiplomatic enough to remind the French national assembly of this (quoting Chirac: 'We are building a united Europe of states, not a United States of Europe': speech to French Foreign Affairs Committee, 20 November 2000: quoted in Edwards and Wiessala (eds) 2001: 2). The silence following the Franco-German 'workshop' of 19 May was deafening. At the end of June and Chirac's 'pre-presidency' Bundestag speech, France's Europe Minister Pierre Moscovici proclaimed: 'We have no plans to reinvent Europe. The French Presidency will be a small-scale affair' (*ER 2513*: 1 July, I: 3).

It is instructive to compare the 'visions' on offer during 2000, from these three major players.

### *Fischer*

Joschka Fischer was first into the ring (on 12 May 2000, almost 50 years to the day, he reminded his audience, after Schuman's declaration) and with by far the 'widest' vision. He began (www.rewi.hu-berlin.de) by stressing the 'rejection of the European balance of power principle and the hegemonic ambitions of individual states', but acknowledged that 'it is this process of European integration that is now being called into question by many people'. He asked to be allowed to cast aside the mantle of foreign minister while thinking out loud, about the 'possible strategic prospects for European integration *far beyond the coming decade* and the IGC'. (*idem*, emphasis added). He described the recent informal foreign ministers' meeting (in the Azores) on 'finality' as 'a discussion that will surely have consequences'.

His message, predictably, was 'onward to completion'; no holding back! 'We must put into place the last brick … namely political integration' (*idem*). Playing to the gallery of 'European saints' by rather oddly describing World War II as 'also a Franco-German war', he averred that again developments 'will depend decisively on France and Germany'. Of the euro, he said:

> In Maastricht, one of the three essential sovereign rights of the modern nation-state – currency, internal security and external security – was, for the first time,

transferred to the sole responsibility of a European institution ... [I]t was a profoundly political act ... symbol[ising] *the power of the sovereign who guarantees it.*

(emphasis added)

Enlargement and deepening would make it possible '*to lastingly overcome the risks and temptations inherent in Germany's dimensions and central situation*' (emphasis added). For a self-proclaimed 'postmodern' and 'green', that sounded to some a little like a threat. 'And all the eurosceptics on this and the other side of the Channel would be well advised not to immediately produce the big headlines again' (*Und auch allen Euroskeptikern ... sei empfohlen, jetzt nicht gleich wieder die dicksten Schlagzeilen zu produzieren*). So did that. His list of the issues facing the EU was similar to that of others: but his 'very simple answer: the *transition from a union of states* to full parliamentarisation as a European federation ... based on a constituent treaty', was very different. Although this looked like a recipe *à l'allemande*, he stressed that member states in such an arrangement would have more powers than the *Länder* vis-à-vis the German federation. It should be based on a 'division of sovereignty'. There should be a bicameral EP, with one chamber 'for elected members *who are also members of their national parliaments*'. (Quite how these super-Ian Paisleys were to function effectively in both places was not made clear.) The second chamber would be either a (US) senate- or a Bundesrat-type body. There were, similarly, two options for a 'European executive or government': either 'formed from the national governments' (again, clearly consisting of people on steroids?) or, 'taking the existing Commission structure as a starting-point' [with] 'direct election of a president with far-reaching executive powers'. Fischer's speech was indeed 'hedged with ambiguities' (Norman 2003: 12).

In this 'lean federation', the 'core sovereignties and matters which absolutely have to be regulated at European level' would be 'the domain of the federation, whereas everything else would remain the responsibility of the nation-states'. The 'urgent' question was whether this could be done without a complete change of the very 'Monnet method' he had begun by praising. The 'steps' proposed were couched in terms of 'avant-garde' and 'core groups': even though these 'must never be exclusive', it was clear that those on board at the start would set the agenda; those initially not on board would again have to do all the adapting, or leave. This was a strange notion of 'consensual'; perhaps 'hegemonic ambition of an "avant-garde"' would not be an inappropriate description after all.

### *Chirac*

From there on, it was bound to be all downhill. Next was Chirac, also in Berlin, this time to the Bundestag, on 27 June, 4 days before the start of France's presidency (text: French Embassy London: *SAC/00/675*, 29 June 2000). He spoke of the 'responsibility of us founder members' (i.e. not the British!) 'continually to pose the question of what Europe means, the direction ... its future'. He noticeably failed to enthuse over enlargement: it was 'an achievement ... But ... [t]he enlargement won't go ahead regardless. We shall not allow the unravelling of the European enterprise.'

But 'I believe too that the *pace of European construction can't be decreed*' (emphasis added). 'Our nations are the source of our identities and our roots ... the nations will remain the first reference points ... Let's ... at last agree that the Union's institutions are, and will remain original and specific.' This was not the Fischer vision, although there were points of agreement. It was less federal, more 'nation state centred' and more concerned with the international *persona* of the Union (see Norman 2003: 13). He wanted 'to clarify, but *without* setting it in stone, the division of responsibilities' in the European system. Following the (Nice) IGC would begin 'the "great transition" period at the end of which *the EU's institutions and borders will have to have been stabilised*' (i.e. no Turkey etc.?) (*SAC/00/675*: 1–8, 29 June 2000).

Equally predictable was the emphasis on 'making the Franco-German *tandem* the engine of a powerful centre of European industry': yet he recognised that 'we are most lacking ... a better understanding ... of the business culture prevailing in each other's country'. And (France and Germany) 'must together fight the great battle for cultural diversity in the world': 'Anglo-Saxons' beware! (*idem*: 8). Chirac, in his frequent evocation of 'we alone' (France and Germany) caused some to think that, desperately hanging on to Germany's coattails and claiming co-primacy, he 'doth protest too much'.

The speech was important for another reason: it was here that Chirac set forth the possibility of 'an approach modelled on the convention which is drafting our charter of fundamental rights'.

### Blair

Tony Blair's audience at the Warsaw Stock Exchange on 6 October included Czech, Polish and Slovak prime ministers and the Hungarian foreign minister. After praising his hosts and lamenting 'gross misjudgements' in British policy 'over half a century' (and revealing that his summer reading had included Lacouture's biography of de Gaulle), he claimed yet again in ways that many on the continent found annoying: 'Britain can be the bridge between the EU and the US'.

His theme was 'Europe, yes, but what sort of Europe?': his approach, to ask first what one wanted the EU to *do*, then to construct the institutional arrangements to do that. On the latter, he rejected both a 'NAFTA-type' straw man and the 'classic federalist model'. He referred to a '*so-called* democratic deficit': 'The truth is the primary sources of democratic accountability in Europe are the directly elected and representative institutions of the nations of Europe, national parliaments and governments.' Europe had not yet developed 'its own strong demos or polity'; the EU would *remain* a unique combination of the intergovernmental and the supranational; 'a superpower, but not a superstate'. The 'steering' role of the European Council was strongly affirmed; the debate on a constitution 'must not necessarily end up with a single, legally binding document called a constitution for an entity as dynamic as the EU'. Rather, a *political* statement of principles, 'a kind of charter of competences' was to be preferred. Likewise with 'pioneers' (here differing from Chirac): 'greater flexibility ... must not lead to a hard core'; 'enhanced cooperation must not be used to undermine the single market or other common policies' (www.number-10.gov.uk; also www.europaworld.org/speeches/tonyblairpoland61000). His coded reply to the 'avant-garde' concept was: 'We are building a Europe of equal partners.' 'Blair's government prided itself on "joined-up thinking". His remarks in Warsaw amounted to an incipient, but not yet fully joined up, version of the UK's stance in the Convention' (Norman 2003: 15).

## The Convention

Nice had called for a 'debate on the future of Europe': a call taken up at the Laeken European Council a year later (December 2001) which led to the establishment of the Convention in February 2002. In July 2003 the convention was to adopt its 'draft treaty establishing a constitution'. That October, the IGC began its discussions on treaty reform which, after hiccoughs and acrimony at the year's end, were resumed under the Irish presidency in March 2004 and the Constitutional Treaty itself was approved at the Brussels European Council in June. It proceeded to be ratified in many states before the French and Dutch 'nos' of May–June 2005. Despite that negative, it is worth devoting some time to the Convention and the resultant draft treaty. As with the SEA and the TEU, it tells us a lot about 'felt needs' and ambition. It also tells us much about lack of public support.

The idea of again invoking the 'Convention' method, this time for treaty reform, had been floated by several people in 2000, including Chirac and Finnish PM Paavo Lipponen. They were then supported by the EP in May 2001, then by the Benelux states and finally the Swedish presidency (EP: *Resolution on the Treaty of Nice and the Future of the EU*: 31 May; Benelux, *Memorandum on the Future of Europe*, June 22; European Council Presidency Conclusions, Göteborg, June 2001; Dinan in Serfaty (ed.) 2003: 29). The ensuing 'eurofederalist' Belgian presidency pressed the accelerator all the way to Laeken in December.

The Convention was a most unusual body with a very unclear remit: was it there to set out 'options'; to draft something specific; to muse; or what? It would do its work and *then* would come the IGC, which might, in principle, ignore it. It was an 'independent' body and one about which views diverged quite sharply. While for Dinan, an observer, the 'majority ... had a pragmatic approach to European integration' (Dinan in Miles (ed.) 2003: 29), Stuart, a participant, thought it heavily stacked in favour of euro-maximalists: 'a self-selected group of the European political elite, many of whom have their eyes on a career at the European level, which is dependent on more and more integration and who see national governments and national parliaments as an obstacle' (Stuart 2003: 3). It was made up of 105 full members, plus 102 'alternates', most from the governments and parliaments of 28 states, including the pre-accession and pre-pre- accession ones, or from the Union institutions EP, Council and Commission. (The European Council had three representatives – Giscard and his two vice-presidents; leaders of the 28 states one each and their national parliaments two each; the Commission two, the EP 16.) Given this composition, it was open (in principle) to the ensuing IGC to ignore it completely. Possible, but unlikely.

The notably immodest chair of the Convention, Giscard, showed his true colours when urging his troops, 'This is what you have to do if you want the people to build statues of you on horseback back in the villages you all come from' (quoted in Stuart 2003: 57). It is, alas, not clear that he was intending to be witty. Giscard did not need to remind his colleagues that the (intergovernmental) European Council had been his 'baby' back in 1974: but he did so anyway, saying that he was a 'Council man' (Dinan in Miles (ed.) 2003: 32).

He had been chosen at the Laeken European Council over Wim de Kok, to the dismay of the presiding Verhofstadt and of many others who thought him too old or too remote. Chirac had successfully pushed him: though whether to keep him *out* of the French presidential election campaign of 2002 was unclear (Norman 2003: 27): Giscard's 'Council man' credentials were probably decisive in Chirac's eyes. But Verhofstadt did succeed in creating a 'triumvirate': Giscard was to be flanked by Amato and Dehaene, both also chosen 'because of prevailing political realities' (Dinan in Serfaty (ed.) 2003: 30).

Giscard was also to be ably assisted, however, by Sir John Kerr, ex-permanent secretary of the FCO, as Secretary-General. Not merely had Sir John previously also been UK permanent representative to the EU; but also uncommonly close to the action (at one point under the table, literally) of the final stages of the negotiations over 'Maastricht' at the Edinburgh Summit of December 1992; he was also renowned as Mr Fixit. For good measure, Kerr, too, was to be based in the Council secretariat.

The Laeken Council took other key organisational decisions which powerfully loaded membership of the convention in favour of smaller states: each state (including the 13 'in the wings') having, as we have seen, one member representing its head of state or government and two from its national parliament. But this over-representation helped Giscard to claim that votes in the Convention would distort reality and hence should be avoided: in turn, he found himself accused by 'small state' representatives such as Finland's Lipponen, of operating a cabal of the large against the smaller.

The consensus view was that the most effective grouping was the national government representatives; next those of the EP; then those from national parliaments; and, in 'unloved' fourth place – 'apprehensive and insecure' (Dinan in Miles (ed.) 2004: 30) – those of the Commission. This is not altogether surprising. National governments, after all, had the advantages of machinery and resources; but also the European Council, 'their' body, had originally (1974) been Giscard's baby; and further, he reminded the 'conventionnels' that their handiwork would in any case have to be agreed (or not) by the governments in the IGC. The EP had all the advantages of 'home team and home turf': they knew each other well and were on the spot, their institution 'in the ascendancy, used to faring well in successive rounds of treaty reform' (Dinan in Miles (ed.) 2004: 30). Further, they had a strong shared interest in *not* conceding ground to national parliaments. By all accounts, the representatives and allies of the EPP were particularly effective, their now somewhat disparate ranks (including, at member state level, mild 'sceptics' such as Aznar and not so mild Berlusconi) marshalled by the redoubtable campaigner, German MEP Elmar Brok, with his full quiver of proposals ready at the start, to be pulled out as required.

The host of uncertainties surrounding the whole Convention-to-IGC-to-draft-Constitutional-Treaty process explains the title of Peter Norman's blow-by-blow account – *The Accidental Constitution*. But right at the start, Giscard won a key victory, when he urged the Convention to 'achieve a broad *consensus* on a *single proposal*' for a Constitutional Treaty (Norman 2003: 47, emphasis added). 'Consensus' meant not voting – hence compromises rather than the registration of 'victories' or 'defeats'; the 'single proposal' replaced Laeken's 'options' – probably to the dismay of maximalists and minimalists alike. The Convention met between February 2002 and July 2003, submitting a full draft 'treaty establishing a Constitution for Europe' (TCE or CT) on 18 July to the Italian presidency which, in October, would initiate the IGC. Thus, born in a 'euro notes-and-coins euphoria', its voyage continued through the stormy waters of the Iraq war.

The Convention's boasted 'openness' was a rather forlorn attempt at PR: certainly, its plenaries were open and screeds of paper appeared on its websites (but was little read outside the self-selected groupies and acolytes); yet its key 13-member praesidium met behind closed doors (Norman 2003: 4). For the most part, the Convention carried blithely on its way, refusing to recognise the sceptical and neuralgic clamour outside. 'Not once in the sixteen months I spent on the Convention did representatives question whether deeper integration is what the people of Europe really want, whether it serves their best interests or ... provides a sustainable structure for an expanding Union. The debates focussed solely on where we could do more at EU level', wrote Gisela Stuart, German-born Labour MP for Birmingham Edgbaston and an increasingly disenchanted member of the praesidium (Stuart 2003: 3). Peter Norman, a close observer, put a similar view more circumspectly: the praesidium had 'an inherently integrationist bias'; eurosceptics were underrepresented, the EP overrepresented (Norman 2003: 33, 38).

By way of contrast, consider the British *government* representation. Once again, they found themselves fighting a rearguard action on behalf of certain others who lacked the nerve. And it was by and large well done. This time, learning from past defeats by default, the British government made sure it had some coherent paperwork to mark out the turf early on. The 'Hain' paper (CONV 345/1/02) was mainly the work of Prof Alan Dashwood of Cambridge and, significantly a former member of the *Council* legal services – another 'Council man'. It began with a fine aspirational flourish, but was quite clear in its driving principles: a union of 'sovereign states' not a European superstate. Its introduction claimed that it provided a short, clear and inspiring answer to the questions: 'what is the EU for, and – constitutionally speaking – what sort of animal is it?' (CONV 345/1/02 REV 1: 7). Its proclamation listed the EU's 'defining characteristics':

  – The Member States have chosen, in some measure, to exercise their sovereignties in common, through the institutions of the Union.

- In so combining their sovereignties, for defined purposes and within defined limits, the Member States retain their national identities.
- The Union has only those powers which have been *conferred on it by the Member States*. All powers which ... they have not conferred ... remain theirs exclusively.
- Decisions are to be taken as openly as possible and as closely as possible to the citizen. The powers conferred ... are to be exercised in ways that encroach as little as possible on the powers of the Member States.

(ibid.: 8–9)

Was that clear? Yes, indeed, and it was not to the liking of the maximalists: and near the start of proceedings it 'sank without trace' (Norman 2003: 67). But, by the very end of things, it was quite close in important respects – most notably the clear assertion of 'conferral' right at the start of the draft TCE (Art. I–1) to what was to be finally agreed at the level of the European Council in June 2004. That left two things to regret. First, there could be no cheering: no triumphalism that this British view had done so well: for that would guarantee more opposition in predictable quarters. Second, the final document, the Constitutional Treaty, perhaps the best the British could hope for, did not carry: and it remained to be seen whether, in the medium term in which the issue would resurface, an outcome as favourable to non-Napoleonic pragmatism *would* then be able to carry the day.

The very name was a dog's breakfast, as an article in *Le Monde* at the time pointed out: mixing the 'internal-to-a-polity' concept of 'constitution' with the international law instrument of 'treaty'. 'Kind' people might see in this an honest recognition of the Union's ambiguity of status. But the authors of the name probably came to regret it: a more modest title might have evoked less hostility in May–June 2005. Despite Giscard's references to Philadelphia, it bore little resemblance; still less did it have one of the virtues that Napoleon was alleged to prefer in constitutions: brevity.

## Process

There were to be three phases to the Convention's work: first a 'listening' phase; then a 'study' phase; finally the phase of drafting recommendations. Clearly, the 'listening' phase was dominated by 'maximalists', several in more preaching than 'listening' mode; reputations were reinforced (Brok; Duff) or made – Peter Hain was anxious to get the accession states to listen to *him*: allies were going to be needed. Duff worried about an over-mighty praesidium: it proved the wrong target, as Giscard concentrated on reinforcing the power of the secretariat.

The gimmick of a 'youth convention' backfired in acrimony, its members seen as mostly 'the future bureaucrats of the EU institutions' (Voggenhuber, quoted in Norman 2003: 51) – three-quarters producing a strongly 'federal' draft steamrollered over a dissenting eurosceptic minority. But the 'listening phase' did generate a significant sense of occasion: something was stirring and required attention.

In wishing to tame the ambitions of the Commission, the governments of France and Spain shared much in common with the British. These concerns were at the heart of Giscard's negotiations with heads of government over the summer.

The 'study' phase was largely carried out via working groups, eventually 11 in number. 'Largely', not entirely: for there was a 'bypass' and its name was John Kerr: and a secret weapon: the month of August again. A paper from a member of the secretariat, Hervé Bribosia, proposed ways of simplifying and merging the existing treaties; and it made magically rapid way in those becalmed summer days. It bounced in several revisions around the small circle of the triumvirate, Kerr and its author, and became by September the outline of a basic treaty (Norman 2003: 63–5). It was then meant for the praesidium but it appears that when an official hit the wrong email button, it went by mistake (?) to the whole convention (CONV 250/02: Norman 2003: 64).

That autumn, the Nice Treaty stalked like Banquo's ghost: unloved, yet it could not be ignored or abolished: indeed, its 'necessity' had to be proclaimed, as the Irish electorate, having rejected it just days before Göteborg, was cajoled into supporting it in a 'second time round' referendum in October.

## Draft CT outcome

At the turn of 2002–3, matters came to a head and negotiations became serious and fraught. Two aspects were important: one, the crystallising of a 'big' versus 'small' states divide; the other, the *bagarre* over the invasion of Iraq.

Giscard was to lose his 'congress of the peoples of Europe'. The French and German governments used the 40th anniversary of the Élysée Treaty (January 2003) to set forth an influential joint paper on the institutional issues. It proposed a 'dual presidency' formula, where both Commission and European Council presidents would be elected (Pedersen in Miles (ed.) 2003: 20). It reflected a classic compromise: the French (notably Chirac) got a more permanent European Council presidency; the Germans a strengthened Commission, its president elected by the EP. The proposed Council presidency tenure of up to 5 years repeated the earlier 'ABC' proposal, after chief sponsors Aznar, Blair and Chirac. It represented one of the few innovative aspects of what many saw as a rather conservative set of proposals. The British reluctantly went along with day to day usage of the word 'constitution': but the Convention itself – probably wisely – formally retained the terminology 'Constitutional Treaty'. In the end, the 'C word' was probably one part of the project's undoing in the 2005 referenda.

More than a simple tidying-up process, the CT also proposed the effective abolition of the earlier 'pillar' structure: even the CFSP was to become more integrated with the rest of EU external action. It was proposed to retitle Solana's post as union minister for foreign affairs and its holder to be also a member of the Commission. But as Solana himself reiterated, and events – especially Iraq – painfully underlined, a 'common' FSP did not mean a 'single' one. At best, 'the aim was to identify common ambitions and ways of pursuing shared aims that gave "real added value"' (speech in Stockholm, 25 April 2002, quoted in Norman 2003: 109).

Significantly, however, defence was considered by a separate working group under Michel Barnier. Here, with 11 of the EU members also NATO members but four neutrals, and with national sensitivities at their height, modesty and 'flexibility' were mandated. Rather as with the SEA, extension of competence into new areas was prominent, although the content of many smacked of 'gesture politics'.

The EU as a whole was to have legal personality: but the ECJ would not have jurisdiction in all areas: not, notably, in law and order, internal security or most aspects of CFSP and the whole of ESDP (Phinnemore 2004: 4). However, despite the sterling efforts of Amato, the final compromise left the decision mechanisms as complex and obscure as ever: it remained 'difficult to work out how far the draft constitutional treaty extend[ed] QMV' (Norman 2003: 314–15).

In most of the areas where new or expanded activity was discussed, the UK's intergovernmentalist position was in marked contrast to the majority. But it was not alone: prominent examples included Germany's insistence on restricting labour market access and France's tenacious rearguard over the 'cultural exception' in trade negotiations.

As always in EU negotiations, things went right down to the wire. Self-congratulation marked the finalé: the bound volumes of the penultimate draft which the *conventionnels* had been given 'became autograph books, as like children at the end of their first summer camp, the Convention members began rushing around seeking signatures from each other' (Norman 2003: 316). From that point until non-ratification by France and the Netherlands (May–June 2005), there lay some 22 months: then 'different domestic politics' created those No votes 'for very different reasons' (Taggart in Sedelmeier and Young (eds) 2006: 21).

This time also saw the first fruits of the actual enlargement and considerable concerns about yet more enlargement. It also saw the inception, to try to give more continuity to the work of Council presidencies, of '3-year' presidency programmes, beginning with 2004–6.


## EMU limps on

The introduction of euro notes and coins took place on 1 January 2002, the month before the Convention began. It went smoothly and by early March 'four out of five citizens considered the changeover a success, and over two-thirds were happy with the euro' (Beber 2002: 77). This was far from saying that market operators or citizens were happy with the *policies* pursued by the ECB which, '[w]ith merely embryonic fiscal policy waged by Ecofin and its eurogroup' was 'Europe's aggregate demand manager of last resort' (Beber 2002: 77). The whole EMU construction was indeed, as often remarked, 'very lopsided ... with its federal monetary policy and decentralised fiscal policies'; and the appearance of the notes and coins coincided with increased strains within the eurozone (Norman 2003: 108, 122).

Frequent criticisms were heard about ECB chief Duisenberg's communications skills but, most notably in 2001, there was wide acknowledgement of the difficulties amid which the bank was operating. These included a food- and energy-led burst of inflation; the huge uncertainties following 9/11; predictable breaking of the fiscal rules and transatlantic demands for a European expansion to help offset US slowdown. 'If safe driving is boring, the ECB's relative lack of front-page coverage over the past year is strong evidence of its success', opined Beber (2002: 75): but caution was certainly the watchword, as the ECB sought simply to establish some kind of track record with the markets and to avoid reputations for adventurousness or unpredictability.

Doubtless the ECB did its best. The question remained, however, as to how the SGP rules would be implemented. Portugal, 'early warned' on fiscal deficits along with France and Germany, corrected its deficit as required. However, the Franco-German 'anchor', happy enough to castigate others for breach of rules, appeared prepared to affirm: *Les règles ne s'appliquent pas à nous!* (again). The year 2003 thus saw a battle between the Commission (discipline, with a view to sanctions) and the Ecofin council which, on 25 November 2003, decided instead to 'interrupt' the application of the SGP to Germany and France. Thus occurred the 'revision/emasculation' of the SGP (Buiter 2006: 688; Verdun in Sedelmeier and Young (eds) 2006: 199, 205–7).

No less important was the *extent* of the ECB's 'independent power'. Monetary policy was one thing, but: '[T]he Maastricht Treaty was unhappily ambivalent on whether finance ministers or the ECB was in charge of *exchange-rate* policy … Peer Steinbrück, German Finance Minister, last week said that ECB independence related only to monetary policy, and that politicians would take an interest in exchange-rate policy' (Münchau, *FT*, 5 February 2007: 17, emphasis added).

And the policies pursued by national governments continued to diverge significantly. Germany, notably, by pursuing a largely successful wage restraint policy, right through this period markedly improved its competitive position vis-à-vis other eurozone states (and yet more markedly vis-à-vis the UK and USA). This in turn pushed many other eurozone members into higher unemployment and lower growth, a 'beggar-thy-neighbour' situation ominously redolent, in some eyes, of the 1930s. Attacks on the ECB in a 'cross-of-gold' tone became commonplace, not least, and in another fine irony, in France, the lead advocate of EMU since the early days. In the run-up to that country's 2007 presidential election, the tone became strident and the sentiment widely shared. The links between lack of political union and the inadequate policy tools in the hands of the ECB were apparent: the structure was dangerously fragile: but would it fall?

## 9/11: a 'new world'?

In the immediate aftermath of the attacks on New York and Washington on 11 September 2001, *Le Monde* declared: 'We are all Americans now.' NATO Secretary-General Robertson invoked Article V of the Treaty: but was politely told 'Thank you but no, thank you.' The implications for the EU of what Heisbourg called the 'abrupt end' of the 'post-Cold War era itself' (Heisbourg 2001: 143) were to be wide ranging in several of its policy areas and would also severely test the solidarity of member states' relations with one another.

It began well enough. The litmus test in such matters, as usual, was France. 'On

11 September, all the French, all Europeans, felt a bit American', said President Chirac on 4 October. On 7 October, in a televised speech, he said France 'would wage with the United States this battle ... The Taliban regime's refusal to hand over bin Laden ... has led the United States and her allies to launch operations in Afghanistan. *The UN Security Council recognises this action's legitimacy*' (*SAC/01/212:* 11 October 2001, emphasis added). Equally clear was Prime Minister Jospin: alongside the 'solidarity with our American friends' he added '[France's] refusal to enter into a conflict with the Arab and Muslim worlds or wage a war against *anyone* – the only war will be against terrorism' (*SAC/01/214*: 11 October).

And the solidarity had definite limits. Following the Laeken European Council's declaration on the Middle East (December 2001), Foreign Minister Védrine said: 'It is regrettable that whenever the Security Council tries to take up the Middle East issue, the Americans use their veto since, at the Israelis' request, they don't want the Council to deal with it' (*SAC/01/298*: 16 December).

## Iraq: no longer 'all Americans now'

Afghanistan was one thing: Iraq quite another. As the crisis over Iraq came to the boil at the start of 2003, France's position was again hardly unclear. Chirac's New Year greetings speech to the diplomatic corps in Paris on 7 January 2003 was not Delphic. It began with a swipe at an unnamed Fukuyama: 'Some ... saw fit to prophesy the end of history' and moved immediately to Iraq. The 'disarming' (unspecified) of Iraq had to be done through the UN framework: 'It is the only legit-imate one. International action cannot depart from ... legality ... or it will be dis-credited ... Any decision to use force must be explicit and must be taken by the UN Security Council ... France ... intends to remain free to fully exercise her own judgement' (*SAC* 03/03: 10).

There followed the 'ambush' of Colin Powell by the French in New York on 20 January, de Villepin declaring that France would oppose any further Security Council resolution that authorised military action against Iraq (see Peterson in Miles (ed.) 2004: 15).

Iraq was to cause deep divisions both within the EU and in relations with the United States, leading famously to Donald Rumsfeld's 'deliberately unhelpful' characterisation of 'Old' versus 'New' Europe (Allen and Smith in Miles (ed.) 2004: 96). Crucially new was the position and role of Germany, where in the run-up to the September 2002 elections it seemed that both Schröder and, in different ways, his rival Stoiber were playing an anti-American tune. In consequence Germany was effectively 'closed out' by the USA in late 2002. Celebrations of the 40th anniversary of the Franco-German Élyseé Treaty in January 2003 were widely described as 'ostentatious': but it remained true that perceptions of American 'uni-lateralism' encouraged assertions of Franco-German 'solidarity'.

In a diplomatically frantic February, the 10th was one of the busy days. That day, the Germans signed the joint declaration with Russia and France urging that: '[T]here is still an alternative to war. The use of force could only be a last resort. Russia, Germany and France are determined to give every chance to the peaceful disarmament of Iraq' (see *SAC/03/47*: 3); on the same day the French at the UN pre-sented a 'non-paper' on strengthening the Iraq weapons inspection regime and, sep-arately, announced the establishment with Russia of a *bilateral* experts' group on non-proliferation of WMD and delivery systems. At his press conference with Putin the same day, Chirac said: 'I shall tell you what I think deep down: nothing, today, justifies a war … I believe that that region really doesn't need another war. I'm convinced that this is the opinion of a very, very great majority of the people in the world' (*SAC/03/49*: 10). Certainly the mass demonstrations throughout much of the world the following weekend lent credence to that view.

The Greek presidency convened an extraordinary European Council for February 17, whose one and a half page short conclusion attempted to paper over the cracks. By contrast, two choreographed and also controversial letters in February under-lined the divisions, broadly supporting the US line: the 'letter of Eight' – five EU members, Denmark, Italy, Portugal, Spain and the UK, plus the Czech Republic, Hungary and Poland; and that of the 'Vilnius Ten' – the three 'Baltics'; Slovenia and Slovakia; two 'deferred' candidates, Bulgaria and Romania; and three 'not yet can-didates', Albania, Croatia and Macedonia. Chirac's anger was unalloyed: the five candidate countries had 'missed a good opportunity to remain silent'; as for Bulgaria and Romania, their 'position is already very delicate with respect to Europe. If they wanted to reduce their chances of joining Europe, they couldn't find a better way' (*SAC/03/56*: 12). 'Enlargement fatigue' was already apparent and was to grow. 'After early 2003, Iraq effectively ceased to be an EU issue': it affected US–EU rela-tions less than those in NATO and the UN, concluded Peterson (Miles (ed.) 2004: 15). It remained, however, very much a NATO issue, the atmosphere in that part of Brussels poisonous; the relations of the French Ambassador there, Benoit d'Aboville, with most of his fellows at an all-time low.

An atmosphere of vengeful recrimination pervaded transatlantic relations in the months following and reached into all sorts of areas including, predictably, Iraq reconstruction contracts, defence procurement, the transfer of responsibility in Bosnia and proposals for a European military planning 'cell'. As far as the EU was concerned, the issue was whether, yet again, something positive could be dragged out of the failure:

> As one EU Council official put it: 'every cloud has a silver lining. Our history is all about reacting to failure. Without the Balkan wars, we would never have had the CFSP. Without Kosovo, we would never have had ESDP'.
>
> (Peterson in Miles (ed.) 2004: 21)

In this regard, obvious developments in 2003 included the negotiations of the 'EU Three' – France, Germany and the UK, but *without* Solana – with Iran. It was a fine irony that 2003 also saw the publication of *two* new 'security strategies', one either side of the Atlantic – the US 'New National' one hotly followed, in an act of 'me-too-ism' by the first such EU document, agreed at the end of the year. But agreement within the EU remained limited and fragile: it would be sorely tested over the Constitutional Treaty.

## Cyprus and Turkey – again

At the Helsinki Summit of December 1999 a fateful decision had been taken: Cyprus should join even if (as fondly thought unlikely) there was no reunification agreement; and Turkey was recognised as a candidate.

But was the EU serious about having Turkey as a member eventually or not? Or were the Union's constant but constantly changing grounds for delay really in the hope of causing a totally frustrated and increasingly Islamist Turkey to be the one that slammed the door? Would both sides yell 'I told you so!'? Increasingly it appeared so – with incalculable consequences for the EU, the Middle East, NATO and transatlantic relations.

And the eye of the storm was by 2004 a member state: a member state where the government of only one part spoke for the whole, and whose president, Tassos Papadopoulos, threatened to use its veto against every aspect of Turkey's negotiations. Perhaps the wisdom of admitting *Cyprus* might have been questioned. It was, too late: 'Many EU diplomats *now accept* that it was a mistake to allow Cyprus to join at that stage – particularly because of the influence the Greek Cypriot government has thus gained over the negotiations with Turkey' (*FT*, 16 October 2006: 17, emphasis added). 'The fact that Cyprus joined ... as a divided island ... was already one foreign policy failure for the EU [which could directly contribute to] a second and major failure – a breakdown in EU – Turkey relations' (Hughes 2006: 2).

What a masterstroke of timetabling! Cyprus' accession was known to be taking effect, from 1 May 2004. The UN reunification plan was put to the electorates of the divided island in April. It was *accepted* by the Turkish Cypriots, overwhelmingly *rejected* by Greek Cypriots. The EU, which had banked on acceptance by *both* Turkish and Greek Cypriots was, fatally, committed to admitting Cyprus regardless of the result. At the same time, the EU also promised to end the isolation of the Turkish Cypriots. In December 2004 the EU agreed in principle to start accession talks with Turkey. In 2005, and despite the enlargement fatigue factor in the defeat of the 'constitution' referendum, first (in July) the Turks in an additional protocol to their EU customs union agreement agreed to open up their ports and airports to Greek Cypriot traffic from the Republic of Cyprus; then second (in October), the announced accession talks with Turkey actually began.

'Negotiating to join the EU club without recognising one of its 25 Member States [Cyprus] might look ... like a non-starter' (Hughes 2006: 3), yet the talks began. But the Turks refused to open ports and airports until the Cyprus Republic government ended the isolation of Turkish Cypriots: 'issue linkage' which the EU sought to deny. Turkey, the 'goodie' of 2004, had become the 'baddie' of 2005–6, as doubts were piled on doubts. 'Enlargement fatigue' had been apparent in the 2005 French and Dutch referenda. The slowing of political reform in Turkey fuelled the EU's Catch-22 concerns *both* about the role of the (secular) military *and* about the intentions and actions of the not-so-secular Erdogan government, itself facing presidential and parliamentary elections in 2007.These were to be compounded by the (failed) trial of a Turkish author; and by Turkey's insistence that the Armenian 'events' of 1915 were not genocide, while the French chamber of deputies was to vote (October 2006) that Armenian genocide denial should be a criminal offence. There was continuing US pressure for Turkish accession on strategic grounds; but division between 'antis' led by Austria, France and of course Cyprus and 'pros' led by the UK. All made a most unpromising brew (see Hughes 2006; *FT*, 16 October 2006: 17). Meanwhile, the Turkish Republic of North Cyprus (TRNC) remained 'a legal, diplomatic and economic black hole, technically inside the EU but for practical purposes outside it' (*FT*, 16 October 2006: 17).

## Further reading

C. Hill and M. Smith (eds), *International Relations and the European Union*. Oxford: Oxford University Press, 2005.

P. Norman, *The Accidental Constitution: The Story of the European Convention*. Brussels: EuroComment, 2003.

S. Serfaty (ed.), *The European Finality Debate and Its National Dimensions*. Washington, DC: CSIS, 2003.

G. Stuart, *The Making of Europe's Constitution*. London: Fabian Society, 2003.

H. Wallace and W. Wallace (eds), *Policy-Making in the European Union*. Oxford: Oxford University Press, 2005 (5th edn). (Chapters 14–18.)

# 12 New turbulence
## 2005–2008

The future, famously, is 'always open'. The perils of prediction are always great: in regard to the EU, with its frail legitimacy but relative durability, they often seem particularly so. In this chapter, we shall briefly examine some of the developments of the period 2005 to mid-2008, which during that time appeared of undoubted importance, but which, at the time of writing, are too close at hand to permit of anything like a well-reflected view.

At the turn of 2004–05, the institutions themselves underwent major change, consequent on the 'great enlargement'. On the face of it, the changes appeared perhaps more arithmetical and quantitative than qualitative. But everything was affected, not least the critical areas of translation and interpretation, with then 20 official languages; further, the jockeying for position in the Commission official hierarchy was intense. The new Commission, agreed in November 2004, now contained one per member state, following the enlargement from 15 to 25. This alone would guarantee major change of personnel – and a good deal of accompanying turbulence. Once again the choice of its president was not easy. Former Portuguese Prime Minister José Manuel Barroso was a compromise choice and, reputed an economic 'liberal', not a big favourite of either Chirac or Schröder. Verheugen and Wallström were among the few continuing faces on the Commission. Beyond all this lurked the question: how far would this unprecedented – in scope and diversity – enlargement change the ways in which the EU operated?

Once again, this period showed the continuing salience of our four 'battles'. On the 'institutional' front, the defeat of the CT in the French and Dutch referenda of 29 May and 1 June 2005 was never likely to be accepted without a fight – or a subterfuge. Once again, the French and especially German 'motor' got to work. Nicolas Sarkozy had expressed his preference for a 'mini-treaty' in February 2006, while minister of the interior, long before his May 2007 presidential election victory. The proposal for a 'reform' or 'amending' treaty moved forward with a swiftness that surprised some. It should not have been such a surprise, given that so much consisted of an 'unpacking and repackaging' of the material of the original CT. Its essentials were agreed at a special Council, during the German presidency, in October 2007 and signed up to in December. Yet once again (June 2008) it was to fall foul of Ireland's voters, the only ones constitutionally required to pronounce on it.

In regard to 'internal policies', the agenda was no less full. But there was little evidence that, as regards such central matters in a 'common market' as 'economic cultures' – economic philosophies even – and the role of the state in the economy, there was any growing together. In Germany, 'Anglo-Saxon attitudes' were characterised as those of 'locusts'. Sarkozy, in a 'victory' that seemed at the time more pyrrhic than real, managed to snip the reference to 'undistorted' competition out of the main aims of the draft (Lisbon) 'Reform' Treaty (it was promptly reinstated as a protocol). In the UK, by contrast, commentary (about developments elsewhere in particular) referred to a 'slippery slope on the way to economic nationalism'. This was thus a period of major battles over the priorities within the 'other Lisbon' – the Lisbon Strategy. This, post the mid-term November 2004 Kok Review, had tilted toward the 'competitiveness', away from the 'social', aspects of the agenda. This was epitomised by the battles over the 'Bolkestein' services Directive – one of the 'most important internal legislative developments of … arguably the decade' (Howarth in Sedelmeier and Young (eds) 2007: 89).

In regard to the all-important EMU, it was thought a safe bet that its next 10 years would be a good deal more difficult than to date. We shall return to these themes later: but here it is important to recall a point made in the introduction: that 'a good deal depends on the state of the economic barometer'. By summer 2007 the storm signals were hoisted: by mid-2008 it was 'only' the length and strength of the storm which seemed in doubt – and how much consequent wreckage there would be. Inflation was double the ECB's target – and more for some EU non-eurozone states. The ECB raised interest rates to a 7-year high but, with other central banks, promptly went into reverse in the 2008 'credit crunch', faced with acute policy dilemmas as threats of inflation were swiftly proclaimed to have been replaced by threats of deflation and threats to growth.

Movement on the third front –the EU's external persona – was hesitant and variable. There was much huffing and puffing about the nature of representation in international, not least international economic, institutions. Should the eurozone have unitary presence in global councils? How far and how fast would development of the EU's 'external action service' proceed? Would a Doha Round Agreement prove achievable on grounds that most EU member states found satisfactory? Could the EU retain any solidarity of approach over the 'successor to the Kyoto Protocol', as Poland, Italy and others claimed, at the end of 2008, that even modest targets could not be met? Could the 'NATO–ESDP' (perennial) circle finally be squared, as France strongly indicated an intention to return to 'full' NATO participation in 2009, but did not firmly promise it at the time of its – France's – new defence White Paper (the *Livre Blanc*) of June 2008; and as Angela Merkel resisted pressure from the outgoing Bush administration to speed up moves toward NATO membership for Ukraine and Georgia?

Uncertainties remained also over the fourth dimension – geographical scope: particularly over speed, conditionality and sequencing. There were many who thought the admission of Bulgaria and Romania from the start of 2007 overhasty and recriminatory noises were heard about corruption in those two countries. The main bones of contention, of course, remained the ever more balkanised

Balkans – building on the stabilisation and accession agreements (SAAs) decided on at the Thessaloniki European Council of June 2003 – and Turkey. By the end of 2008, the EU had clarified the way it saw its own relations developing with six former Soviet states – Armenia, Azerbaijan, Belarus, Georgia, Moldova and Ukraine: these, under the 'eastern partnership' agreements, would be eligible for a wide-ranging free trade deal, but with no offer of membership in sight.

We shall look at developments in each of these areas, before attempting to sum up where the EU has got to and what *may* be its prospects in the near future.

The Council presidency in the first half of 2005 lay with Luxembourg and its prime minister, Jean-Claude Juncker, highly experienced in the presidency role: and much was expected of it. In the event the expectations were to be disappointed. Significant on the calendar of 'inevitable business' were the mid-term review of the 'Lisbon Agenda'; and attempting to reach agreement on the 'financial perspective' (budget framework) for 2007–13. But other matters obtruded, two in particular: the 'revision' of the terms of the SGP; and the shape and fate of the important ('Bolkestein') services Directive. All caused trouble and there were links between some of them.

Concerning the SGP, the essence of the proposals was to loosen the definition of the circumstances triggering the 'excessive deficit' procedure; and to beef up the pact's 'preventative' aspects – those requiring eurozone member states to abide by *medium term* budgetary objectives (*EI [Europe Information]* 2947: 23 March 2005: II.2–3). The ECB made plain that it was not best pleased with the loosening, insisting that it was 'imperative' that Commission and member states apply the revised pact 'in a rigorous and coherent fashion', or else ... not quite specified! (*EI* 2947: II.3). Some called the result a 'bendy pact'. As finally agreed in June, the new rules 'tried to encourage the Lisbon Agenda reforms, whilst still aiming at fiscal discipline' (Verdun in Sedelmeier and Young (eds) 2006: 207) and giving states more time to carry out fiscal corrections.

The EU was not, however, successful in the first half of 2005 in dealing with its *own* 'medium term budget' issues! In March and June, Tony Blair dug in his heels over the UK rebate: as we shall see, only at year's end was this resolved.

'Liberalisers' set great store by the freeing up of the services sector: unsurprisingly, since it now accounted for more than 70% of EU GDP (although, of course, only a small proportion of intra-EU trade). The issue was, however, *how* to do it. Barroso, under fierce attack from the PES in the EP (on grounds of the threat it posed to the 'European social model' – nowhere defined – and of 'social dumping') and by much of the French political establishment (ditto, but also urged to action against the 'Bolkenstein/Frankenstein monster' by the state of pre-referendum opinion) was obliged to backtrack in February and March (*EI* 2947: 23 March 2005: IV.8; 2948, 25 March, IV. 6–8). Further support for such critical views came, in varying measure, from Schröder, from Swedish, Belgian and Luxembourg sources – and even from John Monks of the UK TUC. It was clear that 'Bolkestein' had elbowed out consideration of the Lisbon Agenda. So overall there was little progress to report. This saga wore a firm 'to be continued' label round its neck, as the EP was again to prove in early 2006.

It was to be little better in June, with another UK rearguard over financing, despite a charm offensive in the EP from freshly re-elected Blair. A frustrated Juncker caricatured the situation as 'two rival philosophies' (liberal free tradeist versus 'solidarist' political union) of what Europe was about and the EU as 'in deep crisis' (*ER* 22 June 2005: 1).

But this last remark referred in no small measure to the 'shock' of the 'double no' in France and the Netherlands: in the French case quite widely anticipated. Several factors underlay the French and Dutch 'nos': some similar in the two countries, others reflecting quite different national situations and perceptions. Similar were the concerns of the generally poorer and of the less skilled: about 'threats' represented by globalisation; competition from workers in and from the new member states; a supposedly triumphant 'Anglo-Saxon model'. In the Netherlands, concerns also included the country's net budget contribution (now the highest per head); and more especially the perception that, when it came to the disciplines and sacrifices supposedly mandated by the SGP 'rules', some (Germany, France) were more equal than others, while the Netherlands economy had suffered from the poor performance of its big neighbours (see Subacchi 2005: 7–8; Wallace 2005: 4–6; Taggart in Sedelmeier and Young (eds) 2006: 7–25).

At the close of his presidency, Juncker, tellingly, said this: 'Europe wishes [*sic*] to listen to its citizens' (*BQE* 8971: 18 June 2005: 5). Clearly 'Europe' found some part of 'no' difficult to comprehend. His 'simplistic polarisation' of 'two rival philosophies' was unwelcome – and inaccurate; his 'tone … unhelpful', thought *EI*'s editorialist (*EI*: 2972: 22 June 2005: 1).

Against this background, few had high hopes of the following UK presidency, the first days of which were scarred by the '7/7' London bombings. The CT was, however, off the agenda – UK ratification suspended; the promised referendum later 'deferred'. The UK's announced priorities were three and unsurprising: economic reform; 'security and stability'; and the EU's international role. Under the first rubric, financial services (the 'action plan') and regulation of chemicals (the 'REACH' Directive) made progress, along with, it seemed, the services Directive. Under the second heading, the main 'progress' was agreement on the retention of email, internet and telecoms data in all EU states for 2 years. The third saw not just several EU-led police and monitoring missions, but a renewed push on the 'post-Kyoto climate change' dossier at the December Montreal Conference.

There were to be two surprise successes. Each, in one way or another, involved incoming German Chancellor Angela Merkel. The December 2004 summit had finally agreed a date – 3 October 2005 – for the opening of negotiations with Turkey. Yet much of 2005 was spent in contorted manoeuvres to set further conditions, open-ended timetables, the possibility of an arrangement short of full membership and so on. In contrast to Schröder, Merkel did not favour Turkey's membership. But advantage was taken of her not yet being in post at the beginning of October (*les absents ont toujours tort*) to go ahead at the same time as beginning negotiations with the Balkan 'lead state', Croatia.

The second was her key 'gift' of funds intended for Germany, to Poland, which finally unblocked the logjam over financing in December. This budget package included a cut in the UK's rebate accompanied by a modest increase in the overall spend; and agreement to hold, during 2008–09, a review of all revenue sources and expenditure priorities. It was predictably another marathon, clinched 'around two o'clock in the morning on December 17' (*EI* 3016, 21 December 2005: I.1). Once done, agreement quickly followed to move FYROM/Macedonia forward to candidate status.

There had certainly been no lack of drama in 2005. What would 2006 – an Austrian followed by a Finnish presidency, both thought sympathetic to a generally liberalising economic agenda – bring? At first it looked like more drama, as the EP, abetted by the Commission, tried to unpick the 'financial perspective' deal and again to increase the size of the budget. In the end, the 'adjustments' agreed were marginal: the budget was to be within a 1.048% GNI ceiling – compared to December's 1.045%. To many observers, on this issue in particular the EP seemed like a terrier with a bone, hurtling around with much sound and fury, not letting go, but achieving very little.

Not so on another hardy perennial and litmus test of the 'liberal agenda', the services Directive, where the EP's 'role, according to the EU Treaties, is to *amend* legislation yet here, virtually unprecedented … it has *de facto* usurped the Commission's role as the *creator* of EU law' (*EI* 3031: 18 Feb 2006, emphases added). A coalition of PES and EPP MEPs had on February 16, 'removed the heart of the European Commission's proposal – the "country of origin" principle' and had also voted to exclude a whole swathe of sectors 'from gambling to healthcare' from the Directive (*EI* 3031: 18 Feb 2006: III.10). The vote was 394:215:33 to replace what many saw as the unworkable country of origin by the weaker 'freedom to provide services' principle; significantly, a high proportion of the 'losers' coming from the CEE new member states. A month later, the spring European Council could only greet the vote 'with satisfaction', hoping that legislation could be passed rapidly; and Barroso was obliged to agree that the EP 'compromise' was the 'only realistic basis for a positive outcome' (*BQE* 9159: 25 March 2006: 8).

There was relief at finding something to agree on. For, for some weeks, accusations had also been flying around, concerning each other's drift toward economic nationalism and protectionism. Italian Finance Minister Tremonti had wanted this discussed at the summit, citing the proposed French GdF/Suez merger as example. In the end, the leaders shied away from a fight: Barroso reported 'no *confrontational* debate'; revealingly he spoke of '*fair* competition and competitive energy markets' (*BQE* 9159: 9, emphases added). Energy, now firmly on the agenda, was to remain so.

More generally however, in terms of 'output', the EU in 2006 managed to do a good deal of mainly unspectacular business: 'despite enlargement and in the absence of treaty reform': non-ratification of the CT had 'not precipitated a crisis in EU decision-making' (Sedelmeier and Young (eds) 2007: 2). There was another side to this, however. The sheer number of member states meant that more than ever there would be domestically driven constraints: at almost any time, someone or other was facing an election. As more governments changed, more new faces appeared; there was less *political* continuity and hence more uncertainty.

At a press conference closing Austria's presidency on 15 June 2006, Chancellor Wolfgang Schüssel let the institutional/'constitutional' cat out of the bag, claiming that living with 'Nice' was not feasible in the longer term; that 'there is also agreement that the substance of the constitutional treaty is sound and should be retained' (*Europolitics* 3107: 19 June 2006: 12). The German presidency of the first half of 2007 was tasked with tabling a report on the CT identifying 'next steps'. As we shall see, it was to do more – playing its cards close to its chest meanwhile. Supporters of the CT placed great faith in the German presidency but in public were keen to deflate excessive expectations, even Juncker claiming to *Die Welt* on 15 June: 'The German government will not make significant progress on this question in 2007' (as quoted in *Europolitics* 3017: 19 June 2006: 12). Not all were so shy: Romano Prodi, back on centre stage now as Italian prime minister, urged a new and ambitious document to be agreed before the next EP elections of 2009, admitting that, though he favoured the term 'constitution', perhaps it ought to be dropped.

Meanwhile, Schüssel also lined up behind Barroso's strategy of 'Europe of results' to try to get away from constitutional navel gazing; producing an impressive looking but merely 'indicative' list of 'projects for Europe' covering the period 2006–10. It was a wish list that appeared to have something for (almost) everybody – though delaying 'implementation of the services Directive' to 2009 and ambiguously slating 'revised' Lisbon Strategy objectives for 2010. 'Bolkestein' slid under cover at the June European Council. The leaders did not want a war over it. Delicate wording papered over the cracks, but in essence 'liberals' gave way before the EP's major amendments of 16 February: notably, as we saw earlier, the abandonment of the 'country of origin' principle in favour of a less 'liberal' 'freedom to provide services' article.

There was much talk of 'all possible improvement of the working of the institutions within the existing treaty framework'. The emphasis was on transparency, improved consultation with – not increased *power for* – national parliaments and revision of 'comitology' to involve the EP more in the process.

The Finnish presidency was yet more strongly identified with championing the 'competitiveness' strand of Lisbon than the Austrians. In concrete terms, the signing of the REACH Regulation (Reg. EC 1907/2006) by Council and EP on 18 December was probably the main event. Some 10 years in the pipeline (!) it was a far more 'industry friendly' and less onerous beast by this stage than in earlier drafts.

Other results were generally judged 'unspectacular'. At the 'informal' October Council in Lahti, the announced intention of EU leaders to 'speak with a single voice on energy' must have amused their dinner guest. President Putin had powerful hands on jugulars: one on Germany's in the shape of long-term energy supply requirements. And while Finland, France, the UK and others were gearing up to 'more nuclear', Germany's main other card was coal: they were hardly going to agree over environmental aspects of the energy agenda (see *Europolitics* 3175: 23 October 2006: 1).

By December, relations with Turkey had worsened over its refusal to sign the protocol extending the customs union to all new member states including Cyprus. Foreign Ministers had agreed on the 11th that negotiations were not to be opened on eight 'chapters' and not to be 'closed' on any meantime. While Turkey was not further discussed at the Council, Serbia and the western Balkans were, the Council approving the changes put forward by the Commission for managing accession negotiations. Notably, learning from the Bulgaria–Romania experience but without naming them, these included tackling the most difficult 'chapters' – such as corruption and judicial reform – from the start. So while Serbia *was* discussed, at the urging of the member states closest to her, any early resumption of talks was not agreed.

Chancellor Merkel, without standing on anyone's foot, urged on consideration of what should be done about the CT. HOSG should appoint 'sherpas' to get on with it, she said. Germany's permanent representative, Schönfelder, had earlier suggested that a text should be agreed during the Portuguese presidency of the second half of 2007, to allow ratification before the 2009 EP elections. Tellingly, Matti Vanhanen for Finland gave his 'personal analysis' of the state of opinion among governments: most member states wished to keep the whole CT text or 'at least most of the text' (*BQE* 9329: 16 December 2006: 6). No very radical changes, then!

Although the priority for the German presidency of the first half of 2007 was preparation of the new IGC, other matters – not least the Doha Round – crowded in as the June European Council approached. On June 19, just 2 days before the start of the Council meeting, the presidency presented its 'draft mandate' for the IGC to the 'sherpas', having 'kept [it] under wraps' (*Europolitics* 3331: 21 June 2007: 1, 4). It dropped the CT's approach of consolidating and replacing the existing treaties. Instead it proposed that the existing treaties – the TEU and TEC (now to be called 'treaty on the functioning of the EU' – TFEU) – would remain in force, but incorporating most of the changes agreed at the 2004 IGC. Dropped were, among others, an article on symbols of the Union; the terms 'constitution' and 'EU minister for foreign affairs'; likewise Regulations, Directives and Decisions were retained and 'law' and 'framework law' dropped.

The Netherlands in particular had wanted more power for national parliaments. What was now proposed was to give them more time to consider legislative proposals and to comment on 'subsidiarity'. If one-third of the parliaments 'contested' the draft, the Commission would have to 'review' it to decide whether to withdraw, amend or retain it. No 'veto' power for national parliaments, however! Final provisions would include articles on the Union's legal personality; on voluntary withdrawal and on procedures for treaty revision – this last, pleasing to the Czechs, might 'increase *or reduce* the competences conferred upon the Union' (*Europolitics* 3331: 4, emphasis added) – although quite how reduction might occur was not clear.

Barroso immediately pushed for a 'tight' mandate for the IGC – i.e. not allowing the reopening of Pandora's box. He used the occasion to 'remind' new member states what an opportunity they had to show that widening did not mean weakening.

It was clear, though, that several states still had 'red lines'. The UK's four were well known: on the status of the charter of fundamental rights (CFR); on the 'minister of foreign affairs'; on extension of QMV in JHA areas; and EU involvement in 'social' areas. Poland's main concern was voting weights; the Czechs (see above) were generally sceptical about 'competence creep' and wanted subsidiarity to work 'in both directions': to enable power to be taken out of Union competence back to that of states. Getting agreement was, as often, declared to be in the balance.

After some 36 hours of negotiations, agreement was reached on the main points. The IGC was to open almost immediately, by the end of July, before any summer break. Both designations 'mini' and 'constitutional' vanished, in favour of 'reform' or 'amending' treaty which should itself be agreed by the October summit, for final signature in December and, it was hoped, ratification in 2008; with entry into force hoped for in 2009. Establishing this tight timetable had entailed some very hard arm twisting, with Merkel at one point allegedly threatening to 'exclude the Poles from the IGC' (!) unless they compromised on the 'double majority' voting system (*Europolitics* 3334: 26 June 2007: 4).

In essence, what was agreed (for full details, see *Bull. EU* 6-2007) was: a more 'permanent' president; a 'foreign minister' without that title; QMV on some 51 further policy areas; revision (but only from 2014) of the 'Nice' Council voting system; more co-decision for the EP; involvement of national parliaments via an 'early warning system' (sometimes called the 'yellow card'); formal acknowledgement of the role of public services; 'free and undistorted competition' moved to a protocol; the CFR legally binding on all except the UK (opt-out). Of this last, *Europolitics* commented, 'It is an odd state of affairs when, in a Union of 27, one of its members can decide that it is not equal to the others by law': little wonder perhaps, that, expected to be the major blockers, 'in the end they [the UK] proved quite cooperative' (3334: 26 June 2007: 4, 5). It was Blair's last summit, Sarkozy's first and, many thought, Merkel's triumph.

Little of substance (beyond minor changes in arithmetic) changed in October, when the name 'Lisbon Treaty' was generally acknowledged. Two outstanding issues were finally resolved: Poland's concerns over QMV in the Council (the 'Ioannina Compromise' of 1994); Italy's about its EP representation. Sarkozy pulled one more rabbit out of his hat, proposing (yet another) 'group of the wise' – this time numbering some 10 or 12 – to reflect on Europe's place in the world in a 10–20 year timeframe. The subplots of this were 'globalisation' and Turkey, thus ticking a couple more boxes with French voters. The presidency, however, warned: '[W]e will not be reopening the institutional debate' (*BQE* 9527: 20 October 2007: 6). A relieved UK Prime Minister Brown urged a return to the substantive agenda and asserted that there was general agreement not to revisit institutional change for a long time. But he had just lost an (albeit rather unwelcome) ally, as (to general but unspoken satisfaction in Brussels) that weekend (21 October) in Poland, Donald Tusk's Civic Platform defeated Jaroslaw Kaczynski's PiS.

The draft reform treaty was hardly greeted with euphoria. It was complex: Giscard called it a 'tool box you have to rummage through to find what you're looking for' (as quoted in *Europolitics* 3407: 7 November 2007: 3). Signature on 13 December would again be prelude to the uncertainties of ratification. The same publication spoke of 'Europeans' dominant scepticism: the feeling that the EU is not responding to economic and social insecurity, the *growing* gap between the EU institutions and citizens', agreeing with Brown that 'there will not be another new treaty for a long time to come' (3407: 7).

Slovenia and France held the presidencies of 2008. Slovenia was the first of the 'class of 2004' to hold the presidency and, with a population of two million, one of the smallest. It had joined the euro at the start of 2007 and Schengen just days before its presidency (21 December 2007). Among its priorities was development of the 'external action service' about which Foreign Minister Rupel expressed 'enthusiasm'; he did not hesitate to call it a 'diplomatic service'. Slovenia had been a key 'sponsor' of speeding Croatia's accession application: but had some 'local difficulties' with her larger neighbour. Rather portentously, Pierre Lemoine suggested that: 'From a geopolitical perspective, Slovenia is obviously a key country' and ominously, that: 'The future of the EU may be played out in the Balkans' (*Europolitics* 3441: 4 January 2008: 4). But the Irish 'no' came at the end of the presidency, throwing many timetables into confusion. The Council conclusions urged others to continue with ratification; the Irish to take stock and report back in October but, said French sources, with 'no obligation of [an] outcome' then (*BQE* 9687: 21 June 2008: 4). The implications of failure, then, were seen as significant for both the EP elections of June 2009 and the subsequent renewal of the Commission. Significantly, the Czechs were reported to expect – and hope? – to conduct their 2009 presidency under 'Nice' rules: that uncelebrated treaty was proving more durable than believed at its inception.

The irony that France, the big founder member 'refusnik', should be charged with picking up the pieces, was not lost on most. One non-eurosceptic British analyst urged that the Irish 'no' should be 'the occasion for a thoroughgoing reassessment of how and why Europe got into this mess. At all costs, this must not be a rerun of the period of reflection … following … rejection … by the French and Dutch when … the EU decided to ignore it'. 'Other countries would have rejected the treaty had they also held referendums, and everyone knows it' (Shepherd, 2008: 6, 8). His more general warning was noteworthy: 'political projects, like individual politicians, can survive being unpopular, but only if they still command respect. If contempt and derision start creeping in, we may enter an entirely new phase' (Shepherd 2008: 5).

As Paris took over, Anand Menon wondered: 'Is France what Europe needs right now?' 'Exercising leadership in an EU of 27 is like herding cats', he wrote (*FT* 27 June 2008: 11). Do mercurial people herd cats well? President Sarkozy did not lack an ambitious agenda, but had hoped not to have it 'tripped up' by non-ratification of the reform treaty. It included environmental protection; agreeing a framework for control of immigration; energy policy – all billed as matters of concrete concern to daily life – plus further steps on the defence front; and the CAP (*Le Monde* 1 July 2008: 1, 16, 17). Related to the last, but indicative of 'blame shifting', within hours of the start of the presidency – and with impeccable timing ahead of crucial 'Doha' talks in Geneva – he had launched a fierce attack on trade Commissioner Peter Mandelson, even blaming *him* for the Irish 'no'. *Plus ça change?*

## Envoi

What, in brief, has been achieved and what, though announced, hoped for or striven after, has not? What have been some of the unintended consequences? As we have seen, it has been a mixed bag.

In one sense, we are back at the starting point: the *economic* centrality of Germany is beyond doubt: and, both for itself and for those around it, much depends on how it acts. In another dimension, successive enlargements have arguably changed the very nature of the 'club': so much so that in Zielonka's view, the EU 'increasingly resembles a neo-medieval empire', rather than any kind of 'Westphalian federation with a central government in charge of a given territory' (Zielonka 2006: 1).

We saw at the start of this book that even agreement on a customs union among six neighbouring states amid the privations of postwar western Europe was far from easy. We have seen that, in the whole intervening period, the fortunes of integration have waxed and waned. We have often had occasion to use such phrases as 'but that was about as far as agreement went'. It has been said often but rightly that, as long as the EC/EU appeared to deliver 'the goods' in prosperity terms, but also not to seem to threaten too much people's senses of political legitimacy and of identity, then the 'permissive consensus' was likely to prevail.

But for some time now these conditions have, for many, not been fulfilled. Turnout for elections to an EP with undoubtedly enhanced powers has fallen steadily in most states: the UK exception in 2004 was mainly the product of increased involvement by 'eurosceptic' parties. *Eurobarometer* data, too, have shown decreasing levels of enthusiasm and support, even for the proposition that membership was a 'good thing' for one's own state, in most countries since 1990 (see *Eurobarometer* 2004: B33–B51; Taylor 2008: 26). There seems to have been a *correlation* between this decline, and more general public disillusion with politics domestically, evident in many of the member states: whether there was any *causal* connection and, if so, which way it ran, was more debatable.

Acknowledgement of the euro's smooth introduction has been balanced by concerns about its governance, workings and consequences in its second decade, especially in the promised economic storms from 2008. As those storms intensified, the EU 'crew' showed itself seriously divided over how to respond. Germany, with its so far burgeoning surpluses and prudent absence of housing bubbles and consumer over-indebtedness, was most reluctant to adopt any major demand stimulus, loudly though the profligate others cried out for it. 'Coordinated response' seemed remote, the costs of its absence unknown but the scope for recrimination considerable. Yet for some hitherto outside the eurozone, the calculation seemed to shift: being 'inside out of the cold' might have benefits, thought not a few in Denmark and Sweden – and even some in the UK. In the trade field, and despite the travails over the Doha Round, the EU can certainly claim successes: it is hard to imagine any recent trade round taking the shape it has done if the EU had not been the main, and relatively unified, bargainer with the USA.

The EU may now propose to offer an 'exit route' but the implied costs of such a choice appear drastic. Thus the whole project has, for some, taken on a 'coercive' face, as unwelcome as it is unfamiliar. It risks evoking the image of the 'bully' rather than the warm welcome of the self-proclaimed 'partnership' or family. This is particularly so where it is made to appear that a 'no' by one state counts, while that of another somehow does not. It seems to have acquired simultaneously a power of attraction to those outside, and a capacity to alienate a good many of those inside. It is routinely used as an 'alibi' by many member state governments: 'Don't blame us: blame Brussels!'

Despite unprecedented prosperity of most of its population, Europe generally appears no longer at the centre of global economic developments. This, despite the striking fact that in 2007, Germany (still) boasted the *world's* largest merchandise exports – ahead of both China and the USA and approaching double those of Japan (*FT* 11 June 2008: 11). The EU's own demography does not bespeak dynamism and its attitudes to both immigration and migration within do not suggest rapid change either. Whatever version of the rather protean term 'globalisation' was considered, many in the EU appeared to wish it to go away. Views that the value of the EU was chiefly as a defensive cartel were widespread. They seemed to become more widespread as the EU – with the rest of the world – entered on an economic recession of unknown length and severity. The talk in France was of 'sovereign wealth funds' to prop up national treasures: while Germany's reluctance to join others in fiscal stimuli equally demonstrated the limits of 'solidarity' and shared priorities.

The development of the EC/EU appears to have fulfilled one of its important early intentions: to transform the relations among the states that made it up. But other costs and strains have become prominent. Notably, the EU's structures, arrangements and proclaimed 'values' are seen as providing separatists, in several member states, with levers to undermine the unity of those states themselves. There is also the risk that arguments over the nature and future of the project could themselves reignite fierce quarrels between members. There is a sense, too, that the capacity of traditional democratic arenas and procedures to influence matters has been declining, without being replaced, or adequately complemented, by any sense of a 'European demos'. Brussels' proliferating lobbies, representative offices and public affairs consultants (so reminiscent of Washington, DC) are more indicative of where influence lies.

The EU was midwife at the (almost) peaceful birth of a new Europe in the 1990s; yet at the same time unable or unwilling to prevent a deadly resurgence of atavistic 'ethnic' quarrels on its southeast flank. Reactions to it 'abroad' have varied widely: from Rifkin's largely admiring 'European dream' (Rifkin 2004) to Kagan's disparagement of the European 'Venus' (Kagan 2003). For the best part of the first decade of the twenty-first century, a large – to many a disproportionate – amount of time and effort was spent in institutional/'constitutional' tinkering. Since the EU is not good at 'multitasking', this has often seemed at the expense of achievement in more concrete and urgent matters such as the whole gamut of environmental pressures, and energy issues. It is easy to think that the EU has fiddled while much of the rest of the world has swept by.

And there yet seems little consensus among the member states about the overall purposes, shape and limits of the enterprise. Several of the main members have seemed to wish to construct a union that closely resembles their own 'state' model – rather than imagining a completely different kind of creature. We have seen how influential French notions were early on: they remain fixed on a protectionist and 'exceptionalist' reflex that believes 'the rules' are there to be bent by arbitrary administrative and bureaucratic fiat. German preferences have almost always taken the form of an insistent federalism – liable to be (wilfully?) misunderstood in the UK – closely modelled on its own constitutional, economic and social arrangements; and, of course, with stern monetary discipline underpinned by an independent central bank. The UK appears to believe that a union as ramshackle as the 'fingers crossed' muddling through that has long characterised its own arrangements (and which has come under enormous strain) is somehow the 'right way to go' or at any rate the 'best that can be hoped for' in the EU context.

The 50th anniversary of the Treaties of Rome was marked in 2007 in distinctly muted tone. There is little doubt that, in Paul Taylor's words, 'in the early twenty-first century the European project needed to be rescued' (Taylor 2008: 1); a good deal more doubt as to whether any of the 'candidate' projects or policies were likely to command support or elicit the required resources – including budgetary ones.

An important part of the debate can be framed in terms of the contrasting views of Siedentop (2000) and Moravcsik (2002). For Siedentop, it is the growing influence of a French-based 'state-like' model – 'bureaucratic ... with its built-in predilection for power rather than authority ... that ... lies behind ... recent pressures to move ahead rapidly ... towards political integration' (Siedentop 2000: 105,107). Were there to be any such move, it might come at a heavy cost to 'the different forms of civic spirit' so central to European democracies: too much might be sacrificed on the altar of 'economism'. '*Today in Europe there is no ... consensus ... [on] which areas of decision-making belong to the centre and which ... the periphery*' (Siedentop 2000: 231, emphasis in original). Neither, it should by now be clear, is there consensus on the best institutional *design* for handling the issues, wherever taken.

For Moravcsik, by way of contrast, concern with the 'democratic deficit' in the EU is 'misplaced' if one bears in mind both the *nature* of most of the EU's activity – ('EU legislative and regulatory activity is inversely correlated with the salience of issues in the minds of European voters'); and also the actual practices of – as opposed to some 'ideal type' of – existing states. 'Insulated institutions', he suggests, are 'often more popular with the public than legislatures'. He admits, however, that the ECB *is* of greater salience, as well as being 'more independent of political pressure than any known national example' (Moravcsik 2002: 615, 621).

This book has sought to survey the trajectory of the EC/EU in terms of the four 'battles' or clusters of issues which we introduced at the start. Their relevance is still apparent: all four will remain both crucial and interconnected, far into the fog of both Europe's and the EU's future.

## Further reading

D. Dinan (ed.), *Origins and Evolution of the European Union*. Oxford: Oxford University Press, 2006. (Chapters 13 and 14.)

P. Taylor, *The End of European Integration*. London: Routledge, 2008.

L. Tsoukalis, *What Kind of Europe?* Oxford: Oxford University Press, 2003.

J. Zielonka, *Europe as Empire. The Nature of the Enlarged European Union*. Oxford: Oxford University Press, 2006.

# Bibliography

Adonnino Report (1985) *A People's Europe: Reports from the Ad Hoc Committee*, Bulletin of the ECs, Supplement 7/85.

Albert, M. (1993) *Capitalism Against Capitalism*, London: Whurr Publishers.

Allen, D., Rummel, R. and Wessels, W. (1982) *European Political Cooperation: Towards a Foreign Policy for Western Europe*, London: Butterworth Scientific.

Andrlik, E. (1981) 'The farmers and the state: agricultural interests in West German polities', *West European Politics* 4 (1): 104–19.

*L'Année Politique* (1973) *L'Anneé politique, économique, sociale et diplomatique*. Paris: Presses Universitaires de France.

*Auf dem Weg zur deutschen Einheit* (1991). Bonn: Inter Nationes.

Aubert de la Rüe, P. (1970) 'Les relations économiques entre l'Europe de l'Est et l'Europe de l'Ouest', *Politique Étrangère* 3: 285–301.

*Aussenpolitik* (1973) (German Foreign Affairs Review). Hamburg: Übersee Verlag.

Beber, M. (2002) '"One careful driver from new": earning the European Central Bank's no-claims bonus', *Journal of Common Market Studies* 40 (Supplement 1): 75–8.

Beetham, D. and Lord, C. (1998) *Legitimacy and the European Union*. London: Longman.

Bell, G. (1973) *The Eurodollar Market and the International System*. London: Macmillan, and New York: John Wiley & Sons Ltd.

Bieber, R. (1984) 'Achievements of the EP 1975–84', *Common Market Law Review* 21: 283–304.

Bieber, R., Dehousse, R., Pinder, J. and Weiler, J. (eds) (1988) *1992: One European Market?* Baden-Baden: Nomos, for European Policy Unit of the European University Institute.

Bomberg, E. and Stubb, A. (2003) *The EU: How Does it Work?* Oxford: Oxford University Press.

Bonn (1977) *Texts Relating to European Political Co-operation*. Bonn: Press and Information Office of the Federal Government.

Bowler, I.R. (1985) *Agriculture under the CAP: A Geography*. Manchester: Manchester University Press.

Brandt, W. (1978) *People and Politics: The Years 1960–1975*. London: Collins.

Brewin, C. (1987) 'The European Community: a union of states without unity of government', *Journal of Common Market Studies* XXVI (1): 1–24.

Brewin, C. and McAllister, R. (1983) *Annual Review of the Activities of the European Communities for 1982*. London: University Association for Contemporary European Studies.

Brewin, C. and McAllister, R. (1986) 'Annual review of the activities of the European Communities in 1985', *Journal of Common Market Studies* XXIV (4): 313–5.

Brewin, C. and McAllister, R. (1988) 'Annual review of the activities of the European Communities in 1987', *Journal of Common Market Studies* XXVI (4): 431–68.

Brewin, C. and McAllister, R. (1989) 'Annual review of the activities of the European Communities in 1988', *Journal of Common Market Studies* XXVII (4): 323–57.

Brewin, C. and McAllister, R. (1991) 'Annual review of the activities of the European Communities in 1990', *Journal of Common Market Studies* XXIX (4): 385–30.

Buckley, M. and Cummings, S. (eds) (2001) *Kosovo: War and its Aftermath*. London: Continuum.

Buiter, W. (1999) 'Alice in Euroland', *Journal of Common Market Studies* 37 (2): 181–209.

Buiter, W. (2006) 'Stabilization in EMU', *Journal of Common Market Studies* 44 (4): 687–710.

Bulmer, S. (1983) 'Domestic politics and European Community policymaking', *Journal of Common Market Studies* XXI (4): 349–64.

Bulmer, S. and Paterson, W. (1987) *The Federal Republic of Germany and the European Community*. London: Allen and Unwin.

Bulmer, S. and Wessels, W. (1987) *The European Council: Decision-Making in European Politics*. Basingstoke: Macmillan.

Burgess, M. (1989) *Federalism and European Union: Political Ideas, Influence and Strategy*. London: Routledge.

Calleo, D. (1999) 'Strategic implications of the euro', *Survival* 41 (1): 5—19.

Cameron, D. (1992) '1992 initiative: causes and consequences', in Sbragia, A. (ed.) *Europolitics: Institutions and Policy-Making in the 'New' European Community*. Washington, DC: Brookings.

Camps, M. (1964) *Britain and the European Community, 1955–63*. Princeton, NJ: Princeton University Press.

Camps, M. (1971) 'European unification in the seventies', *International Affairs* 47 (4): 671–8.

Cappelletti, M., Seccombe, M. and Weiler, J. (eds) (1985–8) *Integration through Law: Europe and the American Federal Experience* (5 vols). Berlin and New York: Walter de Gruyter.

Cecchini Report (1988) *The European Challenge: 1992*. Aldershot: Wildwood House.

Chryssochoou, D.N. (2000) *Democracy in the European Union*. London: I.B. Tauris.

Cini, M (ed.) (2003) *European Union Politics*. Oxford: Oxford University Press.

Clift, B. (2006) 'The new political economy of dirigisme: French macroeconomic policy, unrepentant sinning, and the SGP', *British Journal of Politics and International Relations* 8 (3): 388–409.

Cockfield White Paper (1985) *Completing the Internal Market*. Luxembourg: Office for Official Publications of the European Communities.

Colchester, N. and Buchan, D. (1990) *Europe Relaunched: Truths and Illusions on the way to 1992*. London: Hutchinson.

Commission (of the EC) (1973) *Fifteen Years of Community Policy*. Luxembourg: Office for Official Publications of the European Communities.

Commission (of the EC) (1981) *The Community's Budget*. Brussels/Luxembourg: Office for Official Publications.

Commission (of the EC) (1990) *Political Union: Commission Opinion*. Luxembourg: Office for Official Publications.

Commission (of the EC) COM Documents (various). Luxembourg: Office for Official Publications of the European Communities. (By year followed by number, e.g. (90) 123.)

Connolly, B. (1995) *The Rotten Heart of Europe*. London: Faber & Faber.

Cornford, J. (ed.) (1975) *The Failure of the State*. London: Croom Helm; Totowa, NJ: Rowman & Littlefield.

Cram, L., Dinan, D. and Nugent, N. (1999) *Developments in the European Union*. New York: St Martin's Press.

Croft, S., Redmond, J., Wyn Rees, G. and Webber, M. (1999) *The Enlargement of Europe*. Manchester: Manchester University Press.

Cromwell, W.C. (1992) *The United States and the European Pillar*. London and Basingstoke: Macmillan.

Dahrendorf, R. (1973) 'The foreign policy of the EEC', *The World Today* 29 (ii): 47–57.

Dannreuther, R. (1997) *Eastward Enlargement: NATO and the EU*. Oslo: IFS.

Davidson, R. and White, P. (eds) (1988) *Information and Government: Studies in the Dynamics of Policy-making*. Edinburgh: Edinburgh University Press.

Davis, E., Geroski, P., Kay, J., Manning, A., Smales, C., Smith, S. and Szymanski, S. (1989) *1992: Myths and Realities*. London: London Business School, Centre for Business Strategy.

Debré, M. (1971) 'Europe 1971: deux échecs–deux succès–deux épreuves deux certitudes', *Revue de Défense Nationale* October 1971: 1411–31.

Degimbe Report (1988) *La Dimension sociale du Marché Intérieur*. Brussels: Office for Official Publications of the EC.

Dehaene, J.-L., Simon, D. and von Weizsäcker, R. (1999) *The Institutional Implications of Enlargement*. Brussels: Report to the European Commission.

de la Mahotière, S. (1970) *Towards One Europe*. London: Penguin.

Delarue, M. (1974) 'Frankreich–für ein europäisches Europa', *Aussenpolitik* 2: 134–46.

de la Serre, F. (1970) 'La Grande-Bretagne s'éloigne-t-elle de l'Europe?', *Revue Française de Science Politique* 20 (I): 37–50.

de la Serre, F. (1971) 'La CEE et la Crise de 1965', *Revue Française de Science Politique* 21 (II): 402–20.

de la Serre, F. (1972) *L'adhésion de la Grande Bretagne aux Communautés Européennes* (2 vols), Vol. I: *La seconde candidature 1967–1969*. Paris: La documentation française.

de la Serre, F. (1987) *La Grande Bretagne et la Communauté Européenne*. Paris: Presses Universitaires de France.

Delors Report (1989) *Report on Economic and Monetary Union in the EC*. Luxembourg: Office for Official Publications of the European Communities.

Denton, G. (1967) *Planning in the EEC: The Medium-term Economic Policy Programme of the European Economic Community*. London: Political and Economic Planning.

Denton, G. (1984) 'Re-structuring the EC budget: implications of the Fontainebleau Agreement', *Journal of Common Market Studies* XXIII (2): 117–40.

Denton, G, Harvey, D., Marsh, I, Reichenbach, H., Biehl, D. and Neville-Jones, P. (1983) *Reform of the Common Agricultural Policy and Restructuring of the EEC Budget*. London: University Association for Contemporary European Studies.

DePorte, A. (1979) *Europe between the Superpowers: The Enduring Balance*. New Haven, CT, and London: Yale University Press.

Dinan, D. (1994) *Ever Closer Union?* London: Macmillan.

Dinan, D. (ed.) (2006) *Origins and Evolution of the European Union*. Oxford: Oxford University Press.

*Documents on American Foreign Relations (DAFR)*, several volumes. Washington, DC.

Dooge Committee Report (1985) *Ad Hoc Committee on Institutional Affairs*. Bulletin of the ECs, Interim: 11–1984: 101–6; Final: 3–1985: 101–10.

Drake, H. (2000) *Jacques Delors: Perspectives on a European Leader*. London: Routledge.

Duff, A. (ed.) (1997) *The Treaty of Amsterdam: Text and Commentary*. London: Federal Trust.

Dyson, K. (1994) *Elusive Union: The Process of Economic and Monetary Union in Europe*. London and New York: Longman.

Dyson, K. and Featherstone, K. (1999) *The Road to Maastricht*. Oxford: Oxford University Press.

Eatwell, J., Ellman, M., Karlsson, M., Nuti, D. and Shapiro, J. (1997) *Not 'Just Another Accession'*. London: Institute for Public Policy Research (IPPR).

*ECR: European Court Reports*. Court of Justice of the European Communities: Luxembourg.

Edwards, G. and Wallace, W. (1976) *A Wider European Community?* London: Federal Trust.

Edwards, G. and Wiessala, G. (eds) (1998) *The European Union 1997: Annual Review of Activities, Journal of Common Market Studies, 36*. Oxford: Basil Blackwell.

Edwards, G. and Wiessala, G. (eds) (1999) *The European Union 1998/1999, Journal of Common Market Studies, 37, Annual Review*. Oxford: Basil Blackwell.

Edwards, G. and Wiessala, G. (eds) (2000) *The European Union: Annual Review of the EU 1999/2000, Journal of Common Market Studies, 38*. Oxford: Basil Blackwell.

Edwards, G. and Wiessala, G. (eds) (2001) *The European Union: Annual Review of the EU 2000/2001, Journal of Common Market Studies, 39*. Oxford: Basil Blackwell.

Edwards, G. and Wiessala, G. (eds) (2002) *The European Union 2001/2002, Journal of Common Market Studies, 40*. Oxford: Basil Blackwell.

El-Agraa, A. (ed.) (1980) *The Economics of the European Community*. Oxford: Philip Allan.

Endo, K. (1999) *The Presidency of the European Commission under Jacques Delors*. Basingstoke: Macmillan.

EP (1997) *Background Note on the Enlargement of NATO and the EU:* JPC/CCEE, 28.2.1997. Brussels: European Parliament Committee on Foreign Affairs.

EPC (1997) *Making Sense of the Amsterdam Treaty*. Brussels: European Policy Centre.

Etzioni, A. (1992) 'The evils of self-determination', *Foreign Policy* 89, winter 1992–3: 21–35.

*Europe Documents*, special documents series. Brussels: Agence Internationale d'Information pour la Presse; Agence Europe SA (various dates).

Feld, W. (1976) *The European Community in World Affairs*. Port Washington, NY: Alfred Publishing Co.

Ferri, M. (1982) *Selection of Texts concerning Institutional Matters of the Community from 1950 to 1982*, Luxembourg: European Parliament, Committee on Institutional Affairs.

*Foreign Relations of the United States (FRUS)*, several volumes. Washington DC.

Galloway, D. (2001) *The Treaty of Nice and Beyond*. Sheffield: Sheffield Academic Press.

Gerbet, P. (1956) 'La Genèse du plan Schuman', *Revue Française de Science Politique* 6 (3): 525ff.

Gillingham, J. (1991) *Coal, Steel and the Rebirth of Europe, 1945–1955*. Cambridge: Cambridge University Press.

Gillingham, J. (2003) *European Integration 1950–2003. Superstate or New Market Economy?* Cambridge: Cambridge University Press.

*GRA: General Report on Activities* (of the communities). Annual, cited by volume number. Brussels and Luxembourg: EC Commission.

Grahl, J. (1997) *After Maastricht*. London: Lawrence & Wishart.

Grant, C. (1994) *Delors: Inside the House that Jacques Built*. London: Nicholas Brealey.

Grant, R. (1996) 'France's new relationship with NATO', *Survival*, 38 (1): 58–80.

Grosser, A. (1980) *The Western Alliance: European–American Relations since 1945.* London: Macmillan.

Grosser, A. (1986) 'France–Allemagne, 1936–86' *Politique Étrangère* 1: 247–55.

Guicherd, C. (1999) 'International law and the war on Kosovo', *Survival* 41 (2): 19–33.

Haas, E. (1958) *The Uniting of Europe: Political, Social and Economic Forces.* London: Stevens.

Haas, E. (1975) *The Obsolescence of Regional Integration Theory.* Berkeley, CA: Center for International Studies.

Hansen, N. von (1981) 'Plaidoyer für eine Europaische Union', *EuropaArchiv* 5: 141–8.

Harrison, R. (1974) *Europe in Question: Theories of Regional International Integration.* London: Allen & Unwin.

Hartley, A. (1993) 'Reinventing the politics of Europe', *The World Today* 49 (11): 202–5.

Hartley, T.C. (1988) *The Foundations of European Community Law* (2nd edn). Oxford: Clarendon Press.

Heathcote, N. (1966) 'The crisis of European supranationality', *Journal of Common Market Studies* V (2): 140–71.

Heisbourg, F. (2001) 'The day after: an assessment. Europe and the transformation of the world order', *Survival*, 43 (4): 143–48.

Hill, C. and Smith, M. (eds) (2005) *International Relations and the European Union.* Oxford: Oxford University Press.

Hinsley, F. (1986) *Sovereignty* (2nd edn). Cambridge: Cambridge University Press.

Hirsch, F. (1972) 'The political economics of European monetary integration', *The World Today* 28 (x): 424–33.

Hodges, M. (ed.) (1972) *European Integration: Selected Readings.* London: Penguin.

Hodges, M. and Wallace, W. (eds) (1981) *Economic Divergence in the European Community.* London: Allen & Unwin.

Hogan, M.J. (1987) *The Marshall Plan.* Cambridge: Cambridge University Press.

Hostiou, R. (1969) *Robert Schuman et l'Europe.* Paris: Editions Cujas.

Howe, G. (1996) 'Bearing more of the burden: in search of a European foreign and security policy', *The World Today* 52 (i): 23–6.

Howorth, J. (2000) 'Britain, France and the European defence initiative', *Survival* 42 (2): 43–55.

Hu, Y.-S. (1979) 'German agricultural power: the impact on France and Britain', *The World Today* 35 (xi): 453–61.

Hu, Y.-S. (1981) *Europe Under Stress.* London: Butterworth, for the Royal Institute of International Affairs.

Hughes, K. (2006) *Turkey and the EU: Four Scenarios from Train Crash to Full Steam Ahead.* Brussels: Friends of Europe.

Hyde-Price, A. (1999) 'Berlin republic takes to arms', *The World Today,* 55 (6): 13–15.

International Monetary Fund (1975) *Annual Report on Exchange Restrictions.* Washington, DC: IMF.

Irwin, C. (1971) 'Nuclear aspects of West European defence integration', *International Affairs* 47 (4): 679–91.

Johnson, B. (1970) *The Politics of Money.* London: John Murray.

*Journal of European Integration/Journal d'Integration Européenne* (1983) special number, vol. VI, winter/spring: 'Les Institutions des CE: propositions de réforme et perspectives d'évolution'.

Judah, T. (1999) 'Kosovo's road to war', *Survival* 41 (2): 5–18.

Kagan, R. (2003) *Of Paradise and Power: America and Europe in the New World Order*. New York: Knopf.

Katz, S. (ed.) (1979) *US–European Monetary Relations*. Washington, DC: American Enterprise Institute for Public Policy Research.

*Keesing's Contemporary Archives* (later *Record of World Events*). London and Bristol: Keesing's Publications Ltd. From 1973, London: Longman.

Kirk-Reay Report (1978) EP Working Document 148/78.

Kirschen, E. (1974) The American external seigniorage: origin, cost to Europe and possible defences', *European Economic Review* 5: 355–78.

Kissinger, H. (1982) *Years of Upheaval*. London: Weidenfeld & Nicolson.

Kitzinger, U. (1973) *Diplomacy and Persuasion: How Britain Joined the Common Market*. London: Thames & Hudson.

Klepsch Report (1979) *Two-Way Street: USA-Europe Arms Procurement* (Report to the European Parliament). London: Brassey's; New York: Crane Russack.

Kohl, H. (1991) *Our Future in Europe*. Edinburgh: Europa Institute of Edinburgh University.

Kruse, D. (1980) *Monetary Integration in Western Europe: EMU, EMS and Beyond*. London and Boston: Butterworth.

Lacouture, J. (1998) *Mitterrand: Une histoire de Français*, Paris: Editions du Seuil.

Lambert, J. (1966) 'The constitutional crisis 1965–6', *Journal of Common Market Studies* IV (3): 195–228.

Laughland, J. (1997) *The Tainted Source*. London: Little, Brown.

Laursen, F. (1990) 'The community's policy towards EFTA', *Journal of Common Market Studies* XXVIII (4): 303–25.

Levi, M. and Schütze, W. (1970) 'Les relations économiques de la République Federale avec les pays de l'est', *Politique Étrangère* 4: 439–70.

Lodge, J. (ed.) (1986a) *European Union: The European Community in Search of a Future*. Basingstoke: Macmillan.

Lodge, J. (1986b) 'The Single European Act: towards a new Euro-dynamism?', *Journal of Common Market Studies* XXIV (3): 203–23.

Lodge, J. (ed.) (1989) *The European Community and the Challenge of the Future* (1st edn). London: Pinter.

Lodge, J. (ed.) (1993) *The European Community and the Challenge of the Future* (2nd edn). London: Pinter.

Lord, C. (1998) *Democracy in the European Union*. Sheffield: Sheffield Academic Press.

Ludlow, P. (1982) *The Making of the EMS*. London: Butterworth.

Ludlow, P. and Gros, D. (1992) *The European Union and the Future of Europe*. Brussels: Centre for European Policy Studies (CEPS), mimeo.

Lundestad, G. (1998) *'Empire' by Integration: the US and European Integration 1945–1997*. Oxford: Oxford University Press.

Luxembourg Report (1970) *First Report of the Foreign Ministers to the Heads of State and Government of the Member-States of the EEC*. Luxembourg: Office for Official Publications of the European Communities.

MacDougall Report (1977) *Report of the Study Group on the Role of Public Finance in European Integration* (2 vols). Brussels: EC Commission.

Maldague Report (1976) *Problems of Inflation*. Brussels: EC Commission (reprinted in *Agenor* 64, December 1976).

Maresceau, M. (ed.) (1997) *Enlarging the European Union*. London: Longman.

Marjolin Report (1975) *Report of the Study Group ... (under the Chairmanship of R. Marjolin) to the European Communities* (2 vols). Brussels: EC Commission, Directorate General Economic and Financial Affairs.

Marjolin, R. (1989) *Architect of European Unity: Memoirs 1911–86*. London: Weidenfeld & Nicolson.

Marsh, D. (1992) *The Bundesbank*. London: Heinemann.

McAllister, R. (1971) 'Prospects for decentralisation in a "United Europe"', *The New Atlantis* 3 (2): 136–44.

McAllister, R. (1972) 'Défense quels azimuts? Some recent French attitudes and decisions', Edinburgh: *The Waverley Papers* 4 (2).

McAllister, R. (1975) 'The EEC dimension: intended and unintended consequences', in Cornford, J. (ed.) *The Failure of the State*. London: Croom Helm; Totowa, NJ: Rowman & Littlefield.

McAllister, R. (1978) 'The ironies of European unity', *Futures* June: 246–50.

McAllister, R. (1979) 'Ends and means revisited: some conundra of the fourth medium-term economic policy programme', *Common Market Law Review* 16: 61–76.

McAllister, R. (1988) 'The European Community and the data mountain', in Davidson, R. and White, P. (eds) *Information and Government: Studies in the Dynamics of Policy-Making*. Edinburgh: Edinburgh University Press.

McAllister, R. (2000) 'France and defence: doctrine and restructuring, 1989–2000', Edinburgh: *New Waverley Papers*.

Meade, J., Liesner, H. and Wells, S. (1962) *Case Studies in European Economic Union*. London: Oxford University Press.

Mendl, W. (1970) *Deterrence and Persuasion*. London: Faber & Faber.

Meny, Y. and Wright, V. (eds) (1987) *The Politics of Steel: Western Europe and the Steel Industry*. Berlin and New York: Walter de Gruyter.

Michelmann, H. (1978) *Organizational Effectiveness in a Multinational Bureaucracy*. Farnborough: Saxon House.

Miles, L. (ed.) (2003) *The European Union: Annual Review 2002/2003, Journal of Common Market Studies, 41*. Oxford: Basil Blackwell.

Miles, L. (ed.) (2004) *The European Union: Annual Review 2003/2004, Journal of Common Market Studies, 42*. Oxford: Basil Blackwell.

Miles, L. (ed.) (2005) *The European Union: Annual Review 2004/2005, Journal of Common Market Studies, 43*. Oxford: Basil Blackwell.

Milward, A. (1984) *The Reconstruction of Western Europe, 1945–51*. London: Methuen.

Milward, A. (1992) *The European Rescue of the Nation-State*. London: Routledge.

Milward, A. (2002) *The Rise and Fall of a National Strategy*. London: Frank Cass.

Milward, A., Lynch, F., Ranieri, R., Romero, F. and Sørensen, V. (1993) *The Frontier of National Sovereignty*. London: Routledge.

Mitchell, J. (1976) 'The Tindemans Report: retrospect and prospect', *Common Market Law Review* 13: 455–84.

Monnet, J. (1978) *Memoirs*. London: Collins.

Moore, B. and Rhodes, J. (1973) 'Evaluating the effects of British regional economic policy', *Economic Journal* 83 (329): 83–110.

Moravcsik, A. (1991) 'Negotiating the Single European Act: national interest and conventional statecraft in the European Community', *International Organisation* 45 (1): 19–56.

Moravcsik, A. (1999) *The Choice for Europe*. London: UCL Press.

Moravcsik, A. (2002) 'Reassessing legitimacy in the European Union', *Journal of Common Market Studies,* 40 (4): 603–24.

Moreau Defarges, P. (1985) 'J'ai fait un rêve … Le President François Mitterrand, artisan de l'union européenne', *Politique Étrangère* 2: 359–76.

Moreau Defarges, P. (1986) 'La France et l'Europe: le rêve ambigu ou la mesure du rang', *Politique Étrangère* 1: 199–218.

Morgan, A. (1976) *From Summits to Council: Evolution in the EEC.* London: Chatham House (Royal Institute for International Affairs) and PEP.

Newhouse, J. (1967) *Collision in Brussels: The Common Market Crisis of 30 June, 1965.* New York: Norton.

Nicoll, W (1986) 'From rejection to repudiation: EC budgetary affairs 1985', *Journal of Common Market Studies,* XXV (1), September: 31–50.

Nicoll, W. and Salmon, T. (1990) *Understanding the European Communities.* New York and London: Philip Allan.

Norman, P. (2003) *The Accidental Constitution: The Story of the European Convention.* Brussels: EuroComment.

Nugent, N. (1991) *The Government and Politics of the European Community* (2nd edn). Basingstoke: Macmillan.

Nugent, N. (ed.) (1993) *The European Community 1992: Annual Review of Activities.* Oxford: Basil Blackwell/Journal of Common Market Studies.

Nugent, N. (1994) *The Government and Politics of the European Union* (3rd edn). Basingstoke and London: Macmillan.

Nugent, N. (ed.) (1995) *The European Union 1994, Journal of Common Market Studies, 33, Annual Review.* Oxford: Basil Blackwell.

Nugent, N. (ed.) (1996) *The European Union 1995, Journal of Common Market Studies, 34, Annual Review.* Oxford: Basil Blackwell.

Nugent, N. (ed.) (1997) *The European Union 1996, Journal of Common Market Studies, 35, Annual Review,* Oxford: Basil Blackwell.

Optica Report (1976) *Towards Economic Equilibrium and Monetary Unification.* H/905/75 E Final, Brussels: Commission of the EC.

Padoa-Schioppa, T. (1985) *Money, Economic Policy and Europe.* Brussels and Luxembourg: Office for Official Publications of the European Communities.

Padoa-Schioppa, T. (1987) *Efficiency, Stability and Equity: A Strategy for the Evolution of the Economic System of the EC.* Oxford: Oxford University Press.

Page, S. (1981) 'The revival of protectionism and its consequences for Europe', *Journal of Common Market Studies* XX (1): 17–40.

Palmer, M. (1983) 'The development of the European Parliament's institutional role within the European Community, 1974–83', *Journal of European Integration* VI (2–3): 183–202.

Parfitt, T. (1970) 'Note of the month', *The World Today* 26 (i): 1–4.

Parfitt, T. (1980a) 'Note of the month: the CAP: reconciling the irreconcilable', *The World Today* 36 (iv): 121–5.

Parfitt, T. (1980b) 'The budget and the CAP: a Community crisis avoided', *The World Today* 36 (viii): 313–18.

Paterson, W. (ed.) (1991) *Beyond the Inter-Governmental Conferences.* Edinburgh: Europa Institute of Edinburgh University.

Pelkmans, J. (1986) *Completing the Internal Market for Industrial Products.* Luxembourg: OOP.

Pelkmans, J. (1987) 'The new approach to technical harmonization and standardization', *Journal of Common Market Studies* XXV (3): 249–69.

Pelkmans, J. and Robson, P. (1987) 'The aspirations of the White Paper', *Journal of Common Market Studies* XXV (3): 181–92.

Pelkmans, J. and Winters, A. (1988) *Europe's Domestic Market*. London: Routledge, for RIIA.

Pentland, C. (1973) *International Theory and European Integration*. New York: Free Press/Macmillan.

Peterson, J. and Bomberg, E. (1999) *Decision-Making in the European Union*. Basingstoke: Macmillan.

Petras, J. and Morley, M. (2000) 'Contesting hegemons: US–French relations in the "New World Order"', *Review of International Studies*, 26 (1): 49–67.

Phinnemore, D. (2004) *The Treaty Establishing a Constitution for Europe: An Overview*, Chatham House Briefing Note 04. London: Chatham House.

Pierre, A. (1974) 'What happened to the Year of Europe?', *The World Today* 30 (iii): 110–19.

Pinder, J. (1968) 'Positive integration and negative integration: some problems of economic union in the EEC', *The World Today* 24 (iii): 88–110.

Pinder, J. (1970) 'Prospects for Europe after the summit', *The World Today* 26 (i): 5–18.

Preston, C. (1997) *Enlargement and Integration in the European Union*. London: Routledge.

Pryce, R. (ed.) (1987) *The Dynamics of European Union*. London: Croom Helm.

*RCP: Report on Competition Policy* (annual). Brussels and Luxembourg: Office for Official Publications of the European Communities.

*RCW: Review of the Council's Work* (annual). General Secretariat of the Council, Brussels and Luxembourg: Office for Official Publications of the European Communities.

Rifkin, J. (2004) *The European Dream*. Cambridge: Polity Press.

Roberts, A. (1999) 'NATO's "humanitarian war" over Kosovo', *Survival* 41 (3): 102–23.

Rogers, P. (1999) 'Lessons to learn', *The World Today,* 55 (8/9): 4–5.

Rosamond, B. (2000) *Theories of European Integration*. Basingstoke: Palgrave.

Rosenthal, G. (1975) *The Men behind the Decisions: Cases in European Policymaking*. Lexington, MA, and London: D.C. Heath.

Rosenthal, G. (1982) *The Mediterranean Basin: Its Political Economy and Changing International Relations*. London: Butterworth Scientific.

Ross, G. (1995) *Jacques Delors and European Integration*. Cambridge: Polity Press.

Rutten, M. (2001) *From St Malo to Nice*. Chaillot Paper, 47. Paris: Institute for Security Studies.

Sainte Lorette, L. de (1961) *Le Marché commun* (2nd edn). Paris: A. Colin.

Saint-Ouen, F. (1988) 'Facing European integration: the case of Switzerland', *Journal of Common Market Studies* XXVI (3): 273–85.

Sasse, C., Poullet, E., Coombes, D. and Deprez, G. (1977) *Decision-Making in the European Community*. New York: Praeger.

Sbragia, A. (ed.) (1992) *Europolitics: Institutions and Policy-Making in the 'New' European Community*. Washington, DC: Brookings.

Scheel, W. (1974) 'Europe at the crossroads', *Aussenpolitik* 25 (2): 123–33.

Sedelmeier, U. and Young, A. (eds) (2006) *The JCMS Annual Review of the European Union in 2005, Journal of Common Market Studies, 44*. Oxford: Basil Blackwell.

Sedelmeier, U. and Young, A. (eds) (2007) *The JCMS Annual Review of the European Union in 2006, Journal of Common Market Studies, 45*. Oxford: Basil Blackwell.

Sedelmeier, U. and Young, A. (eds) (2008) *The JCMS Annual Review of the European Union in 2007, Jounal of Common Market Studies, 46*. Oxford: Basil Blackwell.

Serfaty, S. (ed.) (2003) *The European Finality Debate and its National Dimensions.* Washington, DC: CSIS Press.

Shackleton, M. (1990) *Financing the European Community.* London: Pinter/Royal Institute of International Affairs.

Shackleton, M. (1991) The European Community between three ways of life', *Journal of Common Market Studies* XXIX (6): 574–601.

Shepherd, R. (2008) 'European Union Treaty: trust the people', *The World Today,* 64 (7): 4–8.

Shonfield, A. (1973) *Europe: Journey to an Unknown Destination.* London: Allen Lane.

Shonfield, A. (1976) *International Economic Relations of the Western World,* Vol. I: *Politics and Trade.* London and New York: Oxford University Press.

Siedentop, L. (2000) *Democracy in Europe.* London: Penguin Books.

Silj, A. (1967) *Europe's Political Puzzle: A Study of the Fouchet Negotiations and the 1963 Veto.* Cambridge, MA: Center for International Studies, Harvard University.

Simonian, H. (1985) *The Privileged Partnership: Franco-German Relations in the European Community.* Oxford: Clarendon Press.

Single European Act (1986) *Bulletin of the European Communities* Supplement 2/86. Luxembourg: Office for Official Publications of the European Communities.

Smith, A. (1992) 'National identity and the idea of European unity', *International Affairs* 68 (1): 55–76.

Spaak Report (1956) Comité intergouvernemental créé par la conférence de Messine, Rapport des chefs de délégation aux ministres des affaires étrangères, Brussels.

Spierenburg I Report (1975) Advisory Committee on European Union, Netherlands Ministry of Foreign Affairs (unofficial translation), The Hague.

Spierenburg II Report (1979) *Proposals for the Reform of the Commission of the European Communities and its Services.* Brussels: Commission of the European Communities.

Spinelli, A. (1978) 'Reflections on the institutional crisis in the European Community', *West European Politics* 1 (1): 77–88.

Spotts, F. and Wieser, T. (1987) *Italy: A Difficult Democracy.* Cambridge: Cambridge University Press.

Stephens, P. (1996) *Politics and the Pound.* London: Macmillan.

Stirk, P. and Weigall, D. (eds) (1999) *The Origins and Development of European Integration.* London: Pinter.

Strange, S. (1976) *International Economic Relations of the Western World, 1959–72,* Vol. 2: *International Monetary Relations.* London and New York: Oxford University Press, for RIIA.

Strasser, D. (1980) *The Finances of Europe.* Brussels and Luxembourg: Office for Official Publications of the European Communities. (Translation of 2nd edn of *Les Finances de l'Europe.* Brussels: Labor (1980); first edn (1975) Paris: Presses Universitaires de France.)

Stuart, G. (2003) *The Making of Europe's Constitution.* London: Fabian Society.

Subacchi, P. (2005) 'Ghosts return', *The World Today,* 61 (7): 7–8.

Swann, D. (ed.) (1992) *The Single European Market and Beyond: A Study of the Wider Implications of the Single European Act.* London: Routledge.

Swiss Federal Council (1988) *Switzerland's Position with Regard to the Process of European Integration.* Press and Information Service.

Taylor, P (2008) *The End of European Integration.* London: Routledge.

*TEU: Treaty on European Union* (1992). Luxembourg: OOP.

Tew, B. (1977) *The Evolution of the International Monetary System, 1945–77.* London: Hutchinson.

*Texts Relating to European Political Co-operation* (1977). Bonn: Press and Information Office of the Federal Republic of Germany.

'Three Wise Men' Report (1979) *Report on European Institutions by the Committee of Three to the European Council*. Brussels: Commission of the European Communities.

Tindemans Report (1975) *Report on European Union*. Brussels: Ministry of Foreign Affairs (completed 1975, public release 1976).

Twitchett, C. (ed.) (1981) *Harmonization in the EEC*. London: Macmillan.

Twitchett, K. (ed.) (1980) *European Co-operation Today*. London: Europa.

Urwin, D. (1991) *The Community of Europe: A History of European Integration since 1945*. London: Longman.

Urwin, D. (1996) *A Dictionary of European History and Politics, 1945–1995*. London: Longman.

Usher, J. (1981) *European Community Law and National Law: The Irreversible Transfer?* London: Allen & Unwin.

Vedel Report (1972) *Report of the Working Party Examining the Problem of the Enlargement of the Powers of the European Parliament*. Brussels: Commission of the European Communities.

Wallace, H., Wallace, W. and Webb, C. (eds) (1983) *Policy-Making in the European Community* (2nd edn). Chichester: John Wiley & Sons Ltd.

Wallace, W. (2005) 'A treaty too far', *The World Today* 61 (7): 4–6.

Weigall, D. and Stirk, P. (eds) (1992) *The Origins and Development of the European Community*. Leicester: Leicester University Press.

Weiler, J. (1983) The Genscher-Colombo Draft European Act: the politics of indecision', *Journal of European Integration* VI (2–3): 129–53.

Weisenfeld, E. (1986) 'François Mitterrand: l'action extérieure', *Politique Étrangère* 1/86: 131–41.

Weller, M. (1999) 'The Rambouillet conference', *International Affairs* 72 (2): 211–51.

Werner, P. (1971) *Vers l' Union Monétaire Européenne*. Lausanne: Lausanne University (lecture of 22 February 1971).

Willis, F. (1965) *France, Germany and the New Europe 1945–1963*. Stanford, CA: Stanford University Press; London: Oxford University Press.

Woolcock, S. (1982) 'US–European trade relations', *International Affairs* 58 (4): 610–24.

Wyatt, D. and Dashwood, A. (1987) *The Substantive Law of the EEC* (2nd edn). London: Sweet & Maxwell.

Ypersele, J. van and Koeune, J.-C. (1985) *The European Monetary System: Origins, Operations and Outlook*. Luxembourg and Brussels: Office for the Official Publications of the European Communities.

Zielonka, J. (1998) *Explaining Euro-Paralysis: Why Europe is Unable to Act in International Politics*. New York: St Martin's Press.

Zielonka, J. (2006) *Europe as Empire: The Nature of the enlarged European Union*. Oxford: Oxford University Press.

# Index